TOP 10

OF EVERYTHING
2005

TOP 10

OF EVERYTHING
2005
RUSSELL ASH

TED SMART

Contents

DK

LONDON, NEW YORK, MUNICH, MELBOURNE AND DELHI

A PENGUIN COMPANY

Senior Editor Becky Alexander
Senior Art Editor Mark Cavanagh
Production Controller Heather Hughes

Managing Editor Adèle Hayward
Managing Art Editor Karen Self
Category Publisher Stephanie Jackson

Produced for Dorling Kindersley by
The Bridgewater Book Company,
The Old Candlemakers, West Street,
Lewes, East Sussex BN7 2NZ

Editor Howard Spencer
Designer Lisa McCormick
Picture Research Rachael Swann

Author's Project Manager Aylla Macphail
Research Assistant Louise Reip

Published in Great Britain in 2004 by
Dorling Kindersley Limited, 80 Strand,
London WC2R 0RL

This edition produced for The Book People Ltd.
Hall Wood Avenue, Haydock
St. Helens WA11 9UL

2 4 6 8 10 9 7 5 3 1

Copyright © 2004 Dorling Kindersley Limited
Text copyright © 2004 Russell Ash

A CIP catalogue record of this book is available from
the British Library.

ISBN 14053 0406 5

Reproduction by Colourscan, Singapore
Printed and bound by GGP Media GmbH, Germany

See our complete catalogue at
www.dk.com

Contents

Introduction

SWEET SIXTEEN

THIS IS THE 16TH annual edition of *The Top 10 of Everything*. During its lifetime the world has undergone inexorable change, and I have monitored many of these developments, both important and trivial, by presenting a diverse range of lists that reflect everything from the growth of the Internet and the first films to make $1 billion, to the higher-than-ever scores achieved in many sports and the burgeoning of DVD as a home entertainment medium.

A WORLD OF LISTS

We are constantly bombarded with lists. Increasingly, newspapers and TV programmes present rankings based on market research and polls, lists of safest cars, favourite songs, bestsellers, award-winners, crime rates, top schools, and so on. With the ever-faster pace of the Information Age, these and the lists in *The Top 10 of Everything* offer an overview of what might otherwise be a daunting mass of facts and figures.

LIST LIMITS

The *Top 10 of Everything* contains only definitive lists. Although there are some "bests", these are generally bestsellers (most film Top 10s, for example, are based on world box office income), while "worsts" cover such events as crimes and disasters, so all can be quantified. This criterion imposes certain limitations: the top prices paid for works of art and collectables are based on auction sales, and though even higher prices may occasionally have been paid privately for such items as paintings and rare cars, these are seldom made public. Certain sporting seasons inconveniently fail to coincide with our deadline, and there are areas where one must treat data circumspectly: as work was in progress, reports of an explosion in North Korea initially claimed over 3,000 dead; within days this had been revised to 161 – no less tragic, but a graphic indicator of how divergent some figures can be.

INFORMATION SOURCES

My numerous sources include "official" and government departments, commercial and research organizations, and especially private individuals around the world who are specialists in everything from snakes to skyscrapers, and who have been generous enough to share with me the results of their research. My grateful thanks to them all.

KEEP IN CONTACT

Check out and contact me with any comments, corrections or ideas for new lists via *The Top 10 of Everything* website:
http://www.top10ofeverything.com

Other Dorling Kindersley books by Russell Ash:
The Factastic Book of 1,001 Lists
The Factastic Book of Comparisons
Great Wonders of the World
The Top 10 of Sport (with Ian Morrison)
The Top 10 of Film

SPECIAL FEATURES

• Over 700 lists covering everything on Earth – and beyond

• Completely updated with many innovative lists, from the most expensive guitars to the oldest theatres and highest-earning film trilogies

• Includes Top 10 lists that track changes over time, from the richest people in the world to the most common first names and the tallest buildings

• "The First To…" features reveal some of the individuals who were the first in an area of endeavour – including the first woman graduate, the first to sell a million records, and the first boxers to use gloves.

THE UNIVERSE
& THE EARTH

Stars & Galaxies

TOP 10 GALAXIES NEAREST TO THE EARTH

	GALAXY	DISCOVERED	DIAMETER*	APPROX. DISTANCE*
1	Sagittarius Dwarf	1994	10	82
2	Large Magellanic Cloud	Prehist.	30	160
3	Small Magellanic Cloud	Prehist.	16	190
4	= Draco Dwarf	1954	3	205
	= Ursa Minor Dwarf	1954	2	205
6	Sculptor Dwarf	1937	3	254
7	Sextans Dwarf	1990	4	258
8	Carina Dwarf	1977	2	330
9	Fornax Dwarf	1938	6	450
10	Leo II	1950	3	660

* 1,000 light years

Source: Peter Bond, Royal Astronomical Society

These, and other galaxies, are members of the so-called "Local Group", although with vast distances such as these, "local" is clearly a relative term.

TOP 10 STARS NEAREST TO THE EARTH*

	STAR	LIGHT YEARS	KM (MILLIONS)	MILES (MILLIONS)
1	Proxima Centauri	4.22	39,923,310	24,792,500
2	Alpha Centauri	4.39	41,531,595	25,791,250
3	Barnard's Star	5.94	56,195,370	34,897,500
4	Wolf 359	7.78	73,602,690	45,707,500
5	Lalande 21185	8.31	78,616,755	48,821,250
6	Sirius	8.60	81,360,300	50,525,000
7	Luyten 726-8	8.72	82,495,560	51,230,000
8	Ross 154	9.69	91,672,245	56,928,750
9	Ross 248	10.32	97,632,360	60,630,000
10	Epsilon Eridani	10.49	99,240,645	61,628,750

* Excluding the Sun

Source: Peter Bond, Royal Astronomical Society

A spaceship travelling at 40,237 km/h (25,000 mph) – which is faster than any human has yet reached in space – would take more than 113,200 years to reach the Earth's closest star, Proxima Centauri. While the nearest stars in this list lie just over four light years away from the Earth, others within the Milky Way lie at a distance of 2,500 light years.

TOP 10 MOST COMMON ELEMENTS IN THE SUN

	ELEMENT	PARTS PER MILLION*
1	Hydrogen	750,000
2	Helium	230,000
3	Oxygen	9,000
4	Carbon	3,000
5	= Iron	1,000
	= Neon	1,000
	= Nitrogen	1,000
8	Silicon	900
9	Magnesium	700
10	Sulphur	400

* mg per kg

Helium was discovered in the Sun before it was detected on Earth, its name deriving from *helios*, the Greek word for Sun. More than 70 elements have been detected in the Sun, the most common of which correspond closely to those found in the Universe as a whole, with some variations in ratios – including a greater proportion of the principal element, hydrogen. The atoms of hydrogen in the Universe outnumber those of all the other elements combined.

THE 10 TYPES OF STAR

	TYPE	SPECTRUM	MAXIMUM SURFACE TEMPERATURE (°C)
1	W	Bright lines	80,000
2	O	Bright and dark lines	40,000
3	B	Bluish-white	25,000
4	A	White	10,000
5	F	White/slightly yellow	7,500
6	G	Yellowish	6,000
7	K	Orange	5,000
8	M	Orange-red	3,400
9	= C (formerly R and N)	Reddish	2,600
	= S	Red	2,600

Stars are classified by type according to their spectra – the colours by which they appear when viewed with a spectroscope. These vary according to the star's surface temperature. A letter is assigned to each – although there are some variations, Type C sometimes being divided into R and N. One mnemonic for remembering the sequence takes the initial letters of the words in the phrase "Wow! O Be A Fine Girl Kiss Me Right Now Sweetie".

▶ **Bode's well**
Discovered in 1774 by German astronomer Johann Elert Bode (who also suggested the name of the planet Uranus), the classic spiral Bode's Galaxy (M81) can be seen with relatively small telescopes.

GALACTIC PIONEER

IT WAS NOT UNTIL 1923 that American astronomer Edwin Hubble used photographs taken by the 100-inch telescope at Mount Wilson Observatory to prove that the Universe extends far beyond the Milky Way. He observed that the magnitude of the Cepheid variable star in the Andromeda Galaxy (M31) indicated that it was in an entirely separate galaxy, at a distance of 2.2 million light years. The idea that our own galaxy is only one of many had been suggested by earlier observers, but Hubble was the first to demonstrate it as fact.

THE FIRST TO...

BRIGHTEST STARS*

STAR	CONSTELLATION	DISTANCE#	APPARENT MAGNITUDE
1 Sirius	Canis Major	8.65	−1.46
2 Canopus	Carina	313	−0.62
3 Alpha Centauri	Centaurus	4.35	−0.27
4 Arcturus	Boötes	36	−0.04
5 Vega	Lyra	25	+0.03
6 Capella	Auriga	42	+0.08
7 Rigel	Orion	773	+0.18
8 Procyon	Canis Minor	11.4	+0.38
9 Achernar	Eridanus	144	+0.46
10 Beta Centauri	Centaurus	525	+0.61

Excluding the Sun

From the Earth in light years

Source: *Peter Bond, Royal Astronomical Society*

This Top 10 is based on apparent visual magnitude as viewed from Earth – the lower the number, the brighter the star. At its brightest, the variable star Betelgeuse would make the Top 10, but its average magnitude disqualifies it.

BRIGHTEST GALAXIES

GALAXY/NO.	DISTANCE#	APPARENT MAGNITUDE
1 Large Magellanic Cloud	0.17	0.91
2 Small Magellanic Cloud	0.21	2.70
3 Andromeda Galaxy (NGC 224, M31)	2.6	4.36
4 Triangulum Galaxy (NGC 598, M33)	2.8	6.27
5 Centaurus Galaxy (NGC 5128)	12.0	7.84
6 Bode's Galaxy (NGC 3031, M81)	12.0	7.89
7 Silver Coin Galaxy (NGC 253)	8.5	8.04
8 Southern Pinwheel Galaxy (NGC 5236, M83)	15.0	8.20
9 Pinwheel Galaxy (NGC 5457, M101)	24.0	8.31
10 Cigar Galaxy (NGC 55)	4.9	8.42

From the Earth in light years

Messier (M) numbers are named after French astronomer Charles Messier (1730–1817), who in 1781 compiled the first catalogue of galaxies, nebulae, and star clusters. From 1888, these were replaced by New General Catalogue (NGC) numbers. As well as the official names that have been assigned to them, galaxies discovered prior to the change are identified by both M and NGC numbers.

Orbiting the Sun

TOP 10 LARGEST BODIES IN THE SOLAR SYSTEM

BODY	MAXIMUM DIAMETER (KM)	(MILES)
1 Sun	1,392,140	865,036
2 Jupiter	142,984	88,846
3 Saturn	120,536	74,898
4 Uranus	51,118	31,763
5 Neptune	49,532	30,778
6 Earth	12,756	7,926
7 Venus	12,103	7,520
8 Mars	6,794	4,222
9 Ganymede	5,269	3,274
10 Titan	5,150	3,200

Most of the planets are visible with the naked eye and have been observed since ancient times. The exceptions are Uranus, discovered on 13 March 1781 by the British astronomer Sir William Herschel; Neptune, found by German astronomer Johann Galle on 23 September 1846; and, outside the Top 10, Pluto, located using photographic techniques by American astronomer Clyde Tombaugh, who announced his discovery on 13 March 1930.

TOP 10 MOST MASSIVE BODIES IN THE SOLAR SYSTEM*

BODY	MASS#
1 Sun	332,830.000
2 Jupiter	317.828
3 Saturn	95.161
4 Neptune	17.148
5 Uranus	14.536
6 Earth	1.000
7 Venus	0.815
8 Mars	0.10745
9 Mercury	0.05527
10 Pluto	0.0022

* Excluding satellites

Compared with the Earth = 1; the mass of Earth is approximately 73,500,000,000,000 tonnes

The mass of a body – the amount of material it contains – determines its gravitational attraction: Jupiter's high mass means that an object on it would weigh over 144,000 times as much as the same object on Pluto, which has a low mass.

TOP 10 MOST FREQUENTLY SEEN COMETS

COMET	YEARS BETWEEN APPEARANCES
1 Encke	3.302
2 Grigg-Skjellerup	4.908
3 Honda-Mrkós-Pajdusáková	5.210
4 Tempel 2	5.259
5 Neujmin 2	5.437
6 Brorsen	5.463
7 Tuttle-Giacobini-Kresák	5.489
8 Tempel-L. Swift	5.681
9 Tempel 1	5.982
10 Pons-Winnecke	6.125

The comets in the Top 10 and several others return with regularity (although with some notable variations), while others may not be seen again for many thousands of years. The most frequent visitor, Encke's Comet, is named after the German astronomer Johann Franz Encke (1791–1865), who in 1818 calculated the period of its elliptical orbit. It is becoming extremely faint: comets often disappear through disintegration or changes in their orbits.

TOP 10 COMETS COMING NEAREST TO THE EARTH

COMET	DATE*	(AU)#	DISTANCE (KM)	(MILES)
1 Comet of 1491	20 Feb 1491	0.0094	1,406,220	873,784
2 Lexell	1 Jul 1770	0.0151	2,258,928	1,403,633
3 Tempel-Tuttle	26 Oct 1366	0.0229	3,425,791	2,128,688
4 IRAS-Araki-Alcock	11 May 1983	0.0313	4,682,413	2,909,516
5 Halley	10 Apr 837	0.0334	4,996,569	3,104,724
6 Biela	9 Dec 1805	0.0366	5,475,282	3,402,182
7 Grischow	8 Feb 1743	0.0390	5,834,317	3,625,276
8 Pons-Winnecke	26 Jun 1927	0.0394	5,894,156	3,662,458
9 Comet of 1014	24 Feb 1014	0.0407	6,088,633	3,783,301
10 La Hire	20 Apr 1702	0.0437	6,537,427	4,062,168

* Of closest approach to the Earth

Astronomical Units: one AU = mean distance from the Earth to the Sun (149,597,870 km/92,955,793 miles)

As they are composed of water ice and dust particles, the impact of a comet with the Earth poses less potential danger than that of an asteroid, a large solid rock structure. One theory, however, suggests that it was just such a cometary collision 65 million years ago that wiped out the dinosaurs.

TOP 10 BODIES* FURTHEST FROM THE SUN

BODY	AVERAGE DISTANCE FROM THE SUN (KM)	(MILES)
1 Pluto	5,914,000,000	3,675,000,000
2 Neptune	4,497,000,000	2,794,000,000
3 Uranus	2,871,000,000	1,784,000,000
4 Chiron	2,800,000,000	1,740,000,000
5 Saturn	1,427,000,000	887,000,000
6 Jupiter	778,300,000	483,600,000
7 Mars	227,900,000	141,600,000
8 Earth	149,597,870	92,955,793
9 Venus	108,200,000	67,200,000
10 Mercury	57,900,000	36,000,000

* In the Solar System, excluding satellites and asteroids

Chiron, a "mystery object" that may be either a comet (Kowal-Meech-Belton) or an asteroid (Asteroid 2060), was discovered on 1 November 1977 by American astronomer Charles Kowal. It measures 200–300 km (124–186 miles) in diameter and orbits between Saturn and Uranus. "Planet X" (the name proposed by Percival Lowell; "Persephone" has also been suggested) is believed by some to orbit beyond Pluto, and would thus be the furthest planet from the Sun and Earth.

TOP 10 LARGEST PLANETARY MOONS

MOON	PLANET	DIAMETER (KM)	(MILES)
1 Ganymede	Jupiter	5,269	3,274

Discovered by Galileo on 11 January 1610, Ganymede – one of Jupiter's 61 known satellites* and the largest moon in the Solar System – is thought to have a surface of ice about 97 km (60 miles) thick. The 1979 *Voyager 1* and 2 space probes failed to detect evidence of an atmosphere. Launched in 1989, NASA's aptly named *Galileo* probe reached Ganymede in June 1996.

MOON	PLANET	DIAMETER (KM)	(MILES)
2 Titan	Saturn	5,150	3,200

Titan, the largest of Saturn's 30 confirmed moons, is actually larger than two of the planets in the Solar System, Mercury and Pluto. It was discovered by the Dutch astronomer Christian Huygens in 1655. We have no idea what its surface looks like because it has a dense atmosphere containing nitrogen, ethane, and other gases that shroud its surface – not unlike that of the Earth 4 billion years ago – but data sent back by *Voyager 1* during 1980 and recent radio telescope observations suggest that it may have ethane "oceans" and "continents" of ice or other solid matter. Recent research has suggested that gases were deposited there by impacting comets.

3 Callisto	Jupiter	4,800	2,983

Possessing a similar composition to Ganymede, Callisto is heavily pitted with craters, perhaps more so than any other body in the Solar System.

4 Io	Jupiter	3,630	2,256

Most of what we know about Io was reported back by the 1979 *Voyager 1* probe, which revealed a crust of solid sulphur with massive volcanic eruptions in progress, hurling sulphurous material 300 km (186 miles) into space.

5 Moon	Earth	3,475	2,159

Our own satellite is a quarter of the size of the Earth, the fifth largest in the Solar System, and, to date, the only one to have been explored by Man.

6 Europa	Jupiter	3,138	1,950

Although Europa's ice-covered surface is apparently smooth and crater-free, it is covered with mysterious black lines, some of them 64 km (40 miles) wide and resembling canals.

MOON	PLANET	DIAMETER (KM)	(MILES)
7 Triton	Neptune	2,704	1,680

Discovered on 10 October 1846 by British brewer and amateur astronomer William Lassell, 17 days after German astronomer Johann Galle had discovered Neptune itself, Triton is the only known satellite in the Solar System that revolves around its planet in the opposite direction to the planet's rotation. It is getting progressively closer to Neptune, and it is believed that in several million years the force of the planet's gravity may scatter it into a form like the rings of Saturn. Information sent back by *Voyager 2* during August 1989 revealed that Triton has an atmosphere composed largely of nitrogen and methane and a surface partly covered with nitrogen and methane ice glaciers. The ice layer shifts from one pole to the other and back again once every 165 years, the length of time it takes for Neptune to orbit the Sun.

8 Titania	Uranus	1,578	980

The largest of Uranus's seven moons, Titania was discovered by William Herschel (who had discovered the planet six years earlier) in 1787 and has a snowball-like surface of ice. Its size estimate was revised by data from *Voyager 2*.

9 Rhea	Saturn	1,528	949

Saturn's second largest moon was discovered by seventeenth-century Italian-born French astronomer Jean-Dominique (formerly Giovanni) Cassini. *Voyager 1*, which flew past Rhea in November 1980, confirmed that its icy surface is pitted with craters, one of them 225 km (140 miles) in diameter.

10 Oberon	Uranus	1,523	946

Oberon was discovered by Herschel and given the name of the fairy king husband of Queen Titania, both characters in Shakespeare's *A Midsummer Night's Dream*. New information from *Voyager 2* has relegated Oberon from 9th to 10th place in this list.

* *To May 2003*

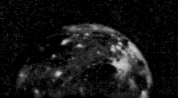

▶ **By Jupiter!**
Four of the largest moons in the Solar System, Io, Europa, Ganymede, and Callisto, are satellites of Jupiter, the largest planet.

Astronauts & Cosmonauts

TOP 10 | OLDEST ASTRONAUTS AND COSMONAUTS *

ASTRONAUT OR COSMONAUT[#]	BORN	LAST FLIGHT	AGE (YRS)	(MTHS)	(DAYS)
1 John H. Glenn	18 Jul 1921	6 Nov 1998	77	3	19
2 F. Story Musgrave	19 Aug 1935	7 Dec 1996	61	3	19
3 Dennis Tito	8 Aug 1940	6 May 2001	60	8	21
4 Vance D. Brand	9 May 1931	11 Dec 1990	59	7	2
5 Jean-Loup Chrétien (France)	30 Aug 1938	6 Oct 1997	59	1	7
6 Valey V. Ryumin (Russia)	16 Aug 1939	12 Jun 1998	58	9	27
7 Karl G. Henize	17 Oct 1926	6 Aug 1985	58	9	20
8 Roger K. Crouch	12 Sep 1940	17 Jul 1997	56	10	5
9 William E. Thornton	14 Apr 1929	6 May 1985	56	0	22
10 Claude Nicollier (Switzerland)	2 Dec 1944	28 Dec 1999	55	0	26

* Including payload specialists, etc.; to 1 January 2004

 # US unless otherwise indicated

John Glenn, who in 1962 had been the first American astronaut to orbit the Earth, re-entered space on 29 October 1998 aboard the Space Shuttle flight STS-95 *Discovery*, becoming the oldest astronaut of all time by a considerable margin.

TOP 10 | LONGEST SPACEWALKS *

ASTRONAUTS[#]	SPACECRAFT	DURATION (DATE)	(HR:MIN)
1 James Voss, Susan Helms	STS-102/ISS[†]	10–11 Mar 2001	8:56
2 Thomas D. Akers, Richard J. Hieb, Pierre J. Thuot	STS-49	13 May 1992	8:29
3 John M. Grunsfeld, Steven L. Smith	STS-103	22 Dec 1999	8:15
4 C. Michael Foale, Claude Nicollier	STS-103	23 Dec 1999	8:10
5 John M. Grunsfeld, Steven L. Smith	STS-103	24 Dec 1999	8:08
6 Daniel T. Barry, Tamara E. Jernigan	STS-96/ISS	29 May 1999	7:55
7 Jeffrey A. Hoffman, F. Story Musgrave	STS-61	4 Dec 1993	7:54
8 Steven S. Smith, Rex J. Walheim	STS 110/ISS	11 Apr 2002	7:48
9 Thomas D. Akers, Kathryn C. Thornton	STS-49	14 May 1992	7:44
10 Takao Doi, Winston E. Scott	STS-87	24 Nov 1997	7:43

* To 1 January 2004

 # All US

† International Space Station

TOP 10 | YOUNGEST ASTRONAUTS AND COSMONAUTS *

ASTRONAUT OR COSMONAUT[#]	BORN	FIRST FLIGHT	AGE (YRS)	(MTHS)	(DAYS)
1 Gherman S. Titov	11 Sep 1935	6 Aug 1961	25	10	25
2 Valentina V. Tereshkova	6 Mar 1937	16 Jun 1963	26	3	10
3 Boris B. Yegorov	26 Nov 1937	15 Oct 1964	26	10	19
4 Yuri A. Gagarin	9 Mar 1934	12 Apr 1961	27	1	3
5 Helen P. Sharman (UK)	30 May 1963	18 May 1991	27	11	19
6 Mark R. Shuttleworth (South Africa)	18 Sep 1973	25 Apr 2002	28	7	7
7 Dumitru D. Prunariu (Romania)	27 Sep 1952	14 May 1981	28	7	24
8 Valery F. Bykovsky	2 Aug 1934	14 Jun 1963	28	10	19
9 Salman Abdel Aziz Al-Saud (Saudi Arabia)	27 Jun 1956	17 Jun 1985	28	11	20
10 Vladimir Remek (Czechoslovakia)	26 Sep 1948	2 Mar 1978	29	5	6

* To 1 January 2004

 # All Soviet, unless otherwise stated

TOP 10 | LONGEST SPACE MISSIONS *

COSMONAUT[#]	MISSION DATES	DURATION (DAYS)	(HRS)	(MIN)
1 Valeri V. Polyakov	8 Jan 1994–22 Mar 1995	437		59
2 Sergei V. Avdeyev	13 Aug 1998–28 Aug 1999	379		52
3 = Musa K. Manarov	21 Dec 1987–21 Dec 1988	365		9
= Vladimir G. Titov	21 Dec 1987–21 Dec 1988	365	22	9
5 Yuri V. Romanenko	5 Feb–5 Dec 1987	326		8
6 Sergei K. Krikalyov	18 May 1991–25 Mar 1992	311		0
7 Valeri V. Polyakov	31 Aug 1988–27 Apr 1989	240		5
8 = Oleg Y. Atkov	8 Feb–2 Oct 1984	236	22	50
= Leonid D. Kizim	8 Feb–2 Oct 1984	236	22	50
= Anatoli Y. Solovyov	8 Feb–2 Oct 1984	236	22	50

* To 1 January 2003

 # All Soviet/Russian

Thirteen Russians and one Kazakh have spent over 200 days on single missions. The longest by US astronauts are the Space Shuttle/International Space Station stays of Daniel W. Bursch and Carl E. Walz, who, with Russian cosmonaut Yuri I. Onufrienko, spent 195 days 19 hours 39 mins 167 secs in space in 2001–2002.

▼ Men on the Moon

Apollo Lunar Module pilot Edwin "Buzz" Aldrin walks on the Moon, 20 July 1969. The module *Eagle* and astronaut Neil Armstrong, who took the photograph, are reflected on Aldrin's visor in this iconic image from the first Moon landing.

THE 10 FIRST MOONWALKERS

	ASTRONAUT	BORN	SPACECRAFT	TOTAL EVA* (HR:MIN)	MISSION DATES
1	Neil A. Armstrong	5 Aug 1930	*Apollo 11*	2:32	16–24 Jul 1969
2	Edwin E. ("Buzz") Aldrin	20 Jan 1930	*Apollo 11*	2:15	16–24 Jul 1969
3	Charles Conrad, Jr.	2 Jun 1930	*Apollo 12*	7:45	14–24 Nov 1969
4	Alan L. Bean	15 Mar 1932	*Apollo 12*	7:45	14–24 Nov 1969
5	Alan B. Shepard	18 Nov 1923	*Apollo 14*	9:23	31 Jan–9 Feb 1971
6	Edgar D. Mitchell	17 Sep 1930	*Apollo 14*	9:23	31 Jan–9 Feb 1971
7	David R. Scott	6 Jun 1932	*Apollo 15*	19:08	26 Jul–7 Aug 1971
8	James B. Irwin	17 Mar 1930	*Apollo 15*	18:35	26 Jul–7 Aug 1971
9	John W. Young	24 Sep 1930	*Apollo 16*	20:14	16–27 Apr 1972
10	Charles M. Duke, Jr.	3 Oct 1935	*Apollo 16*	20:14	16–27 Apr 1972

* Extra Vehicular Activity (i.e. time spent out of the lunar module on the Moon's surface)

Six US *Apollo* missions resulted in successful Moon landings (*Apollo 13*, 11–17 April 1970, was aborted after an oxygen tank exploded). During the last of these (*Apollo 17*; 7–19 December 1972), Eugene A. Cernan (b.14 March 1934) and Harrison H. Schmitt (b.3 July 1935) became the only other astronauts to date who have walked on the surface of the Moon, both spending a total of 22:04 in EVA.

Apollo 14 astronaut Alan B. Shepard made the first ever golf shot on the Moon on 6 February 1971, using a 6-iron head attached to the handle of a rock sample collector. The head is now in the US Golf Association Hall of Fame, New Jersey, but the balls still lie in a lunar bunker. These are not the only evidence of human visits: since there is no wind on the Moon, the astronauts' footprints will be visible for thousands of years. They also left the descent stages of six Apollo modules, three Lunar Rover electric vehicles worth $6 million each, and hundreds of other items they abandoned to reduce the weight of their craft when they took off, including cameras, scientific instruments, clothing, tools, and flags, as well as a memorial to deceased astronauts and cosmonauts. The 12 lunar astronauts collected 2,196 rock samples weighing a total of 381.69 kg (841.6 lb).

THE 10 FIRST PEOPLE TO ORBIT THE EARTH

	NAME	AGE	ORBITS	DURATION (HR:MIN)	SPACECRAFT/ COUNTRY OF ORIGIN	DATE
1	Yuri A. Gagarin	27	1	1:48	*Vostok I*, USSR	12 Apr 1961
2	Gherman S. Titov	25	17	25:18	*Vostok II*, USSR	6–7 Aug 1961
3	John H. Glenn	40	3	4:56	*Friendship 7*, USA	20 Feb 1962
4	Malcolm S. Carpenter	37	3	4:56	*Aurora 7*, USA	24 May 1962
5	Andrian G. Nikolayev	32	64	94:22	*Vostok III*, USSR	11–15 Aug 1962
6	Pavel R. Popovich	31	48	70:57	*Vostok IV*, USSR	12–15 Aug 1962
7	Walter M. Schirra	39	6	9:13	*Sigma 7*, USA	3 Oct 1962
8	Leroy G. Cooper	36	22	34:19	*Faith 7*, USA	15–16 May 1963
9	Valeri F. Bykovsky	28	81	119:6	*Vostok V*, USSR	14–19 Jun 1963
10	Valentina V. Tereshkova	26	48	70:50	*Vostok VI*, USSR	16–19 Jun 1963

No. 2 was the youngest-ever astronaut, aged 25 years 329 days. No. 10 was the first woman in space. Among early pioneering flights, neither Alan Shepard (5 May 1961: *Freedom 7*) nor Gus Grissom (21 July 1961: *Liberty Bell 7*) actually orbited, achieving altitudes of only 185 km (115 miles) and 190 km (118 miles) respectively, and neither flight lasted more than 15 minutes.

Chemical Elements

TOP 10 MOST COMMON ELEMENTS IN SEAWATER

ELEMENT	MG PER LITRE
1 Oxygen*	857,000
2 Hydrogen*	107,800
3 Chlorine	19,870
4 Sodium	11,050
5 Magnesium	1,326
6 Sulphur	928
7 Calcium	422
8 Potassium	416
9 Bromine	67
10 Carbon	28

* Combined as water

There are reckoned to be 5,000 million million tonnes of solids dissolved in the world's oceans – but sodium and chlorine (combined as sodium chloride, or common salt) are the only two that are extracted in substantial quantities.

TOP 10 MOST COMMON ELEMENTS IN THE EARTH'S CRUST

ELEMENT	PARTS PER MILLION*
1 Oxygen	461,000
2 Silicon	282,000
3 Aluminium	82,300
4 Iron	56,300
5 Calcium	41,500
6 Sodium	23,600
7 Magnesium	23,300
8 Potassium	20,900
9 Titanium	5,650
10 Hydrogen	1,400

* mg per kg

Source: *CRC Handbook of Chemistry and Physics* (77th ed.)

This is based on the average percentages of the elements in igneous rock. At an atomic level, out of every million atoms, some 200,000 are silicon, 63,000 aluminium, and 31,000 hydrogen.

EPONYMOUS ELEMENT

THE MINERAL SAMARKSITE was discovered in Russia in 1847 and named in honour of Vasilii Yefrafovich von Samarski-Bykhovets (1803–1870), Chief of Staff of the Russian Corps of Mining Engineers. In 1879 element number 62 was extracted from samarskite by French chemist Paul-Emile Lecoq de Boisbaudran. This was called samarium, the first element to be named after an individual. The most resistant element to demagnetization, it is used in the manufacture of personal stereos, lasers, and film studio lights.

THE FIRST TO...

▼ **Water resource**
Seawater contains a vast quantity of chemical elements, including up to half a tonne of gold in every cubic kilometre, but the costs of extracting them are greater than their value.

TOP 10 MOST COMMON ELEMENTS ON THE MOON

	ELEMENT	PERCENTAGE
1	Oxygen	40.0
2	Silicon	19.2
3	Iron	14.3
4	Calcium	8.0
5	Titanium	5.9
6	Aluminium	5.6
7	Magnesium	4.5
8	Sodium	0.33
9	Potassium	0.14
10	Chromium	0.002

This list is based on the analysis of the 20.77 kg (45.8 lb) of rock samples brought back to the Earth by the crew of the 1969 *Apollo 11* lunar mission.

▶ **Moon rock**
Fragments brought back from the *Apollo 17* Taurus-Littrow landing site have enhanced our knowledge of the moon's elemental make-up.

TOP 10 HEAVIEST ELEMENTS

	ELEMENT	DISCOVERER/ COUNTRY	YEAR DISCOVERED	DENSITY*
1	Osmium	Smithson Tennant, UK	1804	22.59
2	Iridium	Smithson Tennant	1804	22.56
3	Platinum	Julius Caesar Scaliger, Italy/France[#] Charles Wood, UK[†]	1557 1741	21.45
4	Rhenium	Walter K. Noddack *et al.*, Germany	1925	21.01
5	Neptunium	Edwin Mattison McMillan/ Philip H. Abelson, USA	1940	20.47
6	Plutonium	Glenn Theodore Seaborg *et al.*, USA	1940	20.26
7	Gold	–	Prehistoric	19.29
8	Tungsten	Juan José and Fausto de Elhuijar, Spain	1783	19.26
9	Uranium	Martin Heinrich Klaproth, Germany	1789	19.05
10	Tantalum	Anders Gustav Ekeberg, Sweden	1802	16.67

* *Grams per cm³ at 20°C*

[#] *Earliest reference to*

[†] *Discoverer*

The two heaviest elements, the metals osmium and iridium, were discovered at the same time by the British chemist Smithson Tennant (1761–1815), who was also the first to prove that diamonds are made of carbon.

TOP 10 LIGHTEST ELEMENTS*

	ELEMENT	DISCOVERER/ COUNTRY	YEAR DISCOVERED	DENSITY[#]
1	Lithium	Johan August Arfvedson, Sweden	1817	0.533
2	Potassium	Sir Humphry Davy, UK	1807	0.859
3	Sodium	Sir Humphry Davy	1807	0.969
4	Calcium	Sir Humphry Davy	1808	1.526
5	Rubidium	Robert Wilhelm Bunsen, Germany/ Gustav Kirchoff, Germany	1861	1.534
6	Magnesium	Sir Humphry Davy	1808[†]	1.737
7	Phosphorus	Hennig Brandt, Germany	1669	1.825
8	Beryllium	Friedrich Wöhler, Germany/ Antoine-Alexandré Brutus Bussy, France	1828[∞]	1.846
9	Caesium	Robert Wilhelm Bunsen/ Gustav Kirchoff	1860	1.896
10	Sulphur	–	Prehistoric	2.070

* *Solids only*

[#] *Grams per cm³ at 20°C*

[†] *Recognized by Joseph Black, 1755, but not isolated*

[∞] *Recognized by Nicholas Vauquelin, 1797, but not isolated*

High & Mighty

TOP 10 HIGHEST MOUNTAINS IN NORTH AMERICA

	MOUNTAIN	COUNTRY	HEIGHT* (M)	HEIGHT* (FT)
1	McKinley	Alaska, USA	6,194	20,320
2	Logan	Canada	5,959	19,545
3	Citlaltépetl (Orizaba)	Mexico	5,611	18,409
4	St. Elias	Alaska, USA/Canada	5,489	18,008
5	Popocatépetl	Mexico	5,452	17,887
6	Foraker	Alaska, USA	5,304	17,400
7	Ixtaccihuatl	Mexico	5,286	17,343
8	Lucania	Canada	5,226	17,147
9	King	Canada	5,173	16,971
10	Steele	Canada	5,073	16,644

Height of principal peak; lower peaks of the same mountain are excluded

Mount McKinley (or Denali, in the local language) was spotted in 1794 by Captain James Vancouver, and in 1896 named after William McKinley, the then-president of the United States. It was first climbed in 1913 by a party of four, including the Rev. Hudson Stuck, Archdeacon of the Yukon. Today, over 600 people a year ascend its summit.

TOP 10 COUNTRIES WITH THE HIGHEST ELEVATIONS*

	COUNTRY	PEAK	HEIGHT (M)	HEIGHT (FT)
1	= China	Everest	8,850	29,035
	= Nepal	Everest	8,850	29,035
3	Pakistan	K2	8,607	28,238
4	India	Kangchenjunga	8,598	28,208
5	Bhutan	Khula Kangri	7,554	24,784
6	Tajikistan	Mt. Garmo (formerly Kommunizma)	7,495	24,590
7	Afghanistan	Noshaq	7,490	24,581
8	Kyrgystan	Pik Pobedy	7,439	24,406
9	Kazakhstan	Khan Tengri	6,995	22,949
10	Argentina	Cerro Aconcagua	6,960	22,834

Based on the tallest peak in each country

While an elevation of more than 305 m (1,000 ft) is commonly regarded as a mountain, there is no international agreement. Using this criterion, almost every country in the world can claim to have at least one mountain. There are some 54 countries in the world with elevations of greater than 3,048 m (10,000 ft).

TOP 10 HIGHEST MOUNTAINS IN EUROPE

	MOUNTAIN	COUNTRY	HEIGHT* (M)	HEIGHT* (FT)
1	Mont Blanc	France/Italy	4,807	15,771
2	Monte Rosa	Switzerland	4,634	15,203
3	Zumsteinspitze	Italy/Switzerland	4,564	14,970
4	Signalkuppe	Italy/Switzerland	4,555	14,941
5	Dom	Switzerland	4,545	14,911
6	Liskamm	Italy/Switzerland	4,527	14,853
7	Weisshorn	Switzerland	4,505	14,780
8	Täschorn	Switzerland	4,491	14,733
9	Matterhorn	Italy/Switzerland	4,477	14,688
10	Mont Maudit	France/Italy	4,466	14,649

Height of principal peak; lower peaks of the same mountain are excluded

All 10 of Europe's highest mountains are in the Alps; there are, however, at least 15 mountains in the Caucasus (the mountain range that straddles Europe and Asia) that are taller than Mont Blanc. The highest of them, the west peak of Mt. Elbrus, measures 5,642 m (18,510 ft).

▶ **The top of the world**
Mount Everest was first recognized as the world's tallest mountain in 1856. Its height as computed at that time was accurate to within 0.001 per cent of its current official height.

TOP 10 | HIGHEST MOUNTAINS

	MOUNTAIN/LOCATION	FIRST ASCENT	TEAM NATIONALITY	HEIGHT* (M)	(FT)
1	**Everest**, Nepal/China	29 May 1953	British/New Zealand	8,850	29,035
2	**K2 (Chogori)**, Pakistan/China	31 Jul 1954	Italian	8,607	28,238
3	**Kangchenjunga**, Nepal/India	25 May 1955	British	8,598	28,208
4	**Lhotse**, Nepal/China	18 May 1956	Swiss	8,511	27,923
5	**Makalu I**, Nepal/China	15 May 1955	French	8,481	27,824
6	**Lhotse Shar II**, Nepal/China	12 May 1970	Austrian	8,383	27,504
7	**Dhaulagiri I**, Nepal	13 May 1960	Swiss/Austrian	8,172	26,810
8	**Manaslu I (Kutang I)**, Nepal	9 May 1956	Japanese	8,156	26,760
9	**Cho Oyu**, Nepal	19 Oct 1954	Austrian	8,153	26,750
10	**Nanga Parbat (Diamir)**, Kashmir	3 Jul 1953	German/Austrian	8,126	26,660

* Height of principal peak; lower peaks of the same mountain are excluded

Dhaulagiri was once believed to be the world's tallest mountain until Kangchenjunga was surveyed and declared to be even higher. However, when the results of the 19th-century Great Trigonometrical Survey of India were studied it was first realized that Everest (then called "Peak XV") was the tallest, its height being computed as 8,840 m (29,002 ft). The mountain's name was suggested in 1865, as a tribute to Sir George Everest, the Surveyor General of India who had led the Great Trigonometrical Survey. Errors in measurement were corrected in 1955 when it was adjusted to 8,848 m (29,029 ft). On 20 April 1993, using the latest measuring techniques, this was again revised to give a new figure of 8,848 m (29,028 ft). In November 1999 it was announced that an analysis of data beamed from sensors on Everest's summit to GPS (Global Positioning System) satellites had claimed a new height of 8,850 m (29,035 ft). This new height has been accepted and is the current "official" figure. The survey also indicated that Everest is growing higher and moving north-east at a rate of 6 cm (2.4 in) per annum.

TOP 10 | HIGHEST VOLCANOES

	VOLCANO/LOCATION	HEIGHT (M)	(FT)
1	**Ojos del Salado,** Argentina/Chile	6,887	22,595
2	**Llullaillaco,** Argentina/Chile	6,723	22,057
3	**Tipas,** Argentina	6,660	21,850
4	**Cerro El Condor,** Argentina	6,532	21,430
5	**Coropuna,** Peru	6,377	20,922
6	**Parinacota,** Chile	6,348	20,827
7	**Chimborazo,** Ecuador	6,310	20,702
8	**Pular,** Chile	6,233	20,449
9	**Cerro Aucanquilcha,** Chile	6,176	20,262
10	**San Pedro,** Chile	6,145	20,161

Of these volcanoes, only two have erupted in comparatively modern times: Llullaillaco in 1870 and San Pedro in 1960.

Oceans & Seas

TOP 10 SHALLOWEST OCEANS AND SEAS

SEA*/OCEAN	AVERAGE DEPTH (M)	(FT)
1 **Yellow Sea,** Pacific Ocean	36.8	121
2 **Baltic Sea,** Atlantic Ocean	54.8	180
3 **Hudson Bay,** Atlantic Ocean	92.9	305
4 **North Sea,** Atlantic Ocean	93.8	308
5 **Persian Gulf,** Indian Ocean	99.9	328
6 **East China Sea,** Indian Ocean	188.9	620
7 **Red Sea,** Indian Ocean	537.6	1,764
8 **Gulf of California,** Pacific Ocean	723.9	2,375
9 **Sea of Okhotsk,** Pacific Ocean	972.9	3,192
10 **Arctic Ocean**	1,038.4	3,407

* Excludes landlocked seas

The Yellow Sea, or Huang Hai, lies north of the China Sea between China and Korea. It has a maximum depth of 152 m (500 ft) and possesses few deep-water ports. Ice fields form during the winter in parts, while shifting sandbanks make it treacherous for shipping. Its name reflects the colour of mineral deposits from the rivers that discharge into it, which would be dispersed in a deeper body of water. Eventually, it is likely that environmental changes will lead to its disappearance.

TOP 10 DEEPEST OCEANS AND SEAS

SEA/OCEAN	AVERAGE DEPTH (M)	(FT)
1 **Pacific Ocean**	3,939	12,925
2 **Indian Ocean**	3,840	12,598
3 **Atlantic Ocean**	3,575	11,730
4 **Caribbean Sea,** Atlantic Ocean	2,575	8,448
5 **Sea of Japan,** Pacific Ocean	1,666	5,468
6 **Gulf of Mexico,** Atlantic Ocean	1,614	5,297
7 **Mediterranean Sea,** Atlantic Ocean	1,501	4,926
8 **Bering Sea,** Pacific Ocean	1,491	4,893
9 **South China Sea,** Pacific Ocean	1,463	4,802
10 **Black Sea,** Atlantic Ocean	1,190	3,906

The deepest point in the deepest ocean is the Marianas Trench in the Pacific, given as 10,924 m (35,837 ft) in a recent survey, although the slightly lesser depth of 10,916 m (35,814 ft) was recorded on 23 January 1960 by Jacques Piccard (Switzerland) and Donald Walsh (US) in their 17.7-m (58-ft) long bathyscaphe *Trieste 2* during the deepest-ever ocean descent. Whichever is correct, it is close to 11 km (6.8 miles) down, or almost 29 times the height of the Empire State Building.

TOP 10 SMALLEST SEAS

SEA*/OCEAN	APPROXIMATE AREA (SQ KM)	(SQ MILES)
1 **Gulf of California,** Pacific Ocean	153,070	59,100
2 **Persian Gulf,** Indian Ocean	230,000	88,800
3 **Yellow Sea,** Pacific Ocean	293,960	113,500
4 **Baltic Sea,** Atlantic Ocean	382,000	147,500
5 **North Sea,** Atlantic Ocean	427,090	164,900
6 **Red Sea,** Indian Ocean	452,990	174,900
7 **Black Sea,** Atlantic Ocean	507,900	196,100
8 **Andaman Sea,** Indian Ocean	564,880	218,100
9 **East China Sea,** Pacific Ocean	664,590	256,600
10 **Hudson Bay,** Atlantic Ocean	730,120	281,900

* Excludes landlocked seas

The two smallest seas are both gulfs – meaning long bays that extend far inland. The Gulf of California stretches southeast from the mouth of the Colorado River, separating the Baja California Peninsula from the Mexican mainland. It was once known as the Sea of Cortés, after the Spanish conquistador Hernan Cortés, who sent Francisco de Ulloa to explore it in 1540. The Persian Gulf is an arm of the Arabian Sea between Iran and Saudi Arabia.

TOP 10 LARGEST OCEANS AND SEAS

SEA/OCEAN	APPROXIMATE AREA (SQ KM)	(SQ MILES)
1 **Pacific Ocean**	166,241,750	64,186,300
2 **Atlantic Ocean**	86,557,400	33,420,000
3 **Indian Ocean**	73,427,450	28,350,500
4 **Arctic Ocean**	13,223,700	5,105,700
5 **South China Sea,** Pacific Ocean	2,974,600	1,148,500
6 **Caribbean Sea,** Atlantic Ocean	2,515,900	971,400
7 **Mediterranean Sea,** Atlantic Ocean	2,509,960	969,100
8 **Bering Sea,** Pacific Ocean	2,261,100	873,000
9 **Gulf of Mexico,** Atlantic Ocean	1,507,600	582,100
10 **Sea of Okhotsk,** Pacific Ocean	1,392,100	537,500

The geographical term "ocean" encompasses all the world's seawater, with the exception of such landlocked seas as the Caspian. A total of over 70 per cent of the planet's surface is oceanic – the Pacific Ocean alone has an area over 25 per cent greater than that of the land. Smaller divisions of certain oceans are separately identified as seas – including some that are partially landlocked. Wholly landlocked seas are considered alongside lakes, which in many instances are larger than those bearing the name "sea".

TOP 10 LARGEST ISLANDS

ISLAND/COUNTRY	AREA* (SQ KM)	(SQ MILES)
1 **Greenland (Kalaatdlit Nunaat)**	2,175,600	840,004
2 **New Guinea**	785,753	303,381
3 **Borneo** (Indonesia/Malaysia/Brunei)	748,168	288,869
4 **Madagascar** (Malagasy Republic)	587,713	226,917
5 **Baffin Island** (Canada)	503,944	194,574
6 **Sumatra** (Indonesia)	443,065	171,068
7 **Great Britain**	229,957	88,787
8 **Honshu** (Japan)	225,800	87,182
9 **Victoria Island** (Canada)	220,548	85,154
10 **Ellesmere Island** (Canada)	183,964	71,029

* Mainlands, including areas of inland water, but excluding offshore islands

Australia is regarded as a continental land mass rather than an island; otherwise it would rank first, at 7,618,493 sq km (2,941,517 sq miles), or 35 times the size of Great Britain. The largest US island is Hawaii, which measures 10,456 sq km (4,037 sq miles), and the largest off mainland USA is Kodiak, Alaska, at 9,510 sq km (3,672 sq miles).

TOP 10 DEEPEST DEEP-SEA TRENCHES

TRENCH	DEEPEST POINT (M)	(FT)
1 **Marianas**	10,924	35,837
2 **Tonga***	10,800	35,430
3 **Philippine**	10,497	34,436
4 **Kermadec***	10,047	32,960
5 **Bonin**	9,994	32,786
6 **New Britain**	9,940	32,609
7 **Kuril**	9,750	31,985
8 **Izu**	9,695	31,805
9 **Puerto Rico**	8,605	28,229
10 **Yap**	8,527	27,973

* Some authorities consider these parts of the same feature

With the exception of the Puerto Rico (Atlantic), all the trenches in the Top 10 are in the Pacific. Each of the eight deepest trenches would be deep enough to submerge Mount Everest, which is 8,850 m (29,035 ft) above sea level.

▼ **A green and pleasant land**
Reputedly so-named to lure settlers there, Greenland is the world's largest and one of the most sparsely populated islands.

Rivers, Lakes & Waterfalls

TOP 10 HIGHEST WATERFALLS

WATERFALL	RIVER	LOCATION	TOTAL DROP (M)	(FT)
1 Angel	Carrao	Venezuela	979	3,212*
2 Tugela	Tugela	South Africa	850	2,800
3 Utigård	Jostedal Glacier	Nesdale, Norway	800	2,625
4 Mongefossen	Monge	Mongebekk, Norway	774	2,540
5 Mutarazi	Mutarazi River	Zimbabwe	762	2,499
6 Yosemite	Yosemite Creek	California, USA	739	2,425
7 Østre Mardøla Foss	Mardals	Eikisdal, Norway	656	2,152
8 Tyssestrengane	Tysso	Hardanger, Norway	646	2,120
9 Cuquenán	Arabopo	Venezuela	610	2,000
10 Sutherland	Arthur	South Island, New Zealand	580	1,904

Longest single drop 807 m (2,648 ft)

TOP 10 COUNTRIES WITH THE GREATEST AREAS OF INLAND WATER

COUNTRY	PER CENT OF TOTAL AREA	WATER AREA (SQ KM)	(SQ MILES)
1 USA*	4.88	756,600	292,125
2 Canada	7.60	755,170	291,573
3 India	9.56	314,400	121,391
4 China	2.82	270,550	104,460
5 Ethiopia	9.89	120,900	46,680
6 Colombia	8.80	100,210	38,691
7 Indonesia	4.88	93,000	35,908
8 Russia	0.47	79,400	30,657
9 Australia	0.90	68,920	26,610
10 Tanzania	6.25	59,050	22,799

50 states and District of Columbia

 ## LONGEST RIVERS

	RIVER	LOCATION	LENGTH (KM)	(MILES)
1	Nile	Burundi, Dem. Rep. of Congo, Egypt, Eritrea, Ethiopia, Kenya, Rwanda, Sudan, Tanzania, Uganda	6,695	4,158
2	Amazon	Peru, Brazil	6,448	4,007
3	Chang Jiang (Yangtze)	China	6,378	3,964
4	Huang He (Yellow)	China	5,464	3,395
5	Amur	China, Russia	4,415	2,744
6	Lena	Russia	4,400	2,734
7	Congo	Angola, Dem. Rep. of Congo	4,373	2,718
8	Irtysh	China, Kazakhstan, Mongolia, Russia	4,248	2,640
9	Mackenzie	Canada	4,241	2,635
10	Mekong	Tibet, China, Myanmar, Thailand, Laos, Cambodia, Vietnam	4,183	2,600

The source of the Nile was discovered in 1858 when British explorer John Hanning Speke reached Lake Victoria Nyanza, in what is now Burundi. By following the Amazon from its source and up the Rio Pará, it is possible to sail for some 6,750 km (4,195 miles), but because experts do not regard this entire route as part of the Amazon basin, the Nile is still considered the world's longest river.

 ## GREATEST RIVERS*

	RIVER	OUTFLOW/SEA	AVERAGE FLOW (CU M/SEC)
1	Amazon	Brazil/South Atlantic	175,000
2	Zaïre	Angola–Congo/South Atlantic	39,000
3	Negro	Brazil/South Atlantic	35,000
4	Yangtze–Kiang	China/Yellow Sea	32,190
5	Orinoco	Venezuela/South Atlantic	25,200
6	Plata–Paraná–Grande	Uruguay/South Atlantic	22,900
7	Madeira–Mamoré–Grande	Brazil/South Atlantic	21,800
8	Brahmaputra	Bangladesh/Bay of Bengal	19,200
9	Yenisey–Angara–Selenga	Russia/Kara Sea	17,600
10	Lena–Kirenga	Russia/Arctic Ocean	16,600

* Based on rate of discharge at mouth

Rain falls on the Amazon basin on some 200 days a year, a total of over 200 cm (80 in). Fed by more than 1,000 tributaries, the river can reach a rate of almost 250,000 m³ per second in the rainiest month of June. A cubic metre of water weighs a tonne, so every minute, on average, almost 10 million tonnes of water flow out – a discharge so great that it dilutes the salinity of the sea for over 160 km (100 miles) from the mouth.

LARGEST LAKES

	LAKE	LOCATION	APPROXIMATE AREA (SQ KM)	(SQ MILES)
1	Caspian Sea	Azerbaijan/Iran/Kazakhstan/Russia/Turkmenistan	371,000	143,000
2	Michigan/Huron*	Canada/USA	117,610	45,300
3	Superior	Canada/USA	82,100	31,700
4	Victoria	Kenya/Tanzania/Uganda	69,500	26,828
5	Aral Sea	Kazakhstan/Uzbekistan	33,640	12,988
6	Tanganyika	Burundi/Tanzania/Dem. Rep. of Congo/Zambia	32,900	12,700
7	Baikal	Russia	31,500	12,162
8	Great Bear	Canada	31,328	12,096
9	Malawi (Nyasa)	Tanzania/Malawi/Mozambique	28,880	11,150
10	Great Slave	Canada	28,570	11,030

* Now considered as two lobes of the same lake

Lake Michigan/Huron is the world's largest freshwater lake. Lake Baikal (or Baykal) in Siberia, with a depth of as much as 1.63 km (1.02 miles) in parts, is the world's deepest. After two feeder rivers were diverted for irrigation, the area of the Aral Sea fell by so much between 1973 and 1989 that it dropped from 4th to 5th place.

LAKES WITH THE GREATEST VOLUME OF WATER

	LAKE	LOCATION	VOLUME (CU KM)	(CU MILES)
1	Caspian Sea	Azerbaijan/Iran/Kazakhstan/Russia/Turkmenistan	89,600	21,497
2	Baikal	Russia	22,995	5,517
3	Tanganyika	Burundi/Tanzania/Dem. Rep. of Congo/Zambia	18,304	4,391
4	Superior	Canada/USA	12,174	2,921
5	Michigan/Huron*	USA/Canada	8,449	2,642
6	Malawi (Nyasa)	Malawi/Mozambique/Tanzania	6,140	1,473
7	Victoria	Kenya/Tanzania/Uganda	2,518	604
8	Great Bear	Canada	2,258	542
9	Great Slave	Canada	1,771	425
10	Issyk	Kyrgyzstan	1,752	420

* Now considered as two lobes of the same lake

The Caspian Sea is the world's largest inland sea or lake, and receives more water than any other landlocked body of water – an average of 340 km³ (82 cu miles) per annum, which is causing a steady rise in sea level. This environmental change, along with pollution and the overfishing of the Caspian's famed sturgeon population, is among many threats to its future.

World Weather

TOP 10 WETTEST INHABITED PLACES

LOCATION/COUNTRY	HIGHEST TOTAL ANNUAL RAINFALL (MM)	(IN)
1 **Lloro,** Colombia	13,299.4	523.6
2 **Mawsynram,** India	11,872.0	467.4
3 **Mt. Waialeale,** Kauai, Hawaii, USA	11,684.0	460.0
4 **Cherrapuni,** India	10,795.0	425.0
5 **Debundscha,** Cameroon	10,287.0	405.0
6 **Quibdo,** Colombia	8,991.6	354.0
7 **Bellenden Ker,** Queensland, Australia	8,636.0	340.0
8 **Andagoya,** Colombia	7,137.4	281.0
9 **Henderson Lake,** British Colombia, Canada	6,502.4	256.0
10 **Crkvica,** Bosnia	4,648.2	183.0

For the purposes of comparison, Manchester, which is (incorrectly) reputed to be the wettest city in the UK, has an annual rainfall of 800 mm (31 in). Puu Kukui, a mountain in Hawaii, holds the US record for the most rainfall in a single year, receiving 1,790 cm (704.8 in) in 1982.

TOP 10 COLDEST PLACES – EXTREMES

LOCATION*	LOWEST TEMPERATURE (°C)	(°F)
1 **Vostok[#],** Antarctica	-89.2	-138.6
2 **Plateau Station[#],** Antarctica	-84.0	-129.2
3 **Oymyakon,** Russia	-71.1	-96.0
4 **Verkhoyansk,** Russia	-67.7	-90.0
5 **Northice[#],** Greenland	-66.0	-87.0
6 **Eismitte[#],** Greenland	-64.9	-85.0
7 **Snag, Yukon,** Canada	-63.0	-81.4
8 **Prospect Creek,** Alaska, USA	-62.1	-79.8
9 **Fort Selkirk,** Yukon, Canada	-58.9	-74.0
10 **Rogers Pass,** Montana, USA	-56.5	-69.7

* Maximum of two places per country listed

 # Present or former scientific research base

Source: *Philip Eden*

TOP 10 HOTTEST PLACES – EXTREMES

	LOCATION*	HIGHEST TEMPERATURE (°C)	(°F)
1	Al'Azīzīyah, Libya	58.0	136.4
2	Greenland Ranch, Death Valley, USA	56.7	134.0
3 =	Ghudamis, Libya	55.0	131.0
=	Kebili, Tunisia	55.0	131.0
5	Tombouctou, Mali	54.5	130.1
6	Araouane, Mali	54.4	130.0
7	Tirat Tavi, Israel	53.9	129.0
8	Ahwāz, Iran	53.5	128.3
9	Agha Jārī, Iran	53.3	128.0
10	Wadi Halfa, Sudan	52.8	127.0

* Maximum of two places per country listed

Source: Philip Eden

◀ **Rainy days**
Occasional rain is a fact of life in many of the world's cities, but few experience the intense downpours of the world's wettest places, where annual totals can exceed 6 m (20 ft)!

TOP 10 WARMEST PLACES IN THE UK

	WEATHER STATION/LOCATION	AVERAGE ANNUAL TEMPERATURE* (°C)	(°F)
1	St. Helier Harbour, Jersey	12.1	53.8
2	St. Mary's Airport, Isles of Scilly	11.9	53.4
3 =	St. Helier, Jersey	11.8	53.2
=	Lancresse, Guernsey	11.8	53.2
5 =	Central London	11.7	53.1
=	Round Island, Isles of Scilly	11.7	53.1
7	St. Mary's, Isles of Scilly	11.6	52.9
8 =	Pendennis Point, Cornwall	11.4	52.5
=	St. James's Park, London	11.4	52.5
10 =	Greenwich, London	11.3	52.3
=	Isle of Grain, Kent	11.3	52.3
=	Penlee Gardens, Penzance	11.3	52.3
=	Portland, Dorset	11.3	52.3
=	Ryde, Isle of Wight	11.3	52.3
=	St. Ives, Cornwall	11.3	52.3
=	Southsea, Hampshire	11.3	52.3

* Based on the Met Office's 30-year averages for the period 1971–2000

Source: The Met Office

TOP 10 WETTEST PLACES IN THE UK

	WEATHER STATION/LOCATION	AVERAGE ANNUAL RAINFALL* (MM)	(IN)
1	Crib Goch, Snowdonia, Wales	4,472.3	176.0
2	Styhead, Lake District, England	4,392.1	172.9
3	Delta, Snowdonia	4,311.2	169.7
4	Hallival, Isle of Rhum, Scottish Highlands	4,110.1	161.8
5	Beinn Ime, Ben Lomond, Scotland	4,000.2	157.5
6	Llydaw Intake, Snowdonia	3,835.4	150.9
7	Strath Cluanie, Scottish Highlands	3,728.3	146.8
8	Pen-Y-Pass, Snowdonia	3,684.8	145.1
9	Allt Uaine, Southern Grampians, Scotland	3,664.5	144.3
10	Glenshiel Forest, Scottish Highlands	3,588.8	141.3

* Based on the Met Office's 30-year averages for the period 1971–2000

Source: The Met Office

TOP 10 COLDEST PLACES IN THE UK

	WEATHER STATION/LOCATION	HEIGHT (M)	AVERAGE ANNUAL TEMPERATURE* (°C)	(°F)
1	Cairngorm Summit, Scottish Highlands	1,245	0.5	32.9
2	Aonach Mor, Scottish Highlands	1,130	1.2	34.1
3	Cairnwell, Scottish Highlands	933	2.3	36.1
4	Great Dun Fell (No. 2), Lake District	847	3.6	38.5
5	Faelar Lodge, Scottish Highlands	560	4.8	40.6
6	Bealach Na Ba (No. 2), Scottish Highlands	773	5.1	41.2
7	Lowther Hill, Dumfries and Galloway, Scotland	754	5.2	41.3
8 =	Cairngorm Chairlift, Scottish Highlands	663	5.3	41.5
=	Glen Ogle, Scottish Highlands	564	5.3	41.5
=	Moor House, Cumbria	556	5.3	41.5

* Based on the Met Office's 30-year averages for the period 1971–2000

Source: The Met Office

Natural Disasters

WORST VOLCANIC ERUPTIONS

	LOCATION	DATE	ESTIMATED NO. KILLED
1	**Tambora,** Indonesia	5–12 Apr 1815	92,000

The cataclysmic eruption of Tambora on the island of Sumbawa killed about 10,000 islanders immediately, with a further 82,000 dying subsequently (38,000 on Sumbawa and 44,000 on neighbouring Lombok) from disease and famine. An estimated 1.7 million tonnes of ash was expelled, which blocked out sunlight and affected the weather over large areas of the globe during the following year. One effect was to produce brilliant sunsets, depicted strikingly in paintings from the period, especially in the works of J.M.W. Turner.

2	**Unsen,** Japan	1 Apr 1793	53,000

During a period of intense volcanic activity in the area, the island of Unsen, or Unzen, completely disappeared, killing all its inhabitants.

3	**Mont Pelée,** Martinique	8 May 1902	40,000

After lying dormant for centuries, Mont Pelée began to erupt in April 1902. Assured that there was no danger, the 30,000 residents of the main city, St. Pierre, stayed in their homes. At 7.30 am on 8 May the volcano burst apart and showered the port with molten lava, ash, and gas, destroying virtually all life and property.

4	**Krakatoa,** Sumatra/Java	26–27 Aug 1883	36,380

After a series of eruptions over the course of several days, the uninhabited island of Krakatoa exploded with what may have been the biggest bang ever heard by humans, audible up to 4,800 km (3,000 miles) away. Some sources put the fatalities as high as 200,000, most of them killed by subsequent tsunamis that reached 30 m (100 ft) high.

5	**Nevado del Ruiz,** Colombia	13 Nov 1985	22,940

The Andean volcano gave warning signs of erupting, but by the time it was decided to evacuate the local inhabitants, it was too late. The hot steam, rocks, and ash ejected from Nevado del Ruiz melted its icecap, resulting in a mudslide that completely engulfed the town of Armero.

6	**Mount Etna,** Sicily	11 Mar 1669	over 20,000

Europe's largest volcano (3,280 m/10,760 ft) has erupted frequently, but the worst instance occurred in 1669 when the lava flow engulfed the town of Catania, killing at least 20,000.

7	**Laki,** Iceland	Jan–Jun 1783	20,000

Iceland is one the most volcanically active places on the Earth, but since it is sparsely populated, eruptions seldom result in major loss of life. The worst exception was the events at the Laki volcanic ridge, culminating on 11 June with the largest ever recorded lava flow. It engulfed many villages in a river of lava up to 80 km (50 miles) long and 30 m (100 ft) deep.

8	**Vesuvius,** Italy	24 Aug AD 79	16–20,000

When the previously dormant Vesuvius erupted suddenly, the Roman city of Herculaneum was engulfed by a mudflow while Pompeii was buried under a vast layer of pumice and volcanic ash. It was preserved in a near-perfect state, as was uncovered by the archaeological excavations that began in 1738.

9	**Vesuvius,** Italy	16–17 Dec 1631	up to 18,000

Although minor eruptions occurred at intervals after that of AD 79, the next major cataclysm was almost as disastrous, when lava and mudflows gushed down on to the surrounding towns, including Naples.

10	**Mount Etna,** Sicily	1169	over 15,000

Many died in Catania cathedral, where they believed they were safe, and more were killed when a tsunami caused by the eruption hit the port of Messina.

COSTLIEST HURRICANES TO STRIKE THE USA

	HURRICANE	YEAR	DAMAGE ($)*
1	"Great Miami"	1926	83,814,000,000
2	Andrew	1992	38,362,000,000
3	North Texas	1900	30,856,000,000
4	North Texas	1915	26,144,000,000
5	Southwest Florida	1944	19,549,000,000
6	New England	1938	19,275,000,000
7	Southeast Florida/Lake Okeechobee	1928	15,991,000,000
8	Betsy	1965	14,413,000,000
9	Donna	1960	13,967,000,000
10	Camille	1969	12,711,000,000

* Adjusted to 1998 dollars

Source: *Atlantic Oceanographic and Meteorological Laboratory/National Oceanic and Atmospheric Administration*

▼ **After the storm**
The widespread destruction caused by Hurricane Andrew resulted in 725,000 insurance claims in the state of Florida alone, making it the costliest natural disaster of the post-war era.

THE 10 MOST DEADLY TYPES OF DISASTER*

	TYPE OF DISASTER	FREQUENCY (1993–2002)	REPORTED DEATHS (1993–2002)
1	Droughts and famines	263	275,522
2	Floods	1,075	93,561
3	Earthquakes	229	75,391
4	Transportation accidents	1,684	68,106
5	Wind storms	823	60,971
6	Extreme temperatures	135	12,549
7	Industrial accidents	410	10,932
8	Avalanches/landslides	187	9,488
9	Volcanoes	52	511
10	Forest/scrub fires	146	458

* Natural and non-natural

Source: EM-DAT, CRED, University of Louvain, Belgium

At least one of the following criteria must be fulfilled in order that an event be classified as a disaster by EM-DAT: (a) 10 or more people reported killed; (b) 100 people reported affected; (c) a call for international assistance; and/or (d) declaration of a state of emergency.

THE 10 WORST EARTHQUAKES

	LOCATION	DATE	ESTIMATED NO. KILLED
1	Near East/Mediterranean	20 May 1202	1,100,000
2	Shenshi, China	2 Feb 1556	820,000
3	Calcutta, India	11 Oct 1737	300,000
4	Antioch, Syria	20 May 526	250,000
5	Tang-shan, China	28 Jul 1976	242,419
6	Nan-Shan, China	22 May 1927	200,000
7	Yeddo, Japan	30 Dec 1703	190,000
8	Kansu, China	16 Dec 1920	180,000
9	Messina, Italy	28 Dec 1908	160,000
10	Tokyo/Yokohama, Japan	1 Sep 1923	142,807

In some cases there are discrepancies between the "official" death tolls and the estimates of other authorities: a figure of 750,000 is sometimes quoted for the Tang-shan earthquake of 1976, for example, and totals ranging from 58,000 to 250,000 for the Messina quake of 1908. In recent times, the Armenian earthquake of 7 December 1988 and that which struck northwest Iran on 21 June 1990 led to the deaths of more than 55,000 (official estimate 28,854) and 50,000 respectively.

THE 10 WORST FLOODS

	LOCATION	DATE	ESTIMATED NO. KILLED
1	Huang He River, China	Aug 1931	3,700,000
2	Huang He River, China	Spring 1887	1,500,000
3	Holland	1 Nov 1530	400,000
4	Kaifong, China	1642	300,000
5	Henan, China	Sep–Nov 1939	over 200,000
6	Bengal, India	1876	200,000
7	Yangtze River, China	Aug–Sep 1931	140,000
8	Holland	1646	110,000
9	North Vietnam	30 Aug 1971	over 100,000
10 =	Friesland, Holland	1228	100,000
=	Dort, Holland	16 Apr 1421	100,000
=	Canton, China	12 Jun 1915	100,000
=	Yangtze River, China	Sep 1911	100,000

Records of floods caused by China's Huang He, or Yellow River, date back to 2297 BC. Since then, it has flooded at least 1,500 times, resulting in millions of deaths and giving it the nickname "China's Sorrow". According to some accounts, the flood of 1887 may have resulted in as many as six million deaths, as over 2,000 towns and villages were inundated. Even in the 1990s, almost 70 per cent of the 1,026,700,000 people worldwide affected by floods were Chinese.

LIFE ON EARTH

Rare & Many

TOP 10 ORDERS OF MAMMALS WITH THE MOST SPECIES

ORDER	NO. OF SPECIES
1 **Rodents**	1,729
2 **Bats**	981
3 **Insectivores**	374
4 **Carnivores**	252
5 **Marsupials**	248
6 **Even-toed ungulates** (pigs, hippopotamuses, camels, deer, cattle, and antelopes)	194
7 **Primates**	193
8 **Cetaceans** (whales, dolphins, and porpoises)	92
9 **Lagomorphs** (rabbits, hares, and pikas)	66
10 = **Edentates** (armadillos, sloths, and anteaters)	32
= **Seals**	32
Total (including those not in Top 10)	4,237

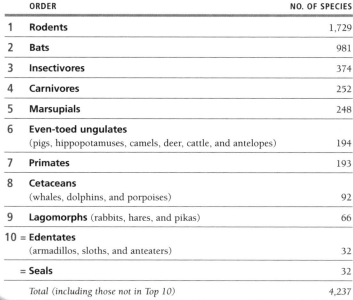

BORN TO BE WILD?

THE FIRST GORILLA born in captivity anywhere in the world was Colo, born on 22 December 1956 at Columbus Zoo, Ohio, USA. The offspring of Millie and Baron Macombo, who had been taken from the wild, Colo herself was successfully paired with Bongo, who had also been born at the zoo. Colo celebrated her 47th birthday in 2003. Improvements in the rearing of great apes in zoos – Columbus Zoo alone has bred over 30 gorillas, including the children and grandchildren of Colo – mean that today few are taken from the wild.

THE FIRST TO...

◄ **Great ape**
Gorillas are the largest representatives of the primate order, which includes lemurs, monkeys, apes, and humans.

THE 10 COUNTRIES WITH THE MOST THREATENED MAMMAL SPECIES

	COUNTRY	TOTAL NO. OF THREATENED MAMMAL SPECIES
1	Indonesia	147
2	India	86
3	China	81
4	Brazil	74
5	Mexico	72
6	Australia	63
7	Papua New Guinea	58
8 =	Kenya	50
=	Madagascar	50
=	Malaysia	50
=	Philippines	50
	UK	12

Source: 2003 IUCN Red List of Threatened Species

The IUCN Red List system classifies the degree of threat posed to wildlife on a sliding scale from Vulnerable (high risk of extinction in the wild) through Endangered (very high risk), to Critically Endangered (extremely high risk). The mammals numbered above belong to all of these categories.

THE 10 COUNTRIES WITH THE MOST THREATENED REPTILE SPECIES

	COUNTRY	TOTAL NO. OF THREATENED REPTILE SPECIES
1	Australia	38
2	China	31
3	Indonesia	28
4	USA	27
5	India	25
6	Vietnam	24
7	Brazil	22
8	Malaysia	21
9 =	Bangladesh	20
=	Myanmar	20
	UK	0

Source: 2003 IUCN Red List of Threatened Species

The actual threats to endangered species of reptiles are many and varied, and include a range of both human activities and natural events, ranging from habitat loss and degradation, invasions by alien species, hunting, and accidental destruction to persecution, pollution, and natural disasters.

TOP 10 MOST COMMON INSECTS*

	SPECIES/SCIENTIFIC NAME	APPROXIMATE NO. OF KNOWN SPECIES
1	Beetles (*Coleoptera*)	400,000
2	Butterflies and moths (*Lepidoptera*)	165,000
3	Ants, bees, and wasps (*Hymenoptera*)	140,000
4	True flies (*Diptera*)	120,000
5	Bugs (*Hemiptera*)	90,000
6	Crickets, grasshoppers, and locusts (*Orthoptera*)	20,000
7	Caddisflies (*Trichoptera*)	10,000
8	Lice (*Phthiraptera/Psocoptera*)	7,000
9	Dragonflies and damselflies (*Odonata*)	5,500
10	Lacewings (*Neuroptera*)	4,700

* By number of known species

This list includes only species that have been discovered and named: it is surmised that many thousands of species still await discovery. It takes no account of the absolute numbers of each species, which are truly colossal: there are at least one million insects for each of the Earth's 6.3 billion humans, which together would weigh at least 12 times as much as the human race. Among the most common insects are ants, flies, beetles, and the little-known springtails, which inhabit moist topsoil the world over. The latter alone probably outweigh the entire

TOP 10 WILD MAMMALS WITH THE LARGEST LITTERS

	SPECIES/SCIENTIFIC NAME	AVERAGE LITTER
1	Common tenrec (*Tenrec ecaudatus*)	25
2	Virginia (common) opossum (*Didelphis virginiana*)	21
3	Southern (black-eared) opossum (*Didelphis marsupialis*)	10
4 =	Ermine (*Mustela erminea*)	9
=	Prairie vole (*Microtus ochrogaster*)	9
=	Syrian (golden) hamster (*Mesocricetus auratus*)	9
7	African hunting dog (*Lycaon pictus*)	8.8
8 =	Dhole (Indian wild dog) (*Cuon alpinus*)	8
=	Pygmy opossum (*Marmosa robinsoni*)	8
=	South American mouse opossum (*Gracilinanus agilis*)	8

The prairie vole probably holds the world record for most offspring produced in a season. It has up to 17 litters in rapid succession, bringing up to 150 young into the world. Rabbits, despite their reputation as fast breeders, fail to make the list with an average litter size of six. All the numbers in the list are averages: the tiny tenrec can produce as many as 31 in a single litter and instances of domestic pigs producing 30 or more piglets at one go are not uncommon. Despite these prodigious reproductive peaks, mammalian litter sizes appear minute when compared with those of other animal groups. Many fish, for instance, can lay more than 10,000 eggs at a time and many amphibians more than 1,000.

Fast & Slow

FASTEST BIRDS

	SPECIES/SCIENTIFIC NAME	MAXIMUM RECORDED SPEED (KM/H)	(MPH)
1	**Common eider** (*Somateria mollissima*)	76	47
2	**Bewick's swan** (*Cygnus columbianus*)	72	44
3	= **Barnacle goose** (*Branta leucopsis*)	68	42
	= **Common crane** (*Grus grus*)	68	42
5	**Mallard** (*Anas platyrhynchos*)	65	40
6	= **Red-throated diver** (*Gavia stellata*)	61	38
	= **Wood pigeon** (*Columba palumbus*)	61	38
8	**Oystercatcher** (*Haematopus ostralegus*)	58	36
9	= **White-fronted goose** (*Anser albifrons*)	54	33
	= **Ring-necked pheasant** (*Phasianus colchichus*)	54	33

Source: *Chris Mead*

▼ Big cat nap
The seemingly leisurely lifestyle of the lion allows it to conserve energy to enable it to achieve bursts of speed when hunting.

FASTEST MAMMALS*

	SPECIES/SCIENTIFIC NAME	MAXIMUM RECORDED SPEED (KM/H)	(MPH)
1	**Cheetah** (*Acinonyx jubatus*)	114	71
2	**Pronghorn antelope** (*Antilocapra americana*)	95	57
3	= **Blue wildebeest (brindled gnu)** (*Connochaetes taurinus*)	80	50
	= **Lion** (*Panthera leo*)	80	50
	= **Springbok** (*Antidorcas marsupialis*)	80	50
6	= **Brown hare** (*Lepus capensis*)	77	48
	= **Red fox** (*Vulpes vulpes*)	77	48
8	= **Grant's gazelle** (*Gazella granti*)	76	47
	= **Thomson's gazelle** (*Gazella thomsonii*)	76	47
10	**Horse** (*Equus caballus*)	72	45

* Of those species for which data available at time of collection

Along with its relatively slow rivals, the cheetah can deliver its astonishing maximum speed over only relatively short distances. For comparison, the human male hundred-metre record stands at 9.78 seconds, equivalent to a speed of 37 km/h (23 mph), so all the mammals in the Top 10, and several others, are capable of outrunning a man. If a human ran the hundred metres at the cheetah's speed, the record would fall to 3 seconds.

SLEEPIEST MAMMALS

	SPECIES/SCIENTIFIC NAME	AVERAGE HOURS OF SLEEP PER DAY
1	= **Lion** (*Panthera leo*)	20
	= **Three-toed sloth** (*Bradypus variegatus*)	20
3	**Little brown bat** (*Myotis lucifugus*)	19.9
4	**Big brown bat** (*Eptesicus fuscus*)	19.7
5	= **Opossum** (*Didelphis virginiana*)	19.4
	= **Water opossum (yapok)** (*Chironectes minimus*)	19.4
7	**Giant armadillo** (*Priodontes maximus*)	18.1
8	**Koala** (*Phascolarctos cinereus*)	up to 18
9	**Nine-banded armadillo** (*Dasypus novemcinctus*)	17.4
10	**Southern owl monkey** (*Aotus azarai*)	17.0

The list excludes periods of hibernation, which can last up to several months among creatures such as the ground squirrel, marmot, and brown bear. At the other end of the scale comes the frantic shrew, which has to hunt and eat constantly or perish: it literally has no time for sleep.

▼ **Designed for speed**
The sprinters of the marine world, sailfish are capable of spurts of speed 13 times that of a champion human swimmer.

 **FASTEST FISH**

	SPECIES/SCIENTIFIC NAME	MAXIMUM RECORDED SPEED (KM/H)	(MPH)
1	**Sailfish** (*Istiophorus platypterus*)	112	69
2	**Striped marlin** (*Tetrapturus audax*)	80	50
3	**Wahoo (peto, jack mackerel)** (*Acanthocybium solandri*)	77	48
4	**Southern bluefin tuna** (*Thunnus maccoyii*)	76	47
5	**Yellowfin tuna** (*Thunnus albacares*)	74	46
6	**Blue shark** (*Prionace glauca*)	69	43
7	= **Bonefish** (*Albula vulpes*)	64	40
	= **Swordfish** (*Xiphias gladius*)	64	40
9	**Tarpon (ox-eye herring)** (*Megalops cyprinoides*)	56	35
10	**Tiger shark** (*Galeocerdo cuvier*)	53	33

Source: Lucy T. Verma

Flying fish are excluded: their top speed in the water is only 37 km/h (23 mph), but airborne they can reach 56 km/h (35 mph). Many sharks other than the two listed are contenders: the Great white shark (of *Jaws* fame) can manage 48 km/h (30 mph) with ease. For smaller fish (up to salmon size) a handy formula for estimating top swimming speed is just over 10 times its own length in centimetres per second: thus a trout 15 cm (6 in) long swims at 160 cm (63 in) per second.

HIBERNATING MAMMALS WITH THE SLOWEST HEARTBEATS*

	SPECIES/SCIENTIFIC NAME	HEARTBEATS PER MINUTE NON-HIBERNATING	HIBERNATING
1	**Franklin's ground squirrel** (*Spermophilus franklinii*)	n/a	2–4
2	**Olympic marmot** (*Marmota olympus*)	130–140	4
3	**Syrian (golden) hamster** (*Mesocricetus auratus*)	500–600	6
4	**American black bear[#]** (*Ursus americanus*)	40–50	8
5	**Hedgehog** (*Erinaceus europaeus*)	190	20
6	**Garden dormouse** (*Eliomys quercinus*)	n/a	25
7	**Eastern pigmy possum (dormouse possum, possum mouse)** (*Cercartetus nanus*)	300–650	28–80
8	**Birch mouse** (*Sicista betulina*)	550–600	30
9	**Big brown bat** (*Eptesicus fuscus*)	450	34
10	**Edible dormouse** (*Myoxus glis*)	450	35

* *Of those species for which data are available; one species per genus listed*

[#] *Not considered true hibernators by some experts – the heartbeat drops although body temperature is not significantly lowered*

Big & Small

SPECIES/SCIENTIFIC NAME	MAXIMUM WEIGHT (KG)	(LB)
1 **Pacific leatherback turtle*** (*Dermochelys coriacea*)	704.4	1,552
2 **Atlantic leatherback turtle*** (*Dermochelys coriacea*)	463.0	1,018
3 **Green sea turtle** (*Chelonia mydas*)	355.3	783
4 **Loggerhead turtle** (*Caretta caretta*)	257.8	568
5 **Alligator snapping turtle#** (*Macroclemys temmincki*)	100.0	220
6 **Flatback (sea) turtle** (*Natator depressus*)	78.2	171
7 **Hawksbill (sea) turtle** (*Eretmochelys imbricata*)	62.7	138
8 **Kemps Ridley turtle** (*Lepidochelys kempi*)	60.5	133
9 **Olive Ridley turtle** (*Lepidochelys olivacea*)	49.9	110
10 **Common snapping turtle#** (*Chelydra serpentina*)	38.5	85

* One species, differing in size according to where they live

Freshwater species

Source: *Lucy T. Verma*

Prehistoric turtles such as *Stupendemys geographicus* may have weighed three times as much as the largest living species, but even these attain an impressive size, with shell lengths of exceptional specimens reaching 2.56 m (8 ft 5 in).

▶ **Turtleweight**
Several turtle species can attain weights of four times that of a typical adult human.

SPECIES*/SCIENTIFIC NAME	WEIGHT# (G)	(OZ)
1 **Pygmy mouse lemur** (*Microcebus myoxinus*)	30	1.0
2 **Hairy-eared dwarf lemur** (*Allocebus trichotis*)	70–100	2.4–3.5
3 ***Tarsius pumilus***	80–165	2.8–5.8
4 **Lesser bush baby** (*Galago moholi*)	140–230	4.9–8.1
5 **Greater dwarf lemur** (*Cheirogaleus major*)	177–600	6.2–21.1
6 **Buffy-headed marmoset** (*Callithrix flaviceps*)	230–453	8.1–15.9
7 **Cotton-top tamarin** (*Saguinus oedipus*)	260–380	9.1–13.4
8 **Golden potto** (*Arctocebus calabarensis*)	266–465	9.3–16.4
9 **Golden-rumped lion tamarin** (*Leontopithecus chrysopygus*)	300–700	10.5–24.6
10 ***Callimico goeldii***	393–860	13.8–30.3

* Lightest species per genus

Weights range across male and female; ranked by lightest in range

The pygmy mouse lemur weighs less than a golf ball and measures just 6.2 cm (2.4 in). Its diminutive size and nocturnal habits resulted in a lack of sightings for over a century, and it was believed to be extinct until it was rediscovered in western Madagascar in 1993.

TOP 10 LIGHTEST TERRESTRIAL MAMMALS

SPECIES*/SCIENTIFIC NAME	LENGTH[#]		WEIGHT[†]	
	(MM)	(IN)	(G)	(OZ)
1 **Pygmy shrew** (*Sorex hoyi*)	46–100	1.8–3.9	2.1–18	0.07–0.63
2 **Pygmy shrew** (*Suncus etruscus*)	35–48	1.4–1.9	2.5	0.22
3 **African pygmy mouse** (*Mus minutoides*)	45–82	1.8–3.2	2.5–12.0	0.09–0.42
4 **Desert shrew** (*Notiosorex crawfordi*)	48–69	1.9–2.7	3.0–5.0	0.1–0.17
5 **Forest musk shrew** (*Sylvisorex* sp.)	45–100	1.8–3.9	3.0–12.0	0.1–0.42
6 **White-toothed shrew** (*Crocidura suaveolens*)	40–100	1.6–3.9	3.0–13.0	0.1–0.46
7 **Asiatic shrew** (*Soriculus salenskii*)	44–99	1.7–3.9	5.0–6.0	0.17–0.21
8 **Delany's swamp mouse** (*Delanymys brooksi*)	50–63	1.9–2.5	5.2–6.5	0.18–0.23
9 **Birch mouse** (*Sicista* sp.)	50–90	1.9–3.5	6.0–14.0	0.21–0.49
10 **Pygmy mouse** (*Baiomys* sp.)	50–81	1.9–3.2	7.0–8.0	0.24–0.59

* Lightest species per genus

\# Some jerboas are smaller, but no weights have yet been recorded

† Ranked by lightest in range

TOP 10 HEAVIEST TERRESTRIAL MAMMALS

SPECIES*/SCIENTIFIC NAME	LENGTH		WEIGHT	
	(M)	(FT)	(KG)	(LB)
1 **African elephant** (*Loxodonta africana*)	7.5	24.6	7,500	16,534
2 **Hippopotamus** (*Hippopotamus amphibius*)	5.0	16.4	4,500	9,920
3 **White rhinoceros** (*Ceratotherium simum*)	4.2	13.7	3,600	7,937
4 **Giraffe** (*Giraffa camelopardalis*)	4.7	15.4	1,930	4,255
5 **American buffalo** (*Bison bison*)	3.5	11.4	1,000	2,205
6 **Moose** (*Alces alces*)	3.1	10.1	825	1,820
7 **Grizzly bear** (*Ursus arctos*)	3.0	9.8	780	1,720
8 **Arabian camel (dromedary)** (*Camelus dromedarius*)	3.45	11.3	690	1,521
9 **Siberian tiger** (*Pantheratigris altaica*)	3.3	10.8	360	793
10 **Gorilla** (*Gorilla gorilla gorilla*)	2.0	6.5	275	606

* Heaviest species per genus

The list excludes domesticated cattle and horses. It also avoids comparing close kin such as the African and Indian elephants, highlighting instead the sumo stars within distinctive large mammal groups such as the bears, deer, big cats, primates, and bovines (ox-like mammals).

Killer Creatures

TOP 10 LARGEST BIRDS OF PREY*

	SPECIES/SCIENTIFIC NAME	MAXIMUM LENGTH (CM)	(IN)
1	Himalayan griffon vulture (*Gyps himalayensis*)	150	59
2	Californian condor (*Gymnogyps californianus*)	134	53
3	Andean condor (*Vultur gryphus*)	130	51
4 =	Lammergeier (*Gypaetus barbatus*)	115	45
=	Lappet-faced vulture (*Torgos tracheliotus*)	115	45
6	Eurasian griffon vulture (*Gyps fulvus*)	110	43
7	European black vulture (*Aegypus monachus*)	107	42
8	Harpy eagle (*Harpia harpyja*)	105	41
9	Wedge-tailed eagle (*Aquila audax*)	104	41
10	Ruppell's griffon (*Gyps rueppellii*)	101	40

* By length; diurnal only – hence excluding owls

The entrants in this Top 10 all measure more than 1 m (39 in) from beak to tail; in all but the vultures, the female will be larger than the male. All these raptors, or aerial hunters, have remarkable eyesight and can spot their victims from great distances, but even if they kill animals heavier than themselves, they are generally unable to take wing with them: stories of eagles carrying off lambs and small children are usually fictitious.

THE 10 TYPES OF SHARKS THAT HAVE KILLED THE MOST HUMANS

	SPECIES/ SCIENTIFIC NAME	UNPROVOKED ATTACKS* (TOTAL)	(FATAL)#
1	Great white (*Carcharodon carcharias*)	205	58
2	Tiger (*Galeocerdo cuvier*)	82	20
3	Bull (*Carcharhinus leucas*)	64	17
4	Requiem (*Carcharhinus*†)	33	8
5	Blue (*Prionace glauca*)	12	4
6	Sand tiger (*Carcharias taurus*)	29	2
7	Shortfin mako (*Isurus oxyrinchus*)	7	1
8	Oceanic whitetip (*Carcharhinus longimanus*)	5	1
9	Dusky (*Carcharhinus obscurus*)	3	1
10 =	Galapagos (*Carcharhinus galapagensis*)	1	1
=	Ganges (*Carcharhinus gangeticus*)	1	1

* 1580–2003

Where fatalities are equal, entries are ranked by total attacks

† Species unspecified

Source: *International Shark Attack File, Florida Museum of Natural History*

TOP 10 WIDEST-RANGING SOLITARY CARNIVORES*

	SPECIES/SCIENTIFIC NAME	MALE RANGE# (SQ KM)
1	Polar bear (*Ursus maritimus*)	500–300,000
2	Siberian tiger (*Panthera tigris altaica*)	3,100–4,140
3	Brown (grizzly) bear (*Ursus arctos*)	293–3,029
4	European lynx (*Lynx lynx*)	275–450
5	Mountain lion (*Felis concolor*)	78–277
6	Canadian lynx (*Lynx canadensis*)	145–243
7	Bobcat (*Lynx rufus*)	13–201
8	Jaguar (*Panthera onca*)	3–200
9	American black bear (*Ursus americanus*)	109–115
10	Tiger (*Panthera tigris*)	60–100

* Of those species for which data are available

Ranked by the furthest in range

The polar bear is the world's largest carnivore. There are an estimated 22,000 to 28,000 in the wild, and although they are not territorial, in their search for food, individual bears and females accompanied by cubs travel across a vast home range, covering an average of 8,850 km (5,500 miles) a year.

THE 10 SNAKES WITH THE DEADLIEST BITES

	SPECIES/SCIENTIFIC NAME	ESTIMATED LETHAL DOSE FOR HUMANS (MG)	AVERAGE VENOM PER BITE (MG)	POTENTIAL HUMAN FATALITIES PER BITE
1	**Coastal taipan** (*Oxyuranus scutellatus*)	1	120	120
2	**Common krait** (*Bungarus caeruleus*)	0.5	42	84
3	**Philippine cobra** (*Naja naja philippinensis*)	2	120	60
4 =	**King cobra** (*Ophiophagus hannah*)	20	1,000	50
=	**Russell's viper** (*Daboia russelli*)	3	150	50
6	**Black mamba** (*Dendroaspis polyepis*)	3	135	45
7	**Yellow-jawed tommygoff** (*Bothrops asper*)	25	1,000	40
8 =	**Multibanded krait** (*Bungarus multicinctus*)	0.8	28	35
=	**Tiger snake** (*Notechis scutatus*)	1	35	35
10	**Jararacussu** (*Bothrops jarararcussu*)	25	800	32

Source: *Russell E. Gough*

In comparing the danger posed by poisonous snakes, this list takes account of such factors as venom strength – and hence its lethality – as well as the amount injected per bite (most snakes inject about 15 per cent of their venom per bite).

▼ Big wings
One of the largest birds of prey, the Andean condor also has the greatest wing area of any bird, with some spanning more than 3 m (10 ft) from tip to tip.

THE 10 DEADLIEST SPIDERS

	SPECIES/SCIENTIFIC NAME	RANGE
1	**Banana spider** (*Phonenutria nigriventer*)	Central and South America
2	**Sydney funnel web** (*Atrax robustus*)	Australia
3	**Wolf spider** (*Lycosa raptoria/erythrognatha*)	Central and South America
4	**Black widow** (*Latrodectus species*)	Widespread
5	**Violin spider/Recluse spider** (*Loxosceles reclusa*)	Widespread
6	**Slender sac spider** (*Cheiracanthium mildei*)	Widespread
7	**Tarantula** (*Eurypelma rubropilosum*)	Neotropics
8	**Tarantula** (*Acanthoscurria atrox*)	Neotropics
9	**Tarantula** (*Lasiodora klugi*)	Neotropics
10	**Tarantula** (*Pamphobeteus species*)	Neotropics

This list ranks spiders according to their "lethal potential" – their venom yield divided by their venom potency. The banana spider, for example, yields 6 mg of venom, with 1 mg the estimated lethal dose in man. However, few spiders are capable of killing humans – there were just 14 recorded deaths caused by black widows in the USA in the whole of the 19th century – since their venom yield is relatively low compared with that of the most dangerous snakes.

TOP 10 HEAVIEST CARNIVORES

	SPECIES/SCIENTIFIC NAME	MAXIMUM LENGTH (M)	(FT)	(IN)	MAXIMUM WEIGHT (KG)	(LB)
1	**Southern elephant seal** (*Mirounga leonina*)	6.5	21	4	3,500	7,716
2	**Walrus** (*Odobenus rosmarus*)	3.8	12	6	1,200	2,646
3	**Steller's sea lion** (*Eumetopias jubatus*)	3.0	9	8	1,100	2,425
4	**Grizzly bear** (*Ursus arctos*)	3.0	9	8	780	1,720
5	**Polar bear** (*Ursus maritimus*)	2.6	8	6	600	1,323
6	**Tiger** (*Panthera tigris*)	2.8	9	2	300	661
7	**Lion** (*Panthera leo*)	1.9	6	3	250	551
8	**American black bear** (*Ursus americanus*)	1.8	6	0	227	500
9	**Giant panda** (*Ailuropoda melanoleuca*)	1.5	5	0	160	353
10	**Spectacled bear** (*Tremarctos ornatus*)	1.8	6	0	140	309

Of the 273 mammal species in the order *Carnivora* or meat-eaters, many (including bears) are in fact omnivorous, and around 40 specialize in eating fish or insects. All, however, share a common ancestry indicated by the butcher's-knife form of their canine teeth. As the Top 10 would otherwise consist exclusively of seals and related marine carnivores, only three representatives have been included in order to enable the terrestrial heavyweight division to make an appearance.

THE 10 MOST COMMON ANIMAL PHOBIAS

	ANIMAL	MEDICAL TERM
1	Spiders	Arachnephobia or arachnophobia
2	Snakes	Ophidiophobia, ophiophobia, ophiciophobia, herpetophobia, or snakephobia
3	Wasps	Spheksophobia
4	Birds (especially pigeons)	Ornithophobia
5	Mice	Musophobia or muriphobia
6	Fish	Ichthyophobia
7	Bees	Apiphobia or apiophobia
8	Dogs	Cynophobia or kynophobia
9	Caterpillars and other insects	Entomophobia
10	Cats	Ailurophobia, elurophobia, felinophbia, galeophbia, or gatophobia

Phobias directed at creatures that may bite or sting or carry disease, such as rabid dogs or rats during the Plague, are understandable. Such fears are so widespread that they have been readily exploited in films including *Arachnophobia* (1990), *The Swarm* (1978), *Venom* (1982), and *The Birds* (1963).

▼ Fear factor
Snakes are the object of one of the most widespread animal phobias, prevalent even in countries where they are rare or unknown.

TOP 10 COUNTRIES WITH THE MOST CAPTIVE ELEPHANTS

	COUNTRY	ELEPHANTS*
1	USA	622
2	Germany	265
3	UK	130
4	Italy	74
5	Sri Lanka	72
6	France	59
7	Spain	49
8	South Africa	46
9	= Canada	45
	= Netherlands	45

* *Total of known elephants in captivity in zoos, circuses, and private collections, 2001*

Source: *Absolut Elephant*

Of the 622 captive elephants in the USA, 340 were in zoos, 241 in circuses, and 41 in private collections, including three at Michael Jackson's Neverland.

TOP 10 ANIMAL CHARITIES IN THE UK

	CHARITY	VOLUNTARY INCOME (£)
1	Royal Society for the Prevention of Cruelty to Animals	60,245,000
2	People's Dispensary for Sick Animals	45,537,000
3	National Canine Defence League	18,647,000
4	Cats Protection League	18,193,000
5	Blue Cross Animals' Hospital	14,997,000
6	The Donkey Sanctuary	12,335,000
7	Battersea Dogs Home	7,039,000
8	Redwings Horse Sanctuary	5,678,000
9	World Society for the Protection of Animals	5,056,000
10	Scottish Society for the Prevention of Cruelty to Animals	4,661,000

Source: *Charities Aid Foundation*

The RSPCA was founded in London in 1824, after the passing two years earlier of an Act of Parliament against animal cruelty. It won royal patronage from Queen Victoria in 1840.

TOP 10 PEARL-FISHING COUNTRIES

	COUNTRY	PEARLS, MOTHER-OF-PEARL, SHELLS (2001) (KG)
1	Croatia	3,125,000
2	Philippines	2,433,000
3	Sri Lanka	498,000
4	Mexico	463,000
5	Tanzania	436,743
6	Papua New Guinea	346,546
7	Australia	250,000
8	Russia	224,000
9	Palau	200,000
10	Fiji	160,000
	World total	*10,275,350*

Source: *Food and Agriculture Organization of the United Nations*

Two French overseas territories are excluded, not being independent states: French Polynesia (820,724 kg catch in 2001) and New Caledonia (342,700 kg).

TOP 10 INSECT AND SPIDER FILMS

	FILM	CREATURE(S)	YEAR
1	A Bug's Life*	Various	1998
2	Antz*	Ants	1998
3	Arachnophobia	Spiders	1990
4	The Fly	Housefly	1986
5	Mimic	Mutant insects	1997
6	James and the Giant Peach#	Various	1996
7	Microcosmos†	Insects	1996
8	The Fly II	Housefly	1989
9	Kingdom of the Spiders	Tarantulas	1977
10	The Swarm	Bees	1978

* *Animated*

Part-animated/part-live action

† *Documentary*

The creatures, which are central to the plots of these films, range from the cute to the terrifying; many exploit widespread phobias relating to insects and spiders. Minor crawl-on roles, such as that of the genetically modified spider that turns Peter Parker into Spider-Man in the 2002 film, have been omitted.

Jaws of death
Although still a rare occurrence, shark attacks have increased in line with the popularity of diving and water-based pursuits.

THE 10 PLACES WHERE SHARK ATTACKS ARE MOST COMMON

LOCATION	FATAL ATTACKS	LAST FATAL ATTACK	TOTAL ATTACKS*
1 USA (excluding Hawaii)	38	2003	737
2 Australia	132	2003	282
3 South Africa	40	2003	199
4 Hawaii	14	1992	96
5 Brazil	19	2002	80
6 Papua New Guinea	26	2000	49
7 New Zealand	9	1968	44
8 Mexico	20	1997	35
9 Iran	8	1985	23
10 The Bahamas	1	1968	21

* Confirmed unprovoked attacks on humans, including non-fatal

Source: *International Shark Attack File/American Elasmobranch Society/Florida Museum of Natural History*

The International Shark Attack File monitors worldwide incidents, a total of more than 2,000 of which have been recorded since the 16th century. The 1990s had the highest attack total (514) of any decade, while 55 unprovoked attacks were recorded in 2003 alone. This upward trend is believed to reflect the increase in the numbers of people engaging in scuba diving and other aquatic activities, rather than any observed increase in the aggressive instincts of sharks.

TOP 10 SPECIES OF FISH MOST CAUGHT*

SPECIES	TOTAL CATCH (2001) (TONNES)
1 Herrings, sardines, and anchovies	20,460,640
2 Carps, barbels, and cyprinid	16,975,250
3 Cods, hakes, and haddocks	9,224,573
4 Tunas, bonitos, and billfish	5,835,258
5 Oysters	4,406,833
6 Shrimps and prawns	4,221,709
7 Clams, cockles, and arkshells	3,917,969
8 Squids, cuttlefish, and octopuses	3,346,844
9 Salmons, trouts, and smelts	2,673,043
10 Tilapias and cichlids	2,068,179
World total	130,207,400

* Including shellfish and molluscs

Source: *Food and Agriculture Organization of the United Nations*

The world's total fishing catch comprises 92,356,034 tonnes caught in the wild, and 37,851,356 tonnes from fish farms – equivalent to 20.6 kilos for each person on the planet, although not all fish caught is for human consumption. The trade is worth $55.9 billion a year, with Thailand and China the leading countries, each exporting around $4 billion-worth.

Dogs & Cats

DOGS' NAMES IN THE UK

FEMALE		MALE
Molly	1	Max
Holly	2	Charlie
Rosie	3	Ben
Poppy	4	Jake
Lucy	5	Barney
Ellie	6	Jack
Tess	7	Buster
Meg	8	Toby
Bonnie	9	Jasper
Daisy	10	Oscar

Source: *Argos Insurance Services*

Recent surveys of dogs' names in the UK have produced slightly differing results, but one thing they agree on is the increasing trend for giving them names that could equally be those of humans.

▼ Top dog

Popular as hunting dogs since the early 19th century, the Labrador retriever heads the list of Britain's leading dog breeds by a considerable margin.

DOG BREEDS IN THE UK

	BREED	NO. REGISTERED BY KENNEL CLUB (2003)
1	Labrador retriever	41,306
2 =	Cocker spaniel	14,892
=	German shepherd (Alsatian)	14,892
4	English springer spaniel	12,599
5	Staffordshire bull terrier	11,325
6	Golden retriever	10,710
7	Cavalier King Charles spaniel	10,614
8	West Highland white terrier	9,823
9	Boxer	9,542
10	Border terrier	6,447

There are perhaps 500 dog breeds in the world, of which The Kennel Club currently recognizes 201 in seven groups: terrier, hound, pastoral, utility, gundog, toy, and working.

PET DOG POPULATIONS

	COUNTRY	ESTIMATED DOG POPULATION (2002)
1	USA	61,080,000
2	Brazil	30,051,000
3	China	22,908,000
4	Japan	9,650,000
5	Russia	9,600,000
6	South Africa	9,100,000
7	France	8,150,000
8	Italy	7,600,000
9	Poland	7,520,000
10	Thailand	6,900,000
	UK	*5,800,000*

Source: *Euromonitor*

Dog ownership in the USA has become increasingly humanized: not only are dogs often considered as "one of the family", but a huge industry has grown up to cater for their nutrition and welfare – to a standard that rivals that enjoyed by many people. In second-placed Brazil, dogs make up almost 43 per cent of the total pet population and account for 77 per cent of pet food sales.

TOP 10 | PET CAT POPULATIONS

	COUNTRY	ESTIMATED CAT POPULATION (2002)
1	USA	76,430,000
2	China	53,100,000
3	Russia	12,700,000
4	Brazil	12,466,000
5	France	9,600,000
6	Italy	9,400,000
7	UK	7,700,000
8	Ukraine	7,350,000
9	Japan	7,300,000
10	Germany	7,000,000

Source: *Euromonitor*

Estimates of the number of domestic cats in the 20 leading countries reveal a total in excess of 221 million, with the greatest increases experienced in Brazil, where the cat population grew by 28.4 per cent, from 9,709,000 in 1998 to 12,466,000 in 2002.

▶ **Persian puss**
Foremost among British non-native and longhaired cat breeds, the Persian has been bred in Europe since the 16th century.

PUT ON A CAT SHOW

BRITISH ARTIST HARRISON WEIR devised the first ever cat show, and provided illustrations of the entrants for the *Illustrated London News*. The show was held at the Crystal Palace, London, on 13 July 1871, when some 160 cats were exhibited. Cat shows became hugely popular, having among their followers Queen Victoria, who owned Persian cats. In the USA, one of the first cat shows took place at Bunnell's Museum, Broadway, New York, in 1881, but the first major national event was held in 1895 at Madison Square Garden – and included wild cats and ocelots.

THE FIRST TO...

TOP 10 | CAT BREEDS IN THE UK

	BREED	NO. REGISTERED BY CAT FANCY (2002)
1	British short hair	5,365
2	Persian	4,264
3	Siamese	3,546
4	Burmese	2,624
5	Bengal	2,126
6	Birman	1,958
7	Ragdoll	1,608
8	Maine coon	1,392
9	Oriental short hair	1,241
10	Exotic short hair	815

This Top 10 is based on a total of 28,970 cats registered with the Governing Council of the Cat Fancy in 2002.

TOP 10 | CATS' NAMES IN THE UK

FEMALE		MALE
Lucy	1	Charlie
Poppy	2	Sammy
Cleo	3	Billy
Holly	4	Oscar
Daisy	5	Oliver
Molly	6	Ben
Tabitha	7	Smokie
Misty	8	Tigger
Amber	9	Sooty
Chloe	10	Leo

Source: *Feline Advisory Bureau/Felix*

Today's cats receive human names to an even greater extent than dogs – three-quarters of the 20 most common cats' names are in the Top 20 babies' names.

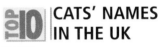

Farm Facts

TOP 10 FRUIT CROPS

	CROP	PRODUCTION (2003) (TONNES)
1	Tomatoes	110,513,591
2	Watermelons	83,199,791
3	Bananas	68,279,192
4	Oranges	62,170,503
5	Grapes	62,150,308
6	Apples	57,938,065
7	Coconuts	50,227,217
8	Plantains	32,796,160
9	Mangoes	26,196,090
10	Cantaloupes and other melons	21,750,512

Source: *Food and Agriculture Organization of the United Nations*

TOP 10 TYPES OF LIVESTOCK

	ANIMAL	STOCKS (2003)
1	Chickens	16,381,477,000
2	Cattle	1,368,054,950
3	Ducks	1,107,445,000
4	Sheep	1,028,594,330
5	Pigs	952,899,660
6	Goats	764,510,558
7	Rabbits	530,066,000
8	Turkeys	257,133,000
9	Geese	247,122,000
10	Buffaloes	170,458,495

Source: *Food and Agriculture Organization of the United Nations*

TOP 10 CATTLE COUNTRIES

	COUNTRY	CATTLE (2003)
1	India	226,100,000
2	Brazil	176,500,000
3	China	108,251,500
4	USA	96,106,000
5	Argentina	50,869,000
6	Sudan	38,325,000
7	Ethiopia	35,500,000
8	Mexico	30,800,000
9	Australia	27,215,000
10	Russia	26,524,540
	UK	10,391,000
	World total	1,368,054,950

Source: *Food and Agriculture Organization of the United Nations*

Since the 1960s, growing and increasingly wealthy populations have raised the demand for milk and meat, prompting an increase in the number of cattle: the world total has risen by over 30 per cent since 1961, while that of China has more than doubled.

TOP 10 VEGETABLE CROPS

	CROP*	PRODUCTION (2003) (TONNES)		CROP*	PRODUCTION (2003) (TONNES)
1	Sugar cane	1,350,293,120	6	Cabbages	62,013,881
2	Potatoes	311,416,329	7	Onions (dry)	52,068,053
3	Sugar beets	238,281,136	8	Yams	39,581,313
4	Soybeans	189,523,638	9	Cucumbers and gherkins	37,607,067
5	Sweet potatoes	136,656,488	10	Aubergines	28,913,000

* Excluding cereals

Source: *Food and Agriculture Organization of the United Nations*

TOP 10 MILK-PRODUCING COUNTRIES

	COUNTRY	PRODUCTION* (2003) (TONNES)
1	USA	78,155,000
2	India	36,500,000
3	Russia	32,800,000
4	Germany	28,012,000
5	France	24,800,000
6	Brazil	23,315,000
7	UK	15,054,000
8	New Zealand	14,200,000
9	Ukraine	13,600,000
10	China	13,333,250
	World total	507,384,506

* Fresh cow's milk

Source: *Food and Agricultural Organization of the United Nations*

▼ The cows come home
First introduced by pioneer settlers in 1624, cattle ranching in the USA became one of the nation's major industries.

TOP 10 COUNTRIES WHERE SHEEP MOST OUTNUMBER PEOPLE

	COUNTRY	SHEEP (2003)	HUMAN POPULATION (2003)	SHEEP PER PERSON (2003)
1	New Zealand	44,700,000	3,951, 307	11.31
2	Australia	98,200,000	19,731,984	4.98
3	Mongolia	11,797,000	2,712,315	4.35
4	Uruguay	11,000,000	3,413,329	3.22
5	Mauritania	8,700,000	2,912,584	2.99
6	Iceland	470,000	280,798	1.67
7	Turkmenistan	6,000,000	4,775,544	1.27
8	= Ireland	4,828,500	3,924,023	1.23
	= Namibia	2,370,000	1,927,447	1.23
	= Sudan	47,000,000	38,114,160	1.23
	UK	35,800,000	60,094,648	0.60
	World total	1,028,594,330	6,302,486,693	0.16

Source: *Food and Agricultural Organization of the United Nations*

The estimated total world sheep population in 2003 was 1,028,594,330 – a global average of one sheep for every 6.08 people (or 0.16 sheep per person) – but, as this Top 10 shows, there are a number of countries where the tables are turned, and sheep far outnumber humans.

Tree Tops

TOP 10 COUNTRIES WITH THE LARGEST AREAS OF FOREST

COUNTRY	AREA (2000) (SQ KM)	(SQ MILES)
1 Russia	8,513,920	3,287,243
2 Brazil	5,439,905	2,100,359
3 Canada	2,445,710	944,294
4 USA	2,259,930	872,564
5 China	1,634,800	631,200
6 Australia	1,545,390	596,678
7 Dem. Rep. of Congo	1,352,070	522,037
8 Indonesia	1,049,860	405,353
9 Angola	697,560	269,329
10 Peru	652,150	251,796
World total	38,561,590	14,888,715
UK	27,940	10,788

Source: *Food and Agriculture Organization of the United Nations*, State of the World's Forests, 2003

TOP 10 COUNTRIES WITH THE LARGEST AREAS OF TROPICAL FOREST

COUNTRY	AREA (SQ KM)	(SQ MILES)
1 Brazil	3,012,730	1,163,222
2 Dem. Rep. of Congo	1,350,710	521,512
3 Indonesia	887,440	343,029
4 Peru	756,360	292,032
5 Bolivia	686,380	265,012
6 Venezuela	556,150	214,730
7 Columbia	531,860	205,352
8 Mexico	457,650	176,700
9 India	444,500	171,622
10 Angola	375,640	145,035
World total	14,076,490	5,434,964

Source: *Food and Agriculture Organization of the United Nations*, State of the World's Forests, 2003

TOP 10 POLLINATORS IN TROPICAL FORESTS*

POLLINATOR	PERCENTAGE OF POLLINATION SYSTEMS
1 Bee	50.6
2 Other insects	15.1
3 Beetle	9.2
4 Bird	8.4
5 Moth	5.6
6 Bat	2.6
7 Butterfly	2.3
8 Wind	2.1
9 Large wasp	1.0
10 Fly	0.5

* *Based on pollination systems in Costa Rican and Malaysian tropical forests*

▼ **Tree Line**
The Olympic National Park, Washington, USA, contains 2,557 sq km (987 sq miles) of forest, including the only rainforest in the northern hemisphere.

TOP 10 LARGEST FORESTS IN THE UK

	FOREST*/LOCATION	LOCATION	AREA (SQ KM)	(SQ MILES)
1	Galloway Forest Park	Dumfries and Galloway	770	297
2	Kielder Forest Park	Northumberland	610	235
3	New Forest	Hampshire	270	104
4	Dornoch Forest	Sutherland	260	100
5	Argyll Forest Park	Argyll	210	81
6	Queen Elizabeth Forest Park	Stirling	200	77
7	Thetford Forest Park	Norfolk/Suffolk	190	73
8	Affric Forest (Fort Augustus)	Inverness-shire	180	69
9	Tay Forest Park	Perthshire	170	65
10	Glengarry Forest (Lochaber Forest District)	Inverness-shire	165	63

* Forestry Commission forests, including areas designated as Forest Parks, which can include areas not covered by woodland

Source: *Forestry Commission*

TOP 10 TIMBER-PRODUCING COUNTRIES

	COUNTRY	ROUNDWOOD PRODUCTION (2002) (CU M)	(CU FT)
1	USA	477,821,131	16,874,095,560
2	India	319,418,047	11,280,142,920
3	China	284,908,256	10,061,441,040
4	Brazil	237,467,063	8,386,070,966
5	Canada	200,326,008	7,074,446,865
6	Russia	176,900,000	6,247,165,123
7	Indonesia	116,052,252	4,098,346,982
8	Ethiopia	92,659,752	3,272,248,564
9	Nigeria	69,482,328	2,453,745,484
10	Sweden	67,500,000	2,383,740,225
	World total	*3,380,456,910*	*119,379,720,200*
	UK	*7,577,000*	*26,757,925*

Source: *Food and Agriculture Organization of the United Nations*

WORLD'S TALLEST TREE

UNTIL RECENTLY a coast redwood at Montgomery State Reserve near Ukiah, California, at 112.01 m (367 ft 6 in), was considered the record-holder, but it has been overtaken by a recent discovery, the so-called "Stratosphere Giant" redwood of 117.8 m (386 ft) in the Rockefeller Forest, Humboldt Redwoods State Park, California. Its location is kept secret to protect it from tourists. Australia once claimed a 150-m (492-ft) eucalyptus tree at Watts River, Victoria, but the tallest surviving example, in the Styx Forest, Tasmania, is 91.6 m (300 ft 6 in).

IT'S A FACT

TOP 10 TALLEST TREES IN THE UK*

	TREE	LOCATION	HEIGHT (M)	(FT)
1	Douglas fir#	Dunans Estate, Argyll and Bute, Scotland	62	203
2	Grand fir	Ardkinglas Woodland Garden, Argyll and Bute, Scotland	61	200
3	Sitka spruce	Randolph's Leap, Moray, Scotland	58	190
4	Giant sequoia#	Benmore Botanical Garden, Argyll and Bute, Scotland	53	174
5	= Noble fir	Ardkinglas Woodland Garden	52	171
	= Norway spruce	Reelig Glen Wood, Moniack, Highland, Scotland	52	171
7	Western hemlock	Benmore Botanical Garden	51	167
8	European silver fir	Benmore Botanical Garden	50	164
9	Nordmann fir	Cragside, Northumberland	48	157
10	Coastal redwood	Bodnant Garden, Colwyn Bay, Conwy, Wales	47	154

* The tallest known example of each of the 10 tallest species

Further examples of same species match this height

Source: *The Tree Register of the British Isles*

THE HUMAN WORLD

Human Body & Health

TOP 10 HEALTHIEST COUNTRIES

	COUNTRY	HEALTHY LIFE EXPECTANCY AT BIRTH*
1	Japan	75.0
2	San Marino	73.4
3	Sweden	73.3
4	Switzerland	73.2
5	Monaco	72.9
6	Iceland	72.8
7	Italy	72.7
8	= Australia	72.6
	= Spain	72.6
10	= Canada	72.0
	= France	72.0
	= Norway	72.0
	UK	70.6

* Average number of years expected to be spent in good health

Source: *World Health Organisation*, World Health Report 2003

▶ **Long life**
Diet and other factors have enabled Japanese healthy life expectancy to top the world league table.

THE 10 MOST COMMON ALLERGENS*

FOOD		ENVIRONMENTAL
Nuts	1	House dust mite
Shellfish/seafood	2	Grass pollens
Milk	3	Tree pollens
Wheat	4	Cats
Eggs	5	Dogs
Fresh fruit (apples, oranges, strawberries, etc.)	6	Horses
Fresh vegetables (potatoes, cucumber, etc.)	7	Moulds (Aspergillus fumigatus, Alternaria Cladosporium, etc.)
Cheese	8	Birch pollen
Yeast	9	Weed pollen
Soya protein	10	Wasp/bee venom

* Substances that cause allergies

Source: *Dr Chris Corrigan, Consultant Allergist, The Allergy Clinic, Guy's Hospital, London*

THE 10 MOST COMMON PHOBIAS

	OBJECT OF PHOBIA	MEDICAL TERM
1	Open spaces	Agoraphobia, cenophobia, or kenophobia
2	Driving	No medical term, can be a symptom of agoraphobia
3	Vomiting	Emetophobia or emitophobia
4	Confined spaces	Claustrophobia, cleisiophobia, cleithrophobia, or clithrophobia
5	Insects	Entemophobia
6	Illness	Nosemophobia
7	Animals	Zoophobia
8	Flying	Aerophobia or aviatophobia
9	Blushing	Erythrophobia
10	Heights	Acrophobia, altophobia, hypsophobia, or hypsiphobia

Source: *National Phobics Society*

TOP 10 LONGEST BONES IN THE HUMAN BODY

BONE	AVERAGE LENGTH (CM)	(IN)
1 **Femur** (thighbone – upper leg)	50.50	19.88
2 **Tibia** (shinbone – inner lower leg)	43.03	16.94
3 **Fibula** (outer lower leg)	40.50	15.94
4 **Humerus** (upper arm)	36.46	14.35
5 **Ulna** (inner lower arm)	28.20	11.10
6 **Radius** (outer lower arm)	26.42	10.40
7 **7th rib**	24.00	9.45
8 **8th rib**	23.00	9.06
9 **Innominate bone** (hipbone – half pelvis)	18.50	7.28
10 **Sternum** (breastbone)	17.00	6.69

These are average dimensions of the bones of an adult male measured from their extremities (ribs are curved, and the pelvis measurement is taken diagonally). The same bones in the female skeleton are usually 6 to 13 per cent smaller, with the exception of the sternum, which is virtually identical.

THE 10 MOST COMMON REASONS FOR HOSPITAL ADMISSIONS IN ENGLAND

REASON	INPATIENTS (1997–98)
1 **Diseases of the cirulatory and respiratory systems**	1,694,000
2 **Complications in pregnancy, birth, and puerperium** (period of time following birth)	1,325,000
3 **Neoplasms** (tumours)	1,190,000
4 **Diseases of the digestive system**	1,180,000
5 **Diseases of the skin, subcutaneous tissue, and muscles**	820,000
6 **Diseases of the genito-urinary system**	763,000
7 **Injuries and poisoning**	736,000
8 **Diseases of the nervous system, eye, and ear**	625,000
9 **Mental disorders**	231,000
10 **Diseases of the blood and blood-forming organs**	143,000

Source: *Department of Health,* Hospital Episode Statistics

TOP 10 LARGEST HUMAN ORGANS

ORGAN		AVERAGE WEIGHT (G)	(OZ)
1 **Skin**		10,886	384.0
2 **Liver**		1,560	55.0
3 **Brain**	male	1,408	49.7
	female	1,263	44.6
4 **Lungs**	total	1,090	38.5
	right	*580*	*20.5*
	left	*510*	*18.0*
5 **Heart**	male	315	11.1
	female	265	9.3
6 **Kidneys**	total	290	10.2
	right	*140*	*4.9*
	left	*150*	*5.3*
7 **Spleen**		170	6.0
8 **Pancreas**		98	3.5
9 **Thyroid**		35	1.2
10 **Prostate**	male only	20	0.7

This list is based on average immediate post-mortem weights, as recorded by St. Bartholomew's Hospital, London, UK, and other sources over a 10-year spell.

THE 10 LEAST HEALTHY COUNTRIES

COUNTRY	HEALTHY LIFE EXPECTANCY AT BIRTH*
1 **Sierra Leone**	28.6
2 **Lesotho**	31.4
3 **Angola**	33.4
4 **Zimbabwe**	33.6
5 **Swaziland**	34.2
6 **= Malawi**	34.9
= Zambia	34.9
8 **Burundi**	35.1
9 **Liberia**	35.3
10 **= Afghanistan**	35.5
= Niger	35.5

* *Average number of years expected to be spent in good health*

Source: *World Health Organisation,* World Health Report 2003

HALE (Health Adjusted Life Expectancy) differs from life expectancy in that an adjustment is made for years spent in ill health as a result of poor diet, disease, lack of health care, and other factors. It is the method used by the World Health Organization, and graphically illustrates the contrast between Western and developing countries.

TOP 10 COUNTRIES THAT SPEND THE MOST ON HEALTH CARE

COUNTRY	HEALTH SPENDING PER CAPITA (1997–2000) ($)
1 **USA**	4,499
2 **Switzerland**	3,573
3 **Japan**	2,908
4 **Norway**	2,832
5 **Denmark**	2,512
6 **Germany**	2,422
7 **Sweden**	2,179
8 **Canada**	2,058
9 **France**	2,057
10 **Belgium**	1,936
UK	1,747

Source: *World Bank,* World Development Indicators 2003

It is estimated that an average spending of $12 per capita per annum is required to provide the minimum of preventive and essential health services, but the spending of many low-income countries falls well short of this figure. Ethiopia, for example, spends only $4 per capita on health care.

Births & Lifespans

TOP 10 COUNTRIES WITH THE MOST BIRTHS

	COUNTRY	EST. BIRTHS (2005)
1	India	24,111,501
2	China	16,759,417
3	Nigeria	5,303,493
4	Indonesia	5,011,279
5	Pakistan	4,381,029
6	Bangladesh	4,331,032
7	USA	4,181,681
8	Brazil	3,132,278
9	Dem. Rep. of Congo	2,666,572
10	Ethiopia	2,665,717
	World	129,217,147
	UK	651,559

Source: *US Census Bureau, International Data Base*

▼ Youth full
The high birth rate in many African countries increasingly contrasts with the single figure and declining rates found in Western Europe.

TOP 10 COUNTRIES WITH THE HIGHEST LIFE EXPECTANCY

	COUNTRY	EST. LIFE EXPECTANCY AT BIRTH (2005)
1	Andorra	83.5
2	San Marino	81.6
3	Japan	81.2
4	Singapore	80.7
5	= Australia	80.4
	= Sweden	80.4
	= Switzerland	80.4
8	Hong Kong	80.2
9	= Canada	80.1
	= Iceland	80.1
	World	64.3
	UK	78.4

Source: *US Census Bureau, International Data Base*

THE 10 COUNTRIES WITH THE HIGHEST BIRTH RATE

	COUNTRY	EST. BIRTH RATE (LIVE BIRTHS PER 1,000, 2005)
1	Niger	48.3
2	Mali	46.8
3	Uganda	46.1
4	Chad	46.0
5	Somalia	45.6
6	Angola	44.6
7	Dem. Rep. of Congo	44.4
8	= Burkina Faso	44.2
	= Liberia	44.2
10	Malawi	44.0
	World	20.0
	UK	10.8

Source: *US Census Bureau, International Data Base*

The countries with the highest birth rates are among the poorest countries in the world. In these countries, people often want to have large families so that the children can help to earn income for the family when they are older.

TOP 10 COUNTRIES WITH THE LOWEST INFANT MORTALITY

	COUNTRY	EST. DEATH RATE PER 1,000 LIVE BIRTHS (2005)
1	Sweden	2.8
2	Japan	3.3
3	= Iceland	3.5
	= Singapore	3.5
5	Finland	3.6
6	Norway	3.7
7	Czech Republic	3.9
8	Andorra	4.0
9	Germany	4.2
10	= France	4.3
	= Slovenia	4.3
	UK	5.2

Source: *US Census Bureau, International Data Base*

The low mortality and small family sizes of these countries reflects the major medical advances of the 20th century: previously, large numbers of babies died before reaching their first birthday.

THE 10 COUNTRIES WITH THE HIGHEST INFANT MORTALITY

	COUNTRY	EST. DEATH RATE PER 1,000 LIVE BIRTHS (2005)
1	Angola	191.2
2	Sierra Leone	143.6
3	Afghanistan	137.9
4	Mozambique	136.4
5	Liberia	128.9
6	Niger	121.7
7	Mali	116.8
8	Somalia	116.7
9	Tajikistan	110.8
10	Guinea-Bissau	107.2
	World	*49.0*

Source: *US Census Bureau, International Data Base*

Deaths as a ratio of live births is a commonly employed measure of a country's medical and social conditions. In sharp contrast to the single-digit mortality rates of many Western countries, these figures represent the most disadvantaged people.

THE 10 COUNTRIES WITH THE LOWEST BIRTH RATE

	COUNTRY	EST. BIRTH RATE (LIVE BIRTHS PER 1,000, 2005)
1	Germany	8.3
2	Austria	8.8
3	Italy	8.9
4	Andorra	9.0
5	= Czech Republic	9.1
	= Slovenia	9.1
7	Latvia	9.2
8	Japan	9.5
9	= Bulgaria	9.7
	= Greece	9.7

Source: *US Census Bureau, International Data Base*

Improvements in birth control, the cost of raising children, and the deliberate decision of many to limit the size of their families are among a range of reasons why the birth rate in many countries has steadily declined in modern times: in 2003, the US birth rate was reported as having fallen to the lowest ever recorded, at 13.9 per 1,000. If counted as an independent country, the Vatican, with a birth rate of zero, would head this list.

INFANT MORTALITY

IT'S A FACT

IN THE PAST 100 YEARS, worldwide infant mortality rates have been driven down by progressive improvements in health care and nutrition. In the period 1901–05, the UK average was 132 deaths per 1,000 children aged under one year, and the figure was as high as 212 in Italy. The large families typical of that era were partly an insurance against this level of risk. In the same period, Scandinavian countries were among the first to achieve levels below 100 deaths per 1,000 – Sweden with a rate of 91 and Norway 81. The rates in many developing countries today are thus comparable to those of Western countries 100 years ago.

THE 10 COUNTRIES WITH THE FEWEST BIRTHS ATTENDED BY SKILLED HEALTH PERSONNEL

	COUNTRY	PERCENTAGE OF ATTENDED BIRTHS*
1	Equatorial Guinea	5
2	Ethiopia	10
3	Bangladesh	13
4	Bhutan	15
5	Chad	16
6	Burundi	19
7	Pakistan	20
8	= Eritrea	21
	= Laos	21
10	Yemen	22

* In those countries/latest year for which data available

Source: *UNICEF*

THE 10 COUNTRIES WITH THE LOWEST LIFE EXPECTANCY

	COUNTRY	EST. LIFE EXPECTANCY AT BIRTH (2005)
1	Botswana	29.4
2	Zambia	35.1
3	Swaziland	35.6
4	Mozambique	36.0
5	Angola	36.6
6	= Lesotho	36.7
	= Zimbabwe	36.7
8	Malawi	37.0
9	Namibia	38.3
10	Rwanda	39.0

Source: *US Census Bureau, International Data Base*

Matters of Life & Death

	EPIDEMIC OR PANDEMIC	LOCATION	DATE	ESTIMATED NO. KILLED
1	Black Death	Europe/Asia	1347–1380s	75,000,000
2	AIDS	Worldwide	1981–	21,800,000
3	Influenza	Worldwide	1918–20	21,640,000
4	Bubonic plague	India	1896–1948	12,000,000
5	Typhus	Eastern Europe	1914–15	3,000,000
6	= "Plague of Justinian"	Europe/Asia	541–90	millions*
	= Cholera	Worldwide	1846–60	millions*
	= Cholera	Europe	1826–37	millions*
	= Cholera	Worldwide	1893–94	millions*
10	Smallpox	Mexico	1530–45	>1,000,000

* No precise figures available

Diseases that spread throughout populations are considered epidemics when more than 400 people out of every 100,000 are affected, while pandemics are those that sweep across wide geographical areas, such as the influenza pandemic that followed the World War I, killing more people than had died during the conflict.

THE 10 MOST COMMON CAUSES OF DEATH BY INFECTIOUS AND PARASITIC DISEASES

	CAUSE	APPROXIMATE NO. OF DEATHS (2002)
1	Lower respiratory infection	3,766,000
2	HIV/AIDS	2,821,000
3	Diarrhoeal diseases	1,767,000
4	Tuberculosis	1,605,000
5	Malaria	1,222,000
6	Measles	760,000
7	Whooping cough (pertussis)	301,000
8	Neonatal tetanus	292,000
9	Meningitis	173,000
10	Syphilis	157,000

Source: *World Health Organization*, World Health Report 2003

In 2002, infectious and parasitic diseases accounted for some 11,122,000 of the 57,027,000 deaths worldwide, or 19.5 per cent of the total. Certain childhood diseases, including measles and whooping cough, showed an increase in this year.

▼ **The scourge of AIDS**
South Africa is the hardest hit of all countries affected by the AIDS pandemic. It has been estimated that by 2008 some 500,000 people will die there every year, and average life expectancy will fall from 60 to 40.

THE 10 | COUNTRIES WITH THE MOST CASES OF AIDS

	COUNTRY	DEATHS (2002)	EST. NO. OF CASES
1	South Africa	360,000	5,000,000
2	India	N/A	3,970,000
3	Nigeria	170,000	3,500,000
4	Kenya	190,000	2,500,000
5	Zimbabwe	200,000	2,300,000
6	Ethiopia	160,000	2,100,000
7	Tanzania	140,000	1,500,000
8	Dem. Rep. of Congo	120,000	1,300,000
9	Zambia	120,000	1,200,000
10	Mozambique	60,000	1,100,000
	World total	*3,000,000*	*40,000,000*
	UK	*460*	*34,000*

Source: *UNAIDS,* Report on the Global HIV/AIDS Epidemic, July 2002

First identified in 1981, AIDS has killed nearly 22 million and affected the social and economic fabric of many African countries by orphaning children, decimating labour forces, and stretching medical resources to their limit.

THE 10 | COUNTRIES WITH THE MOST CREMATIONS

	COUNTRY	PERCENTAGE OF DEATHS	NO. OF CREMATIONS*
1	China	50.60	4,152,000
2	Japan	99.53	1,028,615
3	USA	37.78	676,890
4	UK	71.89	437,124
5	Germany	40.10	338,469
6	France	20.38	109,950
7	Canada	48.50	108,436
8	Czech Republic	77.05	83,406
9	Netherlands	49.51	70,951
10	Sweden	67.84	63,273

* In latest year for which data available

Source: *The Cremation Society of Great Britain*

Cremation is least practised in traditionally Roman Catholic countries, such as Italy (6.91 per cent) and the Republic of Ireland (6.41 per cent). A shortage of land for burials and cultural factors have led to cremation being the dominant means for disposal of the dead in Japan. A typical funeral in Japan costs about 2.3 million yen – approximately £11,000.

THE 10 | COUNTRIES WITH THE MOST DEATHS FROM HEART DISEASE

	COUNTRY	DEATH RATE PER 100,000*
1	Ukraine	935.8
2	Bulgaria	887.8
3	Russia	746.6
4	Latvia	734.7
5	Estonia	715.6
6	Romania	701.6
7	Hungary	687.1
8	Moldova	632.0
9	Croatia	609.6
10	Czech Republic	566.5
	UK	*426.2*

* In those countries latest year for which data available

Source: *United Nations*

High risk factors, including diet and smoking, have contributed to the former Soviet states having high rates of coronary heart disease.

TOP 10 | COUNTRIES WITH THE LOWEST DEATH RATES

	COUNTRY	ESTIMATED DEATH RATE (DEATHS PER 1,000, 2005)
1	Kuwait	2.4
2	Jordan	2.6
3	Brunei	3.4
4	Libya	3.5
5	Oman	3.9
6	Solomon Islands	4.0
7	Bahrain	4.1
8	= Costa Rica	4.3
	= United Arab Emirates	4.3
10	Guam	4.4
	World average	*8.8*
	UK	*10.2*

Source: *US Census Bureau, International Data Base*

The crude death rate is derived by dividing the total number of deaths in a given year by the total population and multiplying by 1,000. These tend to mean that countries with young populations have low death rates and older populations high rates.

THE 10 | COUNTRIES WITH THE HIGHEST DEATH RATES

	COUNTRY	ESTIMATED DEATH RATE (DEATHS PER 1,000, 2005)
1	Botswana	36.5
2	Angola	25.9
3	Swaziland	25.3
4	Lesotho	25.0
5	Mozambique	24.9
6	Zimbabwe	24.7
7	Zambia	24.4
8	Malawi	23.4
9	Namibia	23.1
10	South Africa	23.0

Source: *US Bureau of the Census, International Data Base*

All 10 of the countries with the highest death rates are in sub-Saharan Africa. A decade ago, South Africa had a rate of just 8.7, but the AIDS toll has severely affected the demographic pattern, with a high proportion of young people falling victim.

Accidents & Fires

THE 10 MOST ACCIDENT-PRONE COUNTRIES

	COUNTRY	ACCIDENT DEATH RATE PER 100,000*
1	Estonia	102.8
2	Latvia	101.4
3	Russia	100.2
4	Ukraine	83.0
5	Lithuania	75.2
6	Hungary	58.6
7	Moldova	56.7
8 =	Finland	52.8
=	France	52.8
10	Belarus	51.7
	UK	21.4

* In those countries/latest year for which data available

Source: UN Demographic Yearbook

THE 10 MOST COMMON ACCIDENTS IN UK HOMES

	TYPE OF ACCIDENT	NO OF ACCIDENTS (2002)*
1	Tripping over	417,893
2	Falls on or from stairs or steps	306,168
3	Contact with static object	270,600
4	Cut or tear from sharp object	234,643
5	Struck by moving object	160,351
6	Foreign body	128,023
7	Acute overexertion	90,118
8	Thermal effect	84,460
9	Pinched or crushed by blunt object	79,171
10	Bite/sting	72,673

* National estimates based on actual Home Accident Surveillance System figures for sample population

THE 10 MOST DANGEROUS LOCATIONS IN THE UK HOME

	LOCATION	MOST COMMON ACCIDENT	NO. OF ACCIDENTS (2002)*
1	Living/dining area	Tripping up	311,621
2	Garden/grassed area	Tripping up	299,136
3	Kitchen/utility room	Cut/tear	261,949
4	Bedroom	Falling	231,589
5	Stairs inside	Falling on steps	226,382
6	Yard/driveway/path	Tripping up	127,408
7	Bathroom/toilet	Tripping up	94,854
8	Hallway/lobby	Tripping up	59,881
9	Porch/threshold	Falling on steps	47,827
10	Steps outside	Falling on steps	28,782
	Total		2,701,326

* National estimates based on actual Home Accident Surveillance System figures for sample population

A further 552,024 accidents occurred in unspecified home locations. Storerooms, airing cupboards, and the like, which were the scene of just 451 accidents requiring hospital treatment, are the least dangerous of the domestic location categories.

THE 10 ITEMS MOST FREQUENTLY INVOLVED IN LEISURE ACCIDENTS IN THE UK

ITEM	ACCIDENTS (2002)*
1 **Outdoor surface** (grass, road, ice, etc.)	1,291,295
2 **Clothing/footwear**	894,251
3 **Person** (excluding injured person)	657,374
4 **Sport equipment**	575,845
5 **Construction of a building feature**	437,163
6 **Transport**	345,671
7 **Animal/insect**	137,678
8 **Natural feature of landscape/garden**	113,160
9 **Food/drink**	106,600
10 **Built feature in garden/street**	102,808

* *National estimates based on actual Leisure Accident Surveillance System figures for sample population*

These general categories provide fewer surprises than the often improbable sub-categories: among clothing and footwear, for example, 201 people injured themselves with their trousers, while the animals involved in injuries necessitating hospital visits included fish (12), pigs (11), and rabbits and hamsters (9).

THE 10 WORST SINGLE-BUILDING FIRES

LOCATION/DATE	BUILDING/ STRUCTURE	NO. KILLED
1 **London,** UK, 11 July 1212	London Bridge	3,000*
2 **Santiago,** Chile, 8 Dec 1863	Church of La Compañía	2,500#
3 **Canton,** China, 25 May 1845	Theatre	1,670
4 **Shanghai,** China, June 1871	Theatre	900
5 **Vienna,** Austria, 8 Dec 1881	Ring Theatre	640–850
6 **St. Petersburg,** Russia, 14 Feb 1836	Lehmann Circus	800
7 **Antoung,** China, 13 Feb 1937	Cinema	658
8 **Chicago,** USA, 30 Dec 1903	Iroquois Theatre	602
9 **Mandi Dabwali,** India, 23 Dec 1995	School tent	over 500
10 **Boston,** USA, 28 Nov 1942	Cocoanut Grove Night Club	491

* *Many were burned, crushed, or drowned in the ensuing panic; some chroniclers give the year as 1213*

\# *Precise figure uncertain*

◀ **An accident waiting to happen**
Stairs are among the most dangerous locations in UK homes, with one person in every 233 sustaining a stair-related injury every year.

Marriage & Divorce

THE 10 | COUNTRIES WITH THE LOWEST DIVORCE RATES

	COUNTRY	DIVORCE RATE PER 1,000*
1	Guatemala	0.12
2	Libya	0.25
3	Mongolia	0.34
4	= Armenia	0.35
	= Georgia	0.35
6	Chile	0.42
7	Jamaica	0.44
8	Italy	0.47
9	Turkey	0.49
10	Macedonia	0.52

* In those countries/latest year for which data available

Source: *United Nations*

THE 10 | COUNTRIES WITH THE HIGHEST DIVORCE RATES

	COUNTRY	DIVORCE RATE PER 1,000*
1	Belarus	4.71
2	USA	4.19
3	Russia	3.66
4	Estonia	3.09
5	Ukraine	3.59
6	Aruba	3.40
7	Cuba	3.39
8	Lithuania	3.08
9	Switzerland	2.91
10	Finland	2.72
	UK	2.59

* In those countries/latest year for which data available

Source: *United Nations*

THE 10 | COUNTRIES WHERE WOMEN MARRY THE YOUNGEST

	COUNTRY	AVERAGE AGE AT FIRST MARRIAGE
1	Dem. Rep. of Congo	16.6
2	Niger	17.6
3	= Afghanistan	17.8
	= São Tomé and Principe	17.8
5	= Chad	18.0
	= Mozambique	18.0
7	Bangladesh	18.1
8	Uganda	18.2
9	= Congo	18.4
	= Mali	18.4

Source: *United Nations*

Child bride
Traditionally, Afghan brides are among the youngest in the world. The average age of women marrying is half that of those in certain countries, including Sweden and most Caribbean islands.

TOP 10 COUNTRIES WITH THE HIGHEST MARRIAGE RATE

COUNTRY	MARRIAGES PER 1,000 PER ANNUM*
1 Barbados	13.1
2 Liechtenstein	12.8
3 Cyprus	12.3
4 Seychelles	11.5
5 Jamaica	10.4
6 Ethiopia	10.2
7 Fiji	10.1
8 Bangladesh	9.5
9 Sri Lanka	9.3
10 Iran	8.4
UK	5.1

* In those countries/latest year for which data available

Source: United Nations

The highest figures are actually recorded in places that are not independent countries. Gibraltar, for example, has a marriage rate of 24.9 per 1,000.

TOP 10 COUNTRIES WITH THE LOWEST MARRIAGE RATE

COUNTRY	MARRIAGES PER 1,000 PER ANNUM*
1 United Arab Emirates	2.5
2 Georgia	2.9
3 = Peru	3.2
= Saudi Arabia	3.2
5 St. Lucia	3.3
6 = Andorra	3.4
= Qatar	3.4
8 = South Africa	3.5
= Tajikistan	3.5
10 Panama	3.7

* In those countries/latest year for which data available

Source: United Nations

Marriage rates around the world vary according to a range of religious and cultural factors. These vary from high costs of traditional dowry payments to a shift away from marriage as an institution in Scandinavian countries.

TOP 10 COUNTRIES WITH THE MOST MARRIAGES

COUNTRY	MARRIAGES PER ANNUM*
1 USA	2,329,000
2 Bangladesh	1,181,000
3 Russia	911,162
4 Japan	798,140
5 Mexico	743,856
6 Brazil	731,920
7 Ethiopia	630,290
8 Iran	511,277
9 Egypt	503,651
10 Turkey	485,035
UK	301,083

* In those countries/latest year for which data available

Source: United Nations

This list, based on United Nations statistics, regrettably excludes certain large countries such as India, Indonesia, and Pakistan, which fail to provide accurate data.

MARRIAGE RATES

IT'S A FACT

TODAY THERE ARE BARELY 10 countries in the world with double-figure marriage rates (those with more than 10 marriages annually for every 1,000 of the population). In contrast, 100 years ago only a handful of countries, including Ireland, Uruguay, and Japan, had marriage rates of less than 10 per 1,000, while the rate of 18 or more recorded in Russia and parts of Germany was not uncommon. The institution of marriage has declined to such an extent in certain countries, including the UK, that the rate is less than one-third of that at the beginning of the 20th century, while that of Sweden has plummeted from 11.9 to 3.5.

TOP 10 OVERSEAS HONEYMOON DESTINATIONS FOR UK COUPLES

COUNTRY
1 Maldives
2 Thailand
3 Sri Lanka
4 Mexico
5 Kenya
6 Mauritius
7 St. Lucia
8 USA
9 Bali
10 Antigua

Source: Kuoni Travel

THE 10 MOST COMMON CAUSES OF MARITAL DISCORD AND BREAKDOWN IN THE UK

CAUSE
1 Lack of communication
2 Continual arguments
3 Infidelity
4 Sexual problems
5 Financial problems
6 Work (usually one partner devoting excessive time to work)
7 Physical or verbal abuse
8 Children (whether to have them; attitudes towards their upbringing)
9 Step-parenting
10 Addiction (to drinking, gambling, spending, etc.)

Source: Relate National Marriage Guidance

Names of the Decades 1900s–1990s

TOP 10 FIRST NAMES IN ENGLAND & WALES, 1904

BOYS		GIRLS
William	1	Mary
John	2	Florence
George	3	Doris
Thomas	4	Edith
Arthur	5	Dorothy
James	6	Annie
Charles	7	Margaret
Frederick	8	Alice
Albert	9	Elizabeth
Ernest	10	Elsie

TOP 10 FIRST NAMES IN ENGLAND & WALES, 1914

BOYS		GIRLS
John	1	Mary
William	2	Margaret
George	3	Doris
Thomas	4	Dorothy
James	5	Kathleen
Arthur	6	Florence
Frederick	7	Elsie
Albert	8	Edith
Charles	9	Elizabeth
Robert	10	Winifred

TOP 10 FIRST NAMES IN ENGLAND & WALES, 1924

BOYS		GIRLS
John	1	Margaret
William	2	Mary
George	3	Joan
James	4	Joyce
Thomas	5	Dorothy
Ronald	6	Kathleen
Kenneth	7	Doris
Robert	8	Irene
Arthur	9	Elizabeth
Frederick	10	Eileen

TOP 10 FIRST NAMES IN ENGLAND & WALES, 1964

BOYS		GIRLS
David	1	Susan
Paul	2	Julie
Andrew	3	Karen
Mark	4	Jacqueline
John	5	Deborah
Michael	6	Tracey
Stephen	7	Jane
Ian	8	Helen
Robert	9	Diane
Richard	10	Sharon

TOP 10 FIRST NAMES IN ENGLAND & WALES, 1974

BOYS		GIRLS
Paul	1	Sarah
Mark	2	Claire
David	3	Nicola
Andrew	4	Emma
Richard	5	Lisa
Christopher	6	Joanne
James	7	Michelle
Simon	8	Helen
Michael	9	Samantha
Matthew	10	Karen

The Office for National Statistics and its predecessors have monitored the most popular first names in the middle of each decade, providing a picture of naming fashions over the 20th century.

TOP 10 FIRST NAMES IN ENGLAND & WALES, 1934

BOYS		GIRLS
John	1	Margaret
Peter	2	Jean
William	3	Mary
Brian	4	Joan
David	5	Patricia
James	6	Sheila
Michael	7	Barbara
Ronald	8	Doreen
Kenneth	9	June
George	10	Shirley

TOP 10 FIRST NAMES IN ENGLAND & WALES, 1944

BOYS		GIRLS
John	1	Margaret
David	2	Patricia
Michael	3	Christine
Peter	4	Mary
Robert	5	Jean
Anthony	6	Ann
Brian	7	Susan
Alan	8	Janet
William	9	Maureen
James	10	Barbara

TOP 10 FIRST NAMES IN ENGLAND & WALES, 1954

BOYS		GIRLS
David	1	Susan
John	2	Linda
Stephen	3	Christine
Michael	4	Margaret
Peter	5	Janet
Robert	6	Patricia
Paul	7	Carol
Alan	8	Elizabeth
Christopher	9	Mary
Richard	10	Anne

TOP 10 FIRST NAMES IN ENGLAND & WALES, 1984

BOYS		GIRLS
Christopher	1	Sarah
James	2	Laura
David	3	Gemma
Daniel	4	Emma
Michael	5	Rebecca
Matthew	6	Claire
Andrew	7	Victoria
Richard	8	Samantha
Paul	9	Rachel
Mark	10	Amy

TOP 10 FIRST NAMES IN ENGLAND & WALES, 1994

BOYS		GIRLS
Thomas	1	Rebecca
James	2	Lauren
Jack	3	Jessica
Daniel	4	Charlotte
Matthew	5	Hannah
Ryan	6	Sophie
Joshua	7	Amy
Luke	8	Emily
Samuel	9	Laura
Jordan	10	Emma

◀ **Naming baby**
The choosing of names for babies has taxed generations of parents, with the top choices across the decades combining the traditional and the fashionable.

Rulers & Royals

THE 10 FIRST FEMALE PRIME MINISTERS AND PRESIDENTS

PRIME MINISTER/PRESIDENT	COUNTRY	FIRST PERIOD IN OFFICE
1 Sirimavo Bandaranaike (PM)	Ceylon	Jul 1960–Mar 1965
2 Indira Gandhi (PM)	India	Jan 1966–Mar 1977
3 Golda Meir (PM)	Israel	Mar 1969–Jun 1974
4 Maria Estela Perón (President)	Argentina	Jul 1974–Mar 1976
5 Elisabeth Domitien (PM)	Central African Republic	Jan 1975–Apr 1976
6 Margaret Thatcher (PM)	UK	May 1979–Nov 1990
7 Dr. Maria Lurdes Pintasilgo (PM)	Portugal	Aug 1979–Jan 1980
8 Mary Eugenia Charles (PM)	Dominica	Jul 1980–Jun 1995
9 Vigdís Finnbogadóttir (President)	Iceland	Aug 1980–Aug 1996
10 Gro Harlem Brundtland (PM)	Norway	Feb–Oct 1981

Sirimavo Bandaranaike of Ceylon (now Sri Lanka) became the world's first female prime minister on 21 July 1960. Margaret Thatcher became Britain's first on 4 May 1979. The first 10 were followed by Corazón Aquino, who became president of the Philippines in 1986, and Benazir Bhutto, who was prime minister of Pakistan between 1988 and 1990.

TOP 10 ROYALS IN LINE TO THE BRITISH THRONE

ROYAL

1 HRH The Prince of Wales (Prince Charles Philip Arthur George)
b. 14 Nov 1948 *then his elder son:*

2 HRH Prince William of Wales (Prince William Arthur Philip Louis)
b. 21 June 1982 *then his younger brother:*

3 HRH Prince Henry of Wales (Prince Henry Charles Albert David)
b. 15 Sept 1984 *then his uncle:*

4 HRH The Duke of York (Prince Andrew Albert Christian Edward)
b. 19 Feb 1960 *then his elder daughter:*

5 HRH Princess Beatrice of York (Princess Beatrice Elizabeth Mary)
b. 8 Aug 1988 *then her younger sister:*

6 HRH Princess Eugenie of York (Princess Eugenie Victoria Helena)
b. 23 Mar 1990 *then her uncle:*

7 HRH Prince Edward (Prince Edward Antony Richard Louis)
b. 10 Mar 1964 *then his daughter:*

8 Lady Louise Alice Elizabeth Mary Mountbatten Windsor
b. 8 Nov 2003 *then her aunt:*

9 HRH The Princess Royal (Princess Anne Elizabeth Alice Louise)
b. 15 Aug 1950 *then her son:*

10 Master Peter Mark Andrew Phillips
b. 15 Nov 1977

The birth of Lady Louise Windsor to the Count and Countess of Wessex in November 2003 means that Princess Anne's daughter, Zara Phillips, has now fallen out of the Top 10.

TOP 10 LONGEST-SERVING PRESIDENTS TODAY

PRESIDENT	COUNTRY	TOOK OFFICE
1 General Gnassingbé Eyadéma	Togo	14 Apr 1967
2 El Hadj Omar Bongo	Gabon	2 Dec 1967
3 Colonel Mu'ammar Gadhafi	Libya	1 Sept 1969*
4 Zayid ibn Sultan al-Nuhayyan	United Arab Emirates	2 Dec 1971
5 Fidel Castro	Cuba	2 Dec 1976
6 France-Albert René	Seychelles	5 Jun 1977
7 Ali Abdullah Saleh	Yemen	17 Jul 1978
8 Maumoon Abdul Gayoom	Maldives	11 Nov 1978
9 Teodoro Obiang Nguema Mbasogo	Equatorial Guinea	3 Aug 1979
10 José Eduardo Dos Santos	Angola	21 Sept 1979

* Since a reorganization in 1979, Colonel Gadhafi has held no formal position, but continues to rule under the ceremonial title of "Leader of the Revolution"

All the presidents in this list have been in power for more than 20 years, some for over 30. Fidel Castro was prime minister of Cuba from February 1959 and effectively ruled as dictator from then, but he was not technically president until the Cuban constitution was revised in 1976.

TOP 10 LONGEST-REIGNING LIVING MONARCHS*

MONARCH	COUNTRY	DATE OF BIRTH	ACCESSION
1 Bhumibol Adulyadej	Thailand	5 Dec 1927	9 Jun 1946
2 Prince Rainier III	Monaco	31 May 1923	9 May 1949
3 Elizabeth II	UK	21 Apr 1926	6 Feb 1952
4 Malietoa Tanumafili II	Samoa	4 Jan 1913	1 Jan 1962#
5 Taufa'ahau Tupou IV	Tonga	4 Jul 1918	16 Dec 1965†
6 Haji Hassanal Bolkiah	Brunei	15 July 1946	5 Oct 1967
7 Sayyid Qaboos ibn Said al-Said	Oman	18 Nov 1942	23 Jul 1970
8 Margrethe II	Denmark	16 Apr 1940	14 Jan 1972
9 Jigme Singye Wangchuk	Bhutan	11 Nov 1955	24 Jul 1972
10 Carl XVI Gustaf	Sweden	30 Apr 1946	19 Sept 1973

* Including hereditary rulers of principalities, dukedoms, etc.

Sole ruler since 15 April 1963

† Full sovereignty from 5 June 1970, when British protectorate ended

There are 28 countries that have emperors, kings, queens, princes, dukes, sultans, or other hereditary rulers as their heads of state. This list formerly included Birendra Bir Bikram Shah Dev, King of Nepal since 31 January 1972. On 1 June 2001, he was shot dead by his own son, Crown Prince Dipendra, who then committed suicide. Any further deaths, coups or abdications will elevate, in order, Juan Carlos I of Spain, who ascended to the throne on the death of General Franco and the restoration of the monarchy on 22 November 1975, Shaikh Jabir al-Ahmad al-Jabir al-Sabah, Amir of Kuwait (31 December 1977), and Queen Beatrix of the Netherlands (30 April 1980).

LONGEST-REIGNING MONARCHS

	MONARCH	COUNTRY	REIGN	AGE AT ACCESSION	YEARS REIGNED
1	King Louis XIV	France	1643–1715	5	72
2	King John II	Liechtenstein	1858–1929	18	71
3	Emperor Franz-Josef	Austria-Hungary	1848–1916	18	67
4	Queen Victoria	UK	1837–1901	18	63
5	Emperor Hirohito	Japan	1926–89	25	62
6	Emperor K'ang Hsi	China	1661–1722	8	61
7	King Sobhuza II*	Swaziland	22 Dec 1921–21 Aug 1982	22	60
8	Emperor Ch'ien Lung	China	18 Oct 1735–9 Feb 1796	25	60
9	King Christian IV	Denmark	4 Apr 1588–21 Feb 1648	11	59
10	King George III	UK	26 Oct 1760–29 Jan 1820	22	59

* Paramount chief until 1967, when Great Britain recognised him as king with the granting of internal self-government

King Harald I of Norway is said to have ruled for 70 years from 870–940, and the even longer reigns of 95 years and 94 years are credited respectively to King Mihti of Arakan (Myanmar, as known today) around 1279–1374, and Pharaoh Phiops (Pepi) II of Egypt around 2269–2175 BC, but there is inadequate historical evidence to substantiate any of these claims.

LONGEST-REIGNING QUEENS

	QUEEN*	REIGN COUNTRY	REIGN	YEARS
1	Victoria	UK	1837–1901	63
2	Wilhelmina	Netherlands	1890–1948	58
3	Elizabeth II	UK	1952–	52
4	Wu Chao	China	655–705	50
5	Salote Tubou	Tonga	1918–65	47
6	Elizabeth I	England	1558–1603	44
7	Maria Theresa	Hungary	1740–80	40
8	Maria I	Portugal	1777–1816	39
9	Joanna I	Italy	1343–81	38
10	Suiko Tenno	Japan	592–628	36

* Queens and empresses who ruled in their own right, not as consorts of kings or emperors

◀ **Sun King**
By ascending the French throne as a child and living a then exceptional 77 years, Louis XIV broke all records for the longest substantiated reign.

US Presidents

TOP 10 OLDEST US PRESIDENTS

	PRESIDENT	AGE ON TAKING OFFICE (YEARS)	(DAYS)
1	Ronald W. Reagan	69	349
2	William H. Harrison	68	23
3	James Buchanan	65	315
4	George H.W. Bush	64	223
5	Zachary Taylor	64	100
6	Dwight D. Eisenhower	62	98
7	Andrew Jackson	61	354
8	John Adams	61	125
9	Gerald R. Ford	61	26
10	Harry Truman	60	339

Born on 6 February 1911, Ronald Reagan was 77 years 349 days old when he completed his second term on 20 January 1989. In 2001 Reagan also topped the list of longest-lived former presidents by outliving John Adams, who died on 4 July 1826 at the age of 90 years 247 days. Herbert Hoover is the only other nonagenarian ex-president, dying in 1964 aged 90 years 71 days, but at 31 years 231 days his was the longest lifespan after leaving office.

TOP 10 SHORTEST-SERVING US PRESIDENTS

	PRESIDENT	PERIOD IN OFFICE (YEARS)	(DAYS)
1	William H. Harrison*	—	32
2	James A. Garfield*	—	199
3	Zachary Taylor*	1	127
4	Warren G. Harding*	2	151
5	Gerald R. Ford	2	166
6	Millard Fillmore	2	236
7	John F. Kennedy*	2	306
8	Chester A. Arthur	3	166
9	Andrew Johnson	3	323
10	John Tyler	3	332

* Died in office

Ninth and second-oldest president William Harrison caught pneumonia while delivering an inaugural address in the rain on 4 March 1831. The longest on record, its 8,578 words took him one hour forty five minutes to deliver. He was ill throughout his record shortest term in office, and became the first US president to die in office, and the first to die in the White House. Outside these 10, all other presidents have served either one or two full four-year terms – three in the case of Franklin D. Roosevelt.

TOP 10 YOUNGEST US PRESIDENTS

	PRESIDENT	AGE ON TAKING OFFICE (YEARS)	(DAYS)
1	Theodore Roosevelt	42	322
2	John F. Kennedy	43	236
3	William J. Clinton	46	149
4	Ulysses S. Grant	46	311
5	Grover Cleveland	47	351
6	Franklin Pierce	48	101
7	James A. Garfield	49	105
8	James K. Polk	49	122
9	Millard Fillmore	50	184
10	John Tyler	51	8

Vice-President Theodore Roosevelt assumed the office of president following the assassination of William McKinley. John F. Kennedy was the youngest president to be elected. The US Constitution insists that a president must be at least 35 years old on taking office. George W. Bush was aged 54 years 6 months 14 days when he took office in 2001. Despite his appearance in this list, Polk holds the record for the shortest lifespan after leaving office: he ended his four-year term on 3 March 1849, and died 103 days later at the age of 53 years 225 days.

TOP 10 US PRESIDENTS WITH THE MOST ELECTORAL COLLEGE VOTES

	PRESIDENT	YEAR	VOTES
1	Ronald W. Reagan	1984	525
2	Franklin D. Roosevelt	1936	523
3	Richard M. Nixon	1972	520
4	Ronald W. Reagan	1980	489
5	Lyndon B. Johnson	1964	486
6	Franklin D. Roosevelt	1932	472
7	Dwight D. Eisenhower	1956	457
8	Franklin D. Roosevelt	1940	449
9	Herbert C. Hoover	1928	444
10	Dwight D. Eisenhower	1952	442
	George W. Bush	*2000*	*271*

Each political party in each state is allocated a number of electors equal to the number of its senators (two per state) plus the number of its representatives. Voters vote for the electors, who comprise the Electoral College – and they in turn vote for the presidential and vice-presidential candidates.

TOP 10 PRESIDENTS WITH THE MOST POPULAR VOTES

	PRESIDENT	YEAR	VOTES
1	Ronald W. Reagan	1984	54,281,858
2	George W. Bush	2000	50,459,211
3	George H. W. Bush	1988	48,881,221
4	William J. Clinton	1996	47,401,185
5	Richard M. Nixon	1972	47,165,234
6	William J. Clinton	1992	44,908,254
7	Ronald W. Reagan	1980	43,899,248
8	Lyndon B. Johnson	1964	43,126,506
9	James E. Carter	1976	40,828,929
10	Dwight D. Eisenhower	1956	35,585,316

Despite population increases and the enfranchisement of 18- to 21-year-olds in 1972, the Top 10 ranking shows that it is not the most recent presidential elections that have attracted the greatest number of popular votes for the winning candidate. Also, many presidents have won with less than 50 per cent of the total popular vote: in 1824, John Quincy Adams achieved only 108,740 votes – 30.5 per cent of the total; and in 1860, Abraham Lincoln had 1,865,593 – 39.8 per cent.

▶ Popular President

President John F. Kennedy at the peak of his popularity in 1961. He is pictured on 25 May as he addresses Congress, committing the US to putting a man on the Moon within the decade.

TOP 10 | MOST POPULAR U.S. PRESIDENTS

	PRESIDENT	SURVEY DATE	APPROVAL RATING (%)
1	George W. Bush	21–22 Sept 2001	90
2	George H.W. Bush	28 Feb 1991	89
3	Harry S. Truman	May/June 1945	87
4	Franklin D. Roosevelt	Jan 1942	84
5	John F. Kennedy	28 Apr 1961	83
6	Dwight D. Eisenhower	14 Dec 1956	79
7	Lyndon B. Johnson	5 Dec 1963	78
8	Jimmy Carter	18 Mar 1977	75
9	Gerald R. Ford	16 Aug 1974	71
10	William J. Clinton	30 Jan–1 Feb 1998	69

Source: *The Gallup Organization*

The Gallup Organization began surveying approval and disapproval ratings of US presidents in October 1938. Since then the one president to not make the Top 10 is Richard M. Nixon, whose highest approval rating was 67 per cent on two occasions – November 12, 1969 and January 26, 1973.

TOP 10 | LEAST POPULAR U.S. PRESIDENTS

	PRESIDENT	SURVEY DATE	DISAPPROVAL RATING (%)
1	Richard M. Nixon	2 Aug 1974	66
2	Harry S. Truman	Jan 1952	62
3	George H.W. Bush	31 Jul 1992	60
4	Jimmy Carter	29 Jun 1979	59
5	Ronald W. Reagan	28 Jan 1983	56
6	William J. Clinton	6–7 Sept 1994	54
7	Lyndon B. Johnson	10 Mar 1968; 7 Aug 1968	52
8	= Franklin D. Roosevelt	Nov 1938	46
	= Gerald R. Ford	18 Apr 1975; 21 Nov 1975; 12 Dec 1975	46
10	George W. Bush	7–10 Sep 2001	39

Source: *The Gallup Organization*

Since opinion surveys began, the one president to not make the Top 10 is John F. Kennedy, whose highest disapproval was 30 per cent on 8th November 1963, the last survey compiled before his assassination.

Human Achievements

THE 10 FIRST MOUNTAINEERS TO CLIMB EVEREST

	MOUNTAINEER/COUNTRY OF ORIGIN	DATE
1	**Edmund Hillary,** New Zealand	29 May 1953
2	**Tenzing Norgay,** Nepal	29 May 1953
3	**Jürg Marmet,** Switzerland	23 May 1956
4	**Ernst Schmied,** Switzerland	23 May 1956
5	**Hans-Rudolf von Gunten,** Switzerland	24 May 1956
6	**Adolf Reist,** Switzerland	24 May 1956
7	**Wang Fu-chou,** China	25 May 1960
8	**Chu Ying-hua,** China	25 May 1960
9	**Konbu,** Tibet	25 May 1960
10 =	**Nawang Gombu,** India	1 May 1963
=	**James Whittaker,** USA	1 May 1963

Nawang Gombu and James Whittaker are 10th equal because, neither wishing to deny the other the privilege of being first, they ascended the last steps to the summit side by side.

▶ **On top of the world**
Edmund Hillary (b.1919) and Sherpa Tenzing Norgay (1914–86) celebrate their conquest of Everest.

THE 10 FIRST PEOPLE TO GO OVER NIAGARA FALLS AND SURVIVE

	NAME	METHOD	DATE
1	**Annie Edson Taylor**	Wooden barrel	24 Oct 1901
2	**Bobby Leach**	Steel barrel	25 July 1911
3	**Jean Lussier**	Steel and rubber ball fitted with oxygen cylinders	4 July 1928
4	**William Fitzgerald** (aka Nathan Boya)	Steel and rubber ball fitted with oxygen cylinders	15 July 1961
5	**Karel Soucek**	Barrel	3 July 1984
6	**Steven Trotter**	Barrel	18 Aug 1985
7	**Dave Mundy**	Barrel	5 Oct 1985
8 =	**Peter DeBernardi**	Metal container	28 Sept 1989
=	**Jeffrey Petkovich**	Metal container	28 Sept 1989
10	**Dave Mundy**	Diving bell	26 Sept 1993

Source: *Niagara Falls Museum*

Captain Matthew Webb, the first person to swim the English Channel, was killed on 24 July 1883, attempting to swim the rapids beneath Niagara Falls. Having survived the Falls, Bobby Leach (1842–1920) went on a world lecture tour: while in New Zealand, he slipped on an orange peel and died of his injuries.

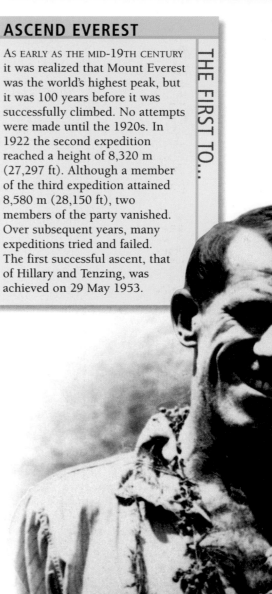

THE FIRST TO...

ASCEND EVEREST

As early as the mid-19th century it was realized that Mount Everest was the world's highest peak, but it was 100 years before it was successfully climbed. No attempts were made until the 1920s. In 1922 the second expedition reached a height of 8,320 m (27,297 ft). Although a member of the third expedition attained 8,580 m (28,150 ft), two members of the party vanished. Over subsequent years, many expeditions tried and failed. The first successful ascent, that of Hillary and Tenzing, was achieved on 29 May 1953.

THE 10 FIRST CROSS-CHANNEL SWIMMERS

	SWIMMER	COUNTRY	TIME (HR:MIN)	DATE
1	Matthew Webb	UK	21:45	24–25 Aug 1875
2	Thomas Burgess	UK	22:35	5–6 Sep 1911
3	Henry Sullivan	USA	26:50	5–6 Aug 1923
4	Enrico Tiraboschi	Italy	16:33	12 Aug 1923
5	Charles Toth	USA	16:58	8–9 Sep 1923
6	Gertrude Ederle	USA	14:39	6 Aug 1926
7	Millie Corson	USA	15:29	27–28 Aug 1926
8	Arnst Wierkotter	Germany	12:40	30 Aug 1926
9	Edward Temme	UK	14:29	5 Aug 1927
10	Mercedes Gleitze	UK	15:15	7 Oct 1927

The first three crossings were from England to France, the rest from France to England. Gertrude Ederle was the first woman to swim the Channel – but it was not until 11 September 1951 that American swimmer Florence Chadwick became the first woman to swim from England to France.

THE 10 FIRST PEOPLE TO REACH THE SOUTH POLE

	NAME/COUNTRY	DATE
1	= Roald Amundsen*, Norway	14 Dec 1911
	= Olav Olavsen Bjaaland, Norway	14 Dec 1911
	= Helmer Julius Hanssen, Norway	14 Dec 1911
	= Helge Sverre Hassel, Norway	14 Dec 1911
	= Oscar Wisting, Norway	14 Dec 1911
6	= Robert Falcon Scott*, UK	17 Jan 1912
	= Henry Robertson Bowers, UK	17 Jan 1912
	= Edgar Evans, UK	17 Jan 1912
	= Lawrence Edward Grace Oates, UK	17 Jan 1912
	= Edward Adrian Wilson, UK	17 Jan 1912

* Expedition leader

Just 33 days separate the first two expeditions to reach the South Pole. Scott's British Antarctic Expedition was organized with its avowed goal "to reach the South Pole and to secure for the British Empire the honour of this achievement". Meanwhile, Norwegian explorer Roald Amundsen also set out on an expedition to the Pole. When Scott eventually reached his goal, he discovered that the Norwegians had beaten them. Demoralized, Scott's team began the arduous return journey, but plagued by illness, hunger, bad weather, and exhaustion, the entire expedition died just as Amundsen's triumph was being reported to the world.

THE 10 FIRST PEOPLE TO REACH THE NORTH POLE

	NAME/COUNTRY OR NATIONALITY	DATE
1	= Robert Edwin Peary, US	6 Apr 1909
	= Matthew Alexander Henson, US	6 Apr 1909
	= Ooqueah, Inuit	6 Apr 1909
	= Ootah, Inuit	6 Apr 1909
	= Egingwah, Inuit	6 Apr 1909
	= Seegloo, Inuit	6 Apr 1909
7	= Pavel Afanaseyevich Geordiyenko, USSR	23 Apr 1948
	= Mikhail Yemel'yenovich Ostrekin, USSR	23 Apr 1948
	= Pavel Kononovich Sen'ko, USSR	23 Apr 1948
	= Mikhail Mikhaylovich Somov, USSR	23 Apr 1948

There remains some doubt as to the validity of Peary's team's claim to have reached the North Pole overland in 1909. The first undisputed "conquest", that of the 1948 Soviet team, was achieved by landing in an aircraft. The first team to attain the Pole overland was led by Ralph S. Plaisted (USA), along with Walter Pederson, Gerald Pitzel, and Jean Luc Bombardier, who arrived on 18 April 1968.

Criminal Records

THE 10 | COUNTRIES WITH THE HIGHEST REPORTED CRIME RATES

	COUNTRY	RATE PER 100,000 (2002*)
1	Finland	14,525.74
2	Sweden	13,350.27
3	Guyana	12,933.18
4	New Zealand	12,586.64
5	England and Wales	11,326.60
6	Grenada	10,177.89
7	Norway	9,822.91
8	Denmark	9,005.77
9	Belgium	8,597.66
10	Canada	8,572.50
	Scotland	*8,225.76*
	Northern Ireland	*2,389.16*

* Or latest year for which data available

Source: *Interpol*

An appearance in this list does not necessarily mark these as the most crime-ridden countries, since the rate of reporting relates closely to factors such as confidence in local law enforcement authorities.

THE 10 | COUNTRIES WITH THE HIGHEST PRISON POPULATION RATE

	COUNTRY	PRISONERS PER 100,000*
1	USA	701
2	Russia	606
3	Kazakhstan	522
4	Turkmenistan	489
5	= Belarus	459
	= Belize	459
7	Suriname	437
8	Dominica	420
9	Ukraine	415
10	Maldives	414
	England and Wales	*141*
	Scotland	*129*

* Most figures relate to dates between 1999–2003

Source: *Home Office,* World Prison Population List (5th ed.)

▼ **Cell multiplication**
In recent years, prison inmate numbers have risen in many countries, putting pressure on often old and inadequate jails.

TOP 10 | COUNTRIES WITH THE LOWEST REPORTED CRIME RATES

	COUNTRY	RATE PER 100,000 (2002*)
1	Georgia	9.00
2	Burkina Faso	9.30
3	Mali	10.03
4	Syria	42.26
5	Cambodia	47.97
6	Yemen	63.22
7	Indonesia	63.48
8	Myanmar	64.54
9	Angola	71.52
10	Cameroon	78.17

* Or latest year for which data available

Source: *Interpol*

It should be noted that for propaganda purposes, many countries do not publish accurate figures, while in certain countries crime is so common and law enforcement so inefficient or corrupt that countless incidents are unreported.

THE 10 COUNTRIES WITH THE MOST PRISONERS

	COUNTRY	PRISONERS*
1	USA	2,033,331
2	China	1,512,194#
3	Russia	864,590
4	India	304,893
5	Brazil	284,989
6	Thailand	258,076
7	Ukraine	198,858
8	South Africa	180,952
9	Iran	163,526
10	Mexico	154,765
	UK	82,241

Most figures relate to dates between 1999–2003

Sentenced prisoners only

Source: *Home Office*, World Prison Population List (5th ed.)

THE 10 MOST COMMON CRIMES IN ENGLAND AND WALES

	CRIME	NO. RECORDED (2002/03)
1	Theft and handling stolen goods (excluding car theft)	1,389,611
2	Criminal damage	1,109,370
3	Car theft (including theft from vehicles)	975,924
4	Violence against the person	835,101
5	Burglary (excluding domestic)	451,307
6	Domestic burglary	437,644
7	Fraud and forgery	330,128
8	Drug offences	141,116
9	Robbery	108,045
10	Sexual offences	48,654
	Total (including those not in Top 10)	*5,899,450*

Source: *Home Office*

Crimes reported to the police in the UK hit an all-time high in 2002–03. Although burglaries declined, incidents of violence against the person showed a marked increase from the 190,339 cases reported in 1991. There were 1,048 murders – the first time this figure had topped 1,000.

THE 10 AREAS OF ENGLAND AND WALES WITH THE HIGHEST CRIME RATES

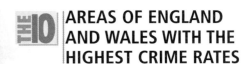

	POLICE FORCE AREA	RECORDED OFFENCES PER 1,000 (2002/03)
1	City of London	1,393
2	Nottinghamshire	159
3	West Yorkshire	155
4	= Greater Manchester	153
	= Humberside	153
6	Metropolitan Police (London)	150
7	West Midlands	137
8	Cleveland	136
9	= Cambridgeshire	120
	= Northumbria	120
	= South Wales	120
	= South Yorkshire	120
	England and Wales average	*113*

Source: *Home Office*

MOST PROLIFIC SERIAL KILLERS*

MURDERER/COUNTRY/CRIMES	VICTIMS

1 Behram (India) — 931

Behram (or Buhram) was the leader of the Thugee cult in India, which it is reckoned was responsible for the deaths of up to 2 million people. At his trial Behram was found guilty of personally committing 931 murders between 1790 and 1830, mostly by ritual strangulation with the cult's traditional cloth, known as a ruhmal. From the end of his reign of terror onwards, the British in India mounted a campaign against Thugee, and the cult was eventually suppressed.

2 Countess Erszébet Báthory (Hungary) — up to 650

In the period up to 1610 in Hungary, Báthory (1560–1614), known as "Countess Dracula" – the title of a 1970 Hammer horror film about her life and crimes – was alleged to have murdered between 300 and 650 girls (her personal list of 610 victims was described at her trial) in the belief that drinking their blood would prevent her from ageing. She was eventually arrested in 1611, tried, and found guilty. She died on 21 August 1614 walled up in her own castle at Csejthe.

3 Pedro Alonso López (Colombia) — 300

Captured in 1980, López, nicknamed the "Monster of the Andes", led police to 53 graves, but probably murdered at least 300 in Colombia, Ecuador, and Peru. He was sentenced to life imprisonment.

4 Dr Harold Shipman (UK) — 215

In January 2000, Manchester doctor Shipman was found guilty of the murder of 15 women patients; the official enquiry into his crimes put the figure at 215, with 45 possible further cases, but some authorities believe that the total could be as high as 400. Shipman hanged himself in his prison cell on 13 January 2004.

5 Henry Lee Lucas (USA) — 200

Lucas (1936–2001) admitted in 1983 to 360 murders, many committed with his partner-in-crime Ottis Toole. He died while on Death Row in Huntsville Prison, Texas.

6 Gilles de Rais (France) — up to 200

A fabulously wealthy French aristocrat, Gilles de Laval, Baron de Rais (1404–40), a one-time supporter of Joan of Arc, allegedly committed murders as sacrifices during black magic rituals. He was accused of having kidnapped and killed between 60 and 200 children, although these figures may have been fabricated by his political enemies. Charged with a catalogue of crimes that included "the conjuration of demons", he was tried, tortured, and found guilty. He was strangled and his body burnt at Nantes on 25 October 1440.

7 Hu Wanlin (China) — 196

Posing as a doctor specializing in ancient Chinese medicine, Hu Wanlin was sentenced on 1 October 2000 to 15 years' imprisonment for three deaths, but authorities believe he was responsible for considerably more, an estimated 20 in Taiyuan, 146 in Shanxi, and 30 in Shangqui.

8 Luis Alfredo Garavito (Colombia) — 189

Garavito confessed in 1999 to a spate of murders. On 28 May 2000 he was sentenced to a total of 835 years' imprisonment.

9 Hermann Webster Mudgett (USA) — up to 150

Also known as "H. H. Holmes", Mudgett (1860–96), a former doctor, may have lured over 150 women to his "castle" on 63rd Street, Chicago, which he operated as a hotel. The bulding contained a warren of secret passages with windowless, soundproofed cells with gas valves. It was fully equipped for torturing, murdering, and dissecting his victims and disposing of their bodies in furnaces or an acid bath. Arrested in 1894 and found guilty of the murder of an ex-partner, Benjamin F. Pitezel, he confessed to killing 27, but may have killed on up to 150 occasions (some authorities have calculated that the remains of 200 victims were found at his home). Mudgett, regarded as America's first mass murderer, was hanged at Moyamensing Prison, Philadelphia, on 7 May 1896.

10 Dr. Jack Kevorkian (USA) — 130

In 1999 Kevorkian, who admitted to assisting in 130 suicides since 1990, was convicted of second-degree murder. His appeal against his 10- to 25-year prison sentence was rejected on 21 November 2001.

* Includes only individual murderers; excludes murders by bandits, those carried out by terrorist groups, political and military atrocities, and gangland slayings.

Because of the secrecy surrounding the horrific crimes of serial killers, and the time-spans involved, it is almost impossible to calculate the precise numbers of their victims. The numbers of murders attributed to the criminals listed should therefore be taken as "best estimates" based on the most reliable evidence available. Such is the magnitude of the crimes of some of the serial killers,

WORST YEARS FOR MURDER IN ENGLAND AND WALES*

YEAR#	RATE PER MILLION	MURDERS TOTAL
1 2003	19.3	1,007
2 2002	15.7	818
3 2001	15.1	778
4 2000	13.1	678
5 1995	13.0	663
6 1999	12.6	650
7 1994	12.4	632
8 1991	12.3	623
9 1997	11.9	610
10 1987	11.9	599

* Since 1951

Prior to 1997, data relate to calendar year; from 1997, data relate to financial year

Source: Home Office, Crime in England and Wales 2002/2003: Supplementary Volume

► **Shoot to kill**
The use of firearms in murders varies around the world. In the USA, they are the most common weapon, whereas the strict prohibition on guns in the UK means they are only rarely used.

 THE 10

MOST COMMON MURDER WEAPONS AND METHODS IN ENGLAND AND WALES

WEAPON OR METHOD	VICTIMS (2002–03)
1 Sharp instrument	272
2 Poison or drugs*	204
3 Hitting and kicking	160
4 Shooting	80
5 Strangulation	68
6 Blunt instrument	47
7 Motor vehicle#	25
8 Burning	23
9 Drowning	8
10 Explosion	4

* Includes 172 of the victims of Dr. Shipman

\# Excludes death by careless/dangerous driving and aggravated vehicle taking

Source: *Home Office*, Crime in England and Wales 2002/2003: Supplementary Volume

 THE 10

COUNTRIES WITH THE HIGHEST MURDER RATES

COUNTRY	REPORTED MURDERS PER 100,000 POPULATION (2002*)
1 Honduras	154.02
2 South Africa	114.84
3 Colombia	69.98
4 Lesotho	50.41
5 Rwanda	45.08
6 Jamaica	43.71
7 El Salvador	34.33
8 Venezuela	33.20
9 Bolivia	31.98
10 Namibia	26.32
England and Wales	2.01

* Or latest year for which data available

Source: *Interpol*

 TOP 10

COUNTRIES WITH THE LOWEST MURDER RATES

COUNTRY	REPORTED MURDERS PER 100,000 POPULATION (2002*)
1 = Burkina Faso	0.38
= Cameroon	0.38
3 Senegal	0.63
4 = Gambia	0.71
= Mali	0.71
= Saudi Arabia	0.71
7 Mauritania	0.76
8 Indonesia	0.80
9 Oman	0.91
10 Hong Kong	1.03

* Or latest year for which data available

Source: *Interpol*

Erratic recording and the desire by some countries to downplay their lack of security may explain some of of the low published figures.

Capital Punishment

THE 10 COUNTRIES WITH THE MOST EXECUTIONS

	COUNTRY	EXECUTIONS* (2002)
1	China	126
2	USA	71
3	Iran	69
4	Saudi Arabia	47
5	Singapore	18
6	Jordan	13
7	Vietnam	12
8	Thailand	6
9	Kuwait	5
10	Pakistan	4

* Verifiable reported executions

Some 112 countries have abolished the death penalty in law or practice, while 83 retain it. Of the latter, a small group of countries execute the most prisoners. According to Amnesty International, in 2002 a total of 1,562 people were executed in 31 countries.

THE 10 FIRST COUNTRIES TO ABOLISH CAPITAL PUNISHMENT

	COUNTRY	ABOLISHED
1	Russia	1826
2	Venezuela	1863
3	Portugal	1867
4	= Brazil	1882
	= Costa Rica	1882
6	Ecuador	1897
7	Panama	1903
8	Norway	1905
9	Uruguay	1907
10	Colombia	1910
	UK	1965

Some countries listed abolished capital punishment in peacetime only, or for all crimes except treason. One US state, Michigan, abolished the death penalty for every offence except treason in 1846.

THE 10 LAST MEN TO BE HANGED FOR MURDER IN THE UK

	NAME	DATE OF EXECUTION
1	John Robson Welby	13 Aug 1964
2	Peter Anthony Allen	13 Aug 1964
3	Dennis Whitty	17 Dec 1963
4	Russell Pascoe	17 Dec 1963
5	Henry Burnett	15 Aug 1963
6	James Smith	28 Nov 1962
7	Oswald Grey	20 Nov 1962
8	James Hanratty	4 Apr 1962
9	Hendryk Niemasz	8 Sept 1961
10	Samuel McLaughlin	25 July 1961

Capital punishment was abolished in the UK on 9 November 1965. Welby and Allen, the last two men to be hanged, were executed on the same day but at different prisons after being found guilty of stabbing John Alan West to death during a robbery. The last woman hanged in the UK was Ruth Ellis, executed on 13 July 1955 for shooting David Blakely.

▲ **Death chamber**
From 1976 to April 2004, a total of 313 executions were carried out at Huntsville, Texas, the most of any state and almost four times as many as Virginia, which recorded the second highest figure.

LAST PUBLIC HANGINGS IN THE UK

	NAME	CRIME	LOCATION	DATE OF EXECUTION
1	Michael Barrett	Murder of Sarah Ann Hodgkinson, one of 12 victims of a bombing in Clerkenwell	London Old Bailey	26 May 1868
2	Robert Smith	Murder of girl, Miss Scott (the last public hanging in Scotland – but the crowd was held back from the scaffold)	Dumfries Prison	12 May 1868
3	Richard Bishop	Stabbing of Alfred Cartwright	Maidstone Prison	30 Apr 1868
4	John Mapp	Murder of a girl	Shrewsbury Prison	9 Apr 1868
5	Frederick Parker	Murder of Daniel Driscoll	York Prison	4 Apr 1868
6	Timothy Faherty	Murder of Mary Hanmer	New Bailey Prison, Manchester	4 Apr 1868
7	Miles Wetherill or Weatherill	Murder of Rev. Plow and his maid	New Bailey Prison, Manchester	4 Apr 1868
8	Frances Kidder	Murder of 12-year-old Louise Kidder-Staple (the last public hanging of a woman)	Maidstone Prison	2 Apr 1868
9	William Worsley	Murder of William Bradbury	Bedford Prison	31 Mar 1868
10	Frederick Baker	Murder and mutilation of 8-year-old Fanny Adams (hence the origin of the phrase "Sweet Fanny Adams")	Winchester Prison	24 Dec 1867

LAST PEOPLE TO BE BEHEADED IN ENGLAND

	NAME/DETAILS	DATE OF EXECUTION
1	**Simon Fraser,** Lord Lovat (b. c.1667) The 80-year-old peer, beheaded for treason at Tower Hill, London, was the last person to be beheaded in Britain.	9 Apr 1747
2	**William Boyd,** Lord Kilmarnock (b.1704) A Jacobite rebel, executed on Tower Hill.	18 Aug 1746
3	**Arthur Elphinstone,** Lord Balmerino (b.1688) A Jacobite rebel, executed on Tower Hill.	18 Aug 1746
4	**Charles Radclyffe** (b.1693) The younger brother of James (No. 6, below), he had escaped when James was caught, but was later recaptured.	8 Dec 1746
5	**William,** Earl of Kenmure (birthdate unknown) A Jacobite rebel, executed on Tower Hill.	24 Feb 1716
6	**Sir James Radclyffe,** Earl of Derwentwater (b.1689) A Jacobite rebel, executed on Tower Hill.	24 Feb 1716
7	**Alice Lisle** (b.c.1614) Although not of noble birth, 71-year-old Lisle was executed in Winchester for treason after being implicated in Monmouth's Rebellion.	2 Sept 1685
8	**James,** Duke of Monmouth (b.1649) Monmouth's beheading on Tower Hill was bungled by executioner Jack Ketch, who had to complete the job with a knife. His head was sewn back on again, so that a portrait could be painted.	15 July 1685
9	**William Russell** (b.1639) The son of the 5th Earl of Bedford, Russell was executed in Lincoln's Inn Fields, London, after being implicated in the "Popish Plot".	21 July 1683
10	**William Howard,** Viscount Stafford (b.1614) Executed for treason on Tower Hill.	29 Dec 1680

LAST PEOPLE TO BE BURNED AT THE STAKE IN ENGLAND

	NAME/DETAILS	DATE OF EXECUTION
1	**Christian (or Catherine) Murphy (or Bowman),** A female member of a gang of coiners (counterfeiters), she was strangled and then burnt at Newgate, London.	18 Mar 1789
2	**Margaret Sullivan** Burned for coining at Newgate.	25 June 1788
3	**Phebe (or Phoebe) Harris** Burned for coining at Newgate.	21 June 1786
4	**Mary Bailey** Mary Bailey was strangled and burnt at Winchester along with John Quinn, for the murder of Cornelius Bailey. She was the last person to be burned at the stake for petty treason (husband murder).	8 Mar 1784
5	**Rebecca Downing** Downing, a servant, was burned at Exeter for murdering her mistress.	29 June 1782
6	**Isabella Condon** Burned for coining at Tyburn, London.	27 Oct 1779
7	**Ann Cruttenden** 80-year-old Cruttenden was burned at the stake in Horsham, Sussex, for the murder of her husband.	8 Aug 1776
8	**Elizabeth Bordingham** Burned at York for husband murder.	30 Mar 1776
9	**Margaret Ryan** Burned at Maidstone, Kent, for husband murder.	18 Mar 1776
10	**Elizabeth Herring** Burned at Tyburn for husband murder.	13 Sept 1773

Burning at the stake was the punishment reserved for women found guilty of treason and "petty treason", which included the murder of husbands and of masters and mistresses by servants. It was abolished on 5 June 1790.

World Wars

TOP 10 | LARGEST ARMED FORCES OF WORLD WAR I

COUNTRY	PERSONNEL*
1 Russia	12,000,000
2 Germany	11,000,000
3 British Empire	8,904,467
4 France	8,410,000
5 Austria-Hungary	7,800,000
6 Italy	5,615,000
7 USA	4,355,000
8 Turkey	2,850,000
9 Bulgaria	1,200,000
10 Japan	800,000

* Total at peak strength

Russia's armed forces were relatively small in relation to the country's population – some six per cent, compared with 17 per cent in Germany. In total, more than 65 million combatants were involved in fighting some of the costliest battles, in terms of numbers killed, that the world has ever known.

THE 10 | COUNTRIES SUFFERING THE GREATEST MILITARY LOSSES IN WORLD WAR I

COUNTRY	NO. KILLED
1 Germany	1,773,700
2 Russia	1,700,000
3 France	1,357,800
4 Austria-Hungary	1,200,000
5 British Empire*	908,371
6 Italy	650,000
7 Romania	335,706
8 Turkey	325,000
9 USA	116,516
10 Bulgaria	87,500

* Including Australia, Canada, India, New Zealand, South Africa, etc.

Romania had the highest military death rate, at 45 per cent of its total mobilized forces; Germany's was 16 per cent, Austria-Hungary's and Russia's 15 per cent, and the British Empire's 10 per cent.

THE 10 | COUNTRIES WITH THE MOST PRISONERS OF WAR CAPTURED IN WORLD WAR I

COUNTRY	NO. CAPTURED
1 Russia	2,500,000
2 Austria-Hungary	2,200,000
3 Germany	1,152,800
4 Italy	600,000
5 France	537,000
6 Turkey	250,000
7 British Empire	191,652
8 Serbia	152,958
9 Romania	80,000
10 Belgium	34,659

▼ **War graves**
The vast extent of many European World War I war cemeteries are a tangible reminder of the military casualties sustained by the participants.

LARGEST ARMED FORCES OF WORLD WAR II

	COUNTRY	PERSONNEL*
1	USSR	12,500,000
2	USA	12,364,000
3	Germany	10,000,000
4	Japan	6,095,000
5	France	5,700,000
6	UK	4,683,000
7	Italy	4,500,000
8	China	3,800,000
9	India	2,150,000
10	Poland	1,000,000

* Total at peak strength

Allowing for deaths and casualties, the total level of forces mobilized during the course of the war is, of course, greater than the peak strength figures: that of the USSR, for example, has been put as high as 20,000,000, the USA 16,354,000, Germany 17,900,000, Japan 9,100,000, and the UK 5,896,000.

COUNTRIES SUFFERING THE GREATEST MILITARY LOSSES IN WORLD WAR II

	COUNTRY	NO. KILLED
1	USSR	13,600,000*
2	Germany	3,300,000
3	China	1,324,516
4	Japan	1,140,429
5	British Empire[†]	357,116
6	Romania	350,000
7	Poland	320,000
8	Yugoslavia	305,000
9	USA	292,131
10	Italy	279,800
	UK alone	*264,000*
	Total	*21,268,992*

* Total, of which 7,800,000 battlefield deaths

[†] Including Australia, Canada, India, New Zealand, etc.

COUNTRIES SUFFERING THE GREATEST MERCHANT SHIPPING LOSSES IN WORLD WAR II

	COUNTRY	VESSELS SUNK NO.	TONNAGE
1	UK	4,786	21,194,000
2	Japan	2,346	8,618,109
3	Germany	1,595	7,064,600
4	USA	578	3,524,983
5	Norway	427	1,728,531
6	Netherlands	286	1,195,204
7	Italy	467	1,155,080
8	Greece	262	883,200
9	Panama	107	542,772
10	Sweden	204	481,864

During 1939–45, Allied losses in the Atlantic alone totalled 3,843 ships (16,899,147 tons). June 1942 was the worst period of the war, with 131 vessels (652,487 tons) lost in the Atlantic and a further 42 vessels (181,709 tons) elsewhere.

Modern Military

COUNTRIES WITH THE HIGHEST MILITARY/ CIVILIAN RATIO

	COUNTRY	RATIO* (2003)
1	North Korea	489
2	Israel	266
3	Qatar	203
4	Jordan	193
5	Syria	188
6	United Arab Emirates	177
7	Iraq	162#
8	Bahrain	155
9	Oman	153
10	Taiwan	130
	UK	36

* Military personnel per 10,000 population

 # Prior to the 2003 conflict

One person in every 20 of North Korea's population is in the military, ten times that of the United States. Despite having the world's largest armed force, China's ratio represents only one in 571 of the total population.

COUNTRIES WITH THE HIGHEST PER CAPITA DEFENCE EXPENDITURE

	COUNTRY	EXPENDITURE PER CAPITA (2002) ($)
1	Qatar	3,115
2	Israel	1,572
3	Kuwait	1,536
4	USA	1,203
5	Singapore	1,072
6	Saudi Arabia	1,038
7	United Arab Emirates	982
8	Oman	846
9	Norway	796
10	Brunei	783
	UK	625

▶ **Strength in numbers**
Other than border conflicts, China's gigantic military force – almost twice as large as that of the USA – has not yet been tested in combat.

COUNTRIES WITH THE LARGEST DEFENCE BUDGETS

	COUNTRY	BUDGET ($)
1	USA	376,200,000,000
2	Japan	41,400,000,000
3	UK	41,300,000,000
4	France	34,900,000,000
5	Germany	27,400,000,000
6	China	22,400,000,000
7	Italy	22,300,000,000
8	Saudi Arabia	18,400,000,000
9	India	15,600,000,000
10	South Korea	14,800,000,000

The so-called "peace dividend" – the savings made as a consequence of the end of the Cold War between the West and the former Soviet Union – was short-lived. In response to the threats of international terrorism and "rogue states", such as Iraq, the budgets of the United States and her allies have increased to record levels.

COUNTRIES WITH THE SMALLEST DEFENCE BUDGETS

	COUNTRY*	BUDGET ($)
1	Gambia	3,400,000
2 =	Antigua and Barbuda	4,000,000
=	Guinea-Bissau	4,000,000
4	Equatorial Guinea	4,500,000
5	Guyana	5,400,000
6	Mauritius	7,200,000
7	Suriname	8,500,000
8	Cape Verde	9,000,000
9	Seychelles	12,000,000
10 =	Barbados	13,000,000
=	Malawi	13,000,000

* Includes only those countries that declare defence budgets

If their defence expenditure is expressed as a proportion of their gross domestic product, several of these countries' spending is actually on a par with many larger and wealthier nations.

THE FIRST TO...

FIRST AIR FORCE

THE WORLD'S FIRST – and smallest – air force was the Aeronautical Division of the US Army Signal Corps, set up under Captain Charles de Forest Chandler on 1 August 1907 to "have charge of all matters pertaining to military ballooning, air machines and all kindred subjects". Initially the force comprised only Chandler and two enlisted men with just two balloons, but in 1909 it acquired its first military aircraft, a Wright Flyer. Chandler went on to achieve another first, on 7 May 1912, becoming the first to fly a plane with a machine gun.

TOP10 COUNTRIES WITH THE SMALLEST ARMED FORCES*

COUNTRY	ESTIMATED TOTAL ACTIVE FORCES#
1 Antigua and Barbuda	170
2 Seychelles	450
3 Barbados	610
4 Gambia	800
5 Bahamas	860
6 Luxembourg	900
7 Belize	1,050
8 Cape Verde	1,200
9 Equatorial Guinea	1,320
10 Guyana	1,600

* Includes only those countries that declare a defence budget

In latest year for which data available

A number of small countries maintain military forces for ceremonial purposes, national prestige, or reasons other than national defence, and would be inadequate to resist an invasion. Luxembourg's army continues a long military tradition, however, and took an active part in peacekeeping operations in former Yugoslavia.

TOP10 COUNTRIES WITH THE LARGEST ARMED FORCES

COUNTRY	ESTIMATED ACTIVE FORCES*			
	ARMY	NAVY	AIR	TOTAL
1 China	1,700,000	250,000	400,000	2,250,000
2 USA	485,000	400,000	367,600	1,427,000#
3 India	1,100,000	55,000	170,000	1,325,000
4 North Korea	950,000	46,000	86,000	1,082,000
5 Russia	321,000	155,000	184,600	960,600†
6 South Korea	560,000	63,000	63,000	686,000
7 Pakistan	550,000	25,000	45,000	620,000
8 Iran	350,000	18,000	52,000	540,000∞
9 Turkey	402,000	52,750	60,100	514,850
10 Vietnam	412,000	42,000	30,000	484,000
UK	116,670	42,370	53,620	212,660

* In latest year for which data available

Includes 174,400 Marine Corps

† Includes Strategic Deterrent Forces, Paramilitary, National Guard, etc.

∞ Includes 120,000 Revolutionary Guards

In addition to the active forces listed here, many of the countries with the largest armies have substantial reserves on standby; South Korea's has been estimated at some 4.5 million, Vietnam's at 3–4 million, and China's at 500–600,000. Russia's former total of 3 million has steadily dwindled as a result both of the end of the Cold War and the economic problems faced by the post-Soviet military establishment.

World Religions

LARGEST MUSLIM POPULATIONS

	COUNTRY	MUSLIM POPULATION (2004)
1	Pakistan	150,850,000
2	India	132,480,000
3	Bangladesh	128,700,000
4	Indonesia	120,670,000*
5	Turkey	70,250,000
6	Iran	66,890,000
7	Egypt	61,900,000
8	Nigeria	53,500,000
9	Algeria	31,300,000
10	Morocco	30,560,000

* An additional 46 million people are considered Muslims by the Indonesian government but are more properly categorized as New Religionists (Islamisized syncretistic religions)

Source: *World Christian Database, www.worldchristiandatabase.org, October 2003*

LARGEST BUDDHIST POPULATIONS

	COUNTRY	BUDDHIST POPULATION (2004)
1	China	110,000,000
2	Japan	70,560,000
3	Thailand	52,580,000
4	Vietnam	40,490,000
5	Myanmar	36,730,000
6	Sri Lanka	13,150,000
7	Cambodia	12,450,000
8	India	7,460,000
9	South Korea	7,350,000
10	Taiwan	4,820,000

Source: *World Christian Database, www.worldchristiandatabase.org, October 2003*

◀ **Path of enlightenment**
Founded in India over 2,500 years ago, Buddhism spread throughout the Far East and beyond to become one of the world's foremost religions.

TOP 10 LARGEST HINDU POPULATIONS

COUNTRY	HINDU POPULATION (2004)
1 India	801,360,000
2 Nepal	19,030,000
3 Bangladesh	18,500,000
4 Indonesia	7,550,000
5 Sri Lanka	2,170,000
6 Pakistan	2,050,000
7 Malaysia	1,830,000
8 USA	1,130,000
9 South Africa	1,080,000
10 Myanmar	1,000,000

Source: *World Christian Database,
www.worldchristiandatabase.org, October 2003*

Hindus constitute some 75 per cent of the
population of India and 70 per cent of that of Nepal,
but only 13 per cent of that of Bangladesh and as
little as three per cent of Indonesia's.

TOP 10 LARGEST JEWISH POPULATIONS

COUNTRY	JEWISH POPULATION (2004)
1 USA	5,795,000
2 Israel	5,096,000
3 France	599,000
4 Argentina	490,000
5 Canada	420,000
6 Palestine	400,000
7 Brazil	379,000
8 UK	312,000
9 Germany	225,000
10 Russia	210,000

Source: World Christian Encyclopedia

The Diaspora – or scattering – of Jewish people has
been in progress for nearly 2,000 years, and as a
result Jewish communities are found in virtually
every country in the world. The worldwide Jewish
population is now estimated to exceed 13 million.

TOP 10 LONGEST-SERVING POPES

POPE	PERIOD IN OFFICE	YRS*
1 Pius IX	16 June 1846–7 Feb 1878	31
2 John Paul II	16 Oct 1978–#	25
3 Leo XIII	20 Feb 1878–20 July 1903	25
4 Peter	between c.32–c.64	c.25
5 Pius VI	15 Feb 1775–29 Aug 1799	24
6 Adrian I	1 Feb 772–25 Dec 795	23
7 Pius VII	14 Mar 1800–20 Aug 1823	23
8 Alexander III	7 Sept 1159–30 Aug 1181	21
9 Sylvester	31 Jan 314–31 Dec 335	21
10 Leo I	29 Sept 440–10 Nov 461	21

* Equal entries are separated by months

 # Still in office; duration as at April 2004

Although St. Peter is regarded as the first pope, some
authorities doubt the historical veracity of his reign.
If he is omitted as unhistorical, Nos. 4–10 all move
up one place and 10th becomes Clement XI (23
September 1700–19 March 1721, a reign of 20 years).

TOP 10 LARGEST CHRISTIAN POPULATIONS

COUNTRY	CHRISTIAN POPULATION (2004)
1 USA	246,543,000
2 Brazil	164,122,000
3 China	106,902,000
4 Mexico	101,541,000
5 Russia	85,234,000
6 Philippines	73,862,000
7 India	68,125,000
8 Germany	62,557,000
9 Nigeria	59,148,000
10 Dem. Rep. of Congo	55,340,000

Source: *World Christian Database*

The Christian populations of these 10 countries
make up 45 per cent of the world total. Although
Christian communities are found in almost every
country in the world, it is difficult to put a precise
figure on nominal membership (a declared religious
persuasion) rather than active participation (regular
attendance at a place of worship).

TOP 10 RELIGIONS IN THE UK

RELIGION	FOLLOWERS (2003)
1 Anglican	28,240,000
2 Roman Catholic	5,840,000
3 Presbyterian	2,900,000
4 Islam	1,700,000
5 Methodist	1,240,000
6 Hinduism	584,000
7 Orthodox Christianity	560,000
8 Pentecostal	523,000
9 Baptist	500,000
10 Sikhism	352,000

Source: *Christian Research*

Membership of Christian churches in the UK has
fallen since the 1970s, while membership of other
religions, particularly Hinduism and Islam, has risen.
This list represents the number of people who have
stated that they belong to a particular religion or
denomination – not necessarily practising members.
Of the 28,240,000 Anglicans in the UK in 2003,
under 1 million regularly attended church services,
although twice as many go at least once a year.

TOP 10 RELIGIOUS BELIEFS

RELIGION	FOLLOWERS (2004)
1 Christianity	2,090,763,000
2 Islam	1,271,884,000
3 Hinduism	841,078,000
4 Agnosticism	774,800,000
5 Chinese folk-religions	400,600,000
6 Buddhism	376,574,000
7 Ethnic religions	242,882,000
8 Atheism	149,564,000
9 New religions	106,937,000
10 Sikhism	24,402,000

Source: *David B. Barrett & Todd M. Johnson,
International Bulletin of Missionary Research,
January 2004*

These authoritative estimates imply that almost
one-third of the world's population are nominally
(self-declared), if not practising, Christians, and
one-fifth are followers of Islam. Most of the major
religions are sectarian: some 17 per cent of
Christians are Roman Catholic, while 83 per cent
of Muslims are Sunni and 16 per cent Shiite.

TOWN & COUNTRY

Countries of the World

TOP 10 SMALLEST COUNTRIES

	COUNTRY	AREA (SQ KM)	(SQ MILES)
1	Vatican City	0.44	0.2
2	Monaco	2	0.7
3	Nauru	21	8
4	Tuvalu	26	10
5	San Marino	60	23
6	Liechtenstein	161	62
7	Marshall Islands	181	70
8	Maldives	300	115
9	Malta	321	124
10	Grenada	339	130

Source: *US Census Bureau, International Data Base*

The "country" status of the Vatican is questionable, since its government and other features are intricately linked with those of Italy. Formerly part of the Papal States, it became part of unified Italy in the 19th century. Its identity as an independent state was enshrined in the Lateran Treaty of 11 February 1929.

TOP 10 LARGEST COUNTRIES

	COUNTRY	% OF WORLD TOTAL	AREA (SQ KM)	(SQ MILES)
1	Russia	13.0	17,075,400	6,592,850
2	Canada	7.6	9,984,670	3,855,103
3	China	7.1	9,326,411	3,600,948
4	USA	6.9	9,166,601	3,539,245
5	Brazil	6.4	8,456,511	3,265,077
6	Australia	5.8	7,617,931	2,941,300
7	India	2.2	2,973,190	1,148,148
8	Argentina	2.1	2,736,690	1,056,642
9	Kazakhstan	2.1	2,717,300	1,049,155
10	Algeria	1.8	2,381,741	919,595
	World total	100.0	131,003,055	50,580,568
	UK	0.2	241,590	93,278

Source: *US Census Bureau, International Data Base/ Statistics Canada*

TOP 10 COUNTRIES WITH THE LONGEST BORDERS

	COUNTRY	TOTAL BORDER LENGTH (KM)	(MILES)
1	China	22,147	13,761
2	Russia	19,961	12,403
3	Brazil	14,691	9,129
4	India	14,103	8,763
5	USA	12,248	7,611
6	Dem. Rep. of Congo	10,744	6,676
7	Argentina	9,665	6,006
8	Canada	8,893	5,526
9	Mongolia	8,162	5,071
10	Sudan	7,687	4,776

This list represents the total length of borders, compiled by adding together the lengths of individual land borders. The wholly European country with the longest total borders is Germany, at 3,618 km (2,248 miles). The total length of the world's land boundaries is reckoned to be approximately 251,480 km (156,262 miles), with shared boundaries counted only once.

▼ Shore thing

The coast of mainland Canada comprises 57,759 km (35,889 miles) of its total coastline length, the balance being the total coastline lengths of its 52,455 offshore islands.

TOP 10 COUNTRIES WITH THE LONGEST COASTLINES

	COUNTRY	TOTAL COASTLINE LENGTH (KM)	(MILES)
1	Canada	202,080	125,566
2	Indonesia	54,716	33,999
3	Russia	37,653	23,396
4	Philippines	36,289	22,559
5	Japan	29,751	18,486
6	Australia	25,760	16,007
7	Norway	21,925	13,624
8	USA	19,924	12,380
9	New Zealand	15,134	9,404
10	China	14,500	9,010

With all its islands, the coastline of Canada is more than six times as long as the distance round the Earth at the Equator (40,076 km/24,901.8 miles). The UK coastline (12,429 km/7,723 miles) is in 13th place after Greece (13,676 km/8,498 miles).

TOP 10 LARGEST LANDLOCKED COUNTRIES

COUNTRY/NEIGHBOURS	AREA (SQ KM)	(SQ ML)
1 **Kazakhstan,** China, Kyrgyzstan, Russia, Turkmenistan, Uzbekistan	2,717,300	1,049,156
2 **Mongolia,** China, Russia	1,565,000	604,250
3 **Niger,** Algeria, Benin, Burkina Faso, Chad, Libya, Mali, Nigeria	1,266,699	489,075
4 **Chad,** Cameroon, Central African Republic, Libya, Niger, Nigeria, Sudan	1,259,201	486,180
5 **Mali,** Algeria, Burkina Faso, Côte d'Ivoire, Guinea, Mauritania, Niger, Senegal	1,219,999	471,044
6 **Ethiopia,** Djibouti, Eritrea, Kenya, Somalia, Sudan	1,119,683	432,312
7 **Bolivia,** Argentina, Brazil, Chile, Paraguay, Peru	1,084,389	418,685
8 **Zambia,** Angola, Dem. Rep. of Congo, Malawi, Mozambique, Namibia, Tanzania, Zimbabwe	740,719	285,993
9 **Afghanistan,** China, Iran, Pakistan, Tajikistan, Turkmenistan, Uzbekistan	647,500	250,001
10 **Central African Republic,** Cameroon, Chad, Congo, Dem. Rep. of Congo, Sudan	622,980	240,534

Source: *US Census Bureau, International Data Base*

There are 42 landlocked countries in the world. Kazakhstan and Turkmenistan both have coasts on the Caspian Sea – which is itself landlocked.

TOP 10 SMALLEST LANDLOCKED COUNTRIES

COUNTRY/NEIGHBOURS	AREA (SQ KM)	(SQ MILES)
1 **Vatican City,** Italy	0.44	0.2
2 **San Marino,** Italy	60	23
3 **Liechtenstein,** Austria, Switzerland	161	62
4 **Andorra,** France, Spain	451	174
5 **Luxembourg,** Belgium, France, Germany	2,585	998
6 **Swaziland,** Mozambique, South Africa	17,200	6,641
7 **Rwanda,** Burundi, Dem. Rep. of Congo, Tanzania, Uganda	24,949	9,633
8 **Burundi,** Dem. Rep.of Congo, Rwanda, Tanzania	25,649	9,903
9 **Macedonia,** Albania, Bulgaria, Greece, Yugoslavia	25,713	9,928
10 **Armenia,** Azerbaijan, Georgia, Iran, Turkey	29,800	11,506

Source: *US Census Bureau, International Data Base*

Landlocked countries – those lacking direct access to the sea – often suffer through having to rely on their neighbours for trade routes. In times of conflict this makes them especially vulnerable to blockades. Two countries in the world are actually doubly-landlocked – completely surrounded by other landlocked countries. They are Liechtenstein, which is surrounded by Austria and Switzerland, and Uzbekistan, surrounded by Afghanistan, Kazakhstan, Kyrgyzstan, Tajikistan, and Turkmenistan.

TOP 10 COUNTRIES WITH THE MOST NEIGHBOURS

COUNTRY/NEIGHBOURS	NO. OF NEIGHBOURS
1 = **China,** Afghanistan, Bhutan, India, Kazakhstan, Kyrgyzstan, Laos, Mongolia, Myanmar, Nepal, North Korea, Pakistan, Russia, Tajikistan, Vietnam	14
= **Russia,** Azerbaijan, Belarus, China, Estonia, Finland, Georgia, Kazakhstan, Latvia, Lithuania, Mongolia, North Korea, Norway, Poland, Ukraine	14
3 **Brazil,** Argentina, Bolivia, Colombia, French Guiana, Guyana, Paraguay, Peru, Suriname, Uruguay, Venezuela	10
4 = **Dem. Rep. of Congo,** Angola, Burundi, Central African Republic, Congo, Rwanda, Sudan, Tanzania, Uganda, Zambia	9
= **Germany,** Austria, Belgium, Czech Republic, Denmark, France, Luxembourg, Netherlands, Poland, Switzerland	9
= **Sudan,** Central African Republic, Chad, Dem. Rep. of Congo, Egypt, Eritrea, Ethiopia, Kenya, Libya, Uganda	9
7 = **Austria,** Czech Republic, Germany, Hungary, Italy, Liechtenstein, Slovakia, Slovenia, Switzerland	8
= **France,** Andorra, Belgium, Germany, Italy, Luxembourg, Monaco, Spain, Switzerland	8
= **Turkey,** Armenia, Azerbaijan, Bulgaria, Georgia, Greece, Iran, Iraq, Syria	8
10 = **Mali,** Algeria, Burkina Faso, Côte d'Ivoire, Guinea, Mauritania, Niger, Senegal	7
= **Niger,** Algeria, Benin, Burkina Faso, Chad, Libya, Mali, Nigeria	7
= **Saudi Arabia,** Iraq, Jordan, Kuwait, Oman, Qatar, United Arab Emirates, Yemen	7
= **Tanzania,** Burundi, Kenya, Malawi, Mozambique, Rwanda, Uganda, Zambia	7
= **Ukraine,** Belarus, Hungary, Moldova, Poland, Romania, Russia, Slovakia	7
= **Zambia,** Angola, Dem. Rep. of Congo, Malawi, Mozambique, Namibia, Tanzania, Zimbabwe	7

It should be noted that some countries have more than one discontinous border with the same country; this has been counted only once.

Country Populations

TOP 10 — MOST POPULATED COUNTRIES

COUNTRY	POPULATION (2005 EST.)
1 China	1,302,207,986
2 India	1,080,264,388
3 USA	295,734,134
4 Indonesia	241,973,879
5 Brazil	186,112,794
6 Pakistan	156,689,148
7 Bangladesh	144,319,628
8 Russia	143,736,793
9 Nigeria	140,601,615
10 Japan	127,417,244
World total	*6,448,780,202*
UK	*60,441,457*

Source: US Census Bureau, International Data Base

TOP 10 — LEAST POPULATED COUNTRIES

COUNTRY	POPULATION (2005 EST.)
1 Tuvalu	11,636
2 Nauru	13,048
3 Palau	20,303
4 San Marino	28,880
5 Monaco	32,409
6 Liechtenstein	33,317
7 St. Kitts and Nevis	38,958
8 Marshall Islands	59,071
9 Antigua and Barbuda	68,722
10 Dominica	69,029

Source: US Census Bureau, International Data Base

TOP 10 — LEAST POPULATED COUNTRIES, 2050

COUNTRY	POPULATION (2050 EST.)
1 Tuvalu	20,018
2 Nauru	22,696
3 Palau	26,300
4 Monaco	32,964
5 San Marino	35,335
6 Liechtenstein	35,776
7 St. Kitts and Nevis	52,348
8 Andorra	69,129
9 Antigua and Barbuda	69,259
10 Aruba	69,990

Source: US Census Bureau, International Data Base

TOP 10 MOST POPULATED COUNTRIES, 2050

	COUNTRY	POPULATION (2050 EST.)
1	India	1,601,004,572
2	China	1,417,630,630
3	US	420,080,587
4	Indonesia	336,247,428
5	Nigeria	307,420,055
6	Bangladesh	279,955,405
7	Pakistan	267,813,495
8	Brazil	228,426,737
9	Dem. Rep. of Congo	181,260,098
10	Mexico	147,907,650
	World total	*9,084,495,405*
	UK	*63,977,435*

Source: *US Census Bureau, International Data Base*

TOP 10 LEAST DENSELY-POPULATED COUNTRIES

	COUNTRY	AREA (SQ KM)	POPULATION (2005 EST.)	POPULATION PER SQ KM
1	Mongolia	1,565,000	2,791,272	1.78
2	Namibia	823,291	1,975,848	2.40
3	Australia	7,617,931	20,090,437	2.61
4	Botswana	585,371	1,545,285	2.64
5	Iceland	100,251	283,443	2.71
6	Surinam	161,471	438,144	2.73
7	Mauritania	1,030,400	3,086,859	2.99
8	Libya	1,759,540	5,765,563	3.28
9	Canada	9,220,970	32,805,041	3.56
10	Guyana	196,850	710,662	3.61
	UK	*241,590*	*60,441,457*	*250.20*

Source: *US Census Bureau, International Data Base*

These sparsely populated countries generally present environmental disadvantages that make human habitation challenging: some contain large tracts of mountain, desert, or dense forest, or have extreme climates.

◄ Population explosion

In 1999 India became only the second country after China with a population of over one billion. If the present rate of increase is maintained, India's population is set to overtake that of China around 2045.

TOP 10 COUNTRIES WITH THE YOUNGEST POPULATIONS

	COUNTRY	PERCENTAGE UNDER 15 (2005 EST.)
1	Uganda	50.3
2	Dem. Rep. of Congo	48.1
3	Chad	47.9
4	São Tomé and Príncipe	47.6
5	Niger	47.3
6	Mali	47.1
7	Malawi	46.9
8	= Benin	46.5
	= Yemen	46.5
10	Burkina Faso	46.0
	World average	*27.8*
	UK	*17.7*

Source: *US Census Bureau, International Data Base*

Countries with high proportions of their population under the age of 15 are usually characterized by high birth rates and high death rates. If regions without country status were included in this list, the Gaza Strip would be at No. 2, with almost one in two people (48.5 per cent) aged under 15.

TOP 10 COUNTRIES WITH THE OLDEST POPULATIONS

	COUNTRY	PERCENTAGE OVER 65 (2005 EST.)
1	Monaco	22.4
2	Japan	19.5
3	Italy	19.4
4	Germany	18.9
5	Greece	18.8
6	Spain	17.6
7	= Belgium	17.4
	= Sweden	17.4
9	Bulgaria	17.2
10	San Marino	16.9
	World average	*7.3*
	UK	*15.8*

Source: *US Census Bureau, International Data Base*

Nine of the 10 countries with the oldest populations are in Europe, implying that this region has lower death rates and a higher life expectancy than the rest of the world. On average, one in every 6.3 people in Europe is over the age of 65 (15.9 per cent). In contrast, the lowest percentages of old people are found in Africa, where the average is only one in every 30 people (3.3 per cent).

World Cities

THE 10 | FIRST CITIES WITH POPULATIONS OF MORE THAN 1 MILLION

	CITY	COUNTRY
1	Rome	Italy
2	Alexandria	Egypt
3	Angkor	Cambodia
4	Hangchow	China
5	London	UK
6	Paris	France
7	Peking	China
8	Canton	China
9	Berlin	Prussia
10	New York	USA

Rome's population was reckoned to have exceeded 1 million some time in the 2nd century BC, and Alexandria soon after. Angkor and Hangchow had both reached this figure by about AD 900 and 1200 respectively, but all three afterwards declined (Angkor was completely abandoned in the 15th century). No other city attained 1 million until London in the early years of the 19th century. The next cities to pass the million mark did so between about 1850 and the late 1870s.

TOP 10 | LARGEST NON-CAPITAL CITIES

	CITY/COUNTRY	CAPITAL	POPULATION (2003 EST.)
1	**New York** (including Newark and Paterson), USA	Washington, DC	21,750,000
2	**São Paulo** (including Guarulhos), Brazil	Brasília	20,200,000
3	**Mumbai** (including Kalyan, Thane, and Ulhasnagar), India	Delhi	18,800,000
4	**Los Angeles** (including Riverside and Anaheim), USA	Washington, DC	17,450,000
5	**Osaka** (including Kobe and Kyoto), Japan	Tokyo	16,700,000
6	**Calcutta*** (including Haora), India	Delhi	14,950,000
7	**Karachi***, Pakistan	Islamabad	13,100,000
8	**Shanghai**, China	Beijing	12,500,000
9	**Rio de Janeiro*** (including Nova Iguaçu and São Gonçalo), Brazil	Brasília	12,150,000
10	**Istanbul***, Turkey	Ankara	10,900,000

* Former capital

Source: *Th. Brinkhoff*: The Principal Agglomerations of the World, *http://www.citypopulation.de, 16.9.2003*

TOP 10 | FASTEST-GROWING CITIES

	CITY/COUNTRY	AVERAGE ANNUAL POPULATION GROWTH RATE* (PERCENTAGE, 2000–05)
1	**Ansan,** South Korea	9.15
2	**Toluca,** Mexico	6.15
3	**Sana'a,** Yemen	5.83
4	**Niamey,** Niger	5.70
5	**Songnam,** South Korea	5.47
6	**P'ohang,** South Korea	5.43
7	**Rajshahi,** Bangladesh	5.29
8	**Kabul,** Afghanistan	5.10
9	= **Antananarivo,** Madagascar	5.05
	= **Campo Grande,** Brazil	5.05
	Tyneside (Newcastle), UK	*0.60*

* Of urban agglomerations with 750,000 inhabitants or more

Source: *United Nations Population Division,* World Urbanization Report: The 2001 Revision

▶ **Capital gain**
Including the adjacent areas of Ecatepec, Nezahualcóyotl, and Naucalpan, Mexico City has undergone phenomenal growth from its 1950 population of 3 million.

TOP 10 | LARGEST CAPITAL CITIES

	CITY/COUNTRY	POPULATION (EST. 2003)
1	**Tokyo** (including Yokohama and Kawasaki), Japan	33,750,000
2	**Mexico City** (including Ecatepec, Nezahualcóyotl, and Naucalpan), Mexico	21,850,000
3	**Seoul** (including Bucheon, Goyang, Incheon, Seongnam, and Suweon), South Korea	21,700,000
4	**Delhi** (including Faridabad and Ghaziabad), India	18,100,000
5	**Jakarta** (including Bekasi, Bogor, Depok, and Tangerang), Indonesia	16,300,000
6	**Cairo** (including Al-Jizah and Shubra al-Khaymah), Egypt	15,600,000
7	**Moscow**, Russia	15,350,000
8	**Manila** (including Kalookan and Quezon City), Philippines	14,000,000
9	**Buenos Aires** (including San Justo and La Plata), Argentina	13,900,000
10	**Dhaka,** Bangladesh	12,050,000

Source: *Th. Brinkhoff: The Principal Agglomerations of the World, http://www.citypopulation.de, 16.9.2003*

TOP 10 | LARGEST CITIES IN THE U.S.

	CITY/STATE	POPULATION (2003)*
1	**New York** (including Newark and Paterson), New York	21,750,000
2	**Los Angeles** (including Riverside and Anaheim), California	17,450,000
3	**Chicago,** Illinois	9,650,000
4	**Washington, DC** (including Baltimore), Dist. of Columbia	7,900,000
5	**San Francisco** (including Oakland and San Jose), California	7,250,000
6	**Philadelphia,** Pennsylvania	5,950,000
7	**Detroit** (including Windsor, ON, Canada), Michigan	5,750,000
8 =	**Boston,** Massachusetts	5,700,000
=	**Dallas** (including Fort Worth), Texas	5,700,000
10	**Miami** (including Fort Lauderdale), Florida	5,400,000

* Of urban agglomeration

Source: *Th. Brinkhoff: The Principal Agglomerations of the World, http://www.citypopulation.de, 16.09.2003*

TOP 10 | COUNTRIES WITH THE MOST MILLION-PLUS CITIES

	COUNTRY	CITIES WITH POPULATIONS OF OVER 1 MILLION
1	**USA**	51
2	**China***	45
3	**India**	40
4	**Brazil**	19
5 =	**Japan**	14
=	**Russia**	14
7	**Germany**	11
8 =	**Indonesia**	8
=	**Pakistan**	8
=	**UK**	8

* Includes Hong Kong

Source: *Th. Brinkhoff: The Principal Agglomerations of the World, http://www.citypopulation.de, 16.09.2003*

There are some 418 cities in the world with populations of more than 1 million people. These cities are found in 100 different countries, but many of these countries contain only one 1 million-plus city (in most instances their capitals). This list thus covers an elite group with more than eight apiece.

US States

MOST POPULOUS STATES

	STATE	POPULATION (1900)	POPULATION (2000)
1	California	1,485,053	33,871,648
2	Texas	3,048,710	20,851,820
3	New York	7,268,894	18,976,457
4	Florida	528,542	15,982,378
5	Illinois	4,821,550	12,419,293
6	Pennsylvania	6,302,115	12,281,054
7	Ohio	4,157,545	11,353,140
8	Michigan	2,420,982	9,938,444
9	New Jersey	1,883,669	8,414,350
10	Georgia	2,216,231	8,186,453

Source: *US Census Bureau*

The total population of the United States according to the 1900 Census was 76,212,168, compared to the preliminary results of the 1 April 2000 Census, which put the total at 281,421,906. Some states have grown faster than others: Florida's population is now over 30 times its 1900 figure.

LEAST POPULOUS STATES

	STATE	POPULATION (2000)
1	Wyoming	493,782
2	Vermont	608,827
3	Alaska	626,932
4	North Dakota	642,200
5	South Dakota	754,844
6	Delaware	783,600
7	Montana	902,195
8	Rhode Island	1,048,319
9	Hawaii	1,211,537
10	New Hampshire	1,235,786
	District of Columbia	572,059

Source: *US Census Bureau*

With a high proportion of its area devoted to agriculture and almost half the land area of Wyoming federally owned, the low population density of the state is likely to be maintained.

MOST DENSELY POPULATED STATES

	STATE	POPULATION* PER (SQ KM)	POPULATION* PER (SQ MILE)
1	New Jersey	437.9	1,134.2
2	Rhode Island	387.3	1,003.2
3	Massachusetts	312.7	810.0
4	Connecticut	271.4	702.9
5	Maryland	209.2	541.8
6	New York	155.1	401.8
7	Delaware	154.7	400.8
8	Florida	114.4	296.3
9	Ohio	107.0	277.2
10	Pennsylvania	105.8	274.0

* Of land area as at 2000

Source: *US Census Bureau*

Population densities have increased dramatically over the past 200 years: that of New Jersey, for example, was 96.8 per sq km (250.7 per sq mile) in 1900, and just 10.8 per sq km (28.1 per sq mile) in 1800.

STATES WITH THE MOST FOREIGN-BORN RESIDENTS

	STATE	FOREIGN-BORN RESIDENTS*
1	California	8,864,255
2	New York	3,868,133
3	Texas	2,899,642
4	Florida	2,670,828
5	Illinois	1,529,058
6	New Jersey	1,476,327
7	Massachusetts	772,983
8	Arizona	656,183
9	Washington	614,457
10	Georgia	577,273
	Total of all states	31,107,889

* Based on 2000 Census

Source: *US Census Bureau*

At the time of the 2000 Census, California had the greatest proportion of foreign-born residents of any state – 26.2 per cent, compared with 11.1 per cent for the United States as a whole.

► **California dreaming**
The 1849 gold rush and the attractions of its climate led to the growth of San Francisco and to California's becoming the most populous of all US states.

TOP 10 LEAST DENSELY POPULATED STATES

STATE	POPULATION* PER (SQ KM)	(SQ MILE)
1 Alaska	0.4	1.1
2 Wyoming	1.9	5.1
3 Montana	2.4	6.2
4 North Dakota	3.6	9.3
5 South Dakota	3.8	10.0
6 New Mexico	5.8	15.0
7 Idaho	6.0	15.6
8 Nevada	7.0	18.2
9 Nebraska	8.6	22.3
10 Utah	10.5	27.2

* Of land area as at 2000

Source: US Census Bureau

TOP 10 SMALLEST STATES

STATE	LAND AREA (SQ KM)	(SQ MILES)
1 Rhode Island	2,706	1,045
2 Delaware	5,063	1,955
3 Connecticut	12,548	4,845
4 Hawaii	16,635	6,423
5 New Jersey	19,215	7,419
6 Massachusetts	20,300	7,838
7 New Hampshire	23,229	8,969
8 Vermont	23,955	9,249
9 Maryland	25,317	9,775
10 West Virginia	62,385	24,087

Smallest state Rhode Island has the longest official name: "State of Rhode Island and Providence Plantations". A total of 546 Rhode Islands – which also includes some 1,295 sq km (500 sq miles) of inland water – could be fitted into the land area of largest state Alaska.

TOP 10 LARGEST STATES

STATE	LAND AREA* (SQ KM)	(SQ MILES)
1 Alaska	1,481,347	571,951
2 Texas	678,051	261,797
3 California	403,933	155,959
4 Montana	376,979	145,552
5 New Mexico	314,309	121,356
6 Arizona	294,312	113,635
7 Nevada	284,448	109,826
8 Colorado	268,627	103,718
9 Wyoming	251,489	97,100
10 Oregon	248,631	95,997

* Excluding water

The admission of Alaska to the Union on 3 January and Hawaii on 20 August 1959 increased the total land area of the United States by almost 20 per cent, bringing it to its present 9,171,146 sq km (3,540,999 sq miles).

Place Names

TOP 10 COUNTRIES WITH THE LONGEST OFFICIAL NAMES

	OFFICIAL NAME*	COMMON ENGLISH NAME	LETTERS
1	al-Jamahīrīyah al-'Arabīyah al-Lībīyah ash-Sha'bīyah al-Ishtirākīyah al-Uẓma	Libya	65
2	al-Jumhūrīyah al-Jazā' irīyah ad-Dīmuqrāṭīyah ash-Sha'bīyah	Algeria	51
3	United Kingdom of Great Britain and Northern Ireland	United Kingdom	45
4	Śri Lanka Prajatantrika Samajavadi Janarajaya	Sri Lanka	41
5	República Democrática de São Tomé e Príncipe	São Tomé and Príncipe	38
6	= al-Jumhūrīyah al-Islāmīyah al-Mūrītanīyah	Mauritania	36
	= Federation of Saint Christopher and Nevis	Saint Kitts and Nevis	36
8	Federal Democratic Republic of Ethiopia	Ethiopia	35
9	= al-Mamlakah al-Urdunnīyah al-Hāshimīyah	Jordan	34
	= Sathalanalat Paxathipatai Paxaxôn Lao	Laos	34

* Some official names have been transliterated from languages that do not use the Roman alphabet; their length may vary according to the method used

There is clearly no connection between the length of names and the longevity of the nation states that bear them, for since this list was first published in 1991, three countries have ceased to exist: Socijalisticka Federativna Republika Jugoslavija (Yugoslavia, 45 letters), Soyuz Sovetskikh Sctsialisticheskikh Respublik (USSR, 43), and Ceskoslovenská Socialistická Republika (Czechoslovakia, 36). Uruguay's official name of La República Oriental del Uruguay is sometimes given in full as the 38-letter La República de la Banda Oriental del Uruguay, which would place it in 6th position.

▶ **The long and the short of it**
A bustling market in Libya. The country's short and commonly used name appeared in Egyptian hieroglyphics 4,000 years ago. Its modern official name, adopted on 8 March 1977, translates as "The Great Socialist People's Libyan Arab Jamahiriya".

LONGEST PLACE NAMES*

NAME	LETTERS
1 **Krung thep mahanakhon amon rattanakosin mahinthara ayuthaya mahadilok phop noppharat ratchathani burirom udomratchaniwet mahasathan amon piman awatan sathit sakkathattiya witsanukam prasit**	168

When the poetic name of Bangkok, capital of Thailand, is used, it is usually abbreviated to "Krung Thep" (city of angels).

2 **Taumatawhakatangihangakoauauotamateaturipukakapiki-maungahoronukupokaiwhenuakitanatahu**	85

This is the longer version (the other has a mere 83 letters) of the Maori name of a hill in New Zealand. It translates as "The place where Tamatea, the man with the big knees, who slid, climbed and swallowed mountains, known as land-eater, played on the flute to his loved one".

3 **Gorsafawddacha'idraigodanheddogleddollônpenrhynareurdraethceredigion**	67

A name contrived by the Fairbourne Steam Railway, Gwynedd, North Wales, for publicity purposes and in order to outdo its rival, No. 4. It means "The Mawddach station and its dragon teeth at the Northern Penrhyn Road on the golden beach of Cardigan Bay".

4 **Llanfairpwllgwyngyllgogerychwyrndrobwllllantysiliogogogoch**	58

This is the place in Gwynedd famed especially for the length of its railway tickets. It means "St. Mary's Church in the hollow of the white hazel near to the rapid whirlpool of the church of St. Tysilo near the Red Cave". Questions have been raised about its authenticity, since its official name comprises only the first 20 letters, and the full name appears to have been invented as a hoax in the 19th century by a local tailor.

5 **El Pueblo de Nuestra Señora la Reina de los Ángeles de la Porciúncula**	57

The site of a Franciscan mission and the full Spanish name of Los Angeles; it means "the town of Our Lady the Queen of the Angels of the Little Portion". Nowadays it is customarily known by its initial letters, "LA", making it also one of the shortest-named cities in the world.

6 **Chargoggagoggmanchaugagoggchaubunagungamaug**	43

Loosely translated, the Indian name of this lake near Webster, Massachusetts, means "You fish on your side, I'll fish on mine, and no one fishes in the middle". It is said to be pronounced "Char-gogg-a-gogg (pause) man-chaugg-a-gog (pause) chau-bun-a-gung-a-maug". It is, however, an invented extension of its real name (Chaubunagungamaug, or "boundary fishing place"), devised in the 1920s by Larry Daly, the editor of the *Webster Times*.

7 = **Lower North Branch Little Southwest Miramichi**	40

Canada's longest place name – a short river in New Brunswick.

= **Villa Real de la Santa Fé de San Francisco de Asis**	40

The full Spanish name of Santa Fe, New Mexico, translates as "Royal city of the holy faith of St. Francis of Assisi".

9 **Te Whakatakanga-o-te-ngarehu-o-te-ahi-a-Tamatea**	38

The Maori name of Hammer Springs, New Zealand; like the second name in this list, it refers to a legend of Tamatea, explaining how the springs were warmed by "the falling of the cinders of the fire of Tamatea". Its name is variously written either hyphenated or as a single word.

10 **Meallan Liath Coire Mhic Dhubhghaill**	32

The longest multiple name in Scotland, a place near Aultanrynie, Highland, alternatively spelled Meallan Liath Coire Mhic Dhughaill (30 letters).

* Including single-word, hyphenated, and multiple names

MOST COMMON HOUSE NAMES IN THE UK

NAME
1 **The Cottage**
2 **Rose Cottage**
3 **The Bungalow**
4 **The Coach House**
5 **Orchard House**
6 **The Lodge**
7 **Woodlands**
8 **The Old School House**
9 **Ivy Cottage**
10 **The Willows**

Source: *Halifax*

Compared with a survey of 1991, this latest overview of UK house names shows a fall in the popularity of former No. 1, The Bungalow, while The Coach House has leapt up from 9th place, pointing to the number of old coach houses now converted into dwellings.

MOST COMMON PLACE NAMES IN GREAT BRITAIN

NAME	OCCURRENCES
1 **Newton**	150
2 **Blackhill/Black Hill**	136
3 **Castlehill/Castle Hill**	128
4 **Mountpleasant/Mount Pleasant**	126
5 **Woodside/Wood Side**	112
6 **Newtown/New Town**	110
7 **Burnside**	107
8 **Greenhill/Green Hill**	105
9 **Woodend/Wood End**	101
10 **Beacon Hill**	95

These entries include the names of towns and villages, as well as woods, hills, and other named locations, but exclude combinations of these names with others (Newton Abbot and Newton-le-Willows, for example, are not counted with the Newtons).

Tallest Buildings 1900–2005

TOP10 TALLEST HABITABLE BUILDINGS IN 1900

BUILDING*/LOCATION#/ YEAR COMPLETED	STOREYS	HEIGHT (M)	(FT)
1 Park Row Building, 1899	30	119.2	391
2 Manhattan Life Insurance Building†, 1894	18	106.1	348
3 Bank of Tokyo, 1896	26	103.0	338
4 St. Paul Building†, 1898	26	96.0	315
5 World Building∞, 1890 spire	20	94.2 106.4	309 349
6 Masonic Temple◊, Chicago, USA, 1892	21	92.1	302
7 Central Tower, San Francisco, USA, 1898	21	91.1	299
8 Park Place Tower, 1895	23	89.0	292
9 Home Life Insurance Building, 1894	16	85.0	279
10 Gillender Building†, 1897	19	82.9	272

* Excluding low-rise habitable buildings with adjoining tower (such as various US city halls)
# All in New York unless otherwise specified
† Demolished 1910
∞ Demolished 1955
◊ Demolished 1939

TOP10 TALLEST HABITABLE BUILDINGS IN 1910

BUILDING*/LOCATION#/ YEAR COMPLETED	STOREYS	HEIGHT (M)	(FT)
1 Metropolitan Life Tower, 1909	50	213.4	700
2 Singer Building†, 1908	47	186.6	612
3 City Investing Building†, 1908	33	148.1	486
4 Park Row Building, 1899	30	119.2	391
5 Hanover National Bank∞, 1903	22	117.4	385
6 Liberty Tower, 1910	33	117.0	384
7 One Times Square, 1905	25	111.0	364
8 Manhattan Life Insurance Building◊, 1894	18	106.1	348
9 Oliver Building, Pittsburgh, USA, 1910	25	105.8	347
10 Land Title & Trust Building Annex, Philadelphia, USA, 1902	23	105.2	345

* Excluding low-rise habitable buildings with adjoining tower (such as various US city halls)
# All in New York unless otherwise specified
† Demolished 1968
∞ Demolished 1931
◊ Demolished 1964

TOP10 TALLEST HABITABLE BUILDINGS IN 1920

BUILDING*/LOCATION#/ YEAR COMPLETED	STOREYS	HEIGHT (M)	(FT)
1 Woolworth Building, 1913	57	241.4	792
2 Metropolitan Life Tower, 1909	50	213.4	700
3 Singer Building†, 1908	47	186.5	612
4 Municipal Building, 1914 spire	34	176.8 182.9	580 600
5 = Bankers Trust Building, 1912	37	164.0	538
= Equitable Building, 1915	39	164.0	538
7 Travelers Tower, Hartford, USA, 1919	24	160.6	527
8 Custom House Tower, Boston, USA, 1915	32	151.2	496
9 PNC Tower, Cincinnati, USA, 1913	31	150.9	495
10 City Investing Building†, 1908	33	148.1	486

* Excluding low-rise habitable buildings with adjoining tower (such as various US city halls)
# All in New York unless otherwise specified
† Demolished 1968

TOP10 TALLEST HABITABLE BUILDINGS IN 1960

BUILDING/LOCATION*/ YEAR COMPLETED	STOREYS	HEIGHT (M)	(FT)
1 Empire State Building, 1931 spire	102	381.0 448.7	1,250 1,472
2 Chrysler Building, 1929 spire	77	281.9 318.8	925 1,046
3 40 Wall Street, 1929 spire	71	264.0 282.4	866 927
4 GE Bulding, 1933	69	259.1	850
5 American International Building, 1932 spire	67	251.8 290.2	826 952
6 1 Chase Manhattan Plaza, 1960	60	247.8	813
7 Woolworth Building, 1913	57	241.4	792
8 20 Exchange Place, 1931 spire	57	225.8 228.0	741 748
9 Terminal Tower, Cleveland, USA, 1930 spire	52	215.8 235.0	708 771
10 Metropolitan Life Tower, 1909	50	213.4	700

* All in New York unless otherwise specified

TOP10 TALLEST HABITABLE BUILDINGS IN 1970

BUILDING/LOCATION*/ YEAR COMPLETED	STOREYS	HEIGHT (M)	(FT)
1 Empire State Building, 1931 spire	102	381.0 448.7	1,250 1,472
2 John Hancock Center, Chicago, USA, 1968 spire	100	343.5 427.2	1,127 1,500
3 Chrysler Building, 1929 spire	77	281.9 318.8	925 1,046
4 40 Wall Street, 1929 spire	71	264.0 282.4	866 927
5 = Bank One Plaza, Chicago, USA, 1969	60	259.1	850
= GE Building, 1933	69	259.1	850
7 US Steel Tower, Pittsburgh, USA, 1970	64	256.0	840
8 American International Building, 1932 spire	67	251.8 290.2	826 952
9 1 Chase Manhattan Plaza, 1960	60	247.8	813
10 Met Life (formerly PanAmerican) Building, 1963	58	246.3	808

* All in New York unless otherwise specified

TOP10 TALLEST HABITABLE BUILDINGS IN 1980

BUILDING/LOCATION*/ YEAR COMPLETED	STOREYS	HEIGHT (M)	(FT)
1 Sears Tower, Chicago, USA, 1974 spire	108	442.0 527.3	1,450 1,730
2 1 World Trade Center#, 1972 spire	110	417.0 526.4	1,368 1,727
3 2 World Trade Center#, 1973 spire	110	415.4 526.4	1,363 1,727
4 Empire State Building, 1931 spire	102	381.0 448.7	1,250 1,472
5 Aon Center, Chicago, USA, 1973	83	346.3	1,136
6 John Hancock Center, Chicago, USA, 1968 spire	100	343.5 427.2	1,127 1,500
7 First Canadian Place, Toronto, Canada, 1975 spire	72	298.1 355.1	978 1,165
8 Chrysler Building, 1929 spire	77	281.9 318.8	925 1,046
9 Citigroup Center, 1977	59	278.9	915
10 40 Wall Street, 1929 spire	71	264.0 282.4	866 927

* All in New York, USA unless otherwise specified
# Destroyed by 9/11 terrorist attacks

TOP 10 | TALLEST HABITABLE BUILDINGS IN 1930

	BUILDING/LOCATION*/ YEAR COMPLETED	STOREYS	HEIGHT (M)	(FT)
1	**Chrysler Building**, 1929	77	281.9	925
	spire		318.8	1,046
2	**40 Wall Street**, 1929	71	264.0	866
	spire		282.6	927
3	**Woolworth Building**, 1913	57	241.4	792
4	**Terminal Tower**, Cleveland, USA, 1930	52	215.8	708
	spire		235.0	771
5	**Metropolitan Life Tower**, 1909	50	213.4	700
6	**Lincoln Building**, 1930	53	205.1	673
7	**Chanin Building**, 1930	56	197.8	649
	spire		207.3	680
8	**Mercantile Building**, 1929	48	189.0	620
9	**New York Life Building**, 1928	40	187.5	615
	spire		202.7	665
10	**Singer Building**#, 1908	47	186.5	612

* All in New York unless otherwise specified
# Demolished 1968

TOP 10 | TALLEST HABITABLE BUILDINGS IN 1940/1950

	BUILDING/LOCATION*/ YEAR COMPLETED	STOREYS	HEIGHT (M)	(FT)
1	**Empire State Building**, 1931	102	381.0	1,250
	spire		448.7	1,472
2	**Chrysler Building**, 1929	77	281.9	925
	spire		318.8	1,046
3	**40 Wall Street**, 1929	71	264.0	866
	spire		282.4	927
4	**GE Building**, 1933	69	259.1	850
5	**American International Building**, 1932	66	251.8	826
	spire		290.2	952
6	**Woolworth Building**, 1913	57	241.4	792
7	**20 Exchange Place**, 1931	57	225.9	741
	spire		228.0	748
8	**Terminal Tower**, Cleveland, USA, 1930	52	215.8	708
	spire		235.0	771
9	**Metropolitan Life Tower**, 1909	50	213.4	700
10	**500 Fifth Avenue**, 1931	60	212.5	697

* All in New York unless otherwise specified

It is of interest to note that the world's Top 10 buildings in 1950 were identical to those in 1940. As this list shows, although several skyscrapers were built during the Depression, economic concerns followed by World War II put a hold on further building, with no rivals to any of these appearing until the 1960s.

TOP 10 | TALLEST HABITABLE BUILDINGS IN 1990

	BUILDING/LOCATION/ YEAR COMPLETED	STOREYS	HEIGHT (M)	(FT)
1	**Sears Tower**, Chicago, USA, 1974	108	442.0	1,450
	spire		527.3	1,730
2	**1 World Trade Center***, New York, USA, 1972	110	417.0	1,368
	spire		526.4	1,727
3	**2 World Trade Center***, New York, USA, 1973	110	415.4	1,363
	spire		526.4	1,727
4	**Empire State Building**, New York, USA, 1931	102	381.0	1,250
	spire		448.7	1,472
5	**Aon Center**, Chicago, USA, 1973	83	346.3	1,136
6	**John Hancock Center**, Chicago, USA, 1968	100	343.5	1,127
	spire		427.2	1,500
7	**Library Tower**, Los Angeles, USA, 1990	73	310.3	1,018
8	**JPMorganChase Tower**, Houston, USA, 1982	75	305.4	1,002
9	**Bank of China Tower**, Hong Kong, 1989	71	305.1	1,001
	spires		367.3	1,205
10	**First Canadian Place**, Toronto, Canada, 1975	72	298.1	978
	spire		355.1	1,165

* Destroyed by 9/11 terrorist attacks

TOP 10 | TALLEST HABITABLE BUILDINGS IN 2000

	BUILDING/LOCATION/ YEAR COMPLETED	STOREYS	HEIGHT (M)	(FT)
1	**Petronas Towers**, Kuala Lumpur, Malaysia, 1998	88	452.0	1,483
2	**Sears Tower**, Chicago, USA, 1974	108	442.0	1,450
	spire		527.3	1,730
3	**1 World Trade Center***, New York, USA, 1972	110	417.0	1,368
	spire		526.4	1,727
4	**2 World Trade Center***, New York, USA, 1973	110	415.4	1,363
	spire		526.4	1,727
5	**Jin Mao Building**, Shanghai, China, 1998	88	382.5	1,255
	spire		420.6	1,380
6	**Empire State Building**, New York, USA, 1931	102	381.0	1,250
	spire		448.7	1,472
7	**Tuntex 85 Sky Tower**, Kao-hsiung, Taiwan, 1997	85	347.5	1,140
	spire		378.0	1,240
8	**Aon Center**, Chicago, USA, 1973	83	346.3	1,136
9	**John Hancock Center**, Chicago, USA, 1968	100	343.5	1,127
	spire		427.2	1,500
10	**Ryogyong Hotel**#, Pyongyang, North Korea, 1992	105	330.1	1,083

* Destroyed by 9/11 terrorist attacks
# Not completed or occupied

TOP 10 | TALLEST HABITABLE BUILDINGS IN 2005

	BUILDING/LOCATION/ YEAR COMPLETED	STOREYS	HEIGHT (M)	(FT)
1	**Petronas Towers**, Kuala Lumpur, Malaysia, 1998	88	452.0	1,483
2	**Taipei 101**, Taipei, Taiwan, 2004	101	448.1	1,470
	spire		508.1	1,667
3	**Sears Tower**, Chicago, USA, 1974	108	442.0	1,450
	spire		527.3	1,730
4	**2 International Finance Centre**, Hong Kong, China, 2003	90	406.9	1,335
	spire		415.8	1,364
5	**Jin Mao Building**, Shanghai, China, 1998	88	382.5	1,255
	spire		420.6	1,380
6	**Empire State Building**, New York, USA, 1931	102	381.0	1,250
	spire		448.7	1,472
7	**Tuntex 85 Sky Tower**, Kao-hsiung, Taiwan, 1997	85	347.5	1,140
	spire		378.0	1,240
8	**Aon Center**, Chicago, USA, 1973	83	346.3	1,136
9	**John Hancock Center**, Chicago, USA, 1968	100	343.5	1,127
	spire		427.2	1,500
10 =	**China World Trade Center**, Beijing, China, 2005	80	330.1	1,083
=	**Ryogyong Hotel***, Pyongyang, North Korea, 1992	105	330.1	1,083

* Not completed or occupied

Bridges & Tunnels

LONGEST ROAD TUNNELS

TUNNEL/LOCATION	YEAR COMPLETED	LENGTH (M)	(FT)
1 **Laerdal,** Norway	2000	24,510	80,413
2 **Zhongnanshan,** China	U/C 2007*	18,040	59,186
3 **St. Gotthard,** Switzerland	1980	16,918	55,505
4 **Arlberg,** Austria	1978	13,972	45,850
5 **Hsuehshan,** Taiwan	U/C 2005*	12,900	42,323
6 **Fréjus,** France/Italy	1980	12,895	42,306
7 **Mont-Blanc,** France/Italy	1965	11,611	38,094
8 **Gudvangen,** Norway	1991	11,428	37,493
9 **Folgefonn,** Norway	2001	11,100	36,417
10 **Kan-Etsu II** (southbound), Japan	1990	11,010	36,122

* Under construction; scheduled completion date

Numbers 1, 3, 4, and 7 have all held the record as "world's longest road tunnel". Previous record-holders include the 5,854 m (19,206 ft) Grand San Bernardo (Italy-Switzerland; 1964), the 5,133 m (16,841) Alfonso XIII or Viella (Spain; 1948), the 3,237 m (10,620 ft) Queensway (Mersey) Tunnel (connecting Liverpool and Birkenhead, UK; 1934), and the 3,186 m (10,453 ft) Col de Tende (France–Italy; 1882), originally built as a rail tunnel and converted in 1928.

LONGEST RAIL TUNNELS

TUNNEL/LOCATION	YEAR COMPLETED	LENGTH (M)	(FT)
1 **AlpTransit Gotthard,** Switzerland	U/C 2010*	57,072	187,244
2 **Seikan,** Japan	1988	53,850	176,673
3 **Channel Tunnel,** France/England	1994	50,450	165,518
4 **Moscow Metro** (Medvedkovo/ Belyaevo section), Russia	1979	38,900	127,625
5 **Guadarrama,** Spain	U/C 2007*	28,377	97,100
6 **London Underground** (East Finchley/ Morden, Northern Line), UK	1939	27,840	91,339
7 **Hakkouda,** Japan	U/C 2013*	26,455	86,795
8 **Iwate,** Japan	U/C 2013*	25,810	84,678
9 **Iiyama,** Japan	U/C 2013*	22,225	72,917
10 **Dai-Shimizu,** Japan	1982	22,221	72,904

* Under construction; scheduled completion date

The world's longest rail tunnel, the Gotthard AlpTransit, Switzerland, was proposed as early as 1947, before finally being given the go-ahead in 1998 after a referendum of the Swiss electorate. When completed, trains will travel through it at 250 km/h (155 mph).

LONGEST SUSPENSION BRIDGES

BRIDGE/LOCATION	YEAR COMPLETED	LENGTH OF MAIN SPAN (M)	(FT)
1 **Akashi-Kaikyo,** Kobe-Naruto, Japan	1998	1,991	6,532
2 **Izmit Bay,** Turkey	U/C*	1,668	5,472
3 **Great Belt,** Denmark	1997	1,624	5,328
4 **Humber Estuary,** UK	1980	1,410	4,626
5 **Jiangyin,** China	1998	1,385	4,544
6 **Tsing Ma,** Hong Kong, China	1997	1,377	4,518
7 **Verrazano Narrows,** New York, USA	1964	1,298	4,260
8 **Golden Gate,** San Francisco, USA	1937	1,280	4,200
9 **Höga Kusten** (High Coast), Veda, Sweden	1997	1,210	3,970
10 **Mackinac Straits,** Michigan, USA	1957	1,158	3,800

* Under construction

Work will begin in 2004–5 on the Messina Strait Bridge between Sicily and Calabria, Italy; it will take 5–6 years and cost €4.6 billion (£3 billion). It will have by far the longest centre span of any bridge at 3,300 m (10,827 ft) although at 3,910 m (12,828 ft) Japan's Akashi-Kaikyo bridge, completed in 1998, and with a main span of 1,990 m (6,529 ft), is the world's longest overall.

TOP 10 LONGEST UNDERWATER TUNNELS

	TUNNEL/LOCATION	YEAR COMPLETED	LENGTH (M)	(FT)
1	**Seikan,** Japan	1988	53,850	176,673
2	**Channel Tunnel,** France/England	1994	50,450	165,518
3	**Dai-Shimizu,** Japan	1982	22,221	72,904
4	**Shin-Kanmon,** Japan	1975	18,680	61,286
5	**Tokyo Bay Aqualine Expressway*,** Japan	1997	9,583	31,440
6	**Great Belt Fixed Link** (Eastern Tunnel), Denmark	1997	8,024	26,325
7	**Bømlafjord*,** Norway	2000	7,921	25,988
8	**Eiksund,*** Norway	U/C 2006†	7,797	25,581
8	**Oslofjord*,** Norway	2000	7,260	23,819
9	**Severn,** UK	1886	7,008	22,992

* Road; others rail

† Under construction; scheduled completion date

The Seikan tunnel connects the Japanese islands of Honshu and Hokkaido, and runs 100 m (328 ft) below the sea bed for 23.3 km (14.4 miles) of its length. It is bored through strata that presented such enormous engineering problems that it took 24 years to complete. The long-mooted Channel Tunnel (pilot borings were undertaken more than 100 years ago) was finally opened to the public in 1994. Its overall length is shorter than the Seikan tunnel, but the undersea portion is longer at 38.0 km (23.6 miles).

TOP 10 LONGEST BRIDGES IN THE UK

	BRIDGE/LOCATION	TYPE*	YEAR COMPLETED	LENGTH OF MAIN SPAN (M)	(FT)
1	**Humber Estuary,** Hessle–Barton-on-Humber	S	1980	1,410	4,626
2	**Forth Road,** North Queensferry–South Queenferry	S	1964	1,006	3,300
3	**Severn Bridge,** Bristol	S	1966	988	3,240
4	**Firth of Forth,** North Queensferry–South Queenferry	CT	1890	521	1,710
5	**Second Severn Crossing,** Bristol	CSG	1996	456	1,496
6	**Queen Elizabeth II,** Dartford	CSG	1991	450	1,476
7	**Tamar,** Saltash–Plymouth	S	1961	335	1,100
8	**Runcorn—Widnes**	SA	1961	330	1,082
9	**Erskine,** Glasgow	CSG	1971	305	1,000
10	**Skye,** Kyleakin-Kyle of Lochalsh	PCG	1995	250	820

* S = Suspension; CT = Cantilever truss; CSG = Cable-stayed steel girder and truss; SA = Steel arch; PCG = Pre-stressed concrete girder

The Humber Estuary bridge, opened in 1981 after eight years in construction, was the longest in the world until the completion in 1997 of the East Bridge section of Denmark's Great Belt. Each of its twin concrete anchorages weighs 400,000 tons and the suspension cables were spun from 66,000 km (41,000 miles) of wire.

TOP 10 LONGEST TUNNELS IN THE UK*

	TUNNEL	LENGTH (KM)	(MILES)
1	**Severn,** Avon/Gwent (rail)	7.02	4.36
2	**Totley,** South Yorkshire (rail)	5.70	3.54
3	**Standedge,** Manchester/West Yorkshire (canal)	5.10	3.17
4	**= Standedge,** Manchester/West Yorkshire (rail)	4.89	3.04
	= Woodhead New, South Yorkshire (rail)	4.89	3.04
6	**Sodbury,** Avon (rail)	4.07	2.53
7	**Strood,** Kent (rail, formerly canal)	3.57	2.22
8	**Disley,** Cheshire (rail)	3.54	2.20
9	**Ffestiniog,** Gwynedd (rail)	3.52	2.19
10	**Sapperton,** Gloucestershire (canal)	3.49	2.17

* Excluding underground railways

◄ Longest bridge so far
The longest, tallest, and most expensive bridge in the world, Japan's Akashi-Kaikyo, measures 3,910 m (12,828 ft) overall. It was built to withstand winds of up to 290 km/h (180 mph) and earthquakes of up to 8.5 on the Richter Scale.

CULTURE & LEARNING

Word for Word

MOST WIDELY SPOKEN LANGUAGES

LANGUAGE	APPROX. NO. OF SPEAKERS*
1 Chinese (Mandarin)	874,000,000
2 Hindustani*	426,000,000
3 Spanish	358,000,000
4 English	341,000,000
5 Bengali	207,000,000
6 Arabic#	206,000,000
7 Portuguese	176,000,000
8 Russian	167,000,000
9 Japanese	125,000,000
10 German (standard)	100,000,000

* Hindi and Urdu are essentially the same language, Hindustani. As the official language of Pakistan it is written in modified Arabic script and called Urdu. As the official language of India it is written in the Devanagari script and called Hindi.

Includes 16 variants of the Arabic language

LANGUAGES OFFICIALLY SPOKEN IN THE MOST COUNTRIES

LANGUAGE	COUNTRIES
1 English	57
2 French	33
3 Arabic	23
4 Spanish	21
5 Portuguese	7
6 = Dutch	5
= German	5
8 = Chinese (Mandarin)	3
= Danish	3
= Italian	3
= Malay	3

There are many countries in the world with more than one official language – both English and French are recognized officially in Canada, for example. English is used in numerous countries as the lingua franca, the common language that enables people who speak mutually unintelligible languages to communicate with each other.

COUNTRIES WITH THE MOST ENGLISH LANGUAGE SPEAKERS

COUNTRY	APPROX. NO. OF SPEAKERS*
1 USA	215,424,000
2 UK	58,190,000
3 Canada	20,000,000
4 Australia	14,987,000
5 Ireland	3,750,000
6 = New Zealand	3,700,000
= South Africa	3,700,000
8 Jamaica#	2,600,000
9 Trinidad and Tobago#	1,145,000
10 Guyana#	650,000

* People for whom English is their mother tongue

Includes English Creole

The Top 10 represents the countries with the greatest numbers of inhabitants who speak English as their mother tongue. The world total is probably in excess of 500 million, in addition to which there are perhaps 1 billion who speak English as a second language.

TOP 10 COUNTRIES WITH THE MOST FRENCH LANGUAGE SPEAKERS

	COUNTRY	APPROX. NO. OF SPEAKERS*
1	France	55,100,000
2	Canada	7,158,000
3	Haiti#	6,868,000
4	Belgium†	3,350,000
5	USA∞	2,250,000
6	Switzerland	1,380,000
7	Mauritius∞	878,000
8	Réunion#	660,000
9	Guadeloupe∞	407,000
10	Martinique∞	372,000

* People for whom French is their mother tongue

French Creole

† Walloon French

∞ French/French Creole

TOP 10 COUNTRIES WITH THE MOST SPANISH LANGUAGE SPEAKERS

	COUNTRY	APPROX. NO. OF SPEAKERS*
1	Mexico	91,080,000
2	Colombia	41,880,000
3	Argentina	35,860,000
4	Spain	29,860,000#
5	Venezuela	23,310,000
6	USA	20,720,000
7	Peru	20,470,000
8	Chile	13,640,000
9	Ecuador	11,760,000
10	Dominican Republic	8,270,000

* People for whom Spanish is their mother tongue

Castilian Spanish

TOP 10 LANGUAGES IN THE WORLD 50 YEARS AGO

	LANGUAGE	APPROX. NO. OF SPEAKERS*
1	Chinese	400,000,000
2	English	200,000,000
3	Russian	140,000,000
4	= Japanese	100,000,000
	= Western Hindi	100,000,000
6	German	80,000,000
7	= French	70,000,000
	= Spanish	70,000,000
9	Portuguese	60,000,000
10	= Bengali	50,000,000
	= Italian	50,000,000

* Mother tongue

A WORLD LANGUAGE

THE FIRST TO...

BEFORE ENGLISH GAINED its pre-eminence as a world language, various artificial languages were proposed to enable international communication. The first to gain a following was Volapük ("World's Speech"), invented by Johann Martin Schleyer (1831–1912), a German priest, in 1879. Volapük clubs were formed all over Europe and America and it had some 100,000 speakers at its peak. It was eclipsed by Esperanto, a much simpler artificial language devised in 1887 by Polish oculist L.L. Zamenhof (1859–1917).

◀ **Big talk**
Some two-thirds of China's 1.3 billion inhabitants, along with millions more in other countries, speak Mandarin, the official version of Chinese.

TOP 10 COUNTRIES WITH THE MOST GERMAN LANGUAGE SPEAKERS

	COUNTRY	APPROX. NO. OF SPEAKERS*
1	Germany	75,060,000
2	Austria	7,444,000
3	Switzerland	4,570,000
4	USA	1,850,000
5	Brazil	910,000
6	Poland	500,000
7	Canada	486,000
8	Kazakhstan	460,000
9	Russia	350,000
10	Italy	310,000

* People for whom German is their mother tongue

As well as these countries, which have historical connections with Germany or contain high numbers of German immigrants or expatriates, several other countries have German speakers, including Denmark, Slovakia, and Luxembourg. Liechtenstein's population of just 33,436 supports a German-language newspaper, *Liechtensteiner Vaterland*.

TOP 10 COUNTRIES WITH THE MOST ARABIC LANGUAGE SPEAKERS

	COUNTRY	APPROX. NO. OF SPEAKERS*
1	Egypt	65,080,000
2	Algeria	26,280,000
3	Saudi Arabia	20,920,000
4	Morocco	18,730,000
5	Iraq	17,490,000
6	Yemen	17,400,000
7	Sudan	17,320,000
8	Syria	14,680,000
9	Tunisia#	6,710,000
10	Libya	4,910,000

* People for whom Arabic is their mother tongue

Another 2,520,000 people speak Arabic-French and 300,000 speak Arabic-English

Written or classical Arabic has changed little since the 7th century, but spoken Arabic varies from country to country. Along with Chinese, English, French, Russian, and Spanish, Arabic is one of the official languages used by the United Nations.

Out of School

TOP 10 COUNTRIES WITH THE MOST STUDENTS IN HIGHER EDUCATION

	COUNTRY	HIGHER EDUCATION STUDENTS*
1	USA	14,350,000
2	India	5,007,000
3	Russia	3,597,900
4	China	3,174,000
5	Japan	3,136,834
6	Indonesia	2,703,886
7	France	2,083,129
8	Philippines	2,022,106
9	Brazil	1,948,200
10	UK	1,820,849

In latest year for which data available

Source: UNESCO

TOP 10 COUNTRIES SPENDING THE MOST ON EDUCATION

	COUNTRY	PUBLIC EXPENDITURE AS PERCENTAGE OF GNP* (2000/01#)
1	Zimbabwe	11.1
2	Yemen	10.6
3	Saudi Arabia	9.3
4	Cuba	8.7
5	Denmark	8.3
6	Botswana	8.1
7	= Lesotho	7.9
	= Namibia	7.9
	= Seychelles	7.9
	= Sweden	7.9
	UK	4.4

Gross National Product

Or latest year available; in those countries for which data available

Source: UNESCO

TOP 10 LARGEST UNIVERSITIES

	UNIVERSITY/COUNTRY	STUDENTS
1	Kameshwara Singh Darbhanga Sanskrit, India	515,000
2	Calcutta, India	300,000
3	Paris, France	279,978
4	Mexico, Mexico	269,000
5	Bombay, India	262,350
6	Chhatrapati Shahuji Maharaj University, India	220,000
7	Utkal, India	200,000
8	Rome, Italy	189,000
9	Buenos Aires, Argentina	183,397
10	Guadalajara, Mexico	180,776

With 594,227 students, the Indira Gandhi National Open University, India, is the world's largest distance learning establishment. Currently 203,744 students are enrolled with the Open University in the UK.

TOP 10 COUNTRIES WITH THE MOST PRIMARY SCHOOL PUPILS

	COUNTRY	PRIMARY SCHOOL PUPILS*
1	China	139,954,000
2	India	110,390,406
3	Brazil	35,838,372
4	Indonesia	29,236,283
5	USA	24,045,967
6	Nigeria	16,190,947
7	Pakistan	15,532,000
8	Mexico	14,650,521
9	Philippines	12,159,495
10	Bangladesh	11,939,949
	UK	5,328,219

In latest year for which data available

Source: UNESCO

This Top 10 reflects the relative proportion of elementary school-age children, thus Brazil, despite having a smaller population than the USA, ranks higher. Despite having populations greater than both Mexico and the Philippines, Russia and Japan, with older population structures, do not feature at all.

TOP 10 COUNTRIES WITH THE MOST SECONDARY SCHOOL PUPILS

	COUNTRY	PERCENTAGE FEMALE	SECONDARY SCHOOL PUPILS*
1	China	45	71,883,000
2	India	38	68,872,393
3	USA	49	21,473,692
4	Indonesia	46	14,209,974
5	Russia	50	13,732,000
6	Japan	49	9,878,568
7	Iran	46	8,776,792
8	Germany	48	8,382,335
9	Mexico	49	7,914,165
10	UK	52	6,548,786

In latest year for which data available

Source: UNESCO

The number of secondary school pupils as a proportion of total population varies from 8 per cent in the USA to 11 in the UK, and 14 in Germany. The figures are surprisingly high in some Asian countries, such as China (6), India (7), and Iran (14), reflecting both these countries' emphasis on education and their large populations of school-age children.

A WOMAN GRADUATES

VENICE-BORN Elena Lucrezia Piscopia Cornaro (1646–84) started studying Latin and Greek at age 7, later mastering a total of seven languages. In addition to languages, she studied mathematics, philosophy, and theology. Although she was not allowed to attend lectures with men and had to work privately, on 25 June 1678, she was awarded a degree by the University of Padua, thus becoming the first woman in the world to be so recognized. She was one of only three female graduates before the 19th century.

THE FIRST TO...

▶ **Prime numbers**

Although primary school education is compulsory in India, and figures as high as 10 per cent of the population have been claimed, many children are employed in rural activities and family businesses and often fail to enrol in or complete their schooling.

LARGEST UNIVERSITIES IN THE UK

	UNIVERSITY*	TOTAL STUDENTS
1	Leeds Metropolitan University	37,282
2	Manchester Metropolitan University	32,085
3	University of Leeds	29,613
4	De Montfort University	27,500
5	University of Birmingham	27,048
6	University of Nottingham	26,500
7	University of Manchester	25,746
8	Thames Valley University	25,741
9	Sheffield Hallam University	24,396
10	University of the West of England	24,343

* Excluding Open University

In the UK in 1992, the distinction between universities, polytechnics, and colleges of higher education ended, and of the 10 largest, six were established as a result of this change. Of the others, Manchester was founded in 1851, Birmingham 1900, Leeds 1904, and Nottingham 1948.

COUNTRIES WITH THE LONGEST SCHOOL ATTENDANCE

	COUNTRY	AVERAGE YEARS IN EDUCATION*		
		GIRLS	BOYS	OVERALL
1	Norway	17.60	16.29	16.94
2	Finland	17.24	16.19	16.71
3	Australia	16.81	16.41	16.60
4	UK	16.82	15.96	16.38
5	Sweden	16.96	15.13	16.02
6	Netherlands	15.76	16.04	15.91
7	Belgium	15.99	15.67	15.83
8	Iceland	16.53	15.08	15.81
9	Denmark	16.01	15.16	15.58
10	France	15.66	15.17	15.41

* In latest year/those countries for which data available

Source: *UNESCO*

The USA is excluded from UNESCO data, but other sources rate its total average school life expectancy at 15.2 years. The world average is reckoned to be 11.97, but there are a number of developing countries where few children spend more than seven years in full-time education.

By the Book

TOP 10 | MOST EXPENSIVE BOOKS AND MANUSCRIPTS

BOOK/MANUSCRIPT/SALE/DETAILS	PRICE (£)*
1 The Codex Hammer (formerly Codex Leicester) Christie's, New York, USA, 11 Nov. 1994 This is one of Leonardo da Vinci's notebooks, which includes many scientific drawings and diagrams. It was purchased by Bill Gates, the billionaire founder of Microsoft.	18,643,190 ($28,800,000)
2 The Rothschild Prayerbook, *c.*1505 Christie's, London, UK, 8 July 1999 This holds the world record price for an illuminated manuscript.	7,800,000
3 The Gospels of Henry the Lion, *c.*1173–75 Sotheby's, London, UK, 6 Dec 1983 At the time of its sale, it became the most expensive manuscript, book, or work of art other than a painting ever sold.	7,400,000
4 John James Audubon's The Birds of America, 1827–38 Christie's, New York, USA, 10 March 2000 The record for any natural history book. Further copies of the same book, a collection of more than 400 large, hand-coloured engravings, have also fetched high prices, including Sotheby's, London, 21 June 1990 (£1,600,000). A facsimile reprint was once listed at $30,000 (£15,000).	5,187,731 ($8,000,000)

BOOK/MANUSCRIPT/SALE/DETAILS	PRICE (£)*
5 The Canterbury Tales, Geoffrey Chaucer, *c.*1476–77 Christie's, London, UK, 8 July 1998 Printed by William Caxton, and purchased by Sir Paul Getty. In 1776, the same volume had changed hands for just £6.	4,621,500
6 Comedies, Histories, and Tragedies, The First Folio of William Shakespeare, 1623 Christie's, New York, USA, 8 Oct 2001 The auction record for a 17th-century book.	4,156,947 ($6,166,000)
7 The Gutenberg Bible, 1455 Christie's, New York, USA, 22 Oct 1987 One of the first books ever printed.	3,264,688 ($5,390,000)
8 The Northumberland Bestiary, *c.*1250–60 Sotheby's, London, UK, 29 Nov 1990	2,700,000
9 The Cornaro Missal, *c.*1503 Christie's, London, UK, 8 July 1999 The world record price for an Italian manuscript.	2,600,000
10 The Burdett Psalter and Hours, *c.*1282–86 Sotheby's, London, UK, 23 June 1998	2,500,000

* Includes buyer's premium

TOP 10 FICTION TITLES IN THE UK, 2003

TITLE/AUTHOR	SALES
1 **The Lovely Bones**, Alice Sebold	584,404
2 **Life of Pi**, Yann Martel	547,727
3 **Can You Keep a Secret?**, Sophie Kinsella	411,247
4 **Harry Potter and the Order of the Phoenix** (Adult Edition), J.K. Rowling	404,938
5 **The No. 1 Ladies' Detective Agency**, (The No. 1 Ladies' Detective Agency series), Alexander McCall Smith	368,646
6 **The Summons**, John Grisham	354,070
7 **I Don't Know How She Does It**, Allison Pearson	333,540
8 **Quentins**, Maeve Binchy	329,359
9 **Man and Wife**, Tony Parsons	323,713
10 **Angels**, Marian Keyes	289,465

Source: *Nielsen BookScan*

◀ High flier
Having sold for £380 ($1,800) in 1909 and $352,000 in 1977, Audubon's *The Birds of America* soared to a new record in 2000 when the ruler of Qatar paid over $8 million for the magnificent book.

TOP 10 BESTSELLING BOOKS

BOOK/AUTHOR/FIRST PUBLISHED	APPROX. SALES
1 **The Bible**, *c.*1451–55	over 6,000,000,000*
2 **Quotations from the Works of Mao Tse-tung**, 1966	900,000,000
3 **The Lord of the Rings**, J.R.R. Tolkien, 1954–55	over 100,000,000
4 **American Spelling Book**, Noah Webster, 1783	up to 100,000,000
5 **Guinness World Records (formerly The Guinness Book of Records)**, 1955	over 95,000,000*#
6 **World Almanac**, 1868	over 80,000,000#
7 **The McGuffey Readers**, William Holmes McGuffey, 1836	60,000,000
8 **The Common Sense Book of Baby and Child Care**, Benjamin Spock, 1946	over 50,000,000
9 **A Message to Garcia**, Elbert Hubbard, 1899	up to 40,000,000
10 = **In His Steps: "What Would Jesus Do?"**, Rev. Charles Monroe Sheldon, 1896	over 30,000,000
= **Valley of the Dolls**, Jacqueline Susann, 1966	over 30,000,000

* *Including translations*

Aggregate sales of annual publication

It is extremely difficult to establish precise sales even of contemporary books, and virtually impossible to do so with books published long ago. Variant editions, translations, and pirated copies all affect the global picture, and few publishers or authors are willing to expose their royalty statements to public scrutiny. As a result, this Top 10 list offers no more than the "best guess" at the great bestsellers of the past, and it may well be that there are other books with a valid claim to a place in it: Margaret Mitchell's *Gone with the Wind* (1936) and Harper Lee's *To Kill a Mockingbird* (1960), for example, may each have sold around 30 million copies.

TOP 10 NON-FICTION TITLES IN THE UK, 2003

TITLE/AUTHOR	SALES
1 **Dr. Atkins' New Diet Revolution: The No-Hunger, Luxurious Weight Loss Plan That Really Works!**, Robert C. Atkins	829,738
2 **Stupid White Men... and Other Sorry Excuses for the State of the Nation**, Michael Moore	522,008
3 **David Beckham: My Side – The Autobiography**, David Beckham	489,652
4 **The Highway Code**, Driving Standards Agency/ Road Safety Directorate	417,738
5 **Schott's Original Miscellany**, Ben Schott	373,184
6 **A Short History of Nearly Everything**, Bill Bryson	371,128
7 **Eats, Shoots & Leaves: The Zero Tolerance Approach to Punctuation**, Lynne Truss	361,935
8 **A Royal Duty**, Paul Burrell	320,178
9 **Guiness World Records: 2004**	300,549
10 **The Kindness of Strangers**, Kate Adie	205,103

Source: *Nielsen BookScan*

TOP 10 CHILDREN'S TITLES IN THE UK, 2003

TITLE/AUTHOR	SALES
1 **Harry Potter and the Order of the Phoenix**, J.K. Rowling	2,977,912
2 **Harry Potter and the Goblet of Fire**, J.K. Rowling	304,930
3 **Harry Potter and the Prisoner of Azkaban**, J.K. Rowling	299,538
4 **The Beano Book: 2004**	229,957
5 **Northern Lights** (His Dark Materials series), Philip Pullman	199,284
6 **Harry Potter and the Chamber of Secrets**, J.K. Rowling	168,760
7 **Harry Potter and the Philosopher's Stone**, J.K. Rowling	168,015
8 **The Subtle Knife** (His Dark Materials series), Philip Pullman	154,357
9 **The Amber Spyglass** (His Dark Materials series), Philip Pullman	150,543
10 **Shadowmancer**, Graham P. Taylor	146,140

Source: *Nielsen BookScan*

Libraries & Borrowing

TOP 10 OLDEST NATIONAL LIBRARIES

	LIBRARY/LOCATION	FOUNDED
1	**Národní Knihovně České Republiky** (National Library of the Czech Republic), Prague, Czech Republic	1366
2	**Österreichische Nationalbibliothek** (National Library of Austria), Vienna, Austria	1368
3	**Biblioteca Nazionale Marciana** (St. Mark's Library), Venice, Italy	1468
4	**Bibliothèque Nationale de France** (National Library of France), Paris, France	1480
5	**National Library of Malta,** Valetta, Malta	1555
6	**Bayericsche Staatsbibliothek** (Bavarian State Library), Munich, Germany	1558
7	**Bibliothèque Royale Albert 1er** (National Library of Belgium), Brussels, Belgium	1559
8	**Nacionalna i Sveučilišna Knjiznica** (Zagreb National and University Library), Zagreb, Croatia	1606
9	**Helsingin Yliopiston Kirjasto** (National Library of Finland), Helsinki, Finland	1640
10	**Kongeligie Bibliotek** (National Library of Denmark), Copenhagen, Denmark	1653

What may claim to be the world's first national library was that in Alexandria, Egypt, founded in about 307 BC by King Ptolemy I Soter. It assembled the world's largest collection of scrolls, which were partly destroyed during Julius Caesar's invasion of 47 BC, and totally by Arab invaders in AD 642, an event that is considered one of the greatest losses to world scholarship. Among national libraries in the English-speaking world, Scotland's dates from 1682 (thus predating the British Library, originally part of the British Museum, established in 1753). The US Library of Congress was founded in 1800.

THE 10 FIRST PUBLIC LIBRARIES IN THE UK

	LIBRARY	FOUNDED
1	**Canterbury**	1847
2	**Warrington**	1848
3	**Salford**	1850
4	**Winchester**	1851
5	= **Liverpool**	1852
	= **Manchester Free**	1852
7	= **Bolton**	1853
	= **Ipswich**	1853
9	**Oxford**	1854
10	= **Cambridge**	1855
	= **Kidderminster**	1855

The Museums Act of 1845 enabled several local authorities to finance libraries attached to museums, with a maximum admission charge of one penny. Following the 1850 Public Libraries Act, the Manchester Free Library, which opened on 2 September 1852, was the country's first free municipally supported public lending library.

▼ Shelf life
Dating from 1366, when Charles IV donated a collection of manuscripts to Prague University, the Czech National Library is considered the most venerable of all national libraries.

MOST BORROWED ADULT AUTHORS IN THE UK, 2002–2003

AUTHOR

1 Danielle Steel
2 Josephine Cox
3 Catherine Cookson
4 Agatha Christie
5 Audrey Howard
6 Jack Higgins
7 James Patterson
8 John Grisham
9 Dick Francis
10 Ian Rankin

Source: *Public Lending Right*

MOST BORROWED CHILDREN'S AUTHORS IN THE UK, 2002–2003

AUTHOR

1 Jacqueline Wilson
2 Mick Inkpen
3 R.L. Stine
4 Janet and Allan Ahlberg
5 Lucy Daniels
6 Roald Dahl
7 Enid Blyton
8 Nick Butterworth
9 Eric Hill
10 Dick King-Smith

Source: *Public Lending Right*

Jacqueline Wilson first entered this Top 10 only five years ago but now heads it – a place often previously occupied by Enid Blyton. Perhaps surprisingly, J.K. Rowling is in 13th place, suggesting that most readers have opted to own, rather than borrow, the *Harry Potter* books.

MOST BORROWED CLASSIC AUTHORS IN THE UK, 2002–2003

AUTHOR

1 J.R.R. Tolkien
2 Georgette Heyer
3 A.A. Milne
4 Beatrix Potter
5 Jane Austen
6 Charles Dickens
7 William Shakespeare
8 Nigel Tranter
9 Daphne du Maurier
10 George Orwell

Source: *Public Lending Right*

Although still a Top 10 resident, Daphne du Maurier has fallen from her No. 1 slot of a decade ago. This is now held by J.R.R. Tolkien, riding high on the interest in his work generated by the *Lord of the Rings* films. Former Top 10 authors include Thomas Hardy (now in 11th place), Anthony Trollope (13th), and D.H. Lawrence, who has dropped out of the Top 20.

LARGEST LIBRARIES

	LIBRARY	LOCATION	FOUNDED	BOOKS
1	Library of Congress	Washington, DC, USA	1800	29,000,000
2	National Library of China	Beijing, China	1909	22,000,000
3	Library of the Russian Academy of Sciences	St. Petersburg, Russia	1714	20,000,000
4	National Library of Canada	Ottawa, Canada	1953	18,800,000
5	Deutsche Bibliothek*	Frankfurt, Germany	1990	18,557,445
6	British Library#	London, UK	1753	16,000,000
7	Institute for Scientific Information on Social Sciences of the Russian Academy of Science	Moscow, Russia	1969	13,500,000
8	Harvard University Library	Cambridge, Massachusetts, USA	1638	13,143,330
9	Vernadsky National Scientific Library of Ukraine	Kiev, Ukraine	1919	13,000,000
10	New York Public Library[†]	New York, USA	1895[†]	11,300,000

*   Formed in 1990 through the unification of the Deutsche Bibliothek, Frankfurt (founded 1947), and the Deutsche Bucherei, Leipzig

\# Founded as part of the British Museum, 1753; became an independent body in 1973

† Astor Library founded 1848, consolidated with Lenox Library and Tilden Trust to form New York Public Library in 1895

Press Power

DAILY NEWSPAPERS

	NEWSPAPER	COUNTRY	AVERAGE DAILY CIRCULATION
1	Yomiuri Shimbun	Japan	14,246,000
2	Asahi Shimbun	Japan	12,326,000
3	Mainichi Shimbun	Japan	5,635,000
4	Nihon Keizai Shimbun	Japan	4,737,000
5	Chunichi Shimbun	Japan	4,571,000
6	Bild-Zeitung	Germany	4,220,000
7	The Sun	UK	3,461,000
8	Sankei Shimbun	Japan	2,665,000
9	USA Today	USA	2,603,000
10	Canako Xiaoxi (Beijing)	China	2,530,000

Source: *World Association of Newspapers*, World Press Trends 2003,
www.wan-press.org

Yomiuri Shimbun was founded in 1874 in emulation of the Western press. The name *Yomiuri*, "selling by reading", refers to the Japanese practice of vendors reading aloud from news-sheets in the era before moveable type.

ENGLISH-LANGUAGE DAILY NEWSPAPERS

	NEWSPAPER	COUNTRY	AVERAGE DAILY CIRCULATION
1	The Sun	UK	3,461,000
2	USA Today	USA	2,603,000
3	Daily Mail	UK	2,411,000
4	The Times of India	India	2,131,000
5	The Mirror	UK	2,117,000
6	The Wall Street Journal	USA	1,821,000
7	The New York Times	USA	1,673,000
8	Los Angeles Times	USA	1,396,000
9	The Washington Post	USA	1,049,000
10	Chicago Tribune	USA	1,016,000

Source: *World Association of Newspapers,* World Press Trends 2003,
www.wan-press.org

The world's bestselling English language dailies represent both long-established publications and relative newcomers: the *Daily Herald*, the first paper ever to sell two million copies, was launched in 1911, became *The Sun* in 1964, and was re-launched as a tabloid in 1969. The *Daily Mail* started in 1896, absorbing the *News Chronicle* in 1960 and *Daily Sketch* in 1971. *USA Today*, launched in 1982, was one of the first newspapers to use computers and to transmit editions for simultaneous publication around the world. *The Times of India* began in 1838 as *The Bombay Times and Journal of Commerce*, changing to its present name in 1861. It is reckoned to have the highest readership (as distinct from sale) of any English language newspaper at some 4.42 million daily.

OLDEST NATIONAL NEWSPAPERS PUBLISHED IN THE UK

	NEWSPAPER	FIRST PUBLISHED
1	**The London Gazette**	16 Nov 1665

Originally published in Oxford as the *Oxford Gazette*, while the royal court resided there during an outbreak of the plague. After 23 issues, it moved to London with the court and changed its name.

2	**Lloyd's List**	1726

Providing shipping news, originally on a weekly basis (as *Lloyd's News*), but since 1734 Britain's oldest daily.

3	**The Times**	1 Jan 1785

First published as the *Daily Universal Register*, it changed its name to *The Times* on 1 March 1788.

4	**The Observer**	4 Dec 1791

Britain's first Sunday newspaper was *Johnson's British Gazette and Sunday Monitor*, first published on 2 March 1780. It survived only until 1829, thus making *The Observer* the longest-running Sunday paper.

5	**Morning Advertiser**	8 Feb 1794

Britain's oldest trade newspaper (a daily established by the Licensed Victuallers Association to earn income for its charity), and the first national paper on Fleet Street, the *Morning Advertiser* changed its name to *The Licensee* and became a twice-weekly news magazine in 1994, before reverting to its original name in 2000.

6	**The Scotsman**	25 Jan 1817

Originally published weekly, the *Daily Scotsman* was published from July 1855 to December 1859, and re-titled *The Scotsman* in January 1860.

7	**The Sunday Times**	Feb 1821

Issued as the *New Observer* until March 1821 and the *Independent Observer* from April 1821 until 22 October 1822, when it changed its name to the *Sunday Times*. On 4 February 1962 it became the first British newspaper to issue a colour supplement.

8	**The Guardian**	5 May 1821

A weekly until 1855 (and called *The Manchester Guardian* until 1959).

9	**News of the World**	1 Oct 1843

The first issue of the national Sunday newspaper declared its aim as being "To give to the poorer classes of society a paper that would suit their means, and to the middle, as well as the rich, a journal which, from its immense circulation, should command their attention." Part of this aspiration was achieved in April 1951, when sales peaked at 8,480,878 copies, the highest-ever circulation of any British newspaper.

10	**The Daily Telegraph**	29 Jun 1855

The first issues were published as the *Daily Telegraph and Courier*, but from 20 August 1855, *Courier* was dropped from the title.

In addition to these, the UK also has several local newspapers that have been published for almost 300 years, led by *Berrow's Worcester Journal*, which dates from about 1709. It first appeared as the *Worcester Post-Man*, changing its name in 1808. The *Lincoln, Rutland and Stamford Mercury* was originally published as the *Stamford Mercury* in about 1710. While these are Britain's oldest newspapers, outside the UK there are three newspapers that are even more venerable than the *London Gazette*, notably the *Post-och Inrikes Tidningar* (Sweden, 1645), *Haarlems Dagblad* (Netherlands, 1656), and *La Gazzetta di Mantova* (Italy, 1664).

TOP 10 TEEN MAGAZINES IN THE UK

	MAGAZINE	AVERAGE CIRCULATION PER ISSUE*
1	Sugar	291,794
2	More!	259,550
3	Bliss	241,664
4	Top of the Pops	230,493
5	Cosmo Girl	198,324
6	J-17	134,650
7	TV Hits	130,164
8	It's Hot	116,515
9	Smash Hits	114,383
10	Sneak	104,174

* In 6 month period to 31 Dec 2003

Source: *Audit Bureau of Circulation Ltd.*

TOP 10 CONSUMER MAGAZINES IN THE UK

	MAGAZINE	AVERAGE UK CIRCULATION PER ISSUE*
1	What's on TV	1,654,843
2	Take a Break	1,227,305
3	Radio Times	1,141,858
4	TV Choice	1,017,468
5	Reader's Digest	778,332
6	Chat	604,582
7	FHM	601,128
8	That's Life	597,420
9	Now	592,076
10	Glamour	580,887

* Actively purchased circulation in 6 month period to 31 Dec 2003

Source: *Audit Bureau of Circulations Ltd.*

▶ **Hot off the press**
Competition from television, the Internet, and other media have done little to assuage the world's passion for newspapers.

Fine Art

TOP 10

MOST EXPENSIVE PAINTINGS

PAINTING/ARTIST/SALE	PRICE (£)
1 Massacre of the Innocents, Sir Peter Paul Rubens (Flemish; 1577–1640), Sotheby's, London, 10 July 2002	45,000,000
2 Portrait du Dr. Gachet, Vincent Van Gogh (Dutch; 1853–90), Christie's, New York, 15 May 1990 Both this painting and the one in the No. 3 position were bought by Ryoei Saito, chairman of the Japanese firm Daishowa Paper Manufacturing.	44,378,696 ($75,000,000)
3 Au Moulin de la Galette, Pierre-Auguste Renoir (French; 1841–1919), Sotheby's, New York, 17 May 1990	42,011,832 ($71,000,000)
4 Portrait de l'Artiste Sans Barbe, Vincent Van Gogh, Christie's, New York, 19 Nov 1998	39,393,940 ($65,000,000)
5 Femme aux Bras Croises, Pablo Picasso (Spanish; 1881–1973), Christie's Rockefeller, New York, 8 Nov 2000	34,965,036 ($50,000,000)
6 Rideau, Cruchon et Compotier, Paul Cézanne (French; 1839–1906), Sotheby's, New York, 10 May 1999	33,950,616 ($55,000,000)

PAINTING/ARTIST/SALE	PRICE (£)
7 Les Noces de Pierrette, Pablo Picasso, Binoche et Godeau, Paris, 30 Nov 1989 This painting was sold by Swedish financier Fredrik Roos and bought by Tomonori Tsurumaki, a Japanese property developer, bidding from Tokyo by telephone.	33,123,028 (F.Fr315,000,000)
8 Irises, Vincent Van Gogh, Sotheby's, New York, 11 Nov 1987 After much speculation, its mystery purchaser was eventually confirmed as Australian businessman Alan Bond. However, as he was unable to pay for it in full, its former status as the world's most expensive work of art has been disputed.	28,000,000 ($49,000,000)
9 Femme Assise Dans un Jardin, Pablo Picasso, Sotheby's, New York, 10 Nov 1999	27,950,310 ($45,000,000)
10 Self Portrait: Yo Picasso, Pablo Picasso, Sotheby's, New York, 9 May 1989 The anonymous purchaser has been identified in unconfirmed reports as Stavros Niarchos, the Greek shipping magnate.	26,687,116 ($43,500,000)

MOST EXPENSIVE BRITISH PAINTINGS

PAINTING/ARTIST/SALE	PRICE (£)
1 **The Lock,** John Constable (1776–1837), Sotheby's, London, 14 Nov 1990	9,800,000
2 **Portrait of Omai, standing in a landscape, wearing robes and a head-dress,** Sir Joshua Reynolds (1723–92), Sotheby's, London, 29 Nov 2001	9,400,000
3 **Seascape, Folkestone,** J.M.W. Turner (1775–1851), Sotheby's, London, 5 July 1984	6,700,000
4 **Cashmere,** John Singer Sargent* (1856–1925), Sotheby's, New York, 5 Dec 1996	6,158,537 ($10,100,000)
5 **St. Cecilia,** John William Waterhouse (1849–1917), Christie's, London, 14 June 2000	6,000,000
6 **Studies of the Human Body,** Francis Bacon (1909–92), Sotheby's, New York, 8 May 2001	5,492,958 ($7,800,000)
7 **In the Garden, Corfu,** John Singer Sargent, Sotheby's, New York, 3 Dec 1997	4,606,061 ($7,600,000)
8 **Spanish Dancer,** John Singer Sargent, Sotheby's, New York, 25 May 1994	4,600,000 ($6,900,000)
9 **Portrait of George Dyer Talking,** Francis Bacon, Christie's Rockefeller, New York, 15 Nov 2000	4,225,352 ($6,000,000)
10 **Study for Portrait of Henrietta Moraes,** Francis Bacon, Phillips, New York, 13 May 2002	4,178,082 ($6,100,000)

* US-born, naturalized British

The highest-priced paintings by British artists represents some of the "greats" and principal styles, led by 18th- and 19th-century masters Constable, Reynolds, and Turner, with Pre-Raphaelite follower John William Waterhouse, Anglo-American Impressionist John Singer Sargent, and modern painter Francis Bacon.

◀ **Record Rubens**
Massacre of the Innocents, a previously neglected painting by Rubens, broke all records when purchased by Canadian collector David Thomson for 10 times its pre-sale estimate.

ARTISTS WITH THE MOST WORKS SOLD FOR MORE THAN ONE MILLION POUNDS

ARTIST	TOTAL VALUE OF WORKS SOLD (£)	NO. OF WORKS SOLD FOR OVER £1 MILLION
1 **Pablo Picasso** (Spanish; 1881–1973)	1,384,883,089	237
2 **Claude Monet** (French; 1840–1926)	1,029,612,975	189
3 **Pierre Auguste Renoir** (French; 1841–1919)	592,987,984	122
4 **Edgar Degas** (French; 1834–1917)	354,127,353	74
5 **Henri Matisse** (French; 1869–1954)	338,458,023	69
6 **Paul Cézanne** (French; 1839–1906)	509,449,001	68
7 **Amedeo Modigliani** (Italian; 1884–1920)	313,953,418	59
8 **Andy Warhol** (American; 1928–87)	159,171,420	56
9 **Vincent van Gogh** (Dutch; 1853–90)	576,442,817	54
10 **Camille Pissaro** (French; 1830–1903)	113,373,094	45

MOST EXPENSIVE PAINTINGS BY WOMEN ARTISTS

PAINTING/ARTIST/SALE	PRICE (£)
1 **Calla Lilies with Red Anemone,** Georgia O'Keeffe (American; 1887–1986), Christie's Rockefeller, New York, 23 May 2001	3,943,662 ($5,600,000)
2 **Cache-cache,** Berthe Morisot (French; 1841–1895), Sotheby's, New York, 9 Nov 2000	2,797,203 ($4,000,000)
3 **Marche au Minho,** Sonia Delaunay (French/Russian; 1885–1979), Laurence Calmels, Paris, 14 June 2002	2,662,338 (€4,100,000)
4 **Black Cross with Stars and Blue,** Georgia O'Keeffe, Christie's Rockefeller, New York, 23 May 2001	2,605,634 ($3,700,000)
5 **In the Box,** Mary Cassatt (American; 1844–1926), Christie's, New York, 23 May 1996	2,450,331 ($3,700,000)
6 **The Conversation,** Mary Cassatt, Christie's, New York, 11 May 1988	2,180,850 ($4,100,000)
7 **Cache-cache,** Berthe Morisot, Sotheby's, New York, 10 May 1999	2,160,494 ($3,500,000)
8 **Rams Head, Blue Morning Glory,** Georgia O'Keeffe, Christie's Rockefeller, New York, 25 Apr 2002	2,152,778 ($3,100,000)
9 **Mother, Sara and the Baby,** Mary Cassatt, Christie's, New York, 10 May 1989	2,147,239 ($3,500,000)
10 **From the Plains,** Georgia O'Keeffe, Sotheby's, New York, 3 Dec 1997	2,000,000 ($3,300,000)

The Top 10 reflects the status of three artists in particular: 20th-century painter Georgia O'Keeffe, whose work focused on natural forms, such as flowers and shells, and Berthe Morisot and Mary Cassatt, whose portraits and intimate domestic scenes are among the most revered works by women of the Impressionist movement.

Art on Show

BEST-ATTENDED ART EXHIBITIONS IN LONDON, 2003

	EXHIBITION/VENUE	DATES	ATTENDANCE TOTAL	DAILY
1	**Art Deco 1910–39,** Victoria and Albert Museum The best-attended show at the V&A for over 50 years, *Art Deco*'s exhibits ranged from furniture to cars.	27 Mar–20 Jul	360,000	3,103
2	**Titian,** National Gallery	19 Feb–18 May	267,939	3,011
3	**Aztecs,** Royal Academy of Arts	16 Nov 2002–11 Apr 2003	436,276	3,009
4	**The Andrew Lloyd Webber Collection,** Royal Academy of Arts	20 Sept–12 Dec	251,738	2,997
5	**The Citibank Photography Prize 2003,** Photographers' Gallery	31 Jan–20 Mar	107,478	2,193
6	**Ron Mueck,** National Gallery	19 Mar–22 June	193,230	2,013
7	**Pissaro in London,** National Gallery	14 May–3 Aug	150,788	1,839
8	**Paradise,** National Gallery	10 July–28 Sept	148,145	1,829
9	**BP Portrait Award,** Victoria and Albert Museum	12 June–21 Sept	160,198	1,571
10	**Confronting Views: The Israeli-Palestinian Conflict,** Photographers' Gallery	2 Apr–4 May	47,489	1,439

Source: The Art Newspaper

BEST-ATTENDED ART EXHIBITIONS, 2003

	EXHIBITION/VENUE/CITY	DATES	ATTENDANCE* TOTAL	DAILY
1	**Leonardo da Vinci, Master Draftsman,** Metropolitan Museum of Art, New York	22 Jan–30 Mar	401,004	6,863
2	**Thomas Struth,** Metropolitan Museum of Art, New York	4 Feb–30 Mar	273,793	5,790
3	**Peter the Great,** State Hermitage, St. Petersburg	2 Jun–31 Aug	450,000	5,759
4	**Leonardo da Vinci: Drawings and Manuscripts,** Musée du Louvre, Paris	8 May–14 July	322,000	5,511
5	**Manet/Velázquez: The French Taste for Spanish Painting,** Metropolitan Museum of Art, New York	4 Mar–29 June	553,622	5,160
6	**Matisse Picasso,** Museum of Modern Art, Queens, New York	13 Feb–19 May	342,223	4,970
7	**Nicolas de Staël,** Centre Georges Pompidou, Paris	12 Mar–30 June	431,492	4,576
8	**Titian,** Museo del Prado, Madrid	10 June–7 Sept	361,522	4,519
9	**Albrecht Dürer,** Albertina, Vienna	5 Sept–8 Dec	427,000	4,495
10	**Vincent's Choice,** Van Gogh Museum, Amsterdam	14 Feb–15 June	527,685	4,325

* Approximate totals provided by museums

Source: The Art Newspaper

► **The genius of Leonardo**
Two of the most popular exhibitions of 2003 provided an opportunity to view drawings by Leonardo da Vinci that are rarely shown publicly.

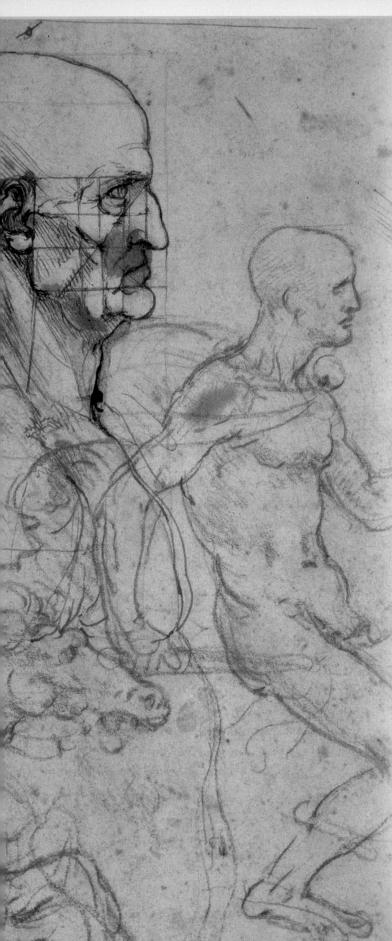

TOP 10 TALLEST FREE-STANDING STATUES

STATUE/LOCATION	HEIGHT (M)	(FT)
1 Chief Crazy Horse, Thunderhead Mountain, South Dakota, USA Started in 1948 by Polish-American sculptor Korczak Ziolkowski and continued after his death in 1982 by his widow and eight of his children, this gigantic equestrian statue remains unfinished.	172	563
2 Buddha, Tokyo, Japan Unveiled in 1993, this statue weighs 1,000 tonnes.	120	394
3 The Indian Rope Trick, Riddersberg Säteri, Jönköping, Sweden Sculptor Calle Örnemark's 144-tonne wooden sculpture depicts a long "rope" held by a fakir, while another figure ascends.	103	337
4 Motherland, 1967, Volgograd, Russia This concrete statue of a woman with a raised sword commemorates the Soviet victory at the Battle of Stalingrad (1942–43).	82	270
5 Kannon, Sanukimachi, Tokyo Bay, Japan This statue of the goddess of mercy was unveiled in 1961.	56	184
6 Statue of Liberty, New York, USA Designed by Auguste Bartholdi and presented to the USA by the people of France, the statue was shipped in sections to Liberty (formerly Bedloes) Island and unveiled on 28 October 1886.	46	151
7 Christ, Rio de Janeiro, Brazil This figure of Christ was unveiled in 1931.	38	125
8 Tian Tan (Temple of Heaven) Buddha, Po Lin Monastery, Hong Kong After 20 years' work this was unveiled on 29 December 1993.	34	112
9 Quantum Cloud, Greenwich, London, UK A gigantic steel human figure surrounded by a matrix of steel struts, it was created in 1999 by Antony Gormley, the sculptor of the similarly gigantic 20-m (66-ft) *Angel of the North*, Gateshead, UK.	29	95
10 Kim Il-Sung, Pyongyang, North Korea Erected to mark the North Korean leader's 60th birthday in 1972.	23	75

TOP 10 BEST-ATTENDED EXHIBITIONS AT THE ROYAL ACADEMY OF ARTS, LONDON*

EXHIBITION	YEAR	TOTAL ATTENDANCE
1 The Genius of China	1974	771,466
2 Monet in the 20th Century	1999	739,324
3 Monet: The Series Paintings	1990	658,289
4 Pompeii AD79	1977	633,347
5 Post-Impressionism	1980	558,573
6 The Great Japan Exhibition	1982	523,005
7 The Genius of Venice	1983	452,885
8 Aztecs	2002–03	436,276
9 J.M.W. Turner	1975	424,629
10 The Great Age of Chivalry	1987–88	349,750

* During the past 40 years, the only period for which detailed comparative figures exist

Collectables

TOP 10 — MOST EXPENSIVE ITEMS OF POP MEMORABILIA

ITEM*/SALE	PRICE (£)#
1 **John Lennon's 1965 Rolls-Royce Phantom V touring limousine,** Sotheby's, New York, 29 June 1985 Finished in psychedelic paintwork.	1,768,462 ($2,299,000)
2 **John Lennon's Steinway Model Z upright piano,** Fleetwood-Owen online auction, Hard Rock Café, London and New York, 17 Oct 2000 Teak veneered, complete with cigarette burns, on which Lennon composed *Imagine*. Lennon also played it at Woodstock in 1969. It was purchased by George Michael.	1,450,000
3 **Bernie Taupin's handwritten lyrics for the rewritten *Candle in the Wind*,** Christie's, Los Angeles, 11 Feb 1998 Played by Sir Elton John at the funeral of Diana, Princess of Wales, sold to Diana's brother Earl Spencer. The sale, part of a charity auction, established a world record for pop lyrics.	278,512 ($400,000)
4 **John Lennon's handwritten lyrics for *Nowhere Man* (1965),** Christie's, New York, 18 Nov 2003	269,526 ($455,500)
5 **Paul McCartney's handwritten lyrics for *Getting Better* (1967),** Sotheby's, London, 14 Sept 1995	161,000
6 **John Lennon's 1970 Mercedes-Benz 600 Pullman four-door limousine,** Christie's, London, 27 Apr 1989	137,500
7 **John Lennon's 1965 Ferrari 330 GT 2+2 two door coupé, right-hand drive,** Fleetwood-Owen online auction, Hard Rock Cafe, London and New York, 17 Oct 2000	130,000
8 **Mal Evan's notebook, compiled 1967–68, which includes a draft by Paul McCartney of the lyrics for *Hey Jude*,** Sotheby's, London, 15 Sept 1998	111,500
9 **Elvis Presley's 1963 Rolls-Royce Phantom V touring limousine,** Sotheby's, London, 28 Aug 1986	110,000
10 **Charlie Parker's Grafton saxophone,** Christie's, London, Sept. 8, 1994	93,000

* Excluding guitars

Including 10 per cent buyer's premium, where appropriate

TOP 10 — MOST VALUABLE AMERICAN COMICS

COMIC	VALUE ($)*
1 **Action Comics No. 1** Published in June 1938, the first issue of *Action Comics* marked the original appearance of Superman.	400,000
2 **Detective Comics No. 27** Issued in May 1939, it is prized as the first comic book to feature Batman.	350,000
3 **Marvel Comics No. 1** The Human Torch and other heroes were first introduced in the issue dated October 1939.	300,000
4 **Superman No. 1** The first comic book devoted to Superman, reprinting the original *Action Comics* story, was published in summer 1939.	240,000
5 **All American Comics No. 16** The Green Lantern made his debut in the issue dated July 1940.	135,000
6 = **Batman No. 1** Published in spring 1940, this was the first comic book devoted to Batman.	115,000
= **Captain America Comics No. 1** Published in March 1941, this was the original comic book in which Captain America appeared.	115,000
8 **Flash Comics No. 1** Dated January 1940, and featuring The Flash, it is rare because it was produced in small numbers for promotional purposes, and was unique as issue #2 was retitled *Whiz Comics*.	92,000
9 **Whiz Comics No. 1** Published in February 1940 – and confusingly numbered "2" – it was the first comic book to feature Captain Marvel.	80,000
10 **More Fun Comics No. 52** The Spectre made his debut in the issue dated February 1940.	78,000

* For example in "Near Mint" condition

TOP 10 — MOST EXPENSIVE GUITARS

GUITAR/SALE	PRICE (£)*
1 **Jerry Garcia's "Tiger" guitar,** Guernsey's at Studio 54, New York, 9 May 2002	657,850 ($957,500)
2 **Jerry Garcia's "Wolf" guitar,** Guernsey's at Studio 54, New York, 9 May 2002	542,425 ($789,500)
3 **Eric Clapton's "Brownie",** Christie's, New York, 24 June 1999 Clapton used the 1956 sunburst Fender Stratocaster, one of his favourite electric guitars, to record the whole *Layla* album.	313,425 ($497,500)
4 **George Harrison's first guitar,** a Spanish-style Egmond "Firewood", Cooper Owen/Hard Rock Café, London, 21 Nov 2003	276,000
5 **George Harrison's rosewood Telecaster,** Odyssey, Los Angeles, 13 Sept 2003	271,244 ($434,750)
6 **Acoustic guitar owned by David Bowie, Paul McCartney, and George Michael,** Christie's, London, 18 May 1994	220,000
7 **Jimi Hendrix's Fender Stratocaster electric guitar,** Sotheby's, London, 25 Apr 1990	198,000
8 **John Lennon's Gallotone Champion,** Sotheby's/Hard Rock Café, London, 14 Sept 1999	155,600
9 **Buddy Holly's Gibson acoustic guitar (c.1945), in a tooled leather case made by Holly,** Sotheby's, New York, 23 June 1990	139,658 ($242,000)
10 **Eric Clapton's 1954 Fender Stratocaster,** Christie's, New York, 24 June 1999	120,333 ($190,000)

* Including buyer's premium, where appropriate

TOP 10 MOST EXPENSIVE PHOTOGRAPHS

PHOTOGRAPH*/PHOTOGRAPHER/SALE	PRICE (£)
1 Athenes, Temple de Jupiter Olympien Pris de l'Est (19th century), Joseph Philibert Girault de Prangey (French; 19th century), Christie's, London, 20 May 2003	500,000
2 Untitled V Andreas Gursky (German; 1955–), Christie's, London, 6 Feb 2002	390,000
3 Mullein, Maine (1927), Paul Strand (American; 1890–1976), Phillips, New York, 15 Apr 2002	384,615 ($550,000)
4 Paris, Montparnasse (1993), Andreas Gursky, Christie's Rockefeller, New York, 15 Nov 2001	380,282 ($540,000)
5 Noir et Blanche (1926), Man Ray (American; 1890–1976), Christie's, New York, 4 Oct 1998	363,076 ($607,500)
6 Karnac, Pylone, Pris de l'Ouest (19th century), Joseph Philibert Girault de Prangey, Christie's, London, 20 May 2003	350,000
7 Light Trap for Henry Moore No. 1 (1967), Bruce Nauman (American; 1941–), Sotheby's, New York, 17 May 2000	324,324 ($480,000)
8 Rome, Colonne Trajane (19th century), Joseph Philibert Girault de Prangey, Christie's, London, 20 May 2003	280,000
9 Georgia O'Keeffe: A Portrait – Hands with Thimble (1930), Alfred Stieglitz (American; 1864–1946), Christie's, New York, 8 Oct 1993	265,578 ($398,500)
10 Klitschko (1999), Andreas Gursky, Phillips, New York, 15 May 2003	256,250 ($410,000)

* Single prints only

The top price paid for a collection of photographs was £500,000 for the *Craven Memorial Album* – an album of photographs taken by William Craven, the 2nd Earl of Craven (British; 1809–66). The album was bought on 12 May 2001 at Bearne's, Exeter, UK. At the same auction *The North American Indian* (1907–30), a 20-volume set of photographs by Edward S. Curtis (American; 1868–1952), was purchased for £440,000.

▼ **Black and White**
The most expensive photograph sold in the 20th century, surrealist Man Ray's *Noire et Blanche*, a portrait of model Kiki de Montparnasse with an African mask, was taken in 1926.

MUSIC & MUSICIANS

Record Firsts

THE 10 | FIRST MILLION-SELLING SINGLES IN THE UK

	TITLE	ARTIST OR GROUP	YEAR
1	Rock Around the Clock	Bill Haley & His Comets	1955
2	Mary's Boy Child	Harry Belafonte	1957
3	Diana	Paul Anka	1957
4	It's Now or Never	Elvis Presley	1960
5	Stranger on the Shore	Mr. Acker Bilk	1961
6	The Young Ones	Cliff Richard	1962
7	I Remember You	Frank Ifield	1962
8	Telstar	The Tornados	1962
9	The Next Time/Bachelor Boy	Cliff Richard and the Shadows	1962
10	She Loves You	The Beatles	1963

Bill Haley had already achieved success in the USA with *Shake, Rattle and Roll*, but it was his influential *Rock Around the Clock,* featured in the 1955 film *Blackboard Jungle,* that established his status as Britain's first million-seller. The Beatles' appearance with the UK's 10th million-selling single was a foretaste of their all-time pre-eminence. They went on to amass five platinum singles during the 1960s, while John Lennon added one with *Imagine* and Paul McCartney another with Wings' *Mull of Kintyre/Girls School*.

THE 10 | FIRST FEMALE SINGERS TO HAVE A NO. 1 IN THE UK

	ARTIST	TITLE	DATE AT NO. 1
1	Jo Stafford	You Belong to Me	16 Jan 1953
2	Kay Starr	Comes A-Long A-Love	23 Jan 1953
3	Lita Roza	(How Much Is That) Doggie in the Window?	17 Apr 1953
4	Doris Day	Secret Love	16 Apr 1954
5	Kitty Kallen	Little Things Mean a Lot	10 Sep 1954
6	Vera Lynn	My Son, My Son	5 Nov 1954
7	Rosemary Clooney	This Ole House	26 Nov 1954
8	Ruby Murray	Softly Softly	18 Feb 1955
9	Alma Cogan	Dreamboat	15 Jul 1955
10	Anne Shelton	Lay Down Your Arms	21 Sep 1956

Source: *Music Information Database*

The UK singles chart was launched in November 1952, and Jo Stafford's *You Belong to Me* was only the second single to reach No. 1 on it, replacing the inaugural chart-topper (Al Martino's *Here in My Heart*). The girls were actually briefly running ahead of their male counterparts in these early days, when Kay Starr's *Comes A-Long A-Love* became the UK's third chart-topper only a week after Ms. Stafford's single. Lita Roza, covering a US No. 1 by Patti Page, was the first UK female artist to reach the summit, six months into the life of the chart.

THE 10 | ALBUMS IN THE FIRST UK ALBUMS TOP 10

	TITLE	ARTIST(S)
1	South Pacific	Soundtrack
2	Come Fly with Me	Frank Sinatra
3	Elvis' Golden Records	Elvis Presley
4	King Creole	Elvis Presley
5	My Fair Lady	Broadway Cast
6	Warm	Johnny Mathis
7	The King and I	Soundtrack
8	Dear Perry	Perry Como
9	Oklahoma!	Soundtrack
10	Songs by Tom Lehrer	Tom Lehrer

Source: Melody Maker

The first Top 10 album chart was printed in *Melody Maker* for the week ending 8 November 1958, and represents a time capsule of the popular music of the era, a transitional period when crooners, comedy singers, and musicals rubbed shoulders with up-and-coming rock artists, such as 23-year-old Elvis Presley. The film soundtrack of *South Pacific* not only hit the top of the chart, but stayed in it for a record 306 weeks, remaining the biggest-selling soundtrack album for eight years, until overtaken by *The Sound of Music*.

THE 10 | SINGLES IN THE FIRST UK TOP 10

	TITLE	ARTIST(S)
1	Here in My Heart	Al Martino
2	You Belong to Me	Jo Stafford
3	Somewhere Along the Way	Nat "King" Cole
4	Isle of Innisfree	Bing Crosby
5	Feet Up	Guy Mitchell
6	Half as Much	Rosemary Clooney
7	= Forget Me Not	Vera Lynn
	= High Noon	Frankie Laine
8	= Sugarbush	Doris Day and Frankie Laine
	= Blue Tango	Ray Martin
9	Homing Waltz	Vera Lynn
10	Auf Wiedersehen (Sweetheart)	Vera Lynn

Source: New Musical Express

The first UK singles chart was published in the *New Musical Express* for the week ending 15 November 1952. Curiously, the Top 10 contained 12 entries because those of equal rank shared the same placing.

THE 10 | FIRST ROLLING STONES SINGLES RELEASED IN THE UK

	TITLE (A SIDE/B SIDE)	RELEASE DATE
1	Come On/I Want to Be Loved	Jun 1963
2	I Wanna Be Your Man/Stoned	Nov 1963
3	Not Fade Away/Little by Little	Feb 1964
4	It's All Over Now/Bad Times	Jun 1964
5	Little Red Rooster/Off the Hook	Nov 1964
6	The Last Time/Play with Fire	Feb 1965
7	(I Can't Get No) Satisfaction/The Spider and the Fly	Aug 1965
8	Get Off of My Cloud/The Singer Not the Song	Oct 1965
9	19th Nervous Breakdown/As Tears Go By	Feb 1966
10	Paint It Black/Long Long While	May 1966

The first five single releases by the Stones were all cover versions (of, in order, songs by Chuck Berry, the Beatles, Buddy Holly, the Valentinos, and Sam Cooke), whereas the remaining five were all Jagger/Richards compositions. All of these titles were released by Decca Records. *Come On* reached No. 21 in the singles chart, *I Wanne Be Your Man* No. 12, and *Not Fade Away* No. 3, with *It's All Over Now* being the first of eight No. 1 Stones hits, all of which date from the 1960s. Since then, the group's singles chart performance has been unspectacular, in contrast to the colossal success of their live stage tours, which have earned them the accolade of "World's Greatest Rock 'n' Roll Band".

THE 10 | FIRST BEATLES SINGLES RELEASED IN THE UK

	TITLE (A SIDE/B SIDE)	RELEASE DATE
1	Love Me Do/P.S. I Love You	Oct 1962
2	Please Please Me/Ask Me Why	Jan 1963
3	From Me to You/Thank You Girl	Apr 1963
4	She Loves You/I'll Get You	Aug 1963
5	I Want to Hold Your Hand/This Boy	Nov 1963
6	Can't Buy Me Love/You Can't Do That	Mar 1964
7	A Hard Day's Night/Things We Said Today	Jul 1964
8	I Feel Fine/She's a Woman	Nov 1964
9	Ticket to Ride/Yes It Is	Apr 1965
10	Help!/I'm Down	Jul 1965

Source: *Music Information Database*

▼ Beatlemania

With a succession of global No. 1 singles and albums and their first US appearances, 1964 marked a high-point in the Beatles' early career. Their first two singles had peaked in the UK charts at 17 and 2 respectively, but *From Me to You* hit No. 1, as did all their follow-ups.

TOP 10 ALBUMS BY FEMALE SOLO SINGERS IN THE UK

TITLE/SINGER	YEAR
1 The Immaculate Collection, Madonna	1990
2 Come on Over, Shania Twain	1997
3 Jagged Little Pill, Alanis Morissette	1995
4 Simply the Best, Tina Turner	1991
5 Falling into You, Celine Dion	1996
6 True Blue, Madonna	1986
7 Whitney, Whitney Houston	1987
8 Ray of Light, Madonna	1998
9 Come Away with Me, Norah Jones	2002
10 Let's Talk About Love, Celine Dion	1997

Source: *Music Information Database*

TOP 10 FEMALE SOLO SINGERS IN THE UK

	SINGER	TOTAL CHART HITS
1	Diana Ross	64
2	Madonna	60
3	Donna Summer	42
4	Janet Jackson	39
5	Kylie Minogue	37
6	Tina Turner	36
7	Whitney Houston	33
8	= Shirley Bassey	31
	= Cher	31
10	Gloria Estefan	26

Source: *Music Information Database*

SELL A MILLION

AMERICAN BLUES SINGER BESSIE SMITH was the first female solo singer to achieve a million-selling disc in the pre-chart era. *Down Hearted Blues*, recorded on 15 February 1923 and the first song that she cut, sold at least 800,000 copies at 75 cents in its first year. It proceeded to sell a total of over two million, making it Columbia Records' first major hit. She went on to become one of the most successful singers of her generation, and one of the most prolific, recording some 160 songs for the Columbia label.

THE FIRST TO...

YOUNGEST FEMALE SOLO SINGERS TO HAVE A NO. 1 SINGLE IN THE UK

SINGER/TITLE	YEAR	AGE (YRS)	(MTHS)	(DAYS)
1 Helen Shapiro, You Don't Know	1961	14	10	13
2 Billie, Because We Want To	1998	15	9	20
3 Tiffany, I Think We're Alone Now	1988	16	3	28
4 Nicole, A Little Peace	1982	17	0	0
5 Britney Spears, ...Baby One More Time	1999	17	2	25
6 Sandie Shaw, (There's) Always Something There to Remind Me	1964	17	7	26
7 LeAnn Rimes, Can't Fight the Moonlight	2000	18	2	29
8 Mary Hopkin, Those Were the Days	1968	18	4	22
9 Sonia, You'll Never Stop Me Loving You	1989	18	5	9
10 Christina Aguilera, Genie in a Bottle	1999	18	9	29

Source: *Music Information Database*

The ages shown are those of each artist on the publication date of the chart in which she achieved her first No. 1 single. All ten of these girls were still in their teens when they had their first taste of chart-topping glory. Billie followed up her No. 1 with another chart-topper, *Girlfriend*, when she was 17 years old.

OLDEST FEMALE SOLO SINGERS TO HAVE A NO. 1 SINGLE IN THE UK

SINGER/TITLE	YEAR	AGE (YRS)	(MTHS)	(DAYS)
1 Cher, Believe	1998	52		2
2 Madonna, Music	2000	42	0	7
3 Barbra Streisand, Woman in Love	1980	38	6	
4 Vera Lynn, My Son My Son	1954	37	7	5
5 Kylie Minogue, Slow	2003	35	5	8
6 Nicole Kidman, Something Stupid	2001	34	6	2
7 Kylie Minogue, Can't Get You out of My Head	2001	33	4	
8 Tammy Wynette, Stand By Your Man	1975	33	0	2
9 Kitty Kallen, Little Things Mean a Lot	1954	32	3	6
10 Robin Beck, First Time	1988	32	2	2

Source: *Music Information Database*

The ages shown are those of each artist on the publication date of the chart in which her last No. 1 single reached the top. Coincidentally, since the other entries are of more recent vintage, two entries date from the same year, 1954, when a decade after acquiring her status as the "Forces' Sweetheart", Vera Lynn achieved her one and only No. 1 record and Kitty Kallen enjoyed her sole chart hit in the UK, which hit the No. 1 slot for a single week.

FEMALE SOLO SINGERS WITH THE LONGEST GAPS BETWEEN NO. 1 HIT SINGLES IN THE UK

SINGER	PERIOD	GAP (YRS)	(MTHS)	(DAYS)
1 Diana Ross	18 Sept 1971–1 Mar 1986	14	5	21
2 Kylie Minogue	3 Feb 1990–24 Jun 2000	10	5	5
3 Madonna	12 May 1990–28 Feb 1998	7	9	16
4 Petula Clark	2 Mar 1961–9 Feb 1967	5	11	7
5 Whitney Houston	29 Oct 1988–28 Nov 1992	4	0	30
6 Cher	8 Jun 1991–18 Mar 1995	3	9	10
7 Cher	1 Apr 1995–24 Oct 1998	3	6	23
8 Celine Dion	25 Mar 1995–7 Mar 1998	2	11	10
9 Shirley Bassey	13 Mar 1959–14 Sep 1961	2	6	1
10 Lisa Stansfield	25 Nov 1990–24 Apr 1993	2	4	30

Source: *Music Information Database*

◀ **Whip hand**
By the time of her 1992 *Erotica* release, Madonna had already achieved more than half her total tally of chart hits in a career spanning just eight years.

SINGLES BY FEMALE SOLO SINGERS IN THE UK

TITLE/SINGER	YEAR
1 Believe, Cher	1998
2 ...Baby One More Time, Britney Spears	1999
3 I Will Always Love You, Whitney Houston	1992
4 The Power of Love, Jennifer Rush	1985
5 My Heart Will Go On, Celine Dion	1998
6 Think Twice, Celine Dion	1994
7 Saturday Night, Whigfield	1994
8 Can't Get You Out of My Head, Kylie Minogue	2001
9 Don't Cry for Me Argentina, Julie Covington	1976
10 Torn, Natalie Imbruglia	7

Perhaps the most significant aspect of this list is how comparatively recent most of its entries are. Only one of these singles was released before 1980.

MALE SINGERS WITH THE LONGEST GAPS BETWEEN NO. 1 HIT SINGLES IN THE UK

	SINGER	PERIOD	GAP (YRS)	(MTHS)	(DAYS)
1	George Harrison	2 Feb 1971–26 Jan 2002	30	11	24
2	Elvis Presley	1 Oct 1977–22 Jun 2002	24	8	21
3	Elton John	4 Sept 1976–16 Jun 1990	13	9	12
4	Frank Sinatra	1 Oct 1954–27 May 1966	11	7	26
5	Cliff Richard	17 Apr 1968–19 Aug 1979	11	4	2
6	Cliff Richard	22 Dec 1990–27 Nov 1999	8	11	5
7	Bryan Adams	2 Nov 1991–11 Mar 2000	8	4	9
8	Don McLean	1 July 1972–14 Jun 1980	7	11	13
9	Elvis Presley	12 Sept 1970–27 Aug 1977	6	11	15
10	Cliff Richard	18 Aug 1979–22 Mar 1986	6	7	4

Source: *Music Information Database*

MALE SOLO SINGERS IN THE UK

	SINGER	TOTAL CHART HITS
1	Elvis Presley	135
2	Cliff Richard	126
3	Elton John	82
4	David Bowie	69
5	Rod Stewart	62
6	Michael Jackson	55
7	Stevie Wonder	54
8	Paul McCartney	52
9	Prince	51
10	Tom Jones	43

Source: *Music Information Database*

Elvis Presley's UK chart career commenced with *Heartbreak Hotel* in 1956, but his success grew more slowly than in the USA, where his first records were all No. 1 hits. In the UK he had 15 chart entries (including re-entries) before he achieved the first of his 17 UK No. 1s with *All Shook Up*, in 1957.

► You wear it well

Rod Stewart has been charting in the UK since 1971, when he scored the first of six UK No. 1s with *Maggie May* – which also had a five-week US run at No. 1.

OLDEST MALE SOLO SINGERS TO HAVE A NO. 1 SINGLE IN THE UK

SINGER/TITLE	YEAR	AGE* (YRS)	(MTHS)	(DAYS)
1 Louis Armstrong, What a Wonderful World	1968	66	9	11
2 Cliff Richard, The Millennium Prayer	1999	59	2	4
3 Elton John, Are You Ready for Love?	2003	56	5	12
4 Isaac Hayes#, Chocolate Salty Balls	1999	56	4	13
5 Elton John, Candle in the Wind 1997/ Something About the Way You Look Tonight	1997	51	6	23
6 Telly Savalas, If	1975	51	1	22
7 Frank Sinatra, Strangers in the Night	1967	50	6	4
8 Charles Aznavour, She	1974	50	1	28
9 Clive Dunn, Grandad	1971	49	0	14
10 Lee Marvin, Wand'rin Star	1970	48	1	2

* During last week of No. 1 UK single
# Credited as "Chef"
Source: Music Information Database

 YOUNGEST MALE SOLO SINGERS TO HAVE A NO. 1 SINGLE IN THE UK

SINGER/TITLE	YEAR	AGE* (YRS)	(MTHS)	(DAYS)
1 Little Jimmy Osmond, Long Haired Lover from Liverpool	1972	9	8	7
2 Donny Osmond, Puppy Love	1972	14		
3 Paul Anka, Diana	1957	16		
4 Gareth Gates#, Unchained Melody	2002	17	8	8
5 Gareth Gates, Anyone of Us (Stupid Mistake)	2002	18		
6 Glenn Medeiros, Nothing's Gonna Change My Love	1988	18	0	15
7 Craig Douglas, Only Sixteen	1959	18		7
8 Gareth Gates, Suspicious Minds	2002	18		
9 Cliff Richard, Living Doll	1959	18	9	8
10 Craig David, Fill Me In	2000	18	1	

* During first week of debut No. 1 UK single
# Youngest British solo No. 1
Source: Music Information Database

 SINGLES BY MALE SOLO SINGERS IN THE UK

TITLE/SINGER/GROUP	YEAR
1 Candle in the Wind (1997)/Something About the Way You Look Tonight, Elton John	1997
2 Anything is Possible/Evergreen, Will Young	2002
3 I Just Called to Say I Love You, Stevie Wonder	1984
4 (Everything I Do) I Do It For You, Bryan Adams	1991
5 Tears, Ken Dodd	1965
6 Imagine, John Lennon	1975
7 Careless Whisper, George Michael	1984
8 Release Me, Engelbert Humperdinck	1967
9 Unchained Melody, Gareth Gates	2002
10 Diana, Paul Anka	1957

Source: The Official UK Charts Company

 ALBUMS BY MALE SOLO SINGERS IN THE UK

TITLE/SINGER	YEAR
1 Bad, Michael Jackson	1987
2 Thriller, Michael Jackson	1982
3 I've Been Expecting You, Robbie Williams	1998
4 The Very Best of Elton John, Elton John	1990
5 White Ladder, David Gray	2000
6 Life Thru a Lens, Robbie Williams	1997
7 But Seriously..., Phil Collins	1989
8 Sing When You're Winning, Robbie Williams	2000
9 Bat Out of Hell, Meat Loaf	1978
10 Swing When You're Winning, Robbie Williams	2001

Source: Music Information Database

The certified sales of the Top 10 albums range from the 13 x platinum of Michael Jackson's *Bad* to the 7 x platinum of Robbie Williams's *Swing When You're Winning*, equivalent to 3.9 million and 2.1 million respectively. Sales at the sort of level achieved by Jackson's *Bad* and *Thriller* (11 x platinum, 3.3 million units sold) mean that approximately one in every six British households, or one in every 15 inhabitants, owns a copy of one or both of these mega-sellers.

Groups & Duos

TOP 10 SINGLES BY DUOS IN THE UK

	TITLE/DUO	YEAR
1	**You're The One That I Want,** John Travolta and Olivia Newton-John	1978
2	**Unchained Melody/(There'll Be Bluebirds Over the) White Cliffs of Dover,** Robson & Jerome	1995
3	**Summer Nights,** John Travolta and Olivia Newton-John	1978
4	**Last Christmas/Everything She Wants,** Wham!	1984
5	**Tainted Love,** Soft Cell	1981
6	**I Believe/Up On the Roof,** Robson & Jerome	1995
7	**Especially For You,** Kylie Minogue and Jason Donovan	1988
8	**Unchained Melody,** Righteous Brothers	1990
9	**Sweet Like Chocolate,** Shanks & Bigfoot	1999
10	**Truly Madly Deeply,** Savage Garden	1998

Released in the UK on 1 May 1978, *You're The One That I Want* from *Grease*, the top film of the year, stayed at No. 1 for eight weeks and was in the charts for 26 weeks, achieving platinum status by 1 July. From the same film came *Summer Nights*, released on 1 September, which stayed at No. 1 for seven weeks and was certified platinum on 1 October.

TOP 10 SINGLES BY GROUPS IN THE UK

	TITLE/GROUP	YEAR
1	**Bohemian Rhapsody,** Queen	1975
2	**Mull of Kintyre/Girls' School,** Wings	1977
3	**Rivers of Babylon/Brown Girl in the Ring,** Boney M	1978
4	**Relax,** Frankie Goes To Hollywood	1984
5	**She Loves You,** The Beatles	1963
6	**Mary's Boy Child/Oh My Lord,** Boney M	1978
7	**Love is All Around,** Wet Wet Wet	1994
8	**I Want to Hold Your Hand,** The Beatles	1963
9	**Can't Buy Me Love,** The Beatles	1964
10	**Barbie Girl,** Aqua	1997

Source: *The Official UK Chart Company*

Not only was Queen's *Bohemian Rhapsody* the biggest-selling single by a group in the UK, but more than one poll has ranked it at the top of a list of "100 Greatest Singles" of all time.

TOP 10 ALBUMS BY GROUPS IN THE UK

	TITLE/GROUP	YEAR
1	**Sgt. Pepper's Lonely Hearts Club Band,** The Beatles	1967
2	**(What's the Story), Morning Glory,** Oasis	1995
3	**Brothers in Arms,** Dire Straits	1985
4	**Stars,** Simply Red	1991
5	**Greatest Hits (Volume One),** Queen	1981
6	**Spice,** The Spice Girls	1996
7	**Abba Gold Greatest Hits,** Abba	1990
8	**Rumours,** Fleetwood Mac	1977
9	**Talk on Corners,** The Corrs	1997
10	**The Man Who,** Travis	1999

Source: *BPI*

The Beatles' *Sgt. Pepper*, the seminal album from the 1967 "Summer of Love", sold 250,000 in the UK in its first week and 500,000 within the month, staying at No. 1 for 27 weeks.

TOP 10 DUOS IN THE UK

	DUO	TOTAL CHART HITS
1	**Pet Shop Boys**	37
2	= **Everly Brothers**	30
	= **T. Rex**	30
4	= **Erasure**	28
	= **Eurythmics**	28
6	**Roxette**	25
7	**Everything But the Girl**	23
8	**The Carpenters**	21
9	**Daryl Hall & John Oates**	17
10	= **Orbital**	16
	= **Tears For Fears**	16

Source: *Music Information Database*

Pet Shop Boys started their chart career hesitantly: *West End Girls* was released in 1984 without charting, and it was not until a re-recorded version appeared over a year later that they began their glittering career, which has included four No. 1s.

TOP 10 GROUPS IN THE UK

	GROUP	TOTAL CHART HITS
1	Status Quo	58
2	Queen	53
3	The Rolling Stones	51
4	UB40	49
5	= The Bee Gees	38
	= Depeche Mode	38
7	Pet Shop Boys	37
8	Slade	36
9	Hot Chocolate	35
10	= Iron Maiden	34
	= The Stranglers	34

Source: *Music Information Database*

TOP 10 FEMALE GROUPS IN THE UK

	GROUP	TOTAL CHART HITS
1	The Supremes	31
2	Bananarama	29
3	Salt 'N Pepa	17
4	= Eternal	15
	= The Three Degrees	15
6	Sister Sledge	14
7	= TLC	11
	= Atomic Kitten	11
9	The Spice Girls	10
10	Sugababes	9

Source: *Music Information Database*

▼ **Supreme achievement**
The world's foremost female group, the Supremes' UK chart career lasted a quarter of a century, from 1964 to 1989 – although they never managed to repeat the success of their sole No.1, *Baby Love*.

Singles of Each Year 1992–2003

TOP 10 SINGLES IN THE UK, 1992

	SINGLE	ARTIST OR GROUP
1	I Will Always Love You	Whitney Houston
2	Rhythm Is a Dancer	Snap!
3	Stay	Shakespears Sister
4	Please Don't Go	K.W.S.
5	Abba-esque (E.P.)	Erasure
6	End of the Road	Boyz II Men
7	Ain't No Doubt	Jimmy Nail
8	Would I Lie to You?	Charles & Eddie
9	Ebeneezer Goode	Shamen
10	Deeply Dippy	Right Said Fred

Source: *The Official Charts Company*

Following a familiar pattern, the single topping the UK chart as 1992 ended proved to be the year's biggest seller. Whitney Houston's *I Will Always Love You*, from the film *The Bodyguard*, sold 1.2 million copies to overtake Jennifer Rush's 1985 hit *The Power of Love* and become the biggest-selling single ever in the UK by a female artist.

TOP 10 SINGLES IN THE UK, 1993

	SINGLE	ARTIST OR GROUP
1	I'd Do Anything for Love (But I Won't Do That)	Meat Loaf
2	All That She Wants	Ace of Base
3	(I Can't Help) Falling in Love with You	UB40
4	Mr. Blobby	Mr. Blobby
5	No Limit	2 Unlimited
6	Dreams	Gabrielle
7	Babe	Take That
8	Mr. Vain	Culture Beat
9	Pray	Take That
10	Oh Carolina	Shaggy

Source: *The Official Charts Company*

The eclectic nature of the UK singles market was once again demonstrated by *Mr. Blobby*, 1993's big Christmas novelty hit, and a record that was reviled by just about everybody other than the 765,000 people who bought it.

TOP 10 SINGLES IN THE UK, 1994

	SINGLE	ARTIST OR GROUP
1	Love Is All Around	Wet Wet Wet
2	Saturday Night	Whigfield
3	Stay Another Day	East 17
4	Baby Come Back	Pato Banton
5	I Swear	All-4-One
6	Without You	Mariah Carey
7	Always	Bon Jovi
8	Crazy for You	Let Loose
9	Things Can Only Get Better	D:ream
10	Doop	Doop

Source: *The Official Charts Company*

Love is All Around was written by Reg Presley of The Troggs and was a hit for them in 1967. Wet Wet Wet's version stayed at UK No. 1 for three months, selling 1,783,827 copies, after being featured in *Four Weddings and a Funeral*, the top film at the UK box office this year. A variation on it, *Christmas is All Around*, was included in *Love Actually* (2003).

TOP 10 SINGLES IN THE UK, 1998

	SINGLE	ARTIST OR GROUP
1	Believe	Cher
2	My Heart Will Go On	Celine Dion
3	It's Like That	Run DMC Vs. Jason Nevins
4	No Matter What	Boyzone
5	C'est La Vie	B*witched
6	How Do I Live	LeAnn Rimes
7	Chocolate Salty Balls	Chef
8	Goodbye	The Spice Girls
9	Ghetto Supastar (That Is What You Are)	Pras Michel featuring ODB & Mya
10	Truly Madly Deeply	Savage Garden

Source: *The Official Charts Company*

Cher's top seller of the 1990s was all the more remarkable, as at 52 she was the oldest female solo singer ever to have a UK No. 1. *Believe* spent seven weeks in the top spot, selling 1,672,108 copies in the UK and won three Ivor Novello awards, including that for "Best Song". It hit US No. 1 the next year, 25 years after her last.

TOP 10 SINGLES IN THE UK, 1999

	SINGLE	ARTIST OR GROUP
1	…Baby One More Time	Britney Spears
2	Blue (Da Ba Dee)	Eiffel 65
3	The Millennium Prayer	Cliff Richard
4	Mambo No. 5 (A Little Bit of...)	Lou Bega
5	9pm (Till I Come)	ATB
6	Livin' La Vida Loca	Ricky Martin
7	That Don't Impress Me Much	Shania Twain
8	Sweet Like Chocolate	Shanks & Bigfoot
9	Flat Beat	Mr. Oizo
10	When the Going Gets Tough	Boyzone

Source: *The Official Charts Company*

Seventeen-year-old Britney Spears' debut disc sold 1,450,154 copies – an unprecedented debut sale for a female solo singer. This and the 1,023,526 of Eiffel 65's singalong euro hit *Blue* were Britain's only million-sellers of the year.

TOP 10 SINGLES IN THE UK, 2000

	SINGLE	ARTIST OR GROUP
1	Can We Fix It	Bob the Builder
2	Pure Shores	All Saints
3	It Feels So Good	Sonique
4	Who Let the Dogs Out	Baha Men
5	Rock DJ	Robbie Williams
6	Stan	Eminem
7	Toca's Miracle	Fragma
8	Groove Jet (If This Ain't Love)	Spiller
9	Never Had a Dream Come True	S Club 7
10	Fill Me In	Craig David

Source: *The Official Charts Company*

A diverse mix of singles in a variety of genres, from ballads to rap and the pervasive Ibiza sound, by both established artists and newcomers, achieved chart success in the first year of the new millennium, with Neil Morrisey's surprise novelty hit from BBC children's show *Bob the Builder* the Christmas and overall leader.

TOP 10 SINGLES IN THE UK, 1995

SINGLE	ARTIST OR GROUP
1 Unchained Melody/ The White Cliffs of Dover	Robson & Jerome
2 Gangsta's Paradise	Coolio featuring LV
3 I Believe/Up on the Roof	Robson & Jerome
4 Back for Good	Take That
5 Think Twice	Celine Dion
6 Earth Song	Michael Jackson
7 Fairground	Simply Red
8 You Are Not Alone	Michael Jackson
9 Missing	Everything but the Girl
10 Wonderwall	Oasis

Source: *The Official Charts Company*

Robson (Green) & Jerome (Flynn)'s version of *Unchained Melody*, a song that had charted on several previous occasions since appearing 40 years earlier in the film *Unchained*, sold a million copies within three weeks and reached a total sale of 1,843,201.

TOP 10 SINGLES IN THE UK, 1996

SINGLE	ARTIST OR GROUP
1 Killing Me Softly	Fugees
2 Wannabe	The Spice Girls
3 Spaceman	Babylon Zoo
4 Say You'll Be There	The Spice Girls
5 Return of the Mack	Mark Morrison
6 Ooh Aah ... Just a Little Bit	Gina G
7 Three Lions	Baddiel & Skinner & the Lightning Seeds
8 Children	Robert Miles
9 Mysterious Girl	Peter Andre featuring Bubbler Ranx
10 2 Become 1	The Spice Girls

Source: *The Official Charts Company*

This was the year in which the Spice Girls exploded on to the pop music scene. The group had three No. 1 hits before the year was out and went on to become Britain's most successful female group of all time.

TOP 10 SINGLES IN THE UK, 1997

SINGLE	ARTIST OR GROUP
1 Something About the Way You Look Tonight/Candle in the Wind 1997	Elton John
2 Barbie Girl	Aqua
3 I'll Be Missing You	Puff Daddy & Faith Evans
4 Perfect Day	Various Artists
5 Teletubbies Say Eh-Oh!	Teletubbies
6 Men in Black	Will Smith
7 Don't Speak	No Doubt
8 Torn	Natalie Imbruglia
9 Tubthumping	Chumbawamba
10 Spice up Your Life	The Spice Girls

Source: *The Official Charts Company*

Elton John's rewrite of *Candle in the Wind*, performed in Westminster Abbey during the funeral service for Princess Diana, not only became the bestselling single of the year in the UK (officially 4,864,611 copies), but the biggest selling single of all time.

TOP 10 SINGLES IN THE UK, 2001

SINGLE	ARTIST OR GROUP
1 It Wasn't Me	Shaggy featuring Rikrok
2 Pure and Simple	Hear'Say
3 Can't Get You Out of My Head	Kylie Minogue
4 Whole Again	Atomic Kitten
5 Uptown Girl	Westlife
6 Hey Baby	DJ Otzi
7 Don't Stop Movin'	S Club 7
8 Angel	Shaggy featuring Rayvon
9 Teenage Dirtbag	Wheatus
10 Because I Got High	Afroman

Source: *The Official Charts Company*

While not the first Jamaican singer to have a UK No. 1 single (although, perhaps surprisingly, this feat had eluded the great Bob Marley), Shaggy was the first to top both the UK singles and album charts simultaneously with *It Wasn't Me* and *Hot Shot* respectively. The single sold 1,180,708 copies.

TOP 10 SINGLES IN THE UK, 2002

SINGLE	ARTIST OR GROUP
1 Anything Is Possible/Evergreen	Will Young
2 Unchained Melody	Gareth Gates
3 Hero	Enrique Iglesias
4 Dilemma	Nelly featuring Kelly Rowland
5 A Little Less Conversation	Elvis Vs. JXL
6 Anyone of Us (Stupid Mistake)	Gareth Gates
7 Whenever Wherever	Shakira
8 The Ketchup Song (Asereje)	Las Ketchup
9 Just a Little	Liberty X
10 Without Me	Eminem

Source: *The Official Charts Company*

With 4.6 million votes under his belt as the winner of TV's sensation of the year, Pop Idol, Will Young's debut single sold 1,108,659 copies in its first week and 1,779,938 in total. Runner-up Gareth Gates had a No. 1 hit – the youngest British artist ever to do so – and a sale of 1,318,714 copies of the eighth version of *Unchained Melody* to chart in the UK.

TOP 10 SINGLES IN THE UK, 2003

SINGLE	ARTIST OR GROUP
1 Where Is the Love	Black Eyed Peas
2 Spirit in the Sky	Gareth Gates featuring the Kumars
3 Ignition Remix	R. Kelly
4 Mad World	Michael Andrews featuring Gary Jules
5 Leave Right Now	Will Young
6 All the Things She Said	t.A.T.u.
7 Changes	Ozzy & Kelly Osbourne
8 Breathe	Blu Cantrell featuring Sean Paul
9 Make Luv	Room 5 featuring Oliver Cheatham
10 Christmas Time (Don't Let the Bells End)	The Darkness

Source: *The Official Charts Company*

Although both Black Eyed Peas' *Where is the Love* and Gareth Gates's collaboration with TV's the Kumars went platinum, Black Eyed Peas sold best (some 625,000 copies during the year) without actually hitting the No. 1. spot in the weekly chart.

Albums of Each Year 1992-2003

ALBUMS IN THE UK, 1992

ALBUM	ARTIST OR GROUP
1 Stars	Simply Red
2 Back to Front	Lionel Richie
3 Diva	Annie Lennox
4 We Can't Dance	Genesis
5 Dangerous	Michael Jackson
6 Cher's Greatest Hits: 1965–1992	Cher
7 Up	Right Said Fred
8 Gold – Greatest Hits	Abba
9 Divine Madness	Madness
10 Glittering Prize '81–'92	Simple Minds

Source: *The Official UK Charts Company*

The Top 10 UK albums of 1992 divided equally between new material and compilations of earlier hits – although both Lionel Richie's and Cher's examples of the latter category shrewdly mixed in some new material with the old. Simply Red's *Stars*, remarkably, was the top seller for the second year running: as 1992 drew to a close its total sales had just passed the 3 million mark.

ALBUMS IN THE UK, 1993

ALBUM	ARTIST OR GROUP
1 Bat out of Hell II – Back into Hell	Meat Loaf
2 The Bodyguard (Original Soundtrack)	Whitney Houston
3 Automatic for the People	R.E.M.
4 So Close	Dina Carroll
5 One Woman – The Ultimate Collection	Diana Ross
6 So Far So Good	Bryan Adams
7 Both Sides	Phil Collins
8 Promises and Lies	UB40
9 Unplugged	Eric Clapton
10 Everything Changes	Take That

Source: *The Official UK Charts Company*

Most of these albums were by established major artists (Whitney Houston being the main attraction of *The Bodyguard*), but Dina Carroll's *So Close* deserves note as a mega-selling debut effort, as does the teen favourite Take That release.

ALBUMS IN THE UK, 1994

ALBUM	ARTIST OR GROUP
1 Cross Road – The Best of Bon Jovi	Bon Jovi
2 Carry on up the Charts – The Best of	Beautiful South
3 Music Box	Mariah Carey
4 Always & Forever	Eternal
5 The Division Bell	Pink Floyd
6 End of Part One (Their Greatest Hits)	Wet Wet Wet
7 Monster	R.E.M.
8 Parklife	Blur
9 Live at the BBC	The Beatles
10 Steam	East 17

Source: *The Official UK Charts Company*

Rockers Bon Jovi and indie pop originals The Beautiful South led the way in the year's listing. Blur's *Parklife*, one of the defining releases of the 'Britpop' phenomenon, features lower in the chart.

ALBUMS IN THE UK, 1998

ALBUM	ARTIST OR GROUP
1 Talk on Corners	The Corrs
2 Ladies and Gentlemen – The Best of	George Michael
3 Where We Belong	Boyzone
4 Life Thru a Lens	Robbie Williams
5 I've Been Expecting You	Robbie Williams
6 Urban Hymns	Verve
7 Ray of Light	Madonna
8 Let's Talk About Love	Celine Dion
9 All Saints	All Saints
10 Titanic (Original Soundtrack)	James Horner

Source: *The Official UK Charts Company*

The sweet vocal harmonies of Irish siblings The Corrs propelled them to the No. 1 position in 1998, as *Talk on Corners* became the soundtrack to a thousand dinner parties. Fellow Irish band Boyzone, featuring Ronan Keating, claimed the third spot.

ALBUMS IN THE UK, 1999

ALBUM	ARTIST OR GROUP
1 Come on Over	Shania Twain
2 By Request	Boyzone
3 The Man Who	Travis
4 Gold – Greatest Hits	Abba
5 Performance and Cocktails	Stereophonics
6 I've Been Expecting You	Robbie Williams
7 Steptacular	Steps
8 Talk on Corners	The Corrs
9 Westlife	Westlife
10 On How Life Is	Macy Gray

Source: *The Official UK Charts Company*

Trailed by the winsomely catchy single *That Don't Impress Me Much*, Shania Twain's *Come on Over* finally brought her the kind of success in the UK that she had long enjoyed in North America, and scored massive sales for her worldwide. Sales of their eponymous album meant that Westlife joined Boyzone in the year's Top 10, thereby doubling the contingent of Irish boybands.

ALBUMS IN THE UK, 2000

ALBUM	ARTIST OR GROUP
1 1	The Beatles
2 Swing When You're Winning	Robbie Williams
3 The Marshall Mathers LP	Eminem
4 Coast to Coast	Westlife
5 Play	Moby
6 Born to Do It	Craig David
7 The Greatest Hits	Texas
8 Parachutes	Coldplay
9 The Greatest Hits	Whitney Houston
10 Music	Madonna

Source: *The Official UK Charts Company*

A compilation of The Beatles' No. 1 singles (on both sides of the Atlantic) topped the 2000 UK album chart, while two other greatest hits packages, from Scottish band Texas and American diva Whitney Houston, also made the list of the year's bestsellers.

TOP 10 ALBUMS IN THE UK, 1995

	ALBUM	ARTIST OR GROUP
1	Robson & Jerome	Robson & Jerome
2	(What's the Story) Morning Glory?	Oasis
3	The Colour of My Life	Celine Dion
4	Life	Simply Red
5	History – Past Present & Future, Book 1	Michael Jackson
6	Made in Heaven	Queen
7	Stanley Road	Paul Weller
8	Picture This	Wet Wet Wet
9	The Great Escape	Blur
10	Different Class	Pulp

Source: *The Official UK Charts Company*

Actor-singers Robson and Jerome scored huge album sales – 6 x platinum by the end of the year – on the back of their appearance in the TV series *Soldier, Soldier*, holding off the challenge of Mancunian 'Britpop' band Oasis to claim the No. 1 spot.

TOP 10 ALBUMS IN THE UK, 1996

	ALBUM	ARTIST OR GROUP
1	Jagged Little Pill	Alanis Morissette
2	(What's the Story) Morning Glory?	Oasis
3	Spice	The Spice Girls
4	Falling Into You	Celine Dion
5	Older	George Michael
6	Take Two	Robson & Jerome
7	The Score	Fugees
8	Greatest Hits	Take That
9	Greatest Hits	Simply Red
10	Blue Is the Colour	Beautiful South

Source: *The Official UK Charts Company*

The Spice Girls scored a big success with their debut album *Spice*, but their upbeat message of 'girl power' was outsold in 1996 by the rather more introspective work of Canadian singer-songwriter Alanis Morissette, whose *Jagged Little Pill* went on to become one of the decade's best sellers.

TOP 10 ALBUMS IN THE UK, 1997

	ALBUM	ARTIST OR GROUP
1	Be Here Now	Oasis
2	Urban Hymns	Verve
3	Spice	The Spice Girls
4	White on Blonde	Texas
5	Spiceworld	The Spice Girls
6	The Fat of the Land	The Prodigy
7	Let's Talk About Love	Celine Dion
8	OK Computer	Radiohead
9	Greatest Hits	Eternal
10	The Best of Wham!	Wham!

Source: *The Official UK Charts Company*

Featured in the listing for the third consecutive year, Oasis finally claimed the No. 1 spot with *Be Here Now*, while the appearance of *The Best of Wham!* in the chart was indicative of a revival of interest in music from the early 1980s.

TOP 10 ALBUMS IN THE UK, 2001

	ALBUM	ARTIST OR GROUP
1	No Angel	Dido
2	Swing When You're Winning	Robbie Williams
3	White Ladder	David Gray
4	The Invisible Band	Travis
5	Songbird	Eva Cassidy
6	Hotshot	Shaggy
7	Dreams Can Come True	Gabrielle
8	Survivor	Destiny's Child
9	Just Enough Education to Perform	Stereophonics
10	Gold	Steps

Source: *The Official UK Charts Company*

Singer-songwriters Dido (real name Florian Cloud de Bouneviale) and David Gray scored highly in 2001; both were widely supposed to be popular with 30-something audiences, with young rock outfits like Travis and Stereophonics appealing, in general, to a somewhat younger demographic.

TOP 10 ALBUMS IN THE UK, 2002

	ALBUM	ARTIST OR GROUP
1	Escapology	Robbie Williams
2	M!ssundaztood	P!nk
3	Escape	Enrique Iglesias
4	A Rush of Blood to the Head	Coldplay
5	One Love	Blue
6	By the Way	Red Hot Chili Peppers
7	The Eminem Show	Eminem
8	Unbreakable – The Greatest Hits Vol. 1	Westlife
9	Elv1s – 30 #1 Hits	Elvis Presley
10	Heathen Chemistry	Oasis

Source: *The Official UK Charts Company*

Making a remarkable fifth consecutive appearance in the annual chart, Robbie Williams finally claimed the number one spot with *Escapology* in 2002. William's willingness to embrace styles ranging from rock to swing has given his music a wide, cross-generational appeal, and the high repute of his stage shows can only have helped his album sales.

TOP 10 ALBUMS IN THE UK, 2003

	ALBUM	ARTIST OR GROUP
1	Life for Rent	Dido
2	Justified	Justin Timberlake
3	Stripped	Christina Aguilera
4	Gotta Get Thru This	Daniel Bedingfield
5	Come Away with Me	Norah Jones
6	Permission to Land	The Darkness
7	A Rush of Blood to the Head	Coldplay
8	Number Ones	Michael Jackson
9	Busted	Busted
10	The Best of R.E.M. – In Time 1988–2003	R.E.M.

Source: *The Official UK Charts Company*

In the 2003 chart Dido scored her second No. 1 in three years; Justin Timberlake, whose success as a solo artist in the UK has far outstripped that of his former band *NSYNC, claimed the runners-up position. Lowestoft's The Darkness, purveying a humorous brand of heavy rock, were among the newcomers to make a major sales impact.

Gold & Platinum

 GROUPS WITH THE MOST GOLD ALBUM AWARDS IN THE UK

	GROUP	GOLD ALBUM AWARDS
1	Queen	24
2	The Rolling Stones	20
3	Status Quo	19
4	The Beatles	16
5	= Abba	15
	= Genesis	15
	= UB40	15
8	Roxy Music	14
9	U2	13
10	= Iron Maiden	12
	= Pink Floyd	12

Source: *BPI*

Having started their careers in the 1960s, several of the groups listed would have qualified for even more gold discs if they had been awarded prior to 1 April 1973, the date of their introduction by the BPI (British Phonographic Industry). Gold awards are made for sales of 100,000 albums, cassettes, or CDs.

 MALE ARTISTS WITH THE MOST PLATINUM ALBUM AWARDS IN THE UK

	ARTIST	PLATINUM ALBUM AWARDS
1	Michael Jackson	42
2	Robbie Williams	39
3	Phil Collins	32
4	Elton John	25
5	George Michael	23
6	= Meat Loaf	17
	= Rod Stewart	17
8	Cliff Richard	15
9	= Bon Jovi	14
	= Chris Rea	14
	= Travis	14

Source: *BPI*

Platinum albums in the UK are those that have achieved sales of 300,000. Relative to the population of the UK, this represents approximately one sale per 196 inhabitants. Multi-platinum albums are those that have sold multiples of 300,000: thus a quadruple platinum album denotes sales of 1.2 million units.

 GROUPS WITH THE MOST PLATINUM ALBUM AWARDS IN THE UK

	GROUP	PLATINUM ALBUM AWARDS
1	Simply Red	39
2	Queen	35
3	U2	34
4	Oasis	30
5	Dire Straits	27
6	Fleetwood Mac	24
7	Abba	21
8	= R.E.M.	20
	= Westlife	20
10	= Boyzone	17
	= UB40	17
	= Wet Wet Wet	17

Source: *BPI*

 MALE ARTISTS WITH THE MOST GOLD ALBUM AWARDS IN THE UK

	ARTIST	GOLD ALBUM AWARDS
1	Rod Stewart	26
2	Elton John	23
3	Cliff Richard*	22
4	Paul McCartney#	20
5	= David Bowie	18
	= Neil Diamond	18
7	Elvis Presley	17
8	Mike Oldfield	16
9	James Last	15
10	Prince†	14

* Including two with the Shadows

Including eight with Wings

† Including one with the New Power Generation

Source: *BPI*

► **Golden Girl Mariah**
In a list comprising predominantly US artistes, Mariah Carey's 10 gold albums span 13 years since 1990.

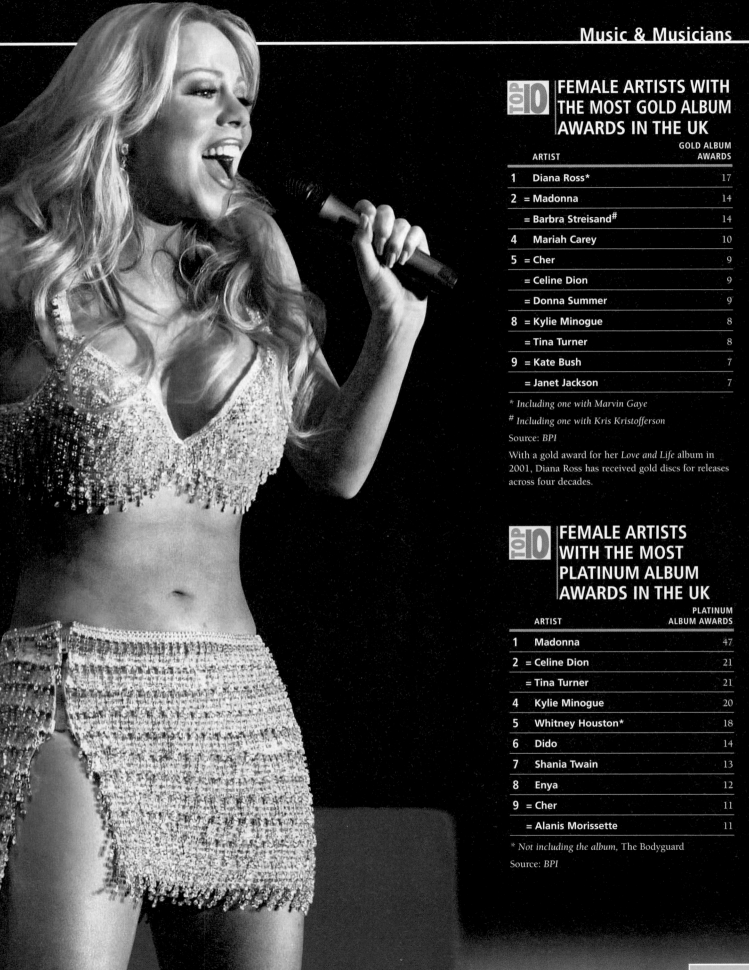

TOP 10 FEMALE ARTISTS WITH THE MOST GOLD ALBUM AWARDS IN THE UK

	ARTIST	GOLD ALBUM AWARDS
1	Diana Ross*	17
2	= Madonna	14
	= Barbra Streisand#	14
4	Mariah Carey	10
5	= Cher	9
	= Celine Dion	9
	= Donna Summer	9
8	= Kylie Minogue	8
	= Tina Turner	8
9	= Kate Bush	7
	= Janet Jackson	7

* *Including one with Marvin Gaye*
# *Including one with Kris Kristofferson*
Source: *BPI*

With a gold award for her *Love and Life* album in 2001, Diana Ross has received gold discs for releases across four decades.

TOP 10 FEMALE ARTISTS WITH THE MOST PLATINUM ALBUM AWARDS IN THE UK

	ARTIST	PLATINUM ALBUM AWARDS
1	Madonna	47
2	= Celine Dion	21
	= Tina Turner	21
4	Kylie Minogue	20
5	Whitney Houston*	18
6	Dido	14
7	Shania Twain	13
8	Enya	12
9	= Cher	11
	= Alanis Morissette	11

* *Not including the album,* The Bodyguard
Source: *BPI*

Music Awards

THE 10 | LATEST GRAMMY RECORDS OF THE YEAR

YEAR	RECORD	ARTIST
2003	**Clocks**	Coldplay
2002	**Don't Know Why**	Norah Jones
2001	**Walk On**	U2
2000	**Beautiful Day**	U2
1999	**Smooth**	Santana featuring Rob Thomas
1998	**My Heart Will Go On**	Celine Dion
1997	**Sunny Came Home**	Shawn Colvin
1996	**Change the World**	Eric Clapton
1995	**Kiss From a Rose**	Seal
1994	**All I Wanna Do**	Sheryl Crow

The Grammys are awarded retrospectively. Thus the 46th awards were presented in 2004 in recognition of musical accomplishment during 2003. At these, Coldplay confirmed their place as the most successful British band in the USA by winning the "Record of the Year" award. They won two Grammys the previous year – "Best Rock Performance by a Duo or Group with a Vocal" for "In My Place" and "Best Alternative Album" with *A Rush of Blood to the Head*.

▶ **Hot Coldplay**
Led by guitarist Chris Martin, Coldplay has won fans and accolades worldwide, gaining Grammy awards in two consecutive years.

THE 10 LATEST WINNERS OF THE BRIT AWARD FOR BEST BRITISH FEMALE SOLO ARTIST

YEAR	ARTIST
2004	Dido
2003	Ms. Dynamite
2002	Dido
2001	Sonique
2000	Beth Orton
1999	Des'ree
1998	Shola Ama
1997	Gabrielle
1996	Annie Lennox
1995	Eddie Reader

The BRIT Awards were first presented in 1982, when the winner in this category was Randy Crawford. Annie Lennox then dominated the award, winning in 1984, 1986, 1989, 1990, and 1993, and for the sixth time in 1996. The only other multiple winners have been Alison Moyet (1985 and 1988) and Lisa Stansfield (1991 and 1992).

THE 10 LATEST WINNERS OF THE BRIT AWARD FOR BEST BRITISH MALE SOLO ARTIST

YEAR	ARTIST
2004	Daniel Bedingfield
2003	Robbie Williams
2002	Robbie Williams
2001	Robbie Williams
2000	Tom Jones
1999	Robbie Williams
1998	Finlay Quaye
1997	George Michael
1996	Paul Weller
1995	Paul Weller

Cliff Richard was the first winner in this category. Robbie Williams's three consecutive wins and total of four are both records; Phil Collins is the other male solo artist to receive the award on three occasions.

THE 10 LATEST WINNERS OF THE BRIT AWARD FOR BEST BRITISH ALBUM*

YEAR	TITLE	ARTIST/OR GROUP
2004	Permission to Land	The Darkness
2003	A Rush of Blood to the Head	Coldplay
2002	No Angel	Dido
2001	Parachutes	Coldplay
2000	The Man Who	Travis
1999	This is My Truth, Tell Me Yours	Manic Street Preachers
1998	Urban Hymns	The Verve
1997	Everything Must Go	Manic Street Preachers
1996	(What's the Story) Morning Glory?	Oasis
1995	Parklife	Blur

* Previously "Best Album"

Kings of the Wild Frontier by Adam and the Ants was the first winner in 1982. Prior to its restriction to British acts, non-British winners in this category included Barbra Streisand's Love Songs (1983) and Michael Jackson's Thriller (1984).

THE 10 LATEST WINNERS OF THE BRIT AWARD FOR BEST BRITISH GROUP

YEAR	GROUP
2004	The Darkness
2003	Coldplay
2002	Travis
2001	Coldplay
2000	Travis
1999	Manic Street Preachers
1998	The Verve
1997	Manic Street Preachers
1996	Oasis
1995	Blur

Police won the debut award in 1982. Twelve years later, former member of the group Sting won in the solo category. George Michael, as part of Wham!, and Mick Hucknall of Simply Red also won in both the group category and subsequently as solo performers.

THE 10 LATEST WINNERS OF THE BRIT AWARD FOR BEST SINGLE BY A BRITISH ARTIST

YEAR	TITLE	ARTIST/GROUP
2004	White Flag	Dido
2003	Just a Little	Liberty X
2002	Don't Stop Movin'	S Club 7
2001	Rock DJ	Robbie Williams
2000	She's the One	Robbie Williams
1999	Angels	Robbie Williams
1998	Never Ever	All Saints
1997	Wannabe	The Spice Girls
1996	Back for Good	Take That
1995	Parklife	Blur

Tainted Love by Soft Cell won the award in 1982. Robbie Williams's triple wins were matched by those of Take That in 1993, 1994, and 1996. They are the only artists with more than one award in this category.

THE 10 LATEST "BEST SONG" OSCAR WINNERS

YEAR	SONG	FILM
2003	Into the West	The Lord of the Rings: The Return of the King
2002	Lose Yourself	8 Mile
2001	If I Didn't Have You	Monsters, Inc.
2000	Things Have Changed	Wonder Boys
1999	You'll Be in My Heart	Tarzan
1998	When You Believe	The Prince of Egypt
1997	My Heart Will Go On	Titanic
1996	You Must Love Me	Evita
1995	Colors of the Wind	Pocahontas
1994	Can You Feel the Love Tonight	The Lion King

The first Oscars were presented during the last days of silent films, and the "Best Song" Oscar was not introduced until the 1934 Academy Awards ceremony. It was then won by "The Continental" from the film The Gay Divorcee.

Classical & Opera

TOP 10 CLASSICAL ALBUMS IN THE UK

	TITLE	PERFORMER(S) OR ORCHESTRA	YEAR
1	The Three Tenors in Concert	José Carreras, Placido Domingo, Luciano Pavarotti	1990
2	The Essential Pavarotti	Luciano Pavarotti	1990
3	Vivaldi: The Four Seasons	Nigel Kennedy/English Chamber Orchestra	1989
4	The Three Tenors – in Concert 1994	José Carreras, Placido Domingo, Luciano Pavarotti	1994
5	The Voice	Russell Watson	2000
6	Voice of an Angel	Charlotte Church	1998
7	Pure	Hayley Westenra	2003
8	Encore	Russell Watson	2002
9	The Essential Pavarotti, 2	Luciano Pavarotti	1991
10	The Pavarotti Collection	Luciano Pavarotti	1986

Source: *Music Information Database*

Sales of classical music boomed to unprecedented heights at the end of the 1980s and in the early 1990s, the rider to this being that it was the records by a select band of superstars – tenors José Carreras, Placido Domingo, and Luciano Pavarotti (particularly the latter, who even had a Top 3 single with "Nessun Dorma"), and young-gun violinist Nigel Kennedy – that soared way ahead of the field as a whole.

TOP 10 OPERAS MOST FREQUENTLY PERFORMED AT THE ROYAL OPERA HOUSE, COVENT GARDEN, 1833–2003

	OPERA	COMPOSER	FIRST PERFORMANCE	TOTAL*
1	La Bohème	Giacomo Puccini	2 Oct 1897	545
2	Carmen	Georges Bizet	27 May 1882	495
3	Aïda	Giuseppi Verdi	22 June 1876	481
4	Rigoletto	Giuseppi Verdi	14 May 1853	455
5	Faust	Charles Gounod	18 July 1863	428
6	Don Giovanni	Wolfgang Amadeus Mozart	17 Apr 1834	414
7	Tosca	Giacomo Puccini	12 July 1900	409
8	La Traviata	Giuseppi Verdi	25 May 1858	391
9	Madama Butterfly	Giacomo Puccini	10 July 1905	366
10	Norma	Vincenzo Bellini	12 July 1833	355

* To 1 January 2004

Most of the works listed were first performed at Covent Garden within a few years of their world premières (in the case of *Tosca*, in the same year). Although some were considered controversial at the time, all of them are now regarded as important components of the classic opera repertoire.

▶ **Voice from the valleys**
Welsh-born Charlotte Church was just 13 when her *Voice of an Angel* album established her the youngest-ever artist with a No. 1 in the UK classical charts.

THE 10 LATEST WINNERS OF THE "BEST OPERA RECORDING" GRAMMY AWARD

YEAR	TITLE/COMPOSER	PRINCIPAL SOLOISTS/ORCHESTRA
2003	**Jenufa,** Leos Janácek	Jerry Hadley, Karita Mattila, Eva Randová, Anja Silja, Jorma Silvasti, Orchestra of the Royal Opera House, Covent Garden
2002	**Tannhäuser,** Richard Wagner	Jane Eaglen, Peter Seiffert, Rene Pape, Thomas Hampson, Waltraud Meier, Staatskapelle Berlin
2001	**Les Troyens,** Hector Belioz	Sir Colin Davis, Ben Heppner, Kenneth Tarver, Michelle De Young, Peter Mattei, Petra Lang, Sara Mingardo, Stephen Milling, London Symphony Orchestra
2000	**Doktor Faust,** Ferruccio Busoni	Kent Nagano, Kim Begley, Dietrich Fischer-Dieskau, Dietrich Henschel, Markus Hollop, Eva Jenis
1999	**The Rake's Progress,** Igor Stravinsky	Ian Bostridge, Bryn Terfel, Anne Sofie von Otter, Deborah York, Monteverdi Choir, London Symphony Orchestra
1998	**Bluebeard's Castle,** Béla Bartók	Jessye Norman, Laszlo Polgar, Karl-August Naegler, Chicago Symphony Orchestra
1997	**Die Meistersinger Von Nürnberg,** Richard Wagner	Ben Heppner, Herbert Lippert, Karita Mattila, Alan Opie, Rene Pape, Jose van Dam, Iris Vermillion, Chicago Symphony Chorus, Chicago Symphony Orchestra
1996	**Peter Grimes,** Benjamin Britten	Philip Langridge, Alan Opie, Janice Watson, Opera London, London Symphony Chorus, City of London Sinfonia
1995	**Les Troyens,** Hector Berlioz	Charles Dutoit, Orchestra Symphonie de Montreal
1994	**Susannah,** Carlisle Floyd	Jerry Hadley, Samuel Ramey, Cheryl Studer, Kenn Chester

Source: *NARAS*

THE 10 LATEST WINNERS OF THE "BEST CLASSICAL ALBUM" GRAMMY AWARD

YEAR	TITLE/COMPOSER	CONDUCTOR/SOLOIST/ORCHESTRA
2003	**Symphony No. 3; Kindertotenlieder;** Gustav Mahler	Michael Tilson Thomas, Michelle DeYoung, San Francisco Symphony
2002	**A Sea Symphony (Symphony No. 1),** Vaughan Williams	Robert Spano, Norman Mackenzie, Brett Polegato, Christine Goerke, Atlanta Symphony Orchestra
2001	**Les Troyens,** Hector Belioz	Sir Colin Davis, Ben Heppner, Kenneth Tarver, Michelle De Young, Peter Mattei, Petra Lang, Sara Mingardo, Stephen Milling, London Symphony Orchestra
2000	**The String Quartets,** Dmitri Shostakovich	Emerson String Quartet
1999	**Firebird; The Right of Spring; Perséphone,** Igor Stravinsky	Michael Tilson Thomas, Stuart Neill, San Francisco Symphony Orchestra
1998	**Prayers of Kierkegaard,** Samuel Barber **Dona Nobis Pacem,** Ralph Vaughan Williams **Cantata Profana,** Béla Bartók	Robert Shaw, Richard Clement, Nathan Gunn, Atlanta Symphony Orchestra and chorus
1997	**Premieres – Cello Concertos,** Richard Danielpour, Leon Kirchner, Christopher Rouse	Yo-Yo Ma, David Zinman, Philadelphia Orchestra
1996	**Of Rage and Remembrance,** John Corigliano	Leonard Slatkin, National Symphony Orchestra
1995	**La Mer,** Claude Debussy	Pierre Boulez, Cleveland Orchestra
1994	**Concerto for Orchestra; Four Orchestral Pieces, Op. 12,** Béla Bartók	Pierre Boulez, Chicago Symphony Orchestra

Source: *NARAS*

STAGE & SCREEN

Stage World

 LATEST WINNERS OF THE LAURENCE OLIVIER AWARD FOR BEST NEW PLAY*

YEAR	PLAY	PLAYWRIGHT
2004	The Pillowman	Martin McDonagh
2003	Vincent in Brixton	Nicholas Wright
2002	Jitney	August Wilson
2001	Blue/Orange	Marie Jones
2000	Goodnight Children Everywhere	Richard Nelson
1999	The Weir	Conor McPherson
1998	Closer	Patrick Marber
1997	Stanley	Pam Gems
1996	Skylight	David Hare
1995	Broken Glass	Arthur Miller

* "BBC Award for Best Play" until 1996; "Best New Play" thereafter; awards are for previous season

Presented by the Society of London Theatres (founded 1908), the award itself depicts Laurence (later Lord) Olivier (1907–89), after whom it is named, in his celebrated role as Henry V at the Old Vic in 1937. Several earlier winners went on to become successful films, among them *Whose Life Is It Anyway?* (play 1978, film 1981), *Children of a Lesser God* (1981/86), *Glengarry Glen Ross* (1983/92), and *Les Liaisons Dangereuses* (1986/88 – as *Dangerous Liaisons*).

 **LONGEST-RUNNING NON-MUSICALS IN THE UK**

SHOW/RUN(S)	PERFORMANCES
1 The Mousetrap (1952–)	21,294*
2 No Sex, Please – We're British (1971–81; 1982–86; 1986–87)	6,761
3 The Woman in Black (1989–)	5,995*
4 Oh! Calcutta! (1970–74; 1974–80)	3,918
5 The Complete Works of William Shakespeare (abridged) (1996–)	3,748*
6 Run for Your Wife (1983–91)	2,638
7 There's a Girl in My Soup (1966–69; 1969–72)	2,547
8 Pyjama Tops (1969–75)	2,498
9 Sleuth (1970; 1972; 1973–75)	2,359
10 Worm's Eye View (1945–51)	2,245

* Still running; total as at 1 January 2004

Oh! Calcutta! is included here as it is regarded as a revue with music, rather than a musical.

▶ **A Hit for Miss**
Composer Claude-Michel Schönberg and lyricist Alain Boublil – who were also responsible for the even longer-running *Les Misérables* – based their hugely successful musical *Miss Saigon* on the opera *Madam Butterfly*.

 OLDEST LONDON THEATRES

THEATRE/LOCATION	DATE OPENED
1 Theatre Royal, Drury Lane	7 May 1663
2 Sadler's Wells, Rosebery Avenue	3 June 1683
3 The Haymarket (Theatre Royal), Haymarket	29 Dec 1720
4 Royal Opera House, Covent Garden	7 Dec 1732
5 The Adelphi (originally Sans Pareil), Strand	27 Nov 1806
6 The Old Vic (originally Royal Coburg), Waterloo Road	11 May 1818
7 The Vaudeville, Strand	16 Apr 1870
8 The Criterion, Piccadilly Circus	21 Mar 1874
9 The Savoy, Strand	10 Oct 1881
10 The Comedy, Panton Street	15 Oct 1881

These are London's 10 oldest theatres still operating on their original sites – although most of them have been rebuilt, some several times. The Lyceum, built in 1771 as "a place of entertainment", was not originally licensed as a theatre and in its early years was used for such events as circuses and exhibitions, with only occasional theatrical performances. The Savoy was gutted by fire in 1990, but was completely rebuilt and reopened in 1993.

 OLDEST AMERICAN THEATRES AND OPERA HOUSES

THEATER OR OPERA HOUSE	LOCATION	BUILT*
1 The Walnut Street Theater	Philadelphia, Pennsylvania	1809
2 The Woodward Opera House	Mount Vernon, Ohio	1851
3 The Fulton Opera House	Lancaster, Pennsylvania	1852
4 Loring Hall	Hingham, Massachusetts	1852
5 Institute Hall	Natchez, Mississippi	1853
6 The Majestic Theater	Chillicothe, Ohio	1853
7 Saco Town Hall	Saco, Maine	1856
8 The Academy of Music	Philadelphia, Pennsylvania	1857
9 Thespian Hall	Boonville, Missouri	1857
10 Thalian Hall	Wilmington, North Carolina	1858

* Most have been remodelled inside and/or outside since

Interdum volgus rectum videt, est ubi peccat. Si veteres ita miratur laudatque poetas, ut nihil anteferat, nihil illis comparet, errat. Si quaedam nimis antique, si peraque dure dicere credit eos, ignave multa fatetur, et sapit et mecum fac Interdum volgus rectum videt, est ubi peccat. Si veteres ita miratur laudatque poetas, ut nihil anteferat, nihil ill. Interdum volgus rectum videt, est ubi peccat.

LONGEST-RUNNING MUSICALS IN THE UK*

MUSICAL/RUN	PERFORMANCES
1 Cats (1981–2002)#	8,949
2 Les Misérables (1985–2004)	7,602†
3 Starlight Express (1984–2002)	7,406
4 The Phantom of the Opera (1986–)	7,162∞
5 Miss Saigon (1989–99)	4,263
6 Oliver! (1960–69)	4,125
7 Jesus Christ, Superstar (1972–80)	3,357
8 Evita (1978–86)	2,900
9 The Sound of Music (1961–67)	2,386
10 Salad Days (1954–60)	2,283

* Continuous runs only

Closed on 12 May 2002, its 21st birthday

† Closed at the Palace Theatre 27 March 2004; opened at Queen's Theatre 3 April 2004

∞ Still running; total as at 1 January 2004

MOST PRODUCED PLAYS BY SHAKESPEARE, 1878–2003

PLAY	PRODUCTIONS
1 As You Like It	78
2 = The Taming of the Shrew	76
= Twelfth Night	76
4 Hamlet	75
5 = A Midsummer Night's Dream	71
= Much Ado About Nothing	71
7 The Merchant of Venice	70
8 Macbeth	64
9 The Merry Wives of Windsor	61
10 Romeo and Juliet	58

Source: Shakespeare Centre

This list is based on analysis of Shakespearean productions (rather than individual performances) from 31 December 1878 to 31 December 2003 at Stratford-upon-Avon and by the Royal Shakespeare Company in London and on tour.

The Film Business

CINEMA-GOING COUNTRIES (PER CAPITA)

	COUNTRY	ATTENDANCE PER INHABITANT (2002)
1	USA	6.09
2	Iceland	5.71
3	Australia	4.95
4	Singapore	4.91
5	New Zealand	4.73
6	Ireland	4.68
7	Canada	4.22
8	Spain	3.58
9	Luxembourg	3.30
10	France	3.14
	UK	*2.98*

Source: Screen Digest

In its relatively short history, cinema has become an important part of the culture of many countries, though one that is being increasingly challenged by television, video, and DVDs.

COUNTRIES SPENDING THE MOST ON CINEMA VISITS

	COUNTRY	AVERAGE SPENDING ON CINEMA VISITS PER CAPITA (2002) ($)
1	Iceland	41.51
2	USA	33.84
3	Switzerland	23.30
4	Australia	23.07
5	Ireland	22.31
6	Norway	19.53
7	Singapore	18.88
8	UK	18.86
9	Canada	18.70
10	Denmark	17.43

Source: Screen Digest

This ranking is a factor of both the level of cinema-going and the average price of tickets. The latter range from $7.62 in Iceland and $5.81 in the USA to as little as 21 cents in India.

COUNTRIES WITH THE HIGHEST BOX OFFICE REVENUE

	COUNTRY	BOX OFFICE REVENUE, (2002) ($)
1	USA	9,519,600,000
2	UK	1,134,400,000
3	France	971,800,000
4	Germany	908,000,000
5	Canada	602,100,000
6	Spain	591,700,000
7	Italy	496,300,000
8	Switzerland	168,300,000
9	Netherlands	147,500,000
10	Sweden	137,300,000

Source: Screen Digest

▶ **Bollywood blockbuster**
The Indian film industry leads the world in terms of output. Big-budget *Devdas* (2002), starring Madhuri Dixit, typifies the Indian take on the sumptuous Hollywood musical.

COUNTRIES WITH THE MOST CINEMAS

	COUNTRY	CINEMA SCREENS (2002)
1	China	65,500
2	USA	35,280
3	India	11,000
4	France	5,280
5	Germany	4,868
6	Spain	4,039
7	Italy	3,495
8	UK	3,402
9	Mexico	2,755
10	Canada	2,753

Source: Screen Digest

For propaganda purposes, the former Soviet Union once claimed to have 176,172 cinemas – locations able to show 35 mm films, the format used for most feature films.

COUNTRIES WITH THE MOST CINEMAS PER MILLION PEOPLE

	COUNTRY	CINEMA SCREENS PER MILLION PEOPLE (2002)
1	Iceland	166.6
2	Sweden	131.9
3	USA	125.4
4	Australia	94.0
5	France	89.3
6	Norway	88.5
7	Canada	85.5
8	Ireland	85.2
9	New Zealand	82.1
10	Czech Republic	76.5
	World average	*26.4*
	UK	*56.6*

Source: Screen Digest

TOP 10 COUNTRIES MAKING THE MOST FILMS PER MILLION PEOPLE

	COUNTRY	FILMS PRODUCED PER MILLION PEOPLE (2002)
1	Iceland	32.12
2	Hong Kong	14.00
3	Switzerland	5.16
4	Slovenia	4.53
5	Denmark	3.56
6	Spain	3.47
7	France	3.40
8	Hungary	3.29
9	Austria	3.21
10	Norway	3.13
	UK	*1.41*

Source: Screen Digest

TOP 10 COUNTRIES SPENDING THE MOST ON FILM PRODUCTION

	COUNTRY	INVESTMENT (2002) ($)
1	USA	14,661,000,000
2	Japan	1,292,130,000
3	UK	851,620,000
4	France	813,040,000
5	Germany	687,000,000
6	Spain	304,320,000
7	Italy	247,970,000
8	India	192,000,000
9	South Korea	133,830,000*
10	Canada	133,090,000

* 2001 figure

Source: Screen Digest

TOP 10 MOST PROLIFIC FILM-PRODUCING COUNTRIES

	COUNTRY	FILMS PRODUCED (2002)
1	India	1,200
2	USA	543
3	Japan	293
4	France	200
5	Spain	137
6	Italy	130
7	Germany	116
8	China	100
9	Philippines	97
10	Hong Kong	92
	UK	*84*

Source: Screen Digest

Based on the number of full-length feature films produced, Hollywood's "golden age" was the 1920s and 1930s, with a peak of 854 films made in 1954, and its nadir 1978 with just 354.

Blockbusters

TOP 10 HIGHEST-GROSSING FILMS

FILM	YEAR	USA	GROSS INCOME ($) REST OF WORLD	WORLD TOTAL
1 Titanic*	1997	600,788,188	1,234,600,000	1,835,388,188
2 The Lord of the Rings: The Return of the King	2003	372,008,809	679,442,744	1,051,431,553
3 Harry Potter and the Philosopher's Stone	2001	317,575,550	649,423,059	966,998,609
4 Star Wars: Episode I – The Phantom Menace	1999	431,088,297	492,048,523	923,136,820
5 Jurassic Park	1993	357,067,947	563,000,000	920,067,947
6 The Lord of the Rings: The Two Towers	2002	339,687,608	579,024,667	918,712,285
7 Harry Potter and the Chamber of Secrets	2002	261,979,634	604,407,177	866,386,811
8 The Lord of the Rings: The Fellowship of the Ring	2001	314,776,170	547,198,215	861,974,385
9 Independence Day	1996	306,169,255	505,000,000	811,169,255
10 Spider-Man	2002	403,706,375	402,000,000	805,706,375

* Winner of "Best Picture" Academy Award

Prior to the release of *Star Wars* in 1977, no film had ever made more than $500 million worldwide. Since then, some 30 films have done so. *Titanic* remains the only film to have grossed more than this amount in the USA alone, while eight of the films listed above have exceeded this total outside the USA. To date, those in the Top 10 are the only films to have earned more than $800 million globally.

TOP 10 FILM BUDGETS

FILM	YEAR	BUDGET ($)
1 = Spider-Man 2	2004	200,000,000
= Titanic	1997	200,000,000
3 = Waterworld	1995	175,000,000
= Wild, Wild West	1999	175,000,000
5 Terminator 3: Rise of the Machines	2003	170,000,000
6 = Master and Commander: The Far Side of the World	2003	150,000,000
= The Polar Express*	2004	150,000,000
8 Tarzan*	1999	145,000,000
9 Die Another Day	2002	142,000,000
10 = Armageddon	1998	140,000,000
= Lethal Weapon 4	1998	140,000,000
= Men in Black II	2002	140,000,000
= Treasure Planet*	2002	140,000,000

* Animated

TOP 10 FILMS WORLDWIDE, 2003

	FILM
1	Finding Nemo
2	The Matrix Reloaded
3	The Lord of the Rings: The Return of the King
4	Pirates of the Caribbean: The Curse of the Black Pearl
5	Bruce Almighty
6	Terminator 3: The Rise of the Machines
7	The Matrix Revolutions
8	X2: X-Men United
9	Bad Boys II
10	Charlie's Angels 2: Full Throttle

While these were the top earners during 2003, *The Lord of the Rings: The Return of the King* was not released until December, and even later in certain countries. If its post-2003 world box office income were taken into account, it would easily head this list, while *The Last Samurai*, another December release, would be in 6th place.

TOP 10 FILM TRILOGIES

TRILOGY	DATES
1 The Lord of the Rings	2001–03
2 Jurassic Park	1993–2002
3 The Matrix	1999–2003
4 Indiana Jones	1981–89
5 Terminator	1984–2003
6 Back to the Future	1985–90
7 The Silence of the Lambs	1991–2001
8 American Pie	1999–2003
9 Die Hard	1988–95
10 Austin Powers	1997–2002

This is based on the cumulative global earnings of all three parts. The first five trilogies in the list have each earned in excess of $1 billion worldwide – $2.5 billion in the case of the *Lord of the Rings* trilogy. *Home Alone* is excluded since *Home Alone 3* was not presented as a sequel to the first two parts, but if it were included, it would be in 7th place.

TOP 10 FILMS IN THE UK, 2003

FILM
1 The Lord of the Rings: The Return of the King
2 Finding Nemo
3 Love Actually
4 The Matrix Reloaded
5 Pirates of the Caribbean: The Curse of the Black Pearl
6 Bruce Almighty
7 X2: X-Men United
8 Calendar Girls
9 Johnny English
10 Terminator 3: The Rise of the Machines

◄ **Sword and sorcery**
The Lord of the Rings: The Return of the King outstripped even the colossal success of its predecessors, becoming only the second film ever to earn more than $1 billion.

Oscar-winning Films

THE 10 "BEST PICTURE" OSCAR WINNERS OF THE 1930s*

YEAR	FILM
1930	All Quiet on the Western Front#
1931	Cimarron
1932	Grand Hotel
1933	Cavalcade#
1934	It Happened One Night#
1935	Mutiny on the Bounty
1936	The Great Ziegfeld
1937	The Life of Emile Zola
1938	You Can't Take It with You#
1939	Gone with the Wind#

* "Oscar"® is a Registered Trade Mark

\# Winner of "Best Director" Academy Award

The first Academy Awards, popularly known as Oscars, were presented on 16 May 1929, and were for films released in 1927–28. *Wings*, the first film to be honored as "Best Picture", was silent. A second ceremony on 31 October of the same year was for films released in 1928–29, and was won by *Broadway Melody*, the first talkie and the first musical to win. *Gone with the Wind* was the first all-colour winner.

THE 10 "BEST PICTURE" OSCAR WINNERS OF THE 1940s

YEAR	FILM
1940	Rebecca
1941	How Green Was My Valley*
1942	Mrs. Miniver*
1943	Casablanca*
1944	Going My Way*
1945	The Lost Weekend*
1946	The Best Years of Our Lives*
1947	Gentleman's Agreement*
1948	Hamlet
1949	All the King's Men

* Winner of "Best Director" Academy Award

Several of the "Best Picture" winners are now regarded as film classics, with many critics rating *Casablanca* among the greatest films of all time. *Mrs. Miniver* (which won a total of six Academy Awards) and *The Best Years of Our Lives* (seven Academy Awards) were both directed by William Wyler and reflected the concerns of wartime and post-war life respectively. *How Green Was My Valley* and *Going My Way* each won five Academy Awards.

THE 10 "BEST PICTURE" OSCAR WINNERS OF THE 1950s

YEAR	FILM
1950	All About Eve*
1951	An American in Paris
1952	The Greatest Show on Earth
1953	From Here to Eternity*
1954	On the Waterfront*
1955	Marty*
1956	Around the World in 80 Days
1957	The Bridge on the River Kwai*
1958	Gigi*
1959	Ben-Hur*

* Winner of "Best Director" Academy Award

The first film of the 1950s, *All About Eve*, received the most nominations (14), while the last, *Ben-Hur*, won the most (11).

THE 10 "BEST PICTURE" OSCAR WINNERS OF THE 1970s

YEAR	FILM
1970	Patton*
1971	The French Connection*
1972	The Godfather
1973	The Sting*
1974	The Godfather, Part II*
1975	One Flew Over the Cuckoo's Nest*
1976	Rocky*
1977	Annie Hall*
1978	The Deer Hunter*
1979	Kramer vs Kramer*

* Winner of "Best Director" Academy Award

THE 10 "BEST PICTURE" OSCAR WINNERS OF THE 1980s

YEAR	FILM
1980	Ordinary People*
1981	Chariots of Fire
1982	Gandhi*
1983	Terms of Endearment*
1984	Amadeus*
1985	Out of Africa*
1986	Platoon*
1987	The Last Emperor*
1988	Rain Man*
1989	Driving Miss Daisy

* Winner of "Best Director" Academy Award

THE 10 "BEST PICTURE" OSCAR WINNERS OF THE 1990s

YEAR	FILM
1990	Dances With Wolves*
1991	The Silence of the Lambs*
1992	Unforgiven*
1993	Schindler's List*
1994	Forrest Gump*
1995	Braveheart*
1996	The English Patient*
1997	Titanic*
1998	Shakespeare in Love
1999	American Beauty*

* Winner of "Best Director" Academy Award

THE 10 "BEST PICTURE" OSCAR WINNERS OF THE 1960s

YEAR	FILM
1960	The Apartment*
1961	West Side Story*
1962	Lawrence of Arabia*
1963	Tom Jones*
1964	My Fair Lady*
1965	The Sound of Music*
1966	A Man for All Seasons*
1967	In the Heat of the Night
1968	Oliver!*
1969	Midnight Cowboy*

* *Winner of "Best Director" Academy Award*

▶ **Epic achievement**
Peter O'Toole in the title role of *Lawrence of Arabia*. The film was nominated for 10 and won seven Oscars. Director David Lean's previous film, *The Bridge on the River Kwai*, had also won a "Best Picture" Oscar.

Oscar-winning Actors

"BEST ACTOR" OSCAR WINNERS OF THE 1930s

YEAR	ACTOR	FILM
1930	George Arliss	Disraeli
1931	Lionel Barrymore	A Free Soul
1932 =	Wallace Beery	The Champ
=	Fredric March	Dr. Jekyll and Mr. Hyde
1933	Charles Laughton	The Private Life of Henry VIII
1934	Clarke Gable	It Happened One Night*#
1935	Victor McLaglen	The Informer#
1936	Paul Muni	The Story of Louis Pasteur
1937	Spencer Tracy	Captains Courageous
1938	Spencer Tracy	Boys Town
1939	Robert Donat	Goodbye, Mr. Chips

*Winner of "Best Picture" Academy Award

#Winner of "Best Director" Academy Award

"BEST ACTOR" OSCAR WINNERS OF THE 1940s

YEAR	ACTOR	FILM
1940	James Stewart	The Philadelphia Story
1941	Gary Cooper	Sergeant York
1942	James Cagney	Yankee Doodle Dandy
1943	Paul Lukas	Watch on the Rhine
1944	Bing Crosby	Going My Way*#
1945	Ray Milland	The Lost Weekend*#
1946	Fredric March	The Best Years of Our Lives*#
1947	Ronald Colman	A Double Life
1948	Laurence Olivier	Hamlet*
1949	Broderick Crawford	All the King's Men*

*Winner of "Best Picture" Academy Award

#Winner of "Best Director" Academy Award

"BEST ACTOR" OSCAR WINNERS OF THE 1950s

YEAR	ACTOR	FILM
1950	Jose Ferrer	Cyrano de Bergerac
1951	Humphrey Bogart	The African Queen
1952	Gary Cooper	High Noon
1953	William Holden	Stalag 17
1954	Marlon Brando	On the Waterfront*#
1955	Ernest Borgnine	Marty*#
1956	Yul Brynner	The King and I
1957	Alec Guinness	The Bridge on the River Kwai*#
1958	David Niven	Separate Tables
1959	Charlton Heston	Ben Hur*#

*Winner of "Best Picture" Academy Award

#Winner of "Best Director" Academy Award

▼ **Out of Africa**
Humphrey Bogart won his one and only Oscar for his role as Charlie Allnut in *The African Queen*, based on a novel by C.S. Forester. His co-star Katharine Hepburn was nominated as "Best Actress", but did not win.

"BEST ACTOR" OSCAR WINNERS OF THE 1960s

YEAR	ACTOR	FILM
1960	Burt Lancaster	Elmer Gantry
1961	Maximilian Schell	Judgement at Nuremberg
1962	Gregory Peck	To Kill a Mockingbird
1963	Sidney Poitier	Lilies of the Field
1964	Rex Harrison	My Fair Lady*#
1965	Lee Marvin	Cat Ballou
1966	Paul Scofield	A Man for All Seasons*#
1967	Rod Steiger	In the Heat of the Night*
1968	Cliff Robertson	Charly
1969	John Wayne	True Grit

* *Winner of "Best Picture" Academy Award*
# *Winner of "Best Director" Academy Award*

Sydney Poitier was the first black actor to win an Academy Award. He subsequently (2002) received an honorary Oscar for his life's work. These were the sole wins of the other recipients of "Best Actor" Oscars during the 1960s, despite being nominated on other occasions, with the exceptions of Lee Marvin and Cliff Robertson, whose wins were achieved as a result of these single nominations in their careers.

"BEST ACTOR" OSCAR WINNERS OF THE 1970s

YEAR	ACTOR	FILM
1970	George C. Scott	Patton*#
1971	Gene Hackman	The French Connection*#
1972	Marlon Brando	The Godfather*
1973	Jack Lemmon	Save the Tiger
1974	Art Carney	Harry and Tonto
1975	Jack Nicholson	One Flew Over the Cuckoo's Nest*#
1976	Peter Finch	Network
1977	Richard Dreyfuss	The Goodbye Girl
1978	John Voight	Coming Home
1979	Dustin Hoffman	Kramer vs Kramer*#

* *Winner of "Best Picture" Academy Award*
# *Winner of "Best Director" Academy Award*

Peter Finch was the first (and so far only) "Best Actor" to be honoured posthumously: he died on 14 January 1977, and the award was announced at the 1976 ceremony held on 28 March 1977. He was not the first posthumous winner of any Academy Award, however: that distinction went to Sidney Howard for his screenplay for *Gone with the Wind*. Howard died on 23 August 1939, and at the award ceremony on 29 February 1940, the Nobel Prize-winning novelist Sinclair Lewis received the Oscar on his behalf.

"BEST ACTOR" OSCAR WINNERS OF THE 1980s

YEAR	ACTOR	FILM
1980	Robert De Niro	Raging Bull
1981	Henry Fonda	On Golden Pond
1982	Ben Kingsley	Gandhi*#
1983	Robert Duvall	Tender Mercies
1984	F. Murray Abraham	Amadeus*#
1985	William Hurt	Kiss of the Spider Woman
1986	Paul Newman	The Color of Money
1987	Michael Douglas	Wall Street
1988	Dustin Hoffman	Rain Man*#
1989	Daniel Day-Lewis	My Left Foot

* *Winner of "Best Picture" Academy Award*
# *Winner of "Best Director" Academy Award*

Although Michael Douglas gained his acting Oscar for *Wall Street*, he had previously won in his capacity as co-producer, with Saul Zaentz, of "Best Picture" *One Flew Over the Cuckoo's Nest* (1975) – a 100 per cent success ratio from his only two nominations. Paul Newman's only Oscar came after being nominated in leading roles seven times from 1958 onwards.

"BEST ACTOR" OSCAR WINNERS OF THE 1990s

YEAR	ACTOR	FILM
1990	Jeremy Irons	Reversal of Fortune
1991	Anthony Hopkins	The Silence of the Lambs*#
1992	Al Pacino	Scent of a Woman
1993	Tom Hanks	Philadelphia
1994	Tom Hanks	Forrest Gump*#
1995	Nicolas Cage	Leaving Las Vegas
1996	Geoffrey Rush	Shine
1997	Jack Nicholson	As Good as It Gets#
1998	Roberto Benigni	Life Is Beautiful
1999	Kevin Spacey	American Beauty*#

* *Winner of "Best Picture" Academy Award*
# *Winner of "Best Director" Academy Award*

Tom Hanks is only the second actor to win in consecutive years since Spencer Tracy (1937 and 1938). The "Best Actor" Oscar winners in the 21st century are: 2000: Russell Crowe for Gladiator; 2001: Denzel Washington for Training Day; 2002: Adrien Brody for The Pianist; and 2003: Sean Penn for Mystic River.

Oscar-winning Actresses

"BEST ACTRESS" OSCAR WINNERS OF THE 1930s

YEAR	ACTRESS	FILM
1930	Norma Shearer	The Divorcee
1931	Marie Dressler	Min and Bill
1932	Helen Hayes	The Sin of Madelon Claudet
1933	Katharine Hepburn	Morning Glory
1934	Claudette Colbert	It Happened One Night*#
1935	Bette Davis	Dangerous
1936	Luise Rainer	The Great Ziegfeld
1937	Luise Rainer	The Good Earth
1938	Bette Davis	Jezebel
1939	Vivien Leigh	Gone With the Wind*#

* Winner of "Best Picture" Academy Award

\# Winner of "Best Director" Academy Award

The first winner of a "Best Actress" Oscar was Janet Gaynor for her roles in three films, *Seventh Heaven* (1927), *Sunrise* (1927), and *Street Angel* (1928), and the second was Mary Pickford for *Coquette* (1929).

"BEST ACTRESS" OSCAR WINNERS OF THE 1940s

YEAR	ACTRESS	FILM
1940	Ginger Rogers	Kitty Foyle
1941	Joan Fontaine	Suspicion
1942	Greer Garson	Mrs. Miniver*#
1943	Jennifer Jones	The Song of Bernadette
1944	Ingrid Bergman	Gaslight
1945	Joan Crawford	Mildred Pierce
1946	Olivia de Havilland	To Each His Own
1947	Loretta Young	The Farmer's Daughter
1948	Jane Wyman	Johnny Belinda
1949	Olivia de Havilland	The Heiress

* Winner of "Best Picture" Academy Award

\# Winner of "Best Director" Academy Award

Joan Fontaine and Olivia de Havilland are the only sisters to win "Best Actress" Oscars. Both also shared the unusual distinction of having been born in Tokyo, Japan, where their British parents had settled.

"BEST ACTRESS" OSCAR WINNERS OF THE 1950s

YEAR	ACTRESS	FILM
1950	Judy Holiday	Born Yesterday
1951	Vivien Leigh	A Streetcar Named Desire
1952	Shirley Booth	Come Back, Little Sheba
1953	Audrey Hepburn	Roman Holiday
1954	Grace Kelly	The Country Girl
1955	Anna Magnani	The Rose Tattoo
1956	Ingrid Bergman	Anastasia
1957	Joanne Woodward	The Three Faces of Eve
1958	Susan Hayward	I Want to Live!
1959	Simone Signoret	Room at the Top

▶ A fair cop

Frances McDormand as police officer Marge Gunderson in black comedy *Fargo,* for which she won the 1996 "Best Actress" Oscar. The film also won an Oscar for "Best Screenplay".

"BEST ACTRESS" OSCAR WINNERS OF THE 1960s

YEAR	ACTRESS	FILM
1960	Elizabeth Taylor	Butterfield 8
1961	Sophia Loren	Two Women
1962	Anne Bancroft	The Miracle Worker
1963	Patricia Neal	Hud
1964	Julie Andrews	Mary Poppins
1965	Julie Christie	Darling
1966	Elizabeth Taylor	Who's Afraid of Virginia Woolf?
1967	Katharine Hepburn	Guess Who's Coming to Dinner
1968	= Katharine Hepburn*	The Lion in Winter
	= Barbra Streisand*	Funny Girl
1969	Maggie Smith	The Prime of Miss Jean Brodie

* The only tie for "Best Actress"

Elizabeth Taylor had been nominated for leading-role Oscars in three consecutive years during the previous decade – for *Raintree County* (1957), *Cat on a Hot Tin Roof* (1958), and *Suddenly, Last Summer* (1959) – but without winning. None of the films listed above won in the "Best Picture" category.

"BEST ACTRESS" OSCAR WINNERS OF THE 1970s

YEAR	ACTRESS	FILM
1970	Glenda Jackson	Women in Love
1971	Jane Fonda	Klute
1972	Liza Minnelli	Cabaret#
1973	Glenda Jackson	A Touch of Class
1974	Ellen Burstyn	Alice Doesn't Live Here Any More
1975	Louise Fletcher	One Flew Over the Cuckoo's Nest*#
1976	Faye Dunaway	Network
1977	Diane Keaton	Annie Hall*#
1978	Jane Fonda	Coming Home
1979	Sally Field	Norma Rae

* Winner of "Best Picture" Academy Award

\# Winner of "Best Director" Academy Award

Glenda Jackson's two wins were garnered from a total of four nominations for leading-role Oscars during the decade: the other two were for *Sunday, Bloody Sunday* (1971) and *Hedda* (1975). Jane Fonda, the other double winner of the decade, was also nominated for her title role in *Julia* (1977).

THE 10 "BEST ACTRESS" OSCAR WINNERS OF THE 1980s

YEAR	ACTRESS	FILM
1980	Sissy Spacek	The Coal Miner's Daughter
1981	Katharine Hepburn	On Golden Pond
1982	Meryl Streep	Sophie's Choice
1983	Shirley MacLaine	Terms of Endearment*#
1984	Sally Field	Places in the Heart
1985	Geraldine Page	The Trip to Bountiful
1986	Marlee Matlin	Children of a Lesser God
1987	Cher	Moonstruck
1988	Jodie Foster	The Accused
1989	Jessica Tandy	Driving Miss Daisy*

* Winner of "Best Picture" Academy Award

\# Winner of "Best Director" Academy Award

As with the "Best Actor" award, only one actress has ever won in consecutive years – Katharine Hepburn in 1967 and 1968. A further 10 have won twice: Ingrid Bergman, Bette Davis, Olivia De Havilland, Sally Field, Jane Fonda, Jodie Foster, Glenda Jackson, Vivien Leigh, Luise Rainer, and Elizabeth Taylor.

THE 10 "BEST ACTRESS" OSCAR WINNERS OF THE 1990s

YEAR	ACTRESS	FILM
1990	Kathy Bates	Misery
1991	Jodie Foster	The Silence of the Lambs*#
1992	Emma Thompson	Howard's End
1993	Holly Hunter	The Piano
1994	Jessica Lange	Blue Sky
1995	Susan Sarandon	Dead Man Walking
1996	Frances McDormand	Fargo
1997	Helen Hunt	As Good as It Gets
1998	Gwyneth Paltrow	Shakespeare in Love*
1999	Hilary Swank	Boys Don't Cry

* Winner of "Best Picture" Academy Award

\# Winner of "Best Director" Academy Award

The "Best Actress" Oscar winners in the 21st century are: 2000: Julia Roberts for *Erin Brockovich*; 2001: Halle Berry for *Monster's Ball*; 2002: Nicole Kidman for *The Hours*; and 2003: Charlize Theron for *Monster*.

Films of the Decades

 FILMS OF THE 1920s

FILM	YEAR
1 The Big Parade	1925
2 The Four Horsemen of the Apocalypse	1921
3 Ben-Hur	1926
4 The Ten Commandments	1923
5 What Price Glory?	1926
6 The Covered Wagon	1923
7 Way Down East	1921
8 The Singing Fool	1928
9 Wings	1927
10 The Gold Rush	1925

Earnings data for early films is unreliable, but if this list were extended back to the first decade of the 20th century, *The Birth of a Nation* (1915) would be a contender as the highest earning film of the silent era. It is also credited as the most successful film made before 1937, when *Snow White and the Seven Dwarfs* took the crown. All the films in this list were black and white, with the exception of *Ben-Hur*, which contains a colour sequence.

FILMS OF THE 1930s

FILM	YEAR
1 Gone with the Wind*	1939
2 Snow White and the Seven Dwarfs	1937
3 The Wizard of Oz	1939
4 Frankenstein	1931
5 King Kong	1933
6 San Francisco	1936
7 = Hell's Angels	1930
= Lost Horizon	1937
= Mr. Smith Goes to Washington	1939
10 Maytime	1937

* *Winner of "Best Picture" Academy Award*

Gone with the Wind and *Snow White and the Seven Dwarfs* have generated more income than any other pre-war film. However, if the income of *Gone with the Wind* is adjusted to allow for inflation in the period since its release, it could be regarded as the most successful film ever. Academy Award-winning *Cavalcade* (1932) is a potential contender for a place in this Top 10, but its earnings have been disputed.

FILMS OF THE 1940s

FILM	YEAR
1 Bambi*	1942
2 Pinocchio*	1940
3 Fantasia*	1940
4 Song of the South#	1946
5 Mom and Dad	1944
6 Samson and Delilah	1949
7 The Best Years of Our Lives†	1946
8 The Bells of St. Mary's	1945
9 Duel in the Sun	1946
10 This Is the Army	1943

* *Animated*

\# *Part animated/part live-action*

† *Winner of "Best Picture" Academy Award*

The top four films of the decade were classic Disney cartoons. Songs from two of them, *When You Wish Upon a Star* from *Pinocchio* and *Zip-A-Dee-Doo-Dah* from *Song of the South*, also won "Best Song" Academy Awards.

FILMS OF THE 1950s

FILM	YEAR
1 Lady and the Tramp*	1955
2 Peter Pan*	1953
3 Cinderella*	1950
4 The Ten Commandments	1956
5 Ben-Hur#	1959
6 Sleeping Beauty*	1959
7 Around the World in 80 Days#	1956
8 This Is Cinerama	1952
9 South Pacific	1958
10 The Robe	1953

* *Animated*

\# *Winner of "Best Picture" Academy Award*

While the popularity of animated films continued, the 1950s was outstanding as the decade of the "big" picture: many of the most successful films were enormous in terms of not only cast and scale, but also the magnitude of the subjects they tackled: three of these were major biblical epics, with *The Robe* the first film to offer the wide screen of CinemaScope.

FILMS OF THE 1960s

FILM	YEAR
1 One Hundred and One Dalmatians*	1961
2 The Jungle Book*	1967
3 The Sound of Music#	1965
4 Thunderball	1965
5 Goldfinger	1964
6 Doctor Zhivago	1965
7 You Only Live Twice	1967
8 The Graduate	1968
9 Butch Cassidy and the Sundance Kid	1969
10 Mary Poppins	1964

* *Animated*

\# *Winner of "Best Picture" Academy Award*

For the first time ever, each of the Top 10 films of the decade earned more than $100 million globally. A high proportion of the top-earning films of the 1960s were musicals, with *The Sound of Music* producing the fastest-selling album ever, while *Mary Poppins* and those featuring the music from *The Jungle Book* and *Doctor Zhivago* were all No. 1

FILMS OF THE 1970s

FILM	YEAR
1 Star Wars*	1977
2 Jaws	1975
3 Grease	1978
4 Close Encounters of the Third Kind	1977
5 The Exorcist	1973
6 Superman	1978
7 Saturday Night Fever	1977
8 Jaws 2	1978
9 Moonraker	1979
10 The Spy Who Loved Me	1977

* *Later retitled* Star Wars: Episode IV – A New Hope

In the 1970s, the arrival of the two prodigies, Steven Spielberg and George Lucas, set the scene for the high adventure blockbusters, the domination of which has continued ever since. Lucas wrote and directed *Star Wars*, while Spielberg directed *Jaws* and wrote and directed *Close Encounters of the Third Kind*. *Grease* and *Saturday Night Fever* continued the musical trend that was established in the 1960s.

FILMS OF THE 1980s

FILM	YEAR
1 E.T. the Extra-Terrestrial	1982
2 Return of the Jedi*	1983
3 The Empire Strikes Back#	1980
4 Indiana Jones and the Last Crusade	1989
5 Rain Man†	1988
6 Raiders of the Lost Ark	1981
7 Batman	1989
8 Back to the Future	1985
9 Who Framed Roger Rabbit	1988
10 Top Gun	1986

* *Later retitled* Star Wars: Episode VI – Return of The Jedi

Later retitled Star Wars: Episode V – The Empire Strikes Back

† *Winner of "Best Picture" Academy Award*

▼ Glittering prize

Indiana Jones prepares to seize a priceless idol in the dramatic opening scene of *Raiders of the Lost Ark* – said to have been inspired by a 1959 Donald Duck comic strip, *The Prize of Pizarro*.

FILMS OF THE 1990s

FILM	YEAR
1 Titanic*	1997
2 Star Wars: Episode I – The Phantom Menace	1999
3 Jurassic Park	1993
4 Independence Day	1996
5 The Lion King#	1994
6 Forrest Gump*	1994
7 The Sixth Sense	1999
8 The Lost World: Jurassic Park	1997
9 Men in Black	1997
10 Armageddon	1998

* *Winner of "Best Picture" Academy Award*

Animated

Each of the Top 10 films of the 1990s has earned more than $550 million around the world, a total of more than $8.4 billion between them.

FILMS OF THE 2000s

FILM	YEAR
1 The Lord of the Rings: The Return of the King	2003
2 Harry Potter and the Philosopher's Stone	2001
3 The Lord of the Rings: The Two Towers	2002
4 Harry Potter and the Chamber of Secrets	2002
5 The Lord of the Rings: The Fellowship of the Ring	2001
6 Finding Nemo	2003
7 Spider-Man	2002
8 The Matrix Reloaded	2003
9 Pirates of the Caribbean: The Curse of the Black Pearl	2003
10 Star Wars: Episode II— Attack of the Clones	2002

As at 1 May 2004

* *Animated*

Star Actors

TOP 10 TOM CRUISE FILMS

FILM	YEAR
1 Mission: Impossible II	2000
2 Mission: Impossible	1996
3 The Last Samurai	2003
4 Rain Man	1988
5 Top Gun	1986
6 Minority Report	2002
7 Jerry Maguire	1996
8 The Firm	1993
9 A Few Good Men	1992
10 Interview with the Vampire: The Vampire Chronicles	1994

Tom Cruise (real name Thomas Cruise Mapother IV) built his career on playing a combination of handsome all-American heroes, military and light comedy roles, but has shown himself equally at home with dramatic parts, for which he has been nominated for Oscars on three occasions. Few actors have matched his commercial success: each of his Top 10 films has earned more than $220 million worldwide, making a total of more than $3.3 billion. Cruise appeared as himself in *Austin Powers in Goldmember*, which has not been included, but if it were it would be ranked 7th.

TOP 10 KEANU REEVES FILMS

FILM	YEAR
1 The Matrix Reloaded	2003
2 The Matrix	1999
3 The Matrix Revolutions	2003
4 Speed	1994
5 Something's Gotta Give	2003
6 Bram Stoker's Dracula	1992
7 The Devil's Advocate	1997
8 Parenthood	1989
9 A Walk in the Clouds	1995
10 Chain Reaction	1996

The son of an English mother and part-Hawaiian, part-Chinese father, Keanu Reeves first came to public attention in the late 1980s with films such as *Dangerous Liaisons* (1988) and *Bill & Ted's Excellent Adventure* (1989). The huge international success of *The Matrix*, which has made more than $450 million worldwide, meant that he was able to command a reputed per-picture salary of $15 million for the two big-budget 2003 sequels.

▶ **Number one**
Keanu Reeves as Neo, "The One" (of which his name is an anagram), star of *The Matrix* trilogy that heads his personal Top 10.

TOP 10 RUSSELL CROWE FILMS

FILM	YEAR
1 Gladiator*	2000
2 A Beautiful Mind	2001
3 Master and Commander: The Far Side of the World	2003
4 L.A. Confidential	1997
5 The Insider	1999
6 The Quick and the Dead	1995
7 Proof of Life	2000
8 Virtuosity	1995
9 Mystery, Alaska	1999
10 The Sum of Us	1994

* *Won Academy Award for "Best Actor"*

TOP 10 JACK NICHOLSON FILMS

FILM	YEAR
1 Batman	1989
2 As Good as It Gets*	1997
3 A Few Good Men	1992
4 Something's Gotta Give	2003
5 Anger Management	2003
6 Terms of Endearment†	1983
7 Wolf	1994
8 One Flew Over the Cuckoo's Nest*	1975
9 Mars Attacks!	1996
10 About Schmidt	2002

* *Won Academy Award for "Best Actor"*

† *Academy Award for "Best Supporting Actor"*

TOP 10 JIM CARREY FILMS

FILM	YEAR
1 Bruce Almighty	2003
2 Dr Seuss's How the Grinch Stole Christmas	2000
3 Batman Forever	1995
4 The Mask	1994
5 Liar Liar	1997
6 The Truman Show	1998
7 Dumb & Dumber	1994
8 Ace Ventura: When Nature Calls	1995
9 Me, Myself & Irene	2000
10 Ace Ventura: Pet Detective	1994

Jim Carrey is a member of an elite club of actors whose Top 10 films have each earned more than $100 million worldwide.

TOP 10 ACTORS AT THE U.S. BOX OFFICE

	ACTOR	FILMS	TOTAL US BOX OFFICE ($)*
1	Harrison Ford	33	3,230,893,589
2	Samuel L. Jackson	59	2,941,724,894
3	Tom Hanks	29	2,803,217,369
4	Eddie Murphy	28	2,403,718,530
5	Robin Williams	39	2,174,174,824
6	Mel Gibson	33	2,157,971,535
7	Tom Cruise	24	2,146,781,940
8	Gene Hackman	76	2,121,529,692
9	Bruce Willis	38	2,094,706,324
10	Bill Paxton	45	2,039,209,824

* As at 20 September 2003

TOP 10 BRAD PITT FILMS

	FILM	YEAR
1	Ocean's Eleven	2001
2	Se7en	1995
3	Interview with the Vampire: The Vampire Chronicles	1994
4	Sleepers	1996
5	Twelve Monkeys	1995
6	Legends of the Fall	1994
7	The Mexican	2001
8	The Devil's Own	1997
9	Meet Joe Black	1998
10	Seven Years in Tibet	1997

Each of Brad (William Bradley) Pitt's 10 highest-earning films have made more than $130 million in total at the world box office.

TOP 10 JOHNNY DEPP FILMS

	FILM	YEAR
1	Pirates of the Carribbean: The Curse of the Black Pearl	2003
2	Sleepy Hollow	1999
3	Platoon	1986
4	Chocolat	2000
5	Donnie Brasco	1997
6	Blow	2001
7	Edward Scissorhands	1990
8	Once Upon a Time in Mexico	2003
9	Don Juan DeMarco	1995
10	The Ninth Gate	1999

Johnny Depp's run of successes means that *Freddy's Dead: The Final Nightmare* (1991), in which his performance was credited as "Oprah Noodlemantra", has now been relegated from his Top 10.

Star Actresses

CAMERON DIAZ FILMS

	FILM	YEAR
1	There's Something About Mary	1998
2	The Mask	1994
3	My Best Friend's Wedding	1997
4	Charlie's Angels	2000
5	Charlie's Angels: Full Throttle	2003
6	Vanilla Sky	2001
7	Gangs of New York	2002
8	Any Given Sunday	1999
9	The Sweetest Thing	2002
10	Being John Malkovich	1999

Cameron Diaz's Top 10 films include several that are among the highest earning of recent years. She also provided the voice of Princess Fiona in *Shrek* (2001) – which has outearned all of them.

DREW BARRYMORE FILMS

	FILM	YEAR
1	E.T. the Extra-Terrestrial	1982
2	Batman Forever	1995
3	Charlie's Angels	2000
4	Charlie's Angels: Full Throttle	2003
5	Scream	1996
6	The Wedding Singer	1998
7	50 First Dates	2004
8	Ever After: A Cinderella Story	1998
9	Never Been Kissed	1999
10	Wayne's World 2	1993

Granddaughter of Hollywood legend John Barrymore, Drew Barrymore's first film role was in *Altered States*, when she was 5; by the time of her part in *E.T. the Extra-Terrestrial* she was aged 7. She commanded a reputed $14 million for her role in *Charlie's Angels: Full Throttle* (2003).

◀ **A fistful of dollars**
Cameron Diaz in *Charlie's Angels: Full Throttle*, one of six of her films that has each earned more than $200 million globally.

TOP 10 NICOLE KIDMAN FILMS

	FILM	YEAR
1	Batman Forever	1995
2	Moulin Rouge!	2001
3	The Others	2001
4	Days of Thunder	1990
5	Eyes Wide Shut	1999
6	Cold Mountain	2003
7	The Peacemaker	1997
8	Practical Magic	1998
9	Far and Away	1992
10	The Hours*	2002

* Won Academy Award for "Best Actress"

Honolulu-born Nicole Kidman was raised in Australia, where she acted on TV before her break into film, in which she has pursued a highly successful career: seven of her Top 10 films have earned over $100 million worldwide.

TOP 10 ACTRESSES AT THE U.S. BOX OFFICE

	ACTRESS	FILMS	TOTAL US BOX OFFICE ($)*
1	Julia Roberts	29	1,885,864,955
2	Carrie Fisher	25	1,546,860,122
3	Whoopi Goldberg	37	1,505,537,440
4	Kathy Bates	34	1,339,011,662
5	Drew Barrymore	34	1,287,426,803
6	Bonnie Hunt	16	1,271,323,335
7	Sally Field	27	1,199,668,305
8	Glenn Close	27	1,191,268,890
9	Meg Ryan	27	1,170,858,199
10	Michelle Pfeiffer	32	1,160,106,123

* As at 2 June 2003

Bonnie Hunt's inclusion, with relatively few but high-earning films, encompasses two animated blockbusters, A Bug's Life (1998) and Monsters, Inc. (2001), for which she provided voices.

TOP 10 UMA THURMAN FILMS

	FILM	YEAR
1	Batman & Robin	1997
2	Pulp Fiction	1994
3	Kill Bill: Vol. 1	2003
4	Paycheck	2003
5	The Truth About Cats and Dogs	1996
6	The Avengers	1998
7	Final Analysis	1992
8	Dangerous Liaisons	1988
9	Beautiful Girls	1996
10	Les Misérables	1998

Although featuring in her Top 10 by virtue of its global box office income, The Avengers did not earn back its substantial production budget, and may thus be regarded as a flop. Conversely, Pulp Fiction had a budget of some $8 million but made more than $200 million globally.

TOP 10 RENÉE ZELLWEGER FILMS

	FILM	YEAR
1	Chicago	2002
2	Bridget Jones's Diary	2001
3	Jerry Maguire	1996
4	Me, Myself & Irene	2000
5	Cold Mountain	2003
6	Nurse Betty	2000
7	Down with Love	2003
8	The Bachelor	1999
9	One True Thing	1998
10	Reality Bites	1994

Since her early roles in films such as The Return of the Texas Chainsaw Massacre (1994), Renée Zellweger has followed an ever-upward trajectory in her film career, gaining consecutive "Best Actress" Oscar nominations for Bridget Jones's Diary (2001) and Chicago (2002), and winning "Best Actress in a Supporting Role" for Cold Mountain (2003).

TOP 10 CATHERINE ZETA-JONES FILMS

	FILM	YEAR
1	Chicago	2002
2	The Mask of Zorro	1998
3	Entrapment	1999
4	Traffic	2000
5	The Haunting	1999
6	America's Sweethearts	2001
7	Intolerable Cruelty	2003
8	High Fidelity	2000
9	The Phantom	1996
10	Christopher Columbus: The Discovery	1992

In little over 10 years, Catherine Zeta-Jones has graduated from stage musicals and TV series The Darling Buds of May, in which she appeared as Mariette Larkin, to starring roles in major Hollywood blockbusters, six of them earning more than $100 million worldwide. She won an Oscar for "Best Actress in a Supporting Role" for her part in Chicago.

TOP 10 JULIA ROBERTS FILMS

	FILM	YEAR
1	Pretty Woman	1990
2	Ocean's Eleven	2001
3	Notting Hill	1999
4	Runaway Bride	1999
5	Hook	1991
6	My Best Friend's Wedding	1997
7	Erin Brockovich*	2000
8	The Pelican Brief	1993
9	Sleeping with the Enemy	1991
10	Stepmom	1998

* Won Academy Award for "Best Actress"

Julia Roberts is in a league of her own: all of her Top 10 films earned more than $155 million worldwide, a cumulative total just short of $3 billion. In addition to these, she has made a further four $100 million-plus films – Conspiracy Theory (1997), America's Sweethearts (2001), The Mexican (2001), and Mona Lisa Smile (2003), a record unmatched by any other actress.

Animated Films

ANIMATED FILM BUDGETS

	FILM	YEAR	BUDGET
1	The Polar Express	2004	150,000,000
2	Tarzan	1999	145,000,000
3	Treasure Planet	2002	140,000,000
4	Final Fantasy: The Spirits Within	2001	137,000,000
5	Dinosaur	2000	128,000,000
6	Monsters, Inc.	2001	115,000,000
7	Home on the Range	2004	110,000,000
8	The Emperor's New Groove	2000	100,000,000
9	The Road to El Dorado	2000	95,000,000
10	Finding Nemo	2003	94,000,000

Animated film budgets have come a long way since *Snow White and the Seven Dwarfs* (1937) established a then record of $1.49 million. The $2.6 million budget for *Pinocchio* (1940) and $2.28 million for the original *Fantasia* (1940) were the two biggest of the 1940s, while *Sleeping Beauty* (1959) at $6 million was the highest of the 1950s. *Robin Hood* (1973) had a budget of $15 million, a record that remained unbroken until 1985, when *The Black Cauldron* (1985) became the first to break the $25 million barrier. Since the 1990s, budgets of $50 million or more have become commonplace: *The Lion King* (1994) cost $79.3 million, while *Tarzan* became the first to break through the $100 million barrier.

▶ Finders keepers
With worldwide earnings of over $850 million and the "Best Animated Feature" Oscar to its credit, *Finding Nemo* has broken every record for an animated film.

NON-DISNEY ANIMATED FEATURE FILMS

	FILM	PRODUCTION COMPANY	YEAR	WORLDWIDE TOTAL GROSS ($)
1	Shrek	DreamWorks	2001	479,000,000
2	Ice Age	Fox Animation	2002	366300,000
3	Casper*	Amblin Entertainment	1995	288,000,000
4	Space Jam*	Warner Bros.	1996	225,400,000
5	Chicken Run	DreamWorks	2000	224,900,000
6	The Prince of Egypt	DreamWorks	1998	218,300,000
7	Cats & Dogs*	Warner Bros.	2001	200,400,000
8	Antz	DreamWorks	1998	181,700,000
9	Mononoke-hime (Princess Mononoke)	Dentsu Inc.	1997	159,400,000
10	Pokémon: The First Movie	4 Kids Entertainment, etc.	1999	155,700,000

* Part animated, part live action

THE 10 | LATEST OSCAR-WINNING ANIMATED FILMS*

YEAR	FILM	DIRECTOR/COUNTRY
2003	Harvie Krumpet	Adam Elliot, Australia
2002	The ChubbChubbs!	Eric Armstrong, Canada
2001	For the Birds	Ralph Eggleston, USA
2000	Father and Daughter	Michael Dudok de Wit, Netherlands
1999	The Old Man and the Sea	Aleksandr Petrov, USA
1998	Bunny	Chris Wedge, USA
1997	Geri's Game	Jan Pinkava, USA
1996	Quest	Tyron Montgomery, UK
1995	Wallace & Gromit: A Close Shave	Nick Park, UK
1994	Bob's Birthday	David Fine and Alison Snowden, UK

* In the category "Short Films (Animated)"

Although *Snow White and the Seven Dwarfs* (1937) received an honorary Academy Award, animated feature films were not eligible for an Oscar until the 2001 ceremony, when the first was won by *Shrek*, followed by *Spirited Away* in 2002 and *Finding Nemo* in 2003.

THE 10 | FIRST OSCAR-WINNING ANIMATED FILMS*

	FILM	DIRECTOR#	YEAR
1	Flowers and Trees	Walt Disney	1931/32
2	The Three Little Pigs	Walt Disney	1932/33
3	The Tortoise and the Hare	Walt Disney	1934
4	Three Orphan Kittens	Walt Disney	1935
5	The Country Cousin	Walt Disney	1936
6	The Old Mill	Walt Disney	1937
7	Ferdinand the Bull	Walt Disney	1938
8	The Ugly Duckling	Walt Disney	1939
9	The Milky Way	Rudolf Ising	1940
10	Lend a Paw	Walt Disney	1941

* In the category "Short Subjects (Cartoons)"
# All USA

Oscars were awarded in the category "Short Subjects (Cartoons)" until 1972, when it was altered to "Short Subjects (Animated Films)", and in 1976 to "Short Films (Animated)". Rudolf Ising (1903–92), the only winner here other than Walt Disney, had originally worked for Disney, but in 1934 had been hired by rivals studio MGM to form their "Happy Harmonies" animation team in competition – even down to its title – with Disney's "Silly Symphonies".

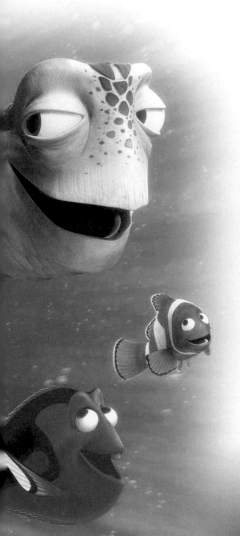

TOP 10 | WALT DISNEY ANIMATED FEATURE FILMS

	FILM	YEAR	WORLDWIDE TOTAL GROSS ($)
1	Finding Nemo	2003	797,700,000
2	The Lion King	1994	787,500,000
3	Monsters, Inc.	2001	529,000,000
4	Aladdin	1992	502,300,000
5	Toy Story 2	1999	485,700,000
6	Tarzan	1999	449,300,000
7	A Bug's Life	1998	363,300,000
8	Toy Story	1995	361,500,000
9	Dinosaur	2000	356,100,000
10	Beauty and the Beast	1991	352,900,000

Within just a month of its 30 May 2003 release, *Finding Nemo* had earned more than $256 million at the US box office, and has more than trebled that figure since its international release. Each film in this Top 10 has made in excess of $350 million worldwide, but even some of the studio's earlier productions, including *Bambi* (1942) and *Snow White and the Seven Dwarfs* (1937), are close runners-up.

TOP 10 | ANIMATED OPENING WEEKENDS IN THE UK

	FILM	UK RELEASE	OPENING WEEKEND GROSS (£)
1	Monsters, Inc.	8 Feb 2002	9,200,257
2	Toy Story 2	11 Feb 2000	7,971,539
3	Finding Nemo	10 Oct 2003	7,381,862
4	Shrek	29 June 2001	4,686,210
5	A Bug's Life	5 Feb 1999	4,204,067
6	Chicken Run	30 June 2000	3,488,755
7	Toy Story	22 Mar 1996	3,387,160
8	Tarzan	22 Oct 1999	3,055,218
9	Ice Age	22 Mar 2002	3,029,738
10	Pokémon: The First Movie	14 Apr 2000	2,833,721

Cautious release in a limited number of venues meant that some animated blockbusters of earlier years failed to make an impact on opening: *Beauty and the Beast* (1992), which became the UK's 6th highest-earning film of 1992, made only £235,499 on its opening weekend, while *Aladdin*, the No. 2 film of 1993, made just £100,706.

Film Genres

TOP 10 MUSICAL FILMS

	FILM	YEAR
1	Grease	1978
2	Chicago	2002
3	Saturday Night Fever	1977
4	8 Mile	2002
5	Moulin Rouge!	2001
6	The Sound of Music	1965
7	Evita	1996
8	The Rocky Horror Picture Show	1975
9	Staying Alive	1983
10	Mary Poppins	1964

Traditional musicals (films in which the cast actually sing) and films in which a musical soundtrack is a major component of the film are included here. The success of *Chicago* suggests that the age of the blockbuster musical film is not yet over, but in recent years films with an important musical content appear to have taken over from them – the film soundtrack album of *Titanic* is the bestselling ever, while animated films' *Beauty and the Beast*, *Aladdin*, *The Lion King*, *Pocahontas*, *The Prince of Egypt*, and *Tarzan* all won "Best Original Song" Oscars.

TOP 10 PIRATE FILMS

	FILM	YEAR
1	Pirates of the Caribbean: The Curse of the Black Pearl	2003
2	Hook	1991
3	Treasure Planet*	2002
4	Peter Pan*	1953
5	Peter Pan: Return to Never Land*	2002
6	The Goonies	1985
7	Muppet Treasure Island	1996
8	Swiss Family Robinson	1960
9	The Island	1980
10	Shipwrecked	1990

* *Animated*

After notable pirate film flops such as *Pirates* (1986) and *Cutthroat Island* (1995), it seemed that the genre was finished, but then along came *Pirates of the Caribbean: The Curse of the Black Pearl*, which has earned so much worldwide that it is ranked as one of the Top 20 films of all time.

TOP 10 VAMPIRE FILMS

	FILM	YEAR
1	Interview with the Vampire: The Vampire Chronicles	1994
2	Bram Stoker's Dracula	1992
3	Blade II	2002
4	Blade	1998
5	Underworld	2003
6	From Dusk Till Dawn	1996
7	Love at First Bite	1979
8	Wes Craven Presents Dracula 2000	2000
9	Queen of the Damned	2002
10	The Lost Boys	1987

Vampires have figured in films since the silent era. The German film *Nächte des Grauens* (1916) was the first to tackle the theme, *The Great London Mystery* (1920) the first to do so in English, and the Hungarian film *Drakula halála* (1921) the first adaptation of Bram Stoker's *Dracula*. Since then, there have been over 400 vampire films, with those in the Top 10 the highest earning worldwide.

▲ **Greased lightning**
With worldwide earnings topping $380 million, *Grease* was not only the blockbuster movie of 1978, but remains unbeaten as the biggest film musical of all time.

TOP 10 JAMES BOND FILMS

	FILM	BOND ACTOR	YEAR
1	Die Another Day	Pierce Brosnan	2002
2	The World is Not Enough	Pierce Brosnan	1999
3	GoldenEye	Pierce Brosnan	1995
4	Tomorrow Never Dies	Pierce Brosnan	1997
5	Moonraker	Roger Moore	1979
6	The Living Daylights	Timothy Dalton	1987
7	For Your Eyes Only	Roger Moore	1981
8	The Spy Who Loved Me	Roger Moore	1977
9	Octopussy	Roger Moore	1983
10	Licence to Kill	Timothy Dalton	1990

Ian Fleming wrote 12 James Bond novels, only two of which, *Moonraker* (1955) and *The Spy Who Loved Me* (1962), figure in this Top 10. After his death in 1964, *For Your Eyes Only, Octopussy, The Living Daylights*, and *GoldenEye* were developed by other writers from his short stories, while subsequent releases were written without reference to Fleming's writings. *Casino Royale* (book 1953, film 1967), featuring 56-year-old David Niven as the retired spy Sir James Bond, is an oddity in that it was presented as a comedy. This and *Never Say Never Again* (1983), effectively a remake of *Thunderball*, are not considered "official" Bond films, making the 2002 release *Die Another Day* the 20th in the canonical series.

TOP 10 DISASTER FILMS

	FILM	YEAR	DISASTER
1	Titanic	1997	Shipwreck
2	Armageddon	1998	Asteroid impact
3	Twister	1996	Tornado
4	Die Hard: With a Vengeance	1995	Terrorist city bomber
5	Apollo 13	1995	Space capsule explosion
6	Deep Impact	1998	Comet impact
7	The Perfect Storm	2000	Storm at sea
8	Die Hard 2: Die Harder	1990	Terrorists at airport
9	Outbreak	1995	Epidemic
10	Dante's Peak	1997	Volcano

Excluding science-fiction subjects (alien attacks, rampaging dinosaurs, and other fantasy themes), disasters involving blazing buildings, natural disasters such as volcanoes, earthquakes, tidal waves, train and air crashes, sinking ships, and terrorist attacks have long been a staple of Hollywood films, while latterly asteroid impact, tornadoes, exploding space capsules, and killer viruses have been added to the genre. The list comprises films that have earned an average of almost $500 million worldwide. Since the real-life tragedy of 9/11, however, Hollywood studios have been understandably reluctant to make films in this genre.

TOP 10 SCIENCE-FICTION FILMS

	FILM	YEAR
1	Star Wars: Episode I – The Phantom Menace	1999
2	Jurassic Park	1993
3	Independence Day	1996
4	Spider-Man	2002
5	Star Wars: Episode IV – A New Hope	1977
6	E.T. the Extra-Terrestrial	1982
7	The Matrix Reloaded	2003
8	Star Wars: Episode II – Attack of the Clones	2002
9	The Lost World: Jurassic Park	1997
10	Men in Black	1997

Science-fiction features more prominently than any other genre among the highest-earning films of all time – within the Top 10, the first five films are also in the all-time Top 10, and all 10 are among the 21 most successful films ever, having earned over $587 million each – a total of more than $7.6 billion at the worldwide box office. The *Star Wars* franchise represents a special achievement: as well as occupying three places in the list, the original film held its commanding place as the biggest money-making film worldwide from 1977 until 1993.

TOP 10 DOCUMENTARY FILMS

	FILM	YEAR	SUBJECT
1	Everest	1998	Exploration
2	To Fly	1976	History of flying
3	Jackass: The Movie	2002	Comedy stunts
4	Mysteries of Egypt	1998	Historical
5	Space Station 3-D	2002	International space station
6	In Search of Noah's Ark	1977	Exploration
7	Grand Canyon: The Hidden Secrets	1984	Exploration
8	The Dream is Alive	1985	Space Shuttle
9	Across the Sea of Time	1995	Historical
10	Eddie Murphy Raw	1987	Comedy

Each of these has earned more than $50 million, with *Everest* making in excess of $100 million worldwide. A number of them are IMAX (large format) films, the earnings of which have accrued from releases over periods of several years, in contrast to the more limited runs of feature films.

Radio Active

RADIO-OWNING COUNTRIES

	COUNTRY	RADIOS PER 1,000 POPULATION (2001)
1	Norway	3,324
2	Sweden	2,811
3	USA	2,117
4	Australia	1,999
5	Finland	1,624
6	UK	1,446
7	Denmark	1,400
8	Estonia	1,136
9	Canada	1,047
10	South Korea	1,034
	World average	419

Source: *World Bank*, World Development Indicators 2003

RADIO STATIONS IN THE UK

	STATION	AVERAGE WEEKLY LISTENER HOURS*
1	BBC Radio 2	172,309
2	BBC Radio 4	123,578
3	BBC Radio 1	82,911
4	BBC Radio FIVE LIVE	47,209
5	Classic FM	46,609
6	95.8 Capital FM	17,352
7	Heart 106.2 FM	15,568
8	talkSPORT (Talk Radio)	15,236
9	BBC Radio 3	14,635
10	Virgin Radio (AM)	10,665
	All UK radio	

* Total number of hours spent by all adults (over 15) listening to the station in an average week, 15 Sept to 14 Dec 2003

Source: *RAJAR*

LATEST RECIPIENTS OF THE SONY RADIO GOLD AWARD*

YEAR	RECIPIENT
2003	John Humphrys
2002	John Peel
2001	Chris Tarrant
2000	Ralph Bernard
1999	Zoë Ball
1998	Chris Evans
1997	Jimmy Young
1996	Richard Baker
1995	Alistair Cooke
1994	Kenny Everett

* *The Gold Award is presented for "Outstanding Contribution to Radio Over the Years".*

THE 10 | LATEST WINNERS OF THE SONY RADIO DRAMA AWARD

YEAR	PROGRAMME	PRODUCERS
2003	Runt	BBC Radio Drama for BBC World Service
2002	A Woman in Waiting	BBC Radio 4
2001	Alpha	BBC World Service Drama for BBC World Service
2000	Plum's War	The Fiction Factory for BBC Radio 4
1999	Bleak House	Goldhawk Universal Productions for BBC Radio 4
1998	The Trick Is to Keep Breathing	BBC Scotland for BBC Radio 4
1997	The Voluptuous Tango	BBC Radio 3
1996	Albion Tower	BBC Radio 3
1995	Mr. McNamara	BBC World Service
1994	Blue	Basilisk Production in association with Channel 4 and BBC Radio 3

THE 10 | LATEST WINNERS OF THE SONY RADIO NEWS COVERAGE AWARD*

YEAR	PROGRAMME	PRODUCERS
2003	Ethiopian Famine	BBC Radio News for Radio 4
2002	Holy Cross Girls School Dispute	BBC Radio Current Affairs for BBC Radio Ulster
2001	The Jon Gaunt Breakfast Show	BBC Three Counties Radio
2000	Late Night Live: Soho Bomb	BBC Current Affairs News for BBC Radio 5 Live
1999	Farming Today	BBC Radio 4
1998	The Death of the Princess of Wales	BBC Radio 4 and BBC Radio 5 Live
1997	Drumcree	BBC Radio Ulster
1996	Dallyn on Saturday	BBC Radio 5 Live
1995	The Magazine: IRA Ceasefire	BBC Radio 5 Live
1994	Today: The Moscow White House Siege	BBC Radio 4

* Previously the "Best Response to a News Event" award

TOP 10 | MOST POPULAR PROGRAMMES ON BBC RADIO 4

PROGRAMME
1 Today
2 The Archers
3 PM
4 Six o'clock News
5 You and Yours
6 The World at One
7 Woman's Hour
8 Daily Service
9 Afternoon Play
10 Front Row

Source: *RAJAR/BBC*

Several popular Radio 4 programmes have a long pedigree: *Today* was first broadcast on 28 October 1957, and *Woman's Hour* dates from 7 October 1946.

 Listen and learn
A century after its invention, radio maintains its value as a medium to educate, inform, and entertain.

TOP 10 | LONGEST-RUNNING PROGRAMMES ON BBC RADIO

PROGRAMME	FIRST BROADCAST
1 The Week's Good Cause	24 Jan 1926
2 The Shipping Forecast	26 Jan 1926
3 Choral Evensong	7 Oct 1926
4 Daily Service	2 Jan 1928*
5 The Week in Westminster	6 Nov 1929
6 Sunday Half Hour	14 July 1940
7 Desert Island Discs	29 Jan 1942
8 Saturday Night Theatre	3 Apr 1943
9 Composer of the Week#	2 Aug 1943
10 From Our Own Correspondent	4 Oct 1946

* *Experimental broadcast; national transmission began December 1929*

Formerly This Week's Composer

A further seven programmes that started in the 1940s are still on the air, including *Down Your Way* (first broadcast on 29 December 1946) and *Any Questions?* (first broadcast on 12 October 1948).

THE FIRST TO...

TALK RADIO PIONEER

THE WORLD'S FIRST professional radio announcer was Harold W. Arlin (1895–1986). He started work for Philadelphia radio station KDKA in January 1921. KDKA was the first station to be licensed in the USA – and at that time operated out of a tent! Arlin broadcast the first US presidential inauguration on 4 March 1921, reading Warren Harding's address on air as the new president read his script. He also provided the first-ever live commentary of a baseball game (Pirates v Phillies, 5 August 1921) and the first football match (Pitt College v University of West Virginia, 8 October 1921). Arlin's commentaries were broadcast abroad; *The Times* once describing him as having "the best known American voice in Europe".

Top TV

TOP 10 PROGRAMMES WITH THE HIGHEST TELEVISION AUDIENCES IN THE UK

	PROGRAMME	DATE	AUDIENCE
1	Royal Wedding of HRH Prince Charles to Lady Diana Spencer	29 July 1981	39,000,000
2	1970 World Cup: Brazil v England	10 June 1970	32,500,000
3 =	1966 World Cup Final: England v West Germany	30 July 1966	32,000,000
=	Cup Final Replay: Chelsea v Leeds	28 Apr 1970	32,000,000
5	Funeral of Diana, Princess of Wales	6 Sept 1997	31,000,000
6	EastEnders Christmas episode	26 Dec 1987	30,000,000
7	Morecambe and Wise Christmas Show	25 Dec 1977	28,000,000
8 =	World Heavyweight Boxing Championship: Joe Frazier v Muhammad Ali	8 Mar 1971	27,000,000
=	Dallas	22 Nov 1980	27,000,000
10	Only Fools and Horses	29 Dec 1996	24,350,000

The funeral of Princess Diana is reckoned to have been seen by 2.5 billion people worldwide, the largest audience in television history. The 22 November 1980 screening of *Dallas* was the most-watched because it was the episode that revealed who shot J.R. Ewing. The most-watched film of all time on British television is *Live and Let Die*. Although already seven years old when it was first broadcast on 20 January 1980, it attracted an audience of 23.5 million.

TOP 10 LIGHT ENTERTAINMENT PROGRAMMES ON UK TELEVISION, 2003

	PROGRAMME*	CHANNEL	DATE	AUDIENCE
1	Only Fools and Horses	BBC1	25 Dec	16,367,000
2	I'm a Celebrity – Get Me Out of Here!	ITV1	12 May	12,728,000
3	Comic Relief	BBC1	14 Mar	11,736,000
4	Pop Idol Live Final	ITV1	20 Dec	11,373,000
5	Children in Need	BBC1	21 Nov	10,485,000
6	My Family	BBC1	4 Apr	10,165,000
7	Coronation Street Christmas Crackers	ITV1	29 Dec	10,137,000
8	It'll Be Alright on the Night All Star	ITV1	31 Aug	9,792,000
9	The British Soap Awards 2003	ITV1	14 May	9,186,000
10	Ant and Dec's Saturday Night Takeaway	ITV1	8 Mar	8,984,000

* The highest-rated episode only of series shown

Source: *BARB/TNS*

▶ **TV time**
In little over 50 years, television has become such an integral part of most people's lives that the pre-TV age is little more than a distant memory.

THE FIRST TO... TRANSMIT TV PICTURES

FOLLOWING EXPERIMENTAL low-definition broadcasts, the first daily high-definition TV service was inaugurated by the BBC in London at 3.00 pm on Monday, 2 November 1936. Up to the end of that year, only 280 sets had been sold, increasing to between 20,000 and 25,000 by September 1939, when the service was put on hold during the War. The first US public service began on 30 April 1939, when an outside broadcast showed President Roosevelt opening the New York World's Fair. Roosevelt thus became the first president of the television age.

TOP 10 CABLE TELEVISION COUNTRIES

	COUNTRY	CABLE TV SUBSCRIBERS (2002) TOTAL	% OF TV HOMES
1	Bhutan	11,200	93.5
2	Netherlands	6,500,000	92.9
3	Belgium	3,880,300	90.5
4	Switzerland	2,739,000	90.4
5	Luxembourg	138,000	86.2
6	Malta	95,100	77.3
7	Israel	1,221,000	73.3
8	Taiwan	4,642,000	69.8
9	USA	73,525,200	68.9
10	Canada	7,868,300	66.7
	World	*351,097,600*	*31.8*
	UK	*3,380,000*	*14.2*

Source: *International Telecommunication Union*, World Telecommunication Development Report, *2003*

THE 10 FIRST COUNTRIES TO HAVE TELEVISION*

	COUNTRY	YEAR
1	UK	1936
2	USA	1939
3	USSR	1939
4	France	1948
5	Brazil	1950
6	Cuba	1950
7	Mexico	1950
8	Argentina	1951
9	Denmark	1951
10	Netherlands	1951

* High-definition regular public broadcasting service

After the pioneer countries listed above, Canada and Germany introduced TV in 1952. Belgium and Japan did the same in 1953 and were followed, ultimately, by almost every other country in the world.

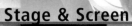

FACTUAL PROGRAMMES ON UK TELEVISION, 2003

	PROGRAMME*	CHANNEL	DATE	AUDIENCE
1	Millionaire Tonight Special	ITV1	21 Apr	16,103,000
2	Michael Jackson Tonight Special	ITV1	3 Feb	15,320,000
3	Antiques Roadshow	BBC1	9 Feb	10,227,000
4	Pompeii – The Last Day	BBC1	20 Oct	10,091,000
5	Celebrity Driving School	BBC1	28 Feb	9,529,000
6	DIY SOS	BBC1	6 Feb	8,231,000
7	Eastenders — The Return of Dirty Den	BBC1	28 Sept	8,179,000
8	Spoilt Rotten	ITV1	27 Feb	7,976,000
9	Airline	ITV1	14 Nov	7,853,000
10	Ground Force America	BBC1	21 July	7,851,000

The highest-rated episode only of series shown

Source: *BARB/TNS*

DRAMAS ON UK TELEVISION, 2003

	PROGRAMME*	CHANNEL	DATE	AUDIENCE
1	Coronation Street	ITV1	24 Feb	19,428,000
2	Eastenders	BBC1	29 Sept	16,657,000
3	Heartbeat	ITV1	12 Jan	12,841,000
4	A Touch of Frost	ITV1	3 Mar	12,236,000
5	The Royal	ITV1	19 Jan	11,959,000
6	Emmerdale	ITV1	10 Feb	11,880,000
7	Rosemary and Thyme	ITV1	31 Aug	11,076,000
8	Cold Feet	ITV1	16 Mar	10,686,000
9	Prime Suspect 6	ITV1	9 Nov	10,498,000
10	The Bill	ITV1	30 Oct	10,407,000

The highest-rated episode only of series shown

Source: *BARB/TNS*

DVD & Video

VIDEOS IN THE UK, 1994

FILM

1 Snow White and the Seven Dwarfs
2 Jurassic Park
3 Mrs. Doubtfire
4 Aladdin
5 Bambi
6 Mr. Motivator – BLT Workout
7 Police Stop!
8 Beauty and the Beast
9 The Jungle Book
10 The Very Best of Torvill and Dean

The success of Disney's programme of re-releasing its classic animated features on video is exemplified by *Snow White and the Seven Dwarfs*, which became the year's top seller as the film celebrated its 57th birthday. Both *Beauty and the Beast* and *The Jungle Book* appeared among the Top 10 for the second year in a row. *Jurassic Park* and *Mrs. Doubtfire* were the predictable big sellers among non-Disney movies.

VIDEOS IN THE UK, 1995

FILM

1 The Lion King
2 Riverdance
3 The Fox and the Hound
4 The Aristocats
5 Four Weddings and a Funeral
6 Pinocchio
7 Coronation Street – Feature-Length Special
8 Batman Forever
9 The Mask
10 Pulp Fiction

The Lion King was to overtake *Aladdin* as the highest-earning animated film of all time worldwide – until itself eventually being beaten by *Finding Nemo*. The success of its 1995 video release established it as not only the top seller of the year but also the bestselling video of the 20th century. The No. 2 title *Riverdance* took less than a year to become the biggest-selling music video ever in the UK.

VIDEOS IN THE UK, 1996

FILM

1 Toy Story
2 101 Dalmatians
3 Lord of the Dance
4 Babe
5 Pocahontas
6 Sleeping Beauty
7 Braveheart
8 The X-Files – The Unopened File
9 Wallis & Gromit – A Close Shave
10 Trainspotting

Disney's *Toy Story*, the first major computer-generated movie, was the biggest film at the 1995 US box office, but in the UK was released both in cinemas (where it became the No. 2 film of the year) and on video in 1996. Disney had four titles in the Top 10, while dancer Michael Flatley's *Lord of the Dance* repeated the success of *Riverdance*, even outselling *Babe*, the UK box office No. 1 of 1995.

VIDEOS IN THE UK, 1997

FILM

1 Independence Day
2 Star Wars – Trilogy
3 101 Dalmatians
4 Matilda
5 Evita
6 Batman and Robin
7 The English Patient
8 Trainspotting
9 Stargate
10 Jumanji

The video success of *Independence Day*, the UK's top film of 1996 by a big margin, was almost inevitable, though the comparatively expensive *Star Wars* trilogy was a less predictable hit. Including the live action *101 Dalmatians*, the previous year's No. 3 at the box office, half the Top 10 videos had been among the Top 10 at the UK box office the previous year.

VIDEOS IN THE UK, 1998

FILM

1 Titanic
2 The Full Monty
3 Lady & the Tramp
4 Men in Black
5 Hercules
6 Flubber
7 Cats
8 Peter Pan
9 Anastasia
10 The Lost World – Jurassic Park

Titanic was released in cinemas and on video in the UK in 1998 and became the top draw in both, beating British-made *The Full Monty*, the top film of 1997 and up to that time the highest-earning film ever at the UK box office.

VIDEOS IN THE UK, 1999

FILM

1 A Bug's Life
2 The Lion King 2 – Simba's Pride
3 The Matrix
4 Notting Hill
5 Saving Private Ryan
6 Mulan
7 Lock, Stock and Two Smoking Barrels
8 Antz
9 Dr. Dolittle
10 George of the Jungle

A mix of adventure and animated (especially insect-infested releases *A Bug's Life* and *Antz*) occupy this last Top 10 of the 20th century. As the new millennium dawned, DVD, launched in the UK in 1998, was becoming the format of choice for increasing numbers of consumers, outselling and progressively replacing the 20-year-old VHS format.

TOP 10 DVDs IN THE UK, 2000

FILM

1 Gladiator
2 The Matrix
3 The Sixth Sense
4 Mission: Impossible 2
5 The Mummy
6 The World is Not Enough
7 Toy Story 2
8 Deep Blue Sea
9 Chicken Run
10 The Perfect Storm

TOP 10 DVDs IN THE UK, 2001

FILM

1 Shrek
2 The Mummy Returns
3 Bridget Jones's Diary
4 Gladiator
5 Pearl Harbor
6 Crouching Tiger, Hidden Dragon
7 Snatch
8 X-Men
9 Lara Croft – Tomb Raider
10 Star Wars: Episode 1 – The Phantom Menace

TOP 10 DVDs IN THE UK, 2002

FILM

1 The Lord of the Rings: The Fellowship of the Ring
2 Harry Potter and the Philosopher's Stone
3 Star Wars: Episode 2 – Attack of the Clones
4 Monsters, Inc.
5 Ocean's Eleven
6 Spider-Man
7 The Fast and the Furious
8 Scooby Doo
9 Ice Age
10 Minority Report

The positions of *The Lord of the Rings: The Fellowship of the Ring*, and *Harry Potter and the Philosopher's Stone* at the UK 2001 box office were reversed in the DVD releases of 2002. Seven of the year's Top 10 had been screened that year as, increasingly, DVDs followed hard on the heels of cinema releases.

TOP 10 DVDs IN THE UK, 2003

FILM

1 The Lord of the Rings: The Two Towers
2 Pirates of the Caribbean: The Curse of the Black Pearl
3 Harry Potter and the Chamber of Secrets
4 The Matrix Reloaded
5 The Lord of the Rings: The Fellowship of the Ring
6 Bruce Almighty
7 Die Another Day
8 X-Men 2
9 Peter Kay – Live at the Bolton Albert Hall
10 8 Mile

Source: *British Video Association*

Once again, the top selling DVDs in many instances mirrored the box office smashes of the year, as DVD became seen as a major source of additional revenue for studios.

◄ **Pirate video**
Despite its December release, *Pirates of the Caribbean* matched its earlier box office success with massive DVD sales in the last few weeks of 2003.

COMMERCIAL
WORLD

Workers of the World

COUNTRIES WITH THE MOST WORKERS

	COUNTRY	WORKERS (2000)
1	China	766,889,000
2	India	442,156,000
3	USA	145,105,000
4	Indonesia	102,561,000
5	Brazil	79,247,000
6	Russia	78,041,000
7	Bangladesh	69,611,000
8	Japan	68,369,000
9	Pakistan	52,077,000
10	Nigeria	45,129,000
	UK	29,890,000

Source: *Food and Agriculture Organization of the United Nations*

As defined by the International Labour Organization, the "labour force" includes people between the ages of 15 and 64 who are currently employed and those who are unemployed. It excludes unpaid groups, such as students, housewives, and retired people. In practice it is difficult to count the unemployed accurately, especially in developing countries.

COUNTRIES WITH THE HIGHEST PROPORTION OF SERVICE INDUSTRY WORKERS

	COUNTRY	PERCENTAGE OF LABOUR FORCE IN SERVICES* (1998–2001) (FEMALE)	(MALE)	COUNTRY	
1	Argentina	89	71	Hong Kong (China)	1
2	= Hong Kong (China)	88	68	Columbia	2
	= Norway	88	67	Peru =	3
	= Panama	88	67	Singapore =	
5	= Canada	87	65	Argentina	5
	= Sweden	87	64	USA	6
	= UK	87	63	Australia =	7
8	= Australia	86	63	Canada =	
	= Belgium	86	63	Ecuador =	
	= France	86	63	France =	
	= Israel	86	63	Morocco =	
	= Peru	86	63	Netherlands =	
	= USA	86	61	UK	

* *Service industries include wholesale and retail trade, restaurants and hotels; transport, communications and storage; finance, insurance, real estate, and business services; and community, social, and personal services*

Source: *World Bank*, World Development Indicators 2003

TYPES OF OCCUPATION IN THE UK AT THE DEATH OF QUEEN VICTORIA

	OCCUPATION	EMPLOYEES* (1901)
1	Farmers and gardeners	2,262,454
2	Domestic service	2,199,517
3	Conveyance (road, rail, canal, etc.)	1,497,629
4	Textile manufacturing	1,462,001
5	Clothing makers and dealers	1,395,795
6	Builders	1,335,820
7	Metal workers	1,175,715
8	Miners and quarry workers	943,880
9	Food trade	865,777
10	Professional (clergymen, teachers, lawyers, etc.)	733,582

* *At the turn of the 20th century, there were 18,261,146 people in the UK labour force.*

Source: *1901 census*

▶ **Screen trade**
In many countries, jobs in service industries – from online banking to call centres – have inexorably overtaken those in "traditional" manufacturing trades.

TOP 10 | OCCUPATIONS IN THE UK

	OCCUPATIONAL SECTOR	EMPLOYEES
1	Real estate renting and business activities	3,907,000
2	Manufacturing	3,668,000
3	Health and social work	2,796,000
4	Retail (except motor and repair of personal/household goods)	2,751,000
5	Education	2,183,000
6	Hotels and restaurants	1,696,000
7	Transport, storage, and communication	1,524,000
8	Public administration and defence	1,443,000
9	Construction	1,186,000
10	Wholesale and commission trade (excluding motor)	1,160,000

The latest survey of employment in the UK indicated that there are a record 28 million in work – 10 million more than a century ago – with these the foremost sectors. Having once headed the list, agricultural workers do not even figure among the Top 10 of today. The trend to self- (3.2 million) and part-time (7.1 million) employment has also notably increased in recent years.

TOP 10 | LARGEST TRADE UNIONS IN THE UK

	TRADE UNION	MEMBERS
1	UNISON	1,272,700
2	Amicus	1,061,199
3	Transport and General Workers' Union (TGWU)	848,809
4	GMB (formerly General, Municipal Boilermakers and Allied Trades Union)	689,276
5	Royal College of Nursing (RCN)	344,192
6	National Union of Teachers (NUT)	314,174
7	Union of Shop, Distributive and Allied Workers (USDAW)	310,337
8	Public and Commercial Services Union	281,923
9	Communications Workers Union (CWU)	279,679
10	National Association of Schoolworkers and Union of Women Teachers (NASUWT)	253,584

Source: *Certification Office,* Annual Report 2002–03

There are 216 trade unions in the UK with a total membership of 7,750,990. This contrasts with 470 unions and a membership of 12,026,000 30 years ago, when there were still unions serving such bygone trades as glass bevelling and felt hat making. Some still retain descriptive names evoking highly specialized industries, among them the Sheffield Wool Shear Workers Union, which has 15 members.

TOP 10 | COUNTRIES WITH THE HIGHEST PROPORTION OF FEMALE WORKERS

	COUNTRY	LABOUR FORCE PERCENTAGE*
1	Cambodia	51.6
2	Latvia	50.5
3	Ghana	50.4
4	Russia	49.2
5	= Belarus	49.0
	= Estonia	49.0
	= Tanzania	49.0
8	= Rwanda	48.8
	= Ukraine	48.8
	= Vietnam	48.8
	World	40.7
	UK	44.2

* *Based on people aged 15–64 who are currently employed; unpaid groups are not included*

Source: *World Bank,* World Development Indicators 2003

Science & Invention

TOP 10 NOBEL PHYSICS PRIZE-WINNING COUNTRIES

	COUNTRY	PHYSICS PRIZES
1	USA	75
2	UK	22
3	Germany	21
4	France	12
5	= Netherlands	8
	= USSR	8
7	= Japan	4
	= Sweden	4
9	= Austria	3
	= Denmark	3
	= Italy	3

TOP 10 CATEGORIES OF PATENTS IN THE UK

	CATEGORY	PATENTS GRANTED (2002)
1	Telecommunications	1,028
2	Civil engineering and building	728
3	Machine elements	606
4	Measuring and testing	571
5	Transport	526
6	Calculating, counting, checking, signalling, and data-handling	485
7	Electric circuit elements and magnets	475
8	Conveying, packing, load handling, hoisting, and storing	423
9	Electric power	318
10	Furniture and household articles	316

Source: *Patent Office*

TOP 10 COUNTRIES WITH THE MOST INDUSTRIAL ROBOTS

	COUNTRY	OPERATIONAL INDUSTRIAL ROBOTS (2002)
1	Japan	350,169
2	Germany	105,217
3	USA	103,515
4	Italy	46,881
5	South Korea	44,265
6	France	24,277
7	Spain	18,352
8	UK	13,651
9	Taiwan	7,491
10	Sweden	6,846

Source: *United Nations Economic Commission for Europe*

TOP 10 COMPANIES REGISTERING THE MOST PATENTS IN THE UK

	COMPANY*	PATENTS REGISTERED (2002)
1	NEC	188
2	Motorola	149
3	Samsung Electronics	126
4	Bosch	117
5	IBM	109
6	Ericsson	100
7	Baker Hughes	91
8	Schlumberger	87
9	Rover Group	81
10	Hewlett Packard	79

* Including subsidiary companies

Source: *Patent Office*

A total of 13,562 patents were applied for and 8,690 granted in the UK in 2002. Although many of these were issued to individuals, 50 were to companies that received 20 or more patents each. The Top 10 are mainly firms engaged in telecommunications and electronics – especially computers – oil exploration, and motor vehicle manufacturing.

TOP 10 COUNTRIES REGISTERING THE MOST PATENTS

	COUNTRY	PATENTS REGISTERED (2001)
1	USA	166,038
2	Japan	121,742
3	Germany	48,207
4	France	42,963
5	UK	39,649
6	South Korea	34,675
7	Italy	25,130
8	Netherlands	20,624
9	Spain	19,709
10	China	16,296

Source: *World Intellectual Property Organization*

A patent is an exclusive licence to manufacture and exploit a unique product or process for a fixed period. This list, based on data from the World Intellectual Property Organization, provides a yardstick of each nation's technological development. A further 34,704 patents were granted by the European Patent Office, which has no national affiliation. The figures refer to the number of patents actually *granted* during 2001: in most instances this represents only a fraction of the patents applied for.

▶ **Rise of the machines**
The number of robots used in motor manufacturing and other industries worldwide was put at 769,888 in 2002, with robot/industrial worker ratios highest in Japan at 308 per 10,000, compared with 36 per 10,000 in the UK.

World Finance

TOP 10 RICHEST COUNTRIES

	COUNTRY	GDP* PER CAPITA (2001) ($)
1	Luxembourg	53,780
2	USA	34,320
3	Ireland	32,410
4	Iceland	29,990
5	Norway	29,620
6	Denmark	29,000
7	Switzerland	28,100
8	Netherlands	27,190
9	Canada	27,130
10	Austria	26,730
	World average	7,376
	UK	24,160

* Gross Domestic Product

Source: *United Nations*, Human Development Indicators, 2003

THE 10 POOREST COUNTRIES

	COUNTRY	GDP* PER CAPITA (2001) ($)
1	Sierra Leone	470
2	Tanzania	520
3	Malawi	570
4	Dem. Rep. of Congo	680
5	Burundi	690
6	Zambia	780
7	Yemen	790
8	= Ethiopia	810
	= Mali	810
10	Madagascar	830

* Gross Domestic Product

Source: *United Nations*, Human Development Indicators, 2003

TOP 10 MOST EXPENSIVE COUNTRIES IN WHICH TO BUY A BIG MAC

	COUNTRY	COST OF A BIG MAC* ($)
1	Switzerland	5.11
2	Denmark	4.72
3	Sweden	4.15
4	Euro area	3.48
5	UK	3.45
6	Turkey	2.94
7	= South Korea	2.80
	= USA	2.80
9	New Zealand	2.70
10	Peru	2.60

* As at 14 Jan 2004; of those countries surveyed

Source: The Economist/*McDonald's* price data

The Big Mac index assesses the value of countries' currencies against the standard US price of a Big Mac, by assuming that an identical amount of goods and services should cost the same in all countries.

THE 10 COUNTRIES MOST IN DEBT

	COUNTRY	TOTAL EXTERNAL DEBT (2001) ($)
1	Brazil	226,362,000,000
2	China	170,110,000,000
3	Mexico	158,290,000,000
4	Russia	152,649,000,000
5	Argentina	136,709,000,000
6	Indonesia	135,704,000,000
7	Turkey	115,118,000,000
8	South Korea	110,109,000,000
9	India	97,071,000,000
10	Thailand	67,384,000,000

Source: *World Bank*, World Development Indicators 2003

TOP 10 SOURCES OF UK GOVERNMENT INCOME

	SOURCE	ESTIMATED INCOME (2002–03) (£)
1	Income Tax	113,300,000,000
2	Social Security contributions	64,300,000,000
3	Value Added Tax	63,600,000,000
4	Corporation Tax	29,900,000,000
5	Fuel duties	22,100,000,000
6	Business rates	18,700,000,000
7	Council Tax	16,600,000,000
8	Tobacco duties	8,100,000,000
9	Stamp duties	7,600,000,000
10	Alcohol duties	7,300,000,000

TOP 10 AREAS OF UK GOVERNMENT EXPENDITURE

	DEPARTMENT	ESTIMATED EXPENDITURE (2002–03) (£)
1	Health	53,628,000,000
2	Local Government	37,396,000,000
3	Education and Skills	20,516,000,000
4	Defence	19,958,000,000
5	Scotland	15,694,000,000
6	Home Office	10,341,000,000
7	Wales	8,455,000,000
8	Work and Pensions	7,146,000,000
9	Northern Ireland Executive	5,378,000,000
10	Social Security Administration	3,962,000,000
	Total estimated expenditure	*203,711,000,000*

Source: *HM Treasury*

▼ Pillars of the establishment
The skyscrapers that dominate Manhattan Island in New York house the financial institutions that control much of the western world's trade.

Big Business

COMPANY/COUNTRY	SECTOR	REVENUE (2002) ($)
1 **Wal-Mart Stores, Inc.,** USA	Retailing	246,525,000,000
2 **General Motors Corp.,** USA	Motor vehicles	186,753,000,000
3 **Exxon Mobil,** USA	Oil, gas, fuel	182,466,000,000
4 **Royal Dutch/Shell Group,** Netherlands/UK	Oil, gas, chemicals	179,431,000,000
5 **BP plc,** UK	Oil, gas	178,721,000,000
6 **Ford Motor Co.,** USA	Motor vehicles	163,871,000,000
7 **DaimlerChrysler AG,** Germany	Motor vehicles	141,421,100,000
8 **Toyota Motor,** Japan	Motor vehicles	131,754,200,000
9 **General Electric,** USA	Electronics, electrical equipment	131,698,000,000
10 **Mitsubishi,** Japan,	Motor vehicles	109,386,100,000

Source: Fortune *magazine,* The 2003 Global 500, *21 July 2003*

Sam Walton opened his first Wal-Mart store in Rogers, Arkansas, in 1962. Since then it has undergone phenomenal growth, becoming the world's No. 1 company. On the day after Thanksgiving, 2001, it achieved the largest single day's sales in retail history, taking $1.25 billion.

COMPANY/COUNTRY	SPECIALITY	RETAIL SALES (2002*) ($)
1 **Home Depot, Inc.,** USA	Home improvement supplies	57,247,000,000
2 **Lowe's Companies, Inc.,** USA	Home improvement supplies	26,491,000,000
3 **Best Buy Co., Inc.,** USA	Consumer electronics	20,946,000,000
4 **Kingfisher plc,** UK	Home imporovement supplies	16,185,000,000
5 **The Gap, Inc.,** USA	Clothing	14,455,000,000
6 **AutoNation, Inc.,** USA	Car dealers	13,463,000,000
7 **TJX Companies, Inc.,** USA	Clothing and accessories	11,981,000,000
8 **Toys "R" Us, Inc.,** USA	Toys	11,305,000,000
9 **IKEA,** Sweden	Home furnishings	10,033,000,000
10 **Circuit City Stores, Inc.,** USA	Consumer electronics	9,954,000,000

* Financial year

Source: Stores *Magazine* Top 200 Global Retailers

▼ Retail giant
The world's largest company Wal-Mart's total sales are almost as great as the Gross National Income of Russia. Five descendants of Sam Walton, the company's founder, are each worth $20.5 billion.

 **OLDEST ESTABLISHED BUSINESSES IN THE UK**

BUSINESS	LOCATION	FOUNDED
1 **The Royal Mint**	Cardiff (formerly London)	886
2 **Kirkstall Forge** (axles, etc.)	Kirkstall, Leeds	1200
3 **The Shore Porters Society of Aberdeen**	Aberdeen	1498
4 **Cambridge University Press** (publishers)	Cambridge	1534
5 **John Brooke and Sons** (property management)	Huddersfield	1541
6 **Child's Bank** (now part of Royal Bank of Scotland)	London	1559
7 **Whitechapel Bell Foundry**	London	1570
8 **Oxford University Press** (publishers)	Oxford	1585
9 **Richard Durtnell and Sons** (builders)	Brasted, near Westerham, Kent	1591
10 **Hays at Guildford** (office services)	Guildford (formerly London)	1651

The companies listed, and certain others, belong to an elite group of tercentarians, firms that have been in business for 300 years or more. A few have even been under the control of the the same family for their entire history.

 **COMPANIES IN THE UK**

COMPANY	SECTOR	GLOBAL REVENUE (2002) ($)
1 **Royal Dutch/Shell Group***	Oil, gas, chemicals	179,431,000,000
2 **BP plc**	Oil, gas	178,721,000,000
3 **Aviva plc, financial services**	Financial services	49,533,300,000
4 **Vodafone Group plc**	Mobile telephones	46,987,000,000
5 **Unilever plc/Unilever NV#**	Food	45,636,200,000
6 **Tesco plc**	Supermarkets	40,387,000,000
7 **HSBC Holdings**	Banking	39,730,000,000
8 **Royal Bank of Scotland**	Banking	36,035,000,000
9 **Prudential plc**	Financial services	35,818,600,000
10 **GlaxoSmithKline plc**	Pharmaceuticals	31,874,200,000

* *Joint venture between UK-based Shell Transport & Trading Company and Royal Dutch Petroleum of the Netherlands*

\# *Unilever NV is Dutch*

Source: Fortune *magazine*, The 2003 Global 500, *21 July 2003*

GLOBAL RETAILERS

COMPANY	COUNTRY	RETAIL SALES (2002*) ($)
1 **Wal-Mart Stores Inc.**	USA	229,617,000,000
2 **Carrefour**	France	65,011,000,000
3 **Home Depot, Inc.**	USA	58,247,000,000
4 **Kroger Co.**	USA	51,760,000,000
5 **METRO AG**	Germany	48,349,000,000
6 **Target**	USA	42,722,000,000
7 **Ahold**	Netherlands	40,755,000,000
8 **Tesco plc**	UK	40,071,000,000
9 **Costco Wholesale Corp.**	USA	37,993,000,000
10 **Sears, Roebuck and Co.**	USA	35,698,000,000

* *Financial year*

Source: Stores *magazine* Top 200 Global Retailers

Each of the world's top 200 retailers achieve sales of $2.4 billion or more. Of them, 42.5 per cent are based in the USA, but they are responsible for 50.6 per cent of these companies' sales. Total retail sales per capita are highest in Japan at $8,522 per annum, followed by the USA at $8,347.

MOST PROFITABLE BANKS

BANK	COUNTRY	PROFITS ($)
1 **Citigroup**	USA	15,276,000,000
2 **Bank of America Corp.**	USA	9,249,200,000
3 **HSBC Holdings**	UK	6,239,700,000
4 **Wells Fargo**	USA	5,434,000,000
5 **Royal Bank of Scotland**	UK	4,619,000,000
6 **Washington Mutual**	USA	3,896,000,000
7 **Wachovia Corp.**	USA	3,579,000,000
8 **Barclays**	UK	3,351,000,000
9 **Bank One Corp.**	USA	3,295,000,000
10 **US Bancorp**	USA	3,289,000,000

Source: Fortune *magazine*, The 2003 Global 500, *21 July 2003*

The world's most profitable bank by a substantial margin, Citgroup began as the City Bank of New York, founded on 16 June 1812 with a capital of $2 million. By 1894, it had grown to be the largest bank in the USA, and in 1919 the first with assets of $1 billion. Following a series of acquisitions and mergers, it became Citigroup Inc. in 1998, and today has some 200 million customers worldwide.

Richest by Year 1994–2003

TOP 10 RICHEST PEOPLE, 1994*

	NAME/COUNTRY	SOURCE	NET WORTH ($)
1	**Bill Gates,** USA	Microsoft	12,900,000,000
2	**Warren Buffett,** USA	Berkshire Hathaway	10,700,000,000
3 =	**Hans Rausing,** Sweden	Packaging	9,000,000,000
=	**Yoshiaki Tsutsumi,** Japan	Property	9,000,000,000
5	**Paul Sacher,** Switzerland	Roche drug company	8,600,000,000
6	**Tsai Wan-lin family,** Taiwan	Insurance, financial services	8,500,000,000
7 =	**Lee Shau Kee,** Hong Kong	Property	6,500,000,000
=	**Kenneth T. Thomson,** Canada	Publishing	6,500,000,000
9	**Chung Ju-yung,** South Korea	Hyundai	6,200,000,000
10	**Li Ka-shing,** Hong Kong	Property, etc.	5,900,000,000

* Excluding royalty
Source: Forbes *magazine*, The World's Richest People, *1995*

TOP 10 RICHEST PEOPLE, 1995

	NAME/COUNTRY	SOURCE	NET WORTH ($)
1	**Bill Gates,** USA	Microsoft	18,500,000,000
2	**Warren Buffett,** USA	Berkshire Hathaway	15,000,000,000
3	**Paul Sacher, Oeri, and Hoffmann family,** Switzerland	Roche drug company	13,000,000,000
4	**Lee Shau Kee,** Hong Kong	Property	12,700,000,000
5	**Tsai Wan-lin family,** Taiwan	Insurance, financial services	12,200,000,000
6	**Kwok brothers,** Hong Kong	Property	11,200,000,000
7	**Li Ka-shing family,** Hong Kong	Property, etc.	10,600,000,000
8	**Yoshiaki Tsutsumi,** Japan	Property, transportation	9,200,000,000
9 =	**Karl and Theo Albrecht,** Germany	Retail	9,000,000,000
=	**Hans and Gad Rausing,** Sweden	Packaging	9,000,000,000

Source: Forbes *magazine*, The World's Richest People, *1996*

TOP 10 RICHEST PEOPLE, 1998

	NAME/COUNTRY	SOURCE	NET WORTH ($)
1	**Bill Gates,** USA	Microsoft	90,000,000,000
2	**Warren Buffett,** USA	Berkshire Hathaway	36,000,000,000
3	**Paul Allen,** USA	Microsoft	30,000,000,000
4	**Steve Ballmer,** USA	Microsoft	19,500,000,000
5	**Oeri, Hoffmann, and Sacher families**	Roche	17,000,000,000
6 =	**Philip F. Anschutz,** Switzerland	Qwest Communications	16,500,000,000
=	**Michael Dell,** USA	Dell Computers	16,500,000,000
8	**S. Robson Walton,** USA	Wal-Mart	15,800,000,000
9	**Prince Alwaleed Bin Talal Alsaud,** Saudi Arabia	Investments	15,000,000,000
10	**Liliane Bettencourt,** France	L'Oreal	13,900,000,000

Source: Forbes *magazine*, The World's Richest People, *1999*

TOP 10 RICHEST PEOPLE, 1999

	NAME/COUNTRY	SOURCE	NET WORTH ($)
1	**Bill Gates,** USA	Microsoft	60,000,000,000
2	**Larry Ellison,** USA	Oracle	47,000,000,000
3	**Paul Allen,** USA	Microsoft	28,000,000,000
4	**Warren Buffett,** USA	Berkshire Hathaway	25,600,000,000
5 =	**Karl and Theo Albrecht,** Germany	Retail	20,000,000,000
=	**Prince Alwaleed Bin Talal Alsaud,** Saudi Arabia	Investments	20,000,000,000
=	**S. Robson Walton,** USA	Wal-Mart	20,000,000,000
8	**Masayoshi Son,** Japan	Softbank	19,400,000,000
9	**Michael Dell,** USA	Dell Computers	19,100,000,000
10	**Kenneth T. Thomson,** Canada	Publishing	16,100,000,000

Source: Forbes *magazine*, The World's Richest People, *2000*

◄ Money, money, money
Despite fluctuations, over the past decade the level of the wealth of the world's billionaires has increased so much that the total worth of today's Top 10 is four times that of their 1994 counterparts.

TOP 10 RICHEST PEOPLE, 1996

	NAME/COUNTRY	SOURCE	NET WORTH ($)
1	Sultan Hassanal Bolkiah, Brunei	Investments	38,000,000,000
2	Bill Gates, USA	Microsoft	36,400,000,000
3	Walton family, USA	Walmart	27,600,000,000
4	Warren Buffett, USA	Berkshire Hathaway	23,200,000,000
5	King Faud Bin Abdul Aziz Alsaud, Saudi Arabia	Investments	20,000,000,000
6	Suharto, Indonesia	Self-made	16,000,000,000
7	Paul Allen, USA	Microsoft	15,314,000,000
8	Sheikh Jaber Al-ahmed Al-jaber Al-sabah, Kuwait	Investments	15,000,000,000
9	Lee Shau Kee, Hong Kong	Property	14,700,000,000
10	Oeri, Hoffmann, and Sacher families, Switzerland	Roche drug company	14,300,000,000

Source: Forbes *magazine*, The World's Richest People, *1997*

TOP 10 RICHEST PEOPLE, 1997

	NAME/COUNTRY	SOURCE	NET WORTH ($)
1	Bill Gates, USA	Microsoft	51,000,000,000
2	Walton family, USA	Walmart	48,000,000,000
3	Sultan Hassanal Bolkiah, Brunei	Investments	36,000,000,000
4	Warren Buffett, USA	Berkshire Hathaway	33,000,000,000
5	King Faud Bin Abdul Aziz Alsaud, Saudi Arabia	Investments	25,000,000,000
6	Paul Allen, USA	Microsoft	21,000,000,000
7	= Sheikh Zayed Bin Sultan Al Nahyan, UAE	Investments	15,000,000,000
	= Sheikh Jaber Al-ahmed Al-jaber Al-sabah, Kuwait	Investments	15,000,000,000
9	Kenneth T. Thomson, Canada	Publishing	14,400,000,000
10	= Forest Edward Mars Sr. & family, US	Confectionary	13,500,000,000
	= Jay A. & Robert A. Pritzker, US	Industry	13,500,000,000

Source: Forbes *magazine*, The World's Richest People, *1998*

TOP 10 RICHEST PEOPLE, 2000

	NAME/COUNTRY	SOURCE	NET WORTH ($)
1	Bill Gates, USA	Microsoft	58,700,000,000
2	Warren Buffett, USA	Berkshire Hathaway	32,300,000,000
3	Paul Allen, USA	Microsoft	30,400,000,000
4	Larry Ellison, USA	Oracle	26,000,000,000
5	Karl and Theo Albrecht, Germany	Retail	25,000,000,000
6	Prince Alwaleed Bin Talal Alsaud, Saudi Arabia	Investments	20,000,000,000
7	Jim C. Walton, USA	Wal-Mart	18,800,000,000
8	John T. Walton, USA	Wal-Mart	18,700,000,000
9	S. Robson Walton, USA	Wal-Mart	18,600,000,000
10	= Alice L. Walton, USA	Wal-Mart	18,500,000,000
	= Helen R. Walton, USA	Wal-Mart	18,500,000,000

Source: Forbes *magazine*, The World's Richest People, *2001*

TOP 10 RICHEST PEOPLE, 2001

	NAME/COUNTRY	SOURCE	NET WORTH ($)
1	Bill Gates, USA	Microsoft	52,800,000,000
2	Warren Buffett, USA	Berkshire Hathaway	35,000,000,000
3	Karl and Theo Albrecht, Germany	Retail	26,800,000,000
4	Paul Allen, USA	Microsoft	25,200,000,000
5	Larry Ellison, USA	Oracle	23,500,000,000
6	Jim C. Walton, USA	Wal-Mart	20,800,000,000
7	John T. Walton, USA	Wal-Mart	20,700,000,000
8	= Alice L. Walton, USA	Wal-Mart	20,500,000,000
	= Helen R. Walton, USA	Wal-Mart	20,500,000,000
10	S. Robson Walton, USA	Wal-Mart	20,400,000,000

Source: Forbes *magazine*, The World's Richest People, *2002*

TOP 10 RICHEST PEOPLE, 2002

	NAME/COUNTRY	SOURCE	NET WORTH ($)
1	Bill Gates, USA	Microsoft	40,700,000,000
2	Warren Buffett, USA	Berkshire Hathaway	30,500,000,000
3	Karl and Theo Albrecht, Germany	Retail	25,600,000,000
4	Paul Allen, USA	Microsoft	20,100,000,000
5	Prince Alwaleed Bin Talal Alsaud, Saudi Arabia	Investments	17,700,000,000
6	Larry Ellison, USA	Oracle	16,600,000,000
7	= Alice L. Walton, USA	Wal-Mart	16,500,000,000
	= Helen R. Walton, USA	Wal-Mart	16,500,000,000
	= Jim C. Walton, USA	Wal-Mart	16,500,000,000
	= John T. Walton, USA	Wal-Mart	16,500,000,000
	= S. Robson Walton, USA	Wal-Mart	16,500,000,000

Source: Forbes *magazine*, The World's Richest People, *2003*

TOP 10 RICHEST PEOPLE, 2003

	NAME/COUNTRY	SOURCE	NET WORTH ($)
1	Bill Gates, USA	Microsoft	46,600,000,000
2	Warren Buffett, USA	Berkshire Hathaway	42,900,000,000
3	Karl Albrecht, Germany	Retail	23,000,000,000
4	Prince Alwaleed Bin Talal Alsaud, Saudi Arabia	Investments	21,500,000,000
5	Paul Allen, USA	Microsoft	21,000,000,000
6	= Alice L. Walton, USA	Wal-Mart	20,000,000,000
	= Helen R. Walton, USA	Wal-Mart	20,000,000,000
	= Jim C. Walton, USA	Wal-Mart	20,000,000,000
	= John T. Walton, USA	Wal-Mart	20,000,000,000
	= S. Robson Walton, USA	Wal-Mart	20,000,000,000

Source: Forbes *magazine*, The World's Richest People, *2004*

Diamonds & Gold

LARGEST POLISHED GEM DIAMONDS

DIAMOND/LAST KNOWN WHEREABOUTS OR OWNER	CARATS
1 **Golden Jubilee,** King of Thailand	545.67
2 **Great Star of Africa/Cullinan I,** British Crown Jewels	530.20
3 **Incomparable/Zale,** auctioned in New York, 1988	407.48
4 **Second Star of Africa/Cullinan II,** British Crown Jewels	317.40
5 **Centenary,** privately owned	273.85
6 **Jubilee,** Paul-Louis Weiller	245.35
7 **De Beers,** sold in Geneva, 1982	234.50
8 **Red Cross,** sold in Geneva, 1973	205.07
9 **De Beers Millennium Star,** De Beers	203.04
10 **Black Star of Africa,** unknown	202.00

Source: De Beers

The De Beers Millennium Star achieved unusual celebrity on 7 November 2000 when it was on display as part of a £350-million ($500-million) collection in the Millennium Dome, Greenwich, London, and armed raiders smashed their way in intent on stealing them. They were caught by police and have since been jailed, but had they succeeded they would have been disappointed: following a tip-off, all the diamonds had been replaced by replicas.

▼ Diamonds are forever
The stuff of legends and a vital component of many world economies, diamonds have long been regarded as the ultimate symbol of durability and wealth.

MOST EXPENSIVE SINGLE DIAMONDS SOLD AT AUCTION

DIAMOND/SALE	PRICE (£)
1 **Star of the Season,** pear-shaped 100.10 carat D* IF# diamond Sotheby's, Geneva, 17 May 1995	10,548,444 (SF19,858,500)
2 **Star of Happiness,** cut cornered rectangular-cut 36 carat D IF diamond Sotheby's, Geneva, 17 Nov 1993	8,183,425 (SF17,823,500)
3 **The Mouawad Splendor,** pear-shaped 101.84 carat D IF diamond Sotheby's, Geneva, 14 Nov 1990	6,510,002 (SF15,950,000)
4 **Fancy blue emerald-cut** 20.17 carat diamond VS2# Sotheby's, New York, 18 Oct 1994	6,145,277 ($9,902,500)
5 **Eternal Light,** pear-shaped 85.91 carat D IF diamond Sotheby's, New York, 19 Apr 1988	4,793,909 ($9,130,000)
6 **Rectangular-cut fancy deep-blue** 13.49 carat diamond IF Christie's, New York, 13 Apr 1995	4,679,487 ($7,482,500)
7 **Fancy pink rectangular-cut** 19.66 carat diamond VVS2# Christie's, Geneva, 17 Nov 1994 (SF9,573,500)	4,675,017 ($7,421,318)
8 **The Jeddah Bride,** rectangular-cut 80.02 carat D IF diamond Sotheby's, New York, 24 Oct 1991	4,185,203 ($7,150,000)
9 **The Agra Diamond,** fancy light pink cushion-shaped 32.24 carat diamond VS1# Christie's, London, 20 June 1990	£4,070,000
10 **Rectangular-cut** 52.59 carat D IF diamond Christie's, New York, 20 Apr 1988	3,953,488 ($7,480,000)

* A colour grade given to a diamond for its whiteness, D being the highest grade

\# A clarity grade, which gives the relative position of a diamond on a flawless-to-imperfect scale. IF = internally flawless, VS = very slightly flawed, VVS = very, very slightly flawed. The numbers indicate the degree of the flaw.

Source: Christie's

DIAMOND PRODUCERS BY VALUE

	COUNTRY	VALUE (2003) ($)
1	**Botswana**	2,200,000,000
2	**Russia**	1,600,000,000
3	= **South Africa**	1,000,000,000
	= **Canada**	1,000,000,000
	= **Angola**	1,000,000,000
6	**Dem. Rep. of Congo**	600,000,000
7	**Namibia**	450,000,000
8	**Australia**	350,000,000
9	**Guinea**	100,000,000
10	**Sierra Leone**	100,000,000

Source: De Beers

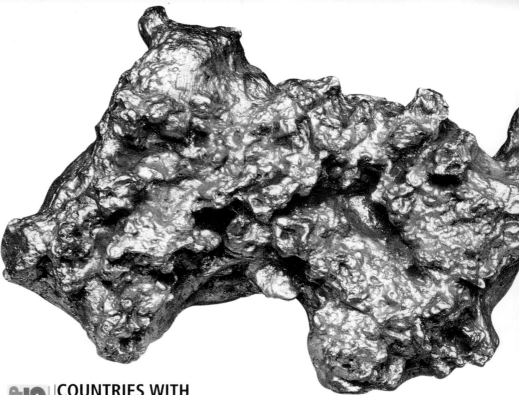

TOP 10 COUNTRIES MAKING GOLD JEWELLERY

	COUNTRY	GOLD USED IN 2002 (TONNES)
1	India	514.0
2	Italy	417.5
3	China	190.0
4	USA	154.1
5	Turkey	146.4
6	Saudi Arabia and Yemen	121.0
7	Indonesia	99.3
8	Egypt	76.0
9	Malaysia	68.7
10	South Korea	68.1
	World	2689.1
	UK	43.4

Source: *Gold Fields Mineral Services Ltd, Gold Survey 2003*

TOP 10 GOLD-PRODUCING COUNTRIES

	COUNTRY	PRODUCTION (2002) (TONNES)
1	South Africa	395.2
2	USA	298.8
3	Australia	263.7
4	China	201.9
5	Russia	180.6
6	Indonesia	157.9
7	Peru	157.3
8	Canada	148.2
9	Uzbekistan	86.6
10	Ghana	70.3
	World	2,587.0

Source: *Gold Fields Mineral Services Ltd, Gold Survey 2003*

The above figures show that output by world-leading gold producer South Africa experienced a decline for the ninth consecutive year since its 1993 all-time high of 619.5 tonnes. Australia's output also fell, after having increased dramatically over recent years: Indonesia and Peru have each escalated production tenfold, while Papua-New Guinea's production of 65.1 tonnes falls only just outside the Top 10.

TOP 10 COUNTRIES WITH THE MOST GOLD

	COUNTRY	GOLD RESERVES* (TROY OUNCES)	(TONNES)
1	USA	261,561,245	8,135.4
2	Germany	110,583,365	3,439.5
3	France	97,250,345	3,024.8
4	Italy	78,827,822	2,451.8
5	Switzerland	53,569,996	1,666.2
6	Netherlands	25,736,876	800.5
7	Japan	24,601,945	765.2
8	China	19,300,245	600.3
9	Spain	16,827,833	523.4
10	Portugal	16,628,497	517.2

* As at October 2003

Source: *World Gold Council*

Gold reserves are the government holdings of gold in each country – which are often far greater than the gold owned by private individuals. In the days of the "Gold Standard", this provided a tangible measure of a country's wealth, guaranteeing the convertibility of its currency, and determined such factors as exchange rates. Though less significant today, gold reserves remain a component in calculating a country's international reserves, alongside its holdings of foreign exchange and

▲ **Glittering prize**
Discovered in Moliagul, Australia, in 1869, the almost pure gold 70.92-kg (156-lb) "Welcome Stranger" nugget was the largest ever found.

THE DEEPEST GOLDMINE

FOR THE PAST 30 YEARS, the Western Deep Levels goldmine, South Africa, has been the deepest in the world. It had reached 3,581 m (11,749 ft) by 1977 and is being extended to 3,841 m (12,600 ft) by the end of 2004, with an ultimate target depth of 4,100 m (13,451 ft). Such depths pose great engineering problems: they require very long lift shafts, but the longer they are, the heavier are the ropes required; they currently weigh 70 tonnes. The temperature this far below the earth's surface is 55° C (131° F), which means that the air has to be refrigerated to make it possible for miners to work there.

IT'S A FACT

Brands & Advertising

TOP 10 MOST VALUABLE GLOBAL BRANDS

	BRAND NAME*	INDUSTRY	BRAND VALUE (2003) ($)
1	Coca-Cola	Beverages	70,450,000,000
2	Microsoft	Technology	65,170,000,000
3	IBM	Technology	51,770,000,000
4	General Electric	Diversified	42,340,000,000
5	Intel	Technology	31,110,000,000
6	Nokia, Finland	Technology	29,440,000,000
7	Disney	Leisure	28,040,000,000
8	McDonald's	Food retail	24,700,000,000
9	Marlboro	Tobacco	22,180,000,000
10	Mercedes, Germany	Automobiles	21,370,000,000

* US-owned unless otherwise stated

Source: *Interbrand/BusinessWeek*

Brand consultants Interbrand use a method of estimating value that takes account of the profitability of individual brands within a business (rather than the companies that own them), as well as such factors as their potential for growth. Well over half of the 75 most valuable global brands surveyed by Interbrand are US-owned, with Europe accounting for another 30 per cent.

▶ **Sign of the Times**
Formerly Longacre Square, New York's Times Square was renamed 100 years ago, becoming the hub of the city's nightlife and its most garish display of advertising.

TOP 10 TYPES OF ADVERTISING IN THE UK

	TYPE OF ADVERTISING	ADVERTISING SPEND (2002) (£)
1	Television	4,326,000,000
2	Regional newspapers	2,870,000,000
3	Direct mail	2,378,000,000
4	National newspapers	1,930,000,000
5	Business and professional journals	1,088,000,000
6	Directories	990,000,000
7	Outdoor and transport	802,000,000
8	Consumer magazines	785,000,000
9	Radio	545,000,000
10	Internet	197,000,000
	UK total	16,734,000,000

Source: *The Advertising Association*

TOP 10 GLOBAL MARKETERS

	COMPANY/BASE	MEASURED MEDIA* SPENDING (2002) ($)
1	Procter & Gamble Company, USA	4,479,000,000
2	Unilever, Netherlands/UK	3,315,000,000
3	General Motors Corporation, USA	3,218,000,000
4	Toyota Motor Corporation, Japan	2,405,000,000
5	Ford Motor Company, USA	2,387,000,000
6	Time Warner, USA	2,349,000,000
7	DaimlerChrysler, Germany/USA	1,800,000,000
8	L'Oréal, France	1,683,000,000
9	Nestlé, Switzerland	1,547,000,000
10	Sony Corporation, Japan	1,513,000,000

* Includes magazines, newspapers, outdoor, television, radio, Internet, and Yellow Pages

Source: *Ad Age Global*

TOP 10 INTERNET ADVERTISERS ACCESSED IN THE UK

	ADVERTISER	IMPRESSIONS*
1	TRUSTe	983,982,000
2	Amazon	156,577,000
3	MSN	151,060,000
4	Capital One	119,208,000
5	Sky.com	115,047,000
6	The Personal Loan Express	97,288,000
7	MBNA Europe Bank	91,940,000
8	eBay	87,967,000
9	Yahoo!	85,192,000
10	VistaPrint.com	83,715,000

*Number of times the advertising banner has been
loaded within a browser during October 2003*

Source: *Nielsen/NetRatings*

TOP 10 COUNTRIES IN WHICH COCA-COLA IS THE TOP COLA BRAND

	COUNTRY	PERCENTAGE OF TOTAL STANDARD COLA MARKET
1	Morocco	98.2
2	Indonesia	90.5
3	France	88.6
4	Australia	86.6
5	Chile	85.0
6	Greece	84.7
7	Bulgaria	84.0
8	Switzerland	83.5
9	= Brazil	83.2
	= South Africa	83.2
	UK	50.7

Source: *Euromonitor*

TOP 10 COUNTRIES THAT SPEND THE MOST ON ADVERTISING

	COUNTRY	EST. ADVERTISING SPEND (2003) ($)
1	USA	144,000,000,000
2	Japan	36,000,000,000
3	Germany	16,000,000,000
4	UK	15,000,000,000
5	China	10,000,000,000
6	France	9,000,000,000
7	Italy	7,000,000,000
8	South Korea	6,000,000,000
9	= Brazil	5,000,000,000
	= Canada	5,000,000,000

Source: *Zenith Optimedia*

Food Favourites

TOP 10 BREAD CONSUMERS

	COUNTRY	CONSUMPTION PER CAPITA (2003) (KG)	(LB	OZ)
1	Turkey	178.6	393	7
2	Bulgaria	155.1	341	9
3	Egypt	146.1	322	1
4	Slovakia	145.2	320	1
5	Saudi Arabia	127.8	281	8
6	Romania	105.0	231	5
7	Norway	97.6	215	2
8	Chile	92.4	203	7
9	Poland	87.6	193	1
10	Belgium	83.2	183	4
	World average	*17.9*	*39*	*5*
	UK	*43.2*	*95*	*2*

Source: *Euromonitor*

◀ Daily bread
Middle Eastern and Eastern European countries lead in bread consumption, with the average Turkish citizen eating three times his own weight in bread every year.

TOP 10 RICE CONSUMERS

	COUNTRY	CONSUMPTION PER CAPITA* (2001) (KG)	(LB	OZ)
1	Myanmar	295.4	651	3
2	Laos	258.7	570	5
3	Vietnam	250.6	552	7
4	Bangladesh	232.8	513	3
5	Cambodia	223.0	491	10
6	Indonesia	222.9	491	6
7	Thailand	163.3	360	0
8	Guinea-Bissau	156.9	345	14
9	Philippines	152.7	336	10
10	Nepal	149.7	330	0
	World average	*84.8*	*186*	*15*
	UK	*4.1*	*9*	*0*

* Paddy equivalent

Source: *Food and Agricultural Organization of the United Nations*

TOP 10 FISH CONSUMERS

	COUNTRY	CONSUMPTION PER CAPITA* (2001) (KG)	(LB	OZ)
1	Maldives	198.5	437	9
2	Iceland	90.1	198	10
3	Portugal	76.1	167	12
4	Kiribati	75.4	166	3
5	Japan	63.8	140	10
6	Guyana	57.3	126	5
7 =	Malaysia	56.8	125	3
=	Seychelles	56.8	125	3
9	Antigua and Barbuda	54.9	121	0
10 =	Norway	51.0	112	6
=	South Korea	51.0	112	6
	World average	*15.8*	*34*	*13*
	UK	*21.6*	*47*	*9*

* Marine only

Source: *Food and Agriculture Organization of the United Nations*

The majority of the fish consumed in the world comes from the sea. The average annual consumption of freshwater fish is 4.4 kg (9 lb 11 oz).

TOP 10 MEAT CONSUMERS

	COUNTRY	CONSUMPTION PER CAPITA (2001) (KG)	(LB	OZ)
1	USA	121.5	267	13
2	Spain	118.1	260	5
3	Denmark	116.8	257	7
4 =	Australia	110.1	242	11
=	Austria	110.1	242	11
6 =	Bahamas	104.0	229	4
=	Cyprus	104.0	229	4
8	New Zealand	103.9	229	0
9	France	102.4	225	12
10	Canada	99.8	220	0
	World average	*38.1*	*83*	*15*
	UK	*77.8*	*171*	*8*

Source: *Food and Agriculture Organization of the United Nations*

FOOD ITEMS CONSUMED IN THE UK BY WEIGHT

ITEM	AVERAGE WEEKLY CONSUMPTION PER CAPITA (KG)	(LB	OZ)
1 Milk and cream	2.012	4	7
2 Meat and meat products	1.032	2	4
3 Bread	0.769	1	11
4 Fresh fruit	0.750	1	10
5 Fresh vegetables (excluding potatoes)	0.732	1	9
6 Fresh potatoes	0.645	1	6
7 Processed vegetables (including processed potatoes)	0.620	1	5
8 Flour and other cereals or cereal products (excluding bread)	0.557	1	3
9 Processed fruit and nuts	0.404	0	14
10 Cakes and biscuits	0.329	0	11

Source: *Department of Environment, Food and Rural Affairs (DEFRA)*, Expenditure and Food Survey 2001–2002

BAKED BEAN CONSUMERS

	COUNTRY	EST. CONSUMPTION PER CAPITA (2004) (KG)	(LB	OZ)
1	Ireland	5.6	12	5
2	UK	4.8	10	9
3	New Zealand	2.3	5	1
4	USA	2.0	4	6
5	Australia	1.9	4	3
6 =	France	1.6	3	8
=	Saudi Arabia	1.6	3	8
8	Switzerland	1.5	3	5
9	Ukraine	1.3	2	13
10 =	Canada	1.2	2	10
=	Mexico	1.2	2	10

Source: *Euromonitor*

Originating among American colonists, baked beans have become a popular and easy meal the world over, with Ireland and the UK the foremost consumers.

VEGETABLE CONSUMERS

	COUNTRY	CONSUMPTION PER CAPITA (2001) (KG)	(LB	OZ)
1	Greece	271.9	599	6
2	United Arab Emirates	257.0	566	9
3	Lebanon	240.1	529	5
4	China	239.4	527	12
5	Libya	237.5	523	9
6	South Korea	229.5	505	15
7	Turkey	228.9	504	10
8	Israel	221.1	487	7
9	Albania	216.7	477	11
10	Kuwait	215.5	475	1
	World average	*111.6*	*246*	*0*
	UK	89.5	197	5

Source: *Food and Agricultural Organization of the United Nations*

▶ **Fruit and veg**
Year-round availability, rising prosperity, and the recommendation that we should eat five portions of fruit or vegetables per day have resulted in their increased consumption.

Sweet Success

TOP 10 SUGAR CONSUMERS

	COUNTRY	CONSUMPTION PER CAPITA* (2001) (KG)	(LB	OZ)
1	United Arab Emirates	250.87	553	1
2	St. Kitts and Nevis	176.97	390	2
3	Israel	160.56	353	15
4	Swaziland	133.35	293	15
5	St. Vincent and the Grenadines	58.54	129	0
6	Cuba	58.13	128	2
7	Trinidad and Tobago	56.93	125	8
8	Austria	55.32	121	15
9	New Zealand	55.01	121	4
10	Barbados	54.84	120	14
	UK	34.32	75	10

* Refined equivalent

Source: Food and Agriculture Organization of the United Nations

TOP 10 CHOCOLATE CONFECTIONERY CONSUMERS

	COUNTRY	CONSUMPTION PER CAPITA (2003*) (KG)	(LB	OZ)
1	Switzerland	11.4	25	0
2	UK	9.5	20	15
3 =	Belgium	8.7	19	2
=	Germany	8.7	19	2
5	Ireland	8.1	17	13
6	Denmark	7.9	17	6
7	USA	6.3	13	14
8	Norway	6.1	13	7
9	Austria	5.6	12	6
10	Poland	5.4	11	14

* Figures are provisional

Source: Euromonitor

TOP 10 SUGAR CONFECTIONERY CONSUMERS

	COUNTRY	CONSUMPTION PER CAPITA (2003*) (KG)	(LB	OZ)
1	Denmark	8.9	19	9
2 =	Finland	6.4	14	2
=	Netherlands	6.4	14	2
4	Sweden	6.0	13	4
5 =	Norway	5.2	11	7
=	Russia	5.2	11	7
7 =	UK	4.3	9	7
=	Ukraine	4.3	9	7
9	Germany	4.1	9	0
10	USA	4.0	8	13

* Figures are provisional

Source: Euromonitor

TOP 10 SWEET BRANDS IN THE UK

	BRAND/ MANUFACTURER	PERCENTAGE OF MARKET SHARE (2002)
1 =	Cadbury's Dairy Milk, Cadbury Trebor Bassett Ltd.	3.2
=	Mars Bar, Masterfoods UK Ltd.	3.2
3	Galaxy, Masterfoods UK Ltd.	2.9
4	Wrigley's Extra, The Wrigley Company Ltd.	2.4
5	Maltesers, Masterfoods UK Ltd.	2.1
6	KitKat, Nestlé UK Ltd.	2.0
7	Terry's, Kraft Foods UK Ltd.	1.9
8	Snickers, Masterfoods UK Ltd.	1.7
9 =	Aero, Nestlé UK Ltd.	1.6
=	Trebor, Cadbury Trebor Bassett Ltd.	1.6

Source: Euromonitor

The leading brands in the list achieve UK sales in excess of £100 million a year, and even those at the bottom an estimated £50 million or more. Celebrating its 70th birthday in 2005, KitKat was launched as Rowntree's Chocolate Crisp, changing its name in 1937 and becoming the company's bestselling confectionery product.

THE 10 FIRST MARS PRODUCTS

	PRODUCT	YEAR INTRODUCED
1 =	Milky Way bar	1923
=	Snickers bar (non-chocolate)	1923
3	Snickers bar (chocolate)	1930
4	3 Musketeers bar	1932
5	Maltesers	1937
6	Kitekat (catfood; now Whiskas)	1939
7	Mars almond bar	1940
8	M&M's plain chocolate candies	1941
9	Uncle Ben's converted brand rice	1942
10 =	M&M's peanut chocolate candies	1954
=	Pal (dogfood)	1954

American candy manufacturer Franklin C. Mars established his first business in Tacoma, Washington, in 1911, and formed the Mar-O-Bar company in Minneapolis (later moving it to Chicago) in 1922, with the first of its internationally known products, the Milky Way bar. The founder's son Forrest E. Mars set up in the UK in 1932, merging the firm with its American counterpart in 1964. Confusingly, outside the USA, the Milky Way bar is known as a Mars Bar, while in the UK a Milky Way is a different product.

TOP 10 OLDEST-ESTABLISHED BRITISH CHOCOLATE PRODUCTS

	PRODUCT	YEAR INTRODUCED
1	Fry's Chocolate Cream	1853
2	Fry's Easter Egg	1873
3	Cadbury's Easter Egg	1875
4	Cadbury's Chocolate Drops*	1904
5	Cadbury's Dairy Milk	1905
6	Cadbury's Bournville	1908
7	Fry's Turkish Delight	1915
8 =	Cadbury's Milk Tray	1920
=	Cadbury's Milk Chocolate Flake	1920
10	Cadbury's Creme Egg#	1923

* Now Chocolate Buttons

Original version

The founders of Fry's and Cadbury's – and Rowntree's too – were all Quakers, whose desire to promote the drinking of chocolate as a healthy alternative to alcohol led to their setting up pioneering chocolate businesses, Joseph Fry in 1761 (or possibly earlier) and John Cadbury from 1824.

TOP 10 | ICE CREAM CONSUMERS

	COUNTRY	CONSUMPTION PER CAPITA (2003) (LITRES)	(PINTS)
1	**Australia**	20.9	36.8
2	**New Zealand**	15.8	27.8
3	**USA**	15.6	27.5
4	**Sweden**	13.5	23.8
5	**Canada**	12.6	22.2
6	**Ireland**	11.7	20.6
7	**Norway**	11.5	20.2
8	**Finland**	11.0	19.4
9	**Denmark**	9.6	16.9
10	**Germany**	9.5	16.7
	UK	*8.6*	*15.1*

Source: *Euromonitor*

◄ **Sundae best**
Total global sales of ice cream in 2003 were estimated at 15,318,682,900 litres, equal to an average of 2.4 litres (4.2 pints) for everyone on the planet.

CONE CONTROVERSY!

THE IDENTITY OF THE INVENTOR of the ice cream cone is disputed. Cones were sold at the St. Louis World's Fair in 1904. There, Ernest A. Hamwi, a Syrian pastry maker, was selling a waffle called a zalabia. When a nearby ice cream vendor, Charles Menches, ran out of bowls, he used Hamwi's zalabia to serve his product. However, New York ice cream maker Italo Marchiony, who was also at the Fair, had been granted a patent for a mould to make cones the previous year, and claimed to have been selling ice cream cones since 1896.

THE FIRST TO...

Beverage Report

▼ A heady brew

With the honourable exception of Australia, the world's top beer drinkers are all Europeans with a long tradition of brewing.

BEER DRINKERS

	COUNTRY	CONSUMPTION PER CAPITA (2001) (LITRES)	(PINTS)
1	Czech Republic	158.1	278.2
2	Ireland	150.8	265.4
3	Germany	123.1	216.6
4	Austria	106.9	188.1
5	Luxembourg	100.9	177.6
6	Denmark	98.6	173.5
7	Belgium	98.0	172.5
8	UK	97.1	170.9
9	Australia	93.0	163.7
10	Slovak Republic	86.4	152.0*

* Estimated from beer production data due to lack of consumption data

Source: *Commission for Distilled Spirits*

Despite being the world's leading beer producer, the USA is ranked 11th in terms of consumption. While no African countries appear above, many Africans do drink beer – usually brews that are made and sold locally, and hence excluded from national statistics.

TEA DRINKERS

	COUNTRY	ANNUAL CONSUMPTION PER CAPITA* (KG)	(LB	OZ)	(CUPS#)
1	Iraq	2.77	6	2	1,219
2	Ireland	2.76	6	1	1,214
3	Libya	2.61	5	7	1,148
4	Qatar	2.29	5	1	1,008
5	UK	2.26	4	15	994
6	Turkey	2.01	4	7	884
7	Kuwait	1.97	4	5	867
8	Iran	1.48	3	4	651
9	= Afghanistan	1.39	3	1	612
	= Morocco	1.39	3	1	612

* 2000–2002

 # Based on 440 cups per kg (2 lb 3 oz)

Source: *International Tea Committee Ltd., London*

Despite the UK's traditional passion for tea, over recent years its consumption has consistently lagged behind that of Ireland. Over the same period, Qatar's tea consumption has dropped from its former world record of 3.97 kg (8 lb 12 oz/1,747 cups) per head.

CHAMPAGNE IMPORTERS

	COUNTRY	BOTTLES IMPORTED (2003)
1	UK	34,465,159
2	USA	18,957,031
3	Germany	11,053,665
4	Belgium	9,143,810
5	Italy	8,506,287
6	Switzerland	5,596,549
7	Japan	5,013,705
8	Netherlands	2,575,838
9	Spain	2,158,056
10	Australia	1,659,441

Source: *Comité Interprofessionnel du Vin de Champagne (CIVC)*

COFFEE DRINKERS

	COUNTRY	CONSUMPTION PER CAPITA (2002) (KG)	(LB	OZ)	(CUPS*)
1	Finland	11.24	24	12	1,686
2	Denmark	9.16	20	3	1,374
3	Norway	9.15	20	2	1,372
4	Belgium and Luxembourg	9.03	19	14	1,354
5	Sweden	8.33	18	6	1,249
6	Austria	7.10	15	10	1,065
7	Switzerland	6.78	14	15	1,017
8	Germany	6.59	14	8	988
9	Netherlands	6.10	13	7	915
10	France	5.54	12	3	831
	UK	2.17	4	12	325

* Based on 150 cups per kg (2 lb 3 oz)

Source: *International Coffee Organization*

TOP 10 BOTTLED WATER DRINKERS

	COUNTRY	CONSUMPTION PER CAPITA (2003) (LITRES)	(PINTS)
1	Italy	177.1	311.7
2	Spain	156.7	275.8
3	France	152.5	268.4
4	Mexico	152.1	267.7
5	Belgium	130.1	229.0
6	Germany	118.6	208.7
7	Switzerland	112.0	197.1
8	Austria	98.0	172.4
9	Portugal	96.8	170.3
10	Argentina	81.4	143.2
	World average	22.9	40.3
	UK	28.7	50.5

Source: *Euromonitor*

Worldwide consumption of bottled mineral water has more than doubled in the past decade, hitting a 2003 total of 144.5 billion litres.

TOP 10 CARBONATED SOFT DRINK CONSUMERS

	COUNTRY	CONSUMPTION PER CAPITA (2003) (LITRES)	(PINTS)
1	USA	195.8	344.5
2	Mexico	126.0	222.0
3	Norway	122.0	215.0
4	Ireland	121.4	214.0
5	Canada	117.1	206.1
6	Belgium	109.3	192.3
7	Australia	103.2	182.0
8	Netherlands	99.8	175.6
9	Chile	99.7	175.4
10	Spain	98.3	173.0
	World average	28.5	50.1
	UK	88.1	155.0

Source: *Euromonitor*

In 2003 the worldwide consumption of soft drinks was 179.4 billion litres – equivalent to almost 60,000 Olympic swimming pools full!

▼ **Soft sell**
Invented over 200 years ago, fizzy drinks became a major global industry in the 20th century, now worth over £125 billion ($200 billion) a year.

TOP 10 WINE PRODUCERS

	COUNTRY	PRODUCTION (1999) (LITRES)	(PINTS)
1	France	6,093,500,000	10,723,000,000
2	Italy	5,811,000,000	10,225,900,000
3	Spain	3,680,200,000	6,476,200,000
4	USA	2,069,100,000	3,641,100,000
5	Argentina	1,588,800,000	2,795,900,000
6	Germany	1,224,400,000	2,154,600,000
7	Australia	851,100,000	1,497,700,000
8	South Africa	796,800,000	1,402,100,000
9	Portugal	780,600,000	1,373,600,000
10	Romania	650,400,000	1,144,500,000
	UK	1,400,000	2,463,600

Source: *Commission for Distilled Spirits*

The rise of New World and Southern Hemisphere wine-producing countries is the most notable development in recent years, ending the centuries-old domination of the winemaking industry by the vineyards of France, Italy, and Spain.

Post & Phone

▼ **Mail drop**
Since the introduction of e-mail, traditional "snail mail" has steadily declined, but the world still sends over 424 billion domestic and 6.7 billion international letters every year.

TOP 10 OLDEST PILLAR BOXES IN DAILY USE IN THE UK

	LOCATION	DATE
1	**Union Street,** St. Peter Port, Guernsey	1853
2	**Barnes Cross,** Bishops Caundle, Dorset	1853
3	**Mount Pleasant/College Road,** Framlingham, Suffolk	1856
4	**Double Street,** Framlingham, Suffolk	1856
5	**Market Place,** Banbury, Oxfordshire	1856
6	**Mudeford Green,** Christchurch, Dorset	1856
7	**Cornwallis/Victoria Road,** Milford-on-Sea, Hampshire	1856
8	**Eastgate,** Warwick	1856
9	**Westgate,** Warwick	1856
10	**High Street,** Eton, Berkshire	1856

The Penny Post was introduced in 1840, and soon afterwards the public pressed for roadside posting boxes, which already existed in Belgium and France. In 1851, Anthony Trollope (best known as the author of *Barchester Towers* and other novels, but at this time a Post Office Surveyor's Clerk) first suggested their use in St Helier, Jersey. They were set up in four locations there on 23 November 1852. No trace of them survives – though it is known that, as today, they were painted red. The following year, on 8 February 1853, one was erected in St. Peter Port, Guernsey – the oldest still in use in the United Kingdom – to be followed by others, of which those in this list are the earliest survivors. A somewhat later model, the hexagonal "Penfold" pillar box dating from 1859–66, is still found in surprising numbers: over 40 are in daily use in London alone.

TOP 10 COUNTRIES WITH THE MOST TELEPHONES

	COUNTRY	TELEPHONE LINES (2002)
1	China	214,420,000
2	USA	186,232,300
3	Japan	71,149,000
4	Germany	53,720,000
5	India	41,420,000
6	Brazil	38,810,000
7	Russia	35,500,000
8	UK	34,898,000
9	France	33,928,700
10	Italy	27,142,000

Source: *International Telecommunication Union*, World Telecommunication Development Report, *2003*

It is estimated that there are some 1,091,575,700 telephone lines in use in the world, of which 329,462,500 are in Europe, 293,448,800 in North and South America, 433,647,800 in Asia, 22,356,500 in Africa, and 12,660,100 in Oceania.

TOP 10 COUNTRIES WITH THE HIGHEST RATIO OF MOBILE PHONE USERS

	COUNTRY	SUBSCRIBERS (2002)	MOBILE PHONES PER 100 INHABITANTS (2002)
1	Luxembourg	473,000	106.50
2	Taiwan	23,905,000	106.15
3	Israel	6,334,000	95.45
4	Hong Kong	6,396,000	94.25
5	Italy	53,003,000	93.87
6	Iceland	261,000	90.60
7	Sweden	7,949,999	88.89
8	Finland	4,517,000	86.74
9	Greece	9,314,000	84.54
10	Norway	3,840,000	84.36
	UK	*49,677,000*	*84.07*

Source: *International Telecommunication Union*, World Telecommunication Development Report, *2003*

The past 20 years has seen a revolution in the use of mobile phones the world over, of which these are the leading countries – with some having more subscribers than inhabitants. As well as the high levels of uptake in these countries, relatively large numbers are encountered as a proportion of total subscribers in certain developing countries, where mobile phones are preferred over often antiquated and unreliable main line networks.

TOP 10 COUNTRIES WITH THE MOST PUBLIC TELEPHONES

	COUNTRY	PUBLIC TELEPHONES PER 1,000 PEOPLE (2002*)
1	South Korea	10.83
2	United Arab Emirates	8.11
3	Brazil	7.87
4	China	7.67
5	Mexico	7.05
6	Malaysia	6.84
7	Taiwan	5.99
8	Greece	5.72
9	Argentina	5.64
10	Japan	5.63
	UK	*2.00*

* Or latest year for which data available

Source: *International Telecommunication Union*, World Telecommunication Development Report, *2003*

World Wide Web

TOP 10 ONLINE LANGUAGES

	LANGUAGE	INTERNET ACCESS*
1	English	280,000,000
2	Chinese	170,000,000
3	Japanese	88,000,000
4	Spanish	70,000,000
5	German	62,000,000
6	Korean	43,000,000
7	French	41,000,000
8	Portuguese	32,000,000
9	Italian	30,000,000
10	Russian	23,000,000
	World total	940,000,000

* Online population estimate for 2004

Source: Global Reach

TOP 10 MOST SEARCHED TERMS OF ALL TIME ON LYCOS

	TERM	WEEKS ON LIST*
1	= Britney Spears	235
	= Dragonball	235
	= Jennifer Lopez	235
	= Las Vegas	235
	= Pamela Anderson	235
	= WWF	235
7	= Final Fantasy	232
	= The Bible	232
9	Tattoos	199
10	Harry Potter	188

* Continuous runs only; as at 14 Feb 2004

Source: Lycos 50

TOP 10 COUNTRIES WITH THE MOST INTERNET USERS

	COUNTRY	ESTIMATED NO. OF INTERNET USERS (2002)
1	USA	182,130,000
2	Japan	56,000,000
3	China	45,800,000
4	Germany	44,130,000
5	UK	34,300,000
6	South Korea	25,600,000
7	France	21,760,000
8	Italy	19,250,000
9	Russia	18,000,000
10	Canada	16,840,000
	World total	580,000,000

Source: CyberAtlas/Nielsen/NetRatings/CIA World Factbook

TOP 10 MOST POPULAR SEARCH ENGINES

	SEARCH ENGINE	PERCENTAGE OF VISITS*
1	Google	13.0
2	Yahoo! Search	10.1
3	MSN Search	7.4
4	Excite	1.3
5	Netscape	1.2
6	iWon	1.1
7	= Ask Jeeves	1.0
	= Google Image Search	0.7
9	Yahoo! Directory	0.6
10	Netscape White Pages	0.5

* Share of visits to both search and portal websties during September 2003; USA traffic only

Source: Hitwise.com/SearchEngineWatch.com

◀ **Cyber café**
The arrival of Internet cafés in 1994 heralded a new era of communications and information gathering for people on the move, those lacking personal Internet access, or as a social activity.

TOP 10 INTERNET FRAUDS

	CATEGORY	PERCENTAGE ALL COMPLAINTS (2003)
1	Online auctions	89
2	General merchandise	5
3	Nigerian money offers	2
4	= Information/adult services	1
	Internet access services	1
6	= Computer equipment/software	0.2
	= Fake cheques	0.2
	= Lotteries	0.2
	= Work-at-home plans	0.2
10	Advance-fee loans	0.1

Source: National Fraud Information Center, National Consumers League

The average loss in the USA to Internet fraud in 2003 per victim was $527. The Nigerian money offer, also known as "Advance fee fraud" or "4-1-9" (after the section of the Nigerian penal code that addresses it), has spread internationally and become so serious that the United States Secret Service devotes considerable resources to combating it – see: http://www.secretservice.gov/alert419.shtml

TOP 10 PARENT COMPANIES FOR UK WEB ACCESS

	PARENT COMPANY	EST. UNIQUE AUDIENCE*
1	Microsoft	14,652,000
2	Google	9,762,000
3	Yahoo!	7,899,000
4	eBay	6,833,000
5	Time Warner	6,381,000
6	BBC	5,996,000
7	Wanadoo	5,131,000
8	Amazon	4,322,000
9	British Telecom	4,184,000
10	RealNetworks	3,627,000

* February 2004

Source: Nielsen/NetRatings

This list ranks the number of home users according to their unique (i.e. unduplicated) visits to at least one of the Internet sites owned by each parent company (defined as "a consolidation of multiple domains and URLs owned by a single entity") during a single month. Users spent an average of anything from 2 hr 05 min 05 sec (Microsoft) down to 32 min 58 sec (RealNetworks) at one or more of the sites within the ownership of the company.

THE WEB INVENTOR

IT'S A FACT

WHEN OXFORD GRADUATE Tim Berners-Lee was working for CERN (the European Particle Physics Laboratory) in 1980, he investigated ways of accessing information on other computers, developing a pioneering programme called "Enquire". However, "browsing" was almost impossible until 1989, when Berners-Lee devised the World Wide Web. This was so named after other names, such as "The Information Mine" (TIM), were rejected. CERN made the Internet available for public use and, rather than earna potential fortune by patenting his invention, Berners-Lee made it freely available.

TOP 10 INTERNET-USING COUNTRIES (PER CAPITA)

	COUNTRIES	USERS	USERS PER 100 INHABITANTS (2002)
1	Iceland	187,000	64.79
2	Sweden	5,125,000	57.31
3	South Korea	8,590,000	55.19
4	USA	159,000,000	55.14
5	= Canada	16,110,000	51.28
	= Denmark	2,756,000	51.28
7	Finland	2,650,000	50.89
8	Netherlands	8,200,000	50.63
9	Singapore	2,100,000	50.44
10	Norway	2,288,000	50.26
	World average	623,023,000	10.22
	UK	25,000,000	42.31

Source: International Telecommunication Union, World Telecommunication Development Report, 2003

Energy Levels

ENERGY-CONSUMING COUNTRIES

COUNTRY	ENERGY CONSUMPTION (2002)*					
	OIL	GAS	COAL	NUCLEAR	HEP#	TOTAL
1 USA	894.3	600.7	553.8	185.8	58.2	2,293.0
2 China	245.7	27.0	663.4	5.9	55.8	997.8
3 Russia	122.9	349.6	98.5	32.0	37.2	640.2
4 Japan	242.6	69.7	105.3	71.3	20.5	509.4
5 Germany	127.2	74.3	84.6	37.3	5.9	329.4
6 India	97.7	25.4	180.8	4.4	16.9	325.1
7 Canada	89.7	72.6	30.7	17.0	78.6	288.7
8 France	92.8	38.5	12.7	98.9	15.0	258.0
9 UK	77.2	85.1	36.5	19.9	1.7	220.3
10 South Korea	105.0	23.6	49.1	27.0	1.2	205.8
World total	3,522.5	2,282.0	2,397.9	610.6	592.1	9,405.0

* *Millions of tonnes of oil equivalent*

Hydroelectric power

Source: BP Statistical Review of World Energy 2003

▼ **Oil and water**
As land sites are exhausted and the demand for oil continues to escalate, increasing numbers of offshore oil rigs have been brought into use.

TOP 10 NATURAL GAS-PRODUCING COUNTRIES

	COUNTRY	PRODUCTION (2002) (TONNES OF OIL EQUIVALENT)
1	Russia	554,900,000
2	USA	547,700,000
3	Canada	183,500,000
4	UK	103,100,000
5	Algeria	80,400,000
6	Indonesia	70,600,000
7	Norway	65,400,000
8	Iran	64,500,000
9	Netherlands	59,900,000
10	Saudi Arabia	56,400,000
	World total	2,527,600,000

Source: BP Statistical Review of World Energy 2003

Russia saw its first increase in natural gas production for several years in 2002 as the huge Zapolyarnoye field was brought on stream. Norwegian output expanded by 21.4 per cent as production from the UK and the Netherlands declined.

TOP 10 COUNTRIES WITH THE MOST NUCLEAR REACTORS

	COUNTRY	REACTORS
1	USA	104
2	France	59
3	Japan	54
4	Russia	30
5	UK	27
6	Germany	19
7	South Korea	18
8	Canada	16
9	India	14
10	Ukraine	13

Source: International Atomic Energy Agency

There are some 440 nuclear power stations in operation in a total of 32 countries around the world, with a further 32 under construction.

TOP 10 OIL-PRODUCING COUNTRIES

	COUNTRY	PRODUCTION (2002) (TONNES)
1	Saudi Arabia	418,100,000
2	Russia	379,600,000
3	USA	350,400,000
4	Mexico	178,400,000
5	China	168,900,000
6	Iran	166,800,000
7	Norway	157,400,000
8	Venezuela	151,400,000
9	Canada	135,600,000
10	UK	115,900,000
	World total	3,556,800,000

Source: BP Statistical Review of World Energy 2003

Restrictions on output by Iraq and a reduction in production by OPEC member countries were countered in 2002 by substantial increases by Canada – up by 170,000 barrels a day – and by oil producers falling outside the Top 10, such as Angola and Brazil.

TOP 10 NATURAL GAS-CONSUMING COUNTRIES

	COUNTRY	CONSUMPTION (2002) (TONNES OF OIL EQUIVALENT)
1	USA	600,700,000
2	Russia	349,600,000
3	UK	85,100,000
4	Germany	74,300,000
5	Canada	72,600,000
6	Japan	69,700,000
7	Ukraine	62,800,000
8	Iran	61,100,000
9	Italy	57,200,000
10	Saudi Arabia	50,800,000
	World total	2,282,000,000

Source: BP Statistical Review of World Energy 2003

World consumption of natural gas grew by 2.8 per cent in 2002, with a figure of 3.9 per cent in the USA. Even higher increases of up to 7 per cent were experienced in the non-OECD Asian Pacific region.

TOP 10 COAL-CONSUMING COUNTRIES

	COUNTRY	CONSUMPTION (2002) (TONNES OF OIL EQUIVALENT)
1	China	663,400,000
2	USA	553,800,000
3	India	180,800,000
4	Japan	105,300,000
5	Russia	98,500,000
6	Germany	84,600,000
7	South Africa	81,800,000
8	Poland	56,400,000
9	Australia	49,500,000
10	South Korea	49,100,000
	World total	2,397,900,000
	UK	36,500,000

Source: BP Statistical Review of World Energy 2003

The rapid expansion of China's economy and industrial output meant that in 2002 the country's coal consumption increased by a remarkable 27.9 per cent, thereby escalating the overall world figure by 6.9 per cent.

TOP 10 OIL-CONSUMING COUNTRIES

	COUNTRY	CONSUMPTION (2002) (TONNES)
1	USA	894,300,000
2	China	245,700,000
3	Japan	242,600,000
4	Germany	127,200,000
5	Russia	122,900,000
6	South Korea	105,000,000
7	India	97,700,000
8	Italy	92,900,000
9	France	92,800,000
10	Canada	89,700,000
	World total	3,522,500,000
	UK	77,200,000

Source: BP Statistical Review of World Energy 2003

Environmental Issues

WIND POWER-
GENERATING
COUNTRIES

COUNTRY	CAPACITY (MEGAWATTS) (2003*)
1 Germany	12,836
2 Spain	5,060
3 USA	4,685
4 Denmark	2,916
5 India	1,702
6 Netherlands	803
7 Italy	800
8 UK	586
9 China	468
10 Japan	415

* 2002 data for non-European countries

Source: *American Wind Energy Association/European Wind Energy Association*

▼ Catching the sun

Technological advances and price falls are starting to make solar panels viable as an alternative and environmentally friendly source of renewable energy.

ALTERNATIVE POWER-
CONSUMING
COUNTRIES

COUNTRY	CONSUMPTION* KW/HR (2001)
1 USA	84,800,000,000
2 Germany	22,600,000,000
3 Japan	19,100,000,000
4 Brazil	14,800,000,000
5 Philippines	12,200,000,000
6 Spain	9,200,000,000
7 Finland	8,400,000,000
8 = Italy	7,800,000,000
= Luxembourg	7,800,000,000
10 Canada	7,200,000,000
World total	251,100,000,000
UK	5,700,000,000

* Includes geothermal, solar, wind, wood, and waste electric power

Source: *Energy Information Administration*

PAPER-RECYCLING
COUNTRIES (PER CAPITA)

COUNTRY	PRODUCTION PER 1,000 PEOPLE (TONNES) (2002)
1 Sweden	168.08
2 Switzerland	161.71
3 Austria	152.81
4 Belgium	152.69
5 Netherlands	148.34
6 Germany	146.82
7 USA	144.17
8 Finland	135.64
9 South Korea	126.59
10 Japan	116.37
World average	22.65
UK	89.60

Source: *Food and Agriculture Organization of the United Nations*

With paper comprising up to 40 per cent of municipal waste, recycling preserves trees and reduces not only energy and water consumption, but also the pollution caused by creating new paper.

CARBON DIOXIDE-EMITTING COUNTRIES

COUNTRY	EMISSIONS PER CAPITA (TONNES OF CARBON) (2001)
1 Qatar	13.66
2 United Arab Emirates	13.31
3 Bahrain	9.47
4 Kuwait	8.32
5 Singapore	7.57
6 Trinidad and Tobago	6.25
7 Luxembourg	5.61
8 USA	5.51
9 Canada	5.22
10 Guam	5.18
World average	*1.07*
UK	*2.59*

Source: *Energy Information Administration*

Carbon dioxide emissions derive from three principal sources – fossil fuel burning, cement manufacturing, and gas flaring. Since World War II, increasing industrialization in many countries has resulted in huge increases in carbon output, a trend that most countries are now actively attempting to reverse.

FRESH WATER-CONSUMING COUNTRIES

COUNTRY	ANNUAL FRESH WATER WITHDRAWALS (CUBIC METRES)*
1 China	525,500,000,000
2 India	500,000,000,000
3 USA	467,300,000,000
4 Pakistan	155,600,000,000
5 Japan	91,400,000,000
6 Mexico	77,800,000,000
7 Russia	77,100,000,000
8 Indonesia	74,300,000,000
9 Iran	70,000,000,000
10 Egypt	66,000,000,000

* In latest year for which data available

Source: *World Bank,* World Development Indicators 2003

Water is used for agriculture, as well as for industrial and domestic purposes. In the cases of China, India, and the USA, agriculture consumes 78, 92, and 42 per cent of the total respectively.

RUBBISH-PRODUCING COUNTRIES

COUNTRY*	DOMESTIC WASTE PER HEAD (2000#) (KG)	(LB)
1 Denmark	580	1,278
2 Netherlands	530	1,168
3 Luxembourg	510	1,124
4 UK	480	1,058
5 USA	460	1,014
6 = Belgium	450	992
= Switzerland	450	992
8 Germany	430	879
9 Australia	400	881
10 = Austria	380	837
= New Zealand	380	837

* In those countries for which data are available

 # Or latest year for which data available

Source: *Organisation for Economic Co-operation and Development*

COUNTRIES PRODUCING THE MOST ELECTRICITY FROM NUCLEAR SOURCES

COUNTRY	NUCLEAR POWER STATIONS IN OPERATION	NUCLEAR AS % OF TOTAL	OUTPUT (MEGAWATT-HOURS)
1 USA	104	20.3	98,230
2 France	59	78.0	63,073
3 Japan	54	36.1	44,287
4 Germany	19	29.9	21,283
5 Russia	30	16.0	20,793
6 South Korea	18	38.6	14,890
7 UK	27	22.4	12,052
8 Canada	16	12.3	11,323
9 Ukraine	13	45.7	11,207
10 Sweden	11	45.7	9,432
World total	*440*	*100.0*	*360,431*

Source: *International Atomic Energy Agency*

If ranked according to reliance on nuclear power, Lithuania would head the list, with 80.1 per cent of its electricity derived from nuclear sources, with France at 78.0 per cent and the UK and USA at a lowly 22.4 and 20.3 per cent respectively.

Hazards at Work

THE 10 MOST DANGEROUS JOBS IN THE UK*

	JOB
1	Bomb disposal officer
2	Deep sea diver
3	Deep sea fisherman
4	Demolition worker
5	Fast jet pilot
6	Oil platform worker
7	Professional motor/motor cycle racer
8	Professional stuntman
9	Steeplejack
10	Tunneller (face worker)

In alphabetical order

Life assurance companies carefully base their premiums on actuarial statistics that take into account the likelihood of people in each job being involved in an accident that injures or kills them at work. This does not mean that companies will not provide cover for such professions, but the riskier the job, the higher the premium.

THE 10 MOST COMMON CAUSES OF INJURY AT WORK IN GREAT BRITAIN

	CAUSE	NONFATAL INJURIES (2002–03)*	
		MAJOR	TOTAL#
1	Handling, lifting or carrying	3,55	9,097
2	Slip, trip or fall on same level	10,458	9,848
3	Struck by moving (including flying or falling) object	3,892	4,466
4	Struck against fixed or stationary object	1,200	5,977
5	Acts of violence	907	5,519
6	Fall from height	3,880	,910
7	Contact with moving machinery	1,35	,989
8	Exposure to or contact with a harmful substance	79	,252
9	Struck by moving vehicle	65	,957
10	Animal	211	911

Provisional figures

Includes all injuries resulting in over 3 days away from work

Source: *Health and Safety Executive*

◀ **Danger on deck**
Deep sea fishing is ranked among the most hazardous of all jobs. Although relatively small numbers are involved in the industry, fishing boats are vulnerable to storms – and workers to such risks as being swept overboard.

WORST INDUSTRIAL DISASTERS*

LOCATION/DATE/INCIDENT	FATALITIES
1 Bhopal, India, 3 Dec 1984 Methylisocyante gas escape at Union Carbide plant	3,849
2 Jesse, Nigeria, 17 Oct 1998 Oil pipeline explosion	more than 700
3 Oppau, Germany, 21 Sept 1921 Chemical plant explosion	561
4 San Juanico, Mexico, 19 Nov 1984 Explosion at a PEMEX liquified petroleum gas plant	540
5 Cubatão, Brazil, 25 Feb 1984 Oil pipeline explosion	508
6 Durunkah, Egypt, 2 Nov 1994 Fuel storage depot fire	more than 500
7 Novosibirsk, USSR, precise date unknown, Apr 1979, Anthrax infection following an accident at a biological and chemical warfare plant	up to 300
8 Adeje, Nigeria, 10 July 2000 Oil pipeline explosion	more than 250
9 Guadalajara, Mexico, 22 Apr 1992 Explosions caused by a gas leak into sewers	230
10 Ludwigshafen, Germany, 28 July 1948 Dimethyl ether explosion in a lacquer plant	184

* *Including industrial sites, factories, and fuel depots and pipelines; excluding military, munitions, bombs, mining, marine and other transport disasters, dam failures, and mass poisonings*

Officially, the meltdown of the nuclear reactor at Chernobyl, Ukraine, on 26 April 1986 caused the immediate death of 31 people, but it has been suggested that by 1992 some 6,000 to 8,000 people had died as a result of radioactive contamination, a toll that will continue to rise for many years. Extending the parameters of "industrial" to include construction work, as many as 25,000 workers may have died during the building of the Panama Canal in the period 1881–1914, largely as a result of diseases such as yellow fever, malaria and cholera, while the building of the Madeira-Mamore railways in Brazil (1870–1912) resulted in over 6,000 deaths from disease, poison arrow attacks, and snakebite. The boring of the Gauley Bridge Water Tunnel, West Virginia, killed some 476 workers in 1935 as a result of inhalation of silica dust, with perhaps 1,500 becoming disabled.

WORST MINING DISASTERS

LOCATION/DATE	FATALITIES
1 Honkeiko, China, 26 Apr 1942	1,549
2 Courrières, France, 10 Mar 1906	1,060
3 Omuta, Japan, 9 Nov 1963	447
4 Senghenydd, UK, 14 Oct 1913	439
5 = Coalbrook, South Africa, 21 Jan 1960	437
= Hokkaido, Japan, 1 Dec 1914	437
7 Wankie, Rhodesia, 6 June 1972	427
8 Tsinan, China, 13 May 1935	400
9 Dhanbad, India, 28 May 1965	375
10 Chasnala, India, 27 Dec 1975	372

A mine disaster at the Fushun mines, Manchuria, on 12 February 1931 may have resulted in up to 3,000 deaths, but information was suppressed by the Chinese government. Soviet security was responsible for obscuring details of an explosion at the East German Johanngeorgendstadt uranium mine on 29 November 1949, when as many as 3,700 may have died. The two worst disasters both resulted from underground explosions: a large numbers of the deaths among mine workers have resulted from that cause, and from asphyxiation by poisonous gases.

MOST COMMON ACCIDENTAL CAUSES OF DEATH AT WORK IN THE UK

ACCIDENT	FATALITIES (2002–03)*
1 Falls from a height	35
2 Struck by a moving vehicle	32
3 Struck by a moving object (including flying/falling)	26
4 Contact with moving machinery	15
5 = Struck against something fixed or stationary	10
= Trapped by something collapsing/overturning	10
7 Contact with electricity	12
8 Drowning or asphyxiation	7
9 Exposure to an explosion	6
10 = Exposure to, or contact with, a harmful substance	5
= Exposure to fire	5
Total (all causes)	*182*

* *Provisional*

Source: *Health and Safety Executive*

TRANSPORT & TOURISM

On the Road

TOP 10 CAR MANUFACTURERS IN THE UK

MANUFACTURER	CAR PRODUCTION (2003)
1 Nissan	331,924
2 Toyota	210,617
3 Peugeot	207,237
4 Honda	184,693
5 BMW	174,191
6 Land Rover	147,545
7 MG Rover	132,789
8 Jaguar/Daimler	126,121
9 Vauxhall	124,061
10 IBC Vehicles	9,576

Source: *Society of Motor Manufacturers and Traders Ltd.*

Named after Nihon Sangyo, one its founding companies, Nissan was established in 1934. The company has had a long association with the UK, in the 1950s assembling British Austin A40 and A50 models under licence in Japan, before setting up in the UK in 1969. Since then Nissan has prospered to become Britain's largest car maker.

TOP 10 OFF-ROAD VEHICLES IN THE UK

VEHICLE	SALES (2003)
1 Land Rover Freelander	21,578
2 Toyota RAV4	15,818
3 Honda CR-V	14,849
4 Land Rover Discovery	11,117
5 Nissan X-trail	8,831
6 BMW X5	8,536
7 Suzuki Grand Vitara	8,343
8 Land Rover Range Rover	6,716
9 Mercedes M-class	5,579
10 Mitsubishi Shogun	4,332

Source: *Society of Motor Manufacturers and Traders Ltd.*

The popularity of 4-wheel-drive off-road vehicles (for use in conditions that surveys show rarely include off-road use) has increased in recent years. The Land Rover Freelander, introduced in 1997 as a scaled down version of the firm's Discovery, has proved to be the bestselling vehicle in the UK and one of the company's most successful export models.

TOP 10 CARS IN THE UK

CAR	SALES (2003)
1 Ford Focus	131,684
2 Vauxhall Corsa	108,387
3 Vauxhall Astra	96,929
4 Ford Fiesta	95,887
5 Renault Clio	83,972
6 Peugeot 206	82,667
7 Renault Megane	71,660
8 Volkswagen Golf	67,226
9 BMW 3 Series	65,489
10 Ford Mondeo	60,046

Source: *Society of Motor Manufacturers and Traders Ltd.*

▶ **Wheels over water**
Recent shifts in the pattern of the world motor industry mean that many cars are imported; even those produced locally are often built by foreign-owned companies.

TOP 10 COUNTRIES WITH THE LONGEST ROAD NETWORKS

COUNTRY	LENGTH (KM)	(MILES)
1 USA	6,334,859	3,936,298
2 India	3,319,644	2,062,731
3 Brazil	1,724,929	1,071,821
4 Canada	1,408,000	874,891
5 China	1,402,698	871,596
6 Japan	1,161,894	721,967
7 France	894,000	555,506
8 Australia	811,603	504,307
9 Spain	663,795	412,463
10 Russia	532,393	330,814
UK	*371,913*	*231,096*

Source: *Central Intelligence Agency*

The CIA's assessment of road lengths includes both paved (mostly tarmac-surfaced) and unpaved highways (gravel and earth-surfaced).

TOP 10 MOTOR VEHICLE MANUFACTURERS

MANUFACTURER	MOTOR VEHICLE PRODUCTION* (2002)
1 General Motors	8,325,835
2 Ford	6,729,499
3 Toyota-Daihatsu-Hino	6,626,387
4 Volkswagen Group	5,017,438
5 DaimlerChrysler	4,456,325
6 PSA Peugeot Citroën	3,262,146
7 Honda	2,988,427
8 Nissan-Nissan diesel	2,718,828
9 Hyundai-Kia	2,641,825
10 Renault-Dacia-Samsung	2,328,508

* Includes cars, light trucks, lorries, buses, and coaches

Source: *OICA Correspondents Survey*

Overall world production in 2002 was reckoned at 58,954,220 vehicles, with the top three manufacturers making 36.8 per cent of the world total. US car companies were responsible for 12,279,582 vehicles, compared with Europe's 19,929,073 and Asia/Oceania's 20,015,264.

MOST EXPENSIVE CAR

ONLY SIX EXAMPLES of the Bugatti Royale were ever produced. One of the largest vehicles of all time, it was 6.7 m (22 ft) long and had a 12.7 litre engine originally designed for aircraft, and sold for $42,000. On 19 November 1987 an example of this rare vehicle – a 1931 Bugatti Type 41 Royale Sports Coupe – established a new world record price for a production car when it was sold at auction in London for £5.5 million ($9,735,000). On 12 April 1990 the same car broke its own record when it was sold privately for $15 million (£9.1 million). Rare examples of the Ferrari 250 GTO, fewer than 40 of which were built between 1962 and 1964, have changed hands for prices close to this.

IT'S A FACT

Track Records

▲ **Like a bullet**
The Japanese Shinkhasen "bullet trains" were introduced in 1964 and have been constantly improved since: the Nozomi 500 is capable of 186 mph (300 km/h)

TOP 10 FASTEST RAIL JOURNEYS*

JOURNEY/COUNTRY	TRAIN	DISTANCE (KM)	(MILES)	SPEED (KM/H)	(MPH)
1 **Hiroshima to Kokura,** Japan	15 Nozomi	192.0	119.3	261.8	162.7
2 **Valence TGV to Avignon TGV,** France	TGV 5102	129.7	80.6	259.4	161.2
3 **Brussels Midi to Valence TGV,** International	ThalysSoleil	831.3	516.5	242.1	150.4
4 **Frankfurt Flughafen (airport) to Siegburg/Bonn,** Germany	19 ICE	143.3	89.0	232.4	144.4
5 **Madrid Atocha to Sevilla (Seville),** Spain	2 AVE	470.5	292.4	209.1	129.9
6 **Alvesta to Hassleholm,** Sweden	X2000 541	98.0	61.0	178.2	111.0
7 **Darlington to York,** UK	6 Voyager	71.0	44.1	177.5	110.3
8 **Roma (Rome) Termini to Firenze (Florence) SMN,** Italy	Eurostar 9458	261.0	162.2	166.6	103.5
9 **Wilmington to Baltimore,** USA	Acela Expresses	110.1	68.4	165.1	102.6
10 **Salo to Karjaa,** Finland	2 Pendolinos	53.1	33.0	151.7	94.3

* Fastest journey for each country; all those in the Top 10 have other similarly or equally fast services

Source: Railway Gazette International

Falling just outside the Top 10, China's Fex T806 between Shenzhen and Guangzhou Dong achieves a speed of 151.6 km/h (94.2 mph), while on the Dorval to Guildwood leg of the Montreal–Toronto journey, Canada's Sunday-only Train 67 averages 149.5 km/h (92.9 mph).

TOP 10 LONGEST RAIL NETWORKS

	COUNTRY	TOTAL RAIL LENGTH (KM)	(MILES)
1	**USA**	194,731	121,000
2	**Russia**	87,157	54,157
3	**China**	71,600	44,490
4	**India**	63,518	39,468
5	**Canada**	49,422	30,709
6	**Germany**	45,514	28,281
7	**Australia**	41,588	25,842
8	**Argentina**	34,463	21,414
9	**France**	32,682	20,308
10	**Brazil**	31,543	19,600
	UK	*16,893*	*10,497*

Source: *Central Intelligence Agency*

The length of the world's rail network is reckoned to be 1,122,650 km (697,582 miles). Some 190,000 to 195,000 km (118,061 to 121,167 miles) is electrified, and 239,430 km (148,775 miles) is narrow gauge. In Europe, 147,760 km (91,814 miles) is electrified, compared with 24,509 km (15,229 miles) in the Far East, 11,050 km (6,866 miles) in Africa, 4,223 km (2,624 miles) in South America, and 4,160 km (2,585 miles) in North America.

TOP 10 OLDEST UNDERGROUND RAILWAY SYSTEMS

	CITY	OPENED
1	**London,** UK	1863
2	**Budapest,** Hungary	1896
3	**Glasgow,** UK	1896
4	**Boston,** USA	1897
5	**Paris,** France	1900
6	**Berlin,** Germay	1902
7	**New York,** USA	1904
8	**Philadelphia,** USA	1907
9	**Hamburg,** Germany	1912
10	**Buenos Aires,** Argentina	1913

Source: *Tony Pattison, Centre for Environmental Initiatives Reasearcher*

The world's first underground system, a section of the Metropolitan Railway from Paddington to Farringdon Street in London, with specially-adapted steam trains, was opened on 10 January 1863. The second opened in Budapest in 1896 to celebrate the 1,000th anniversary of the state of Hungary.

THE 10 FIRST COUNTRIES WITH RAILWAYS

	COUNTRY	FIRST RAILWAY ESTABLISHED
1	**UK**	27 Sep 1825
2	**France**	7 Nov 1829
3	**USA**	24 May 1830
4	**Ireland**	17 Dec 1834
5	**Belgium**	5 May 1835
6	**Germany**	7 Dec 1835
7	**Canada**	21 Jul 1836
8	**Russia**	30 Oct 1837
9	**Austria**	6 Jan 1838
10	**Netherlands**	24 Sep 1839

Although there were earlier horse-drawn railways, the Stockton & Darlington Railway inaugurated the world's first steam service. Some of those listed here had offered earlier limited services, but their opening dates mark the generally accepted beginning of each country's steam railway system. By 1850 several other countries, including Italy (1839), Hungary (1846), Denmark (1847), and Spain (1848), had railways.

TOP 10 MOST COMMON TYPES OF PROPERTY LOST ON LONDON TRANSPORT

	TYPE	NO. OF ITEMS FOUND (2002–03)
1	**Cases and bags**	22,838
2	**Books, cheque books and credit cards**	20,079
3	**Clothing**	19,229
4	**"Value items"** (handbags, purses, wallets, etc.)	13,663
5	**Mobile telephones**	10,694
6	**Umbrellas**	7,932
7	**Keys**	7,454
8	**Spectacles**	5,912
9	**Jewellery, cameras, laptop computers, etc.**	5,610
10	**Gloves** (pairs)	2,432
	Total of the items in Top 10:	*127,817*

Source: *London Transport*

Books (along with cheque books and credit cards, which are included with them) have dropped from their long-standing No. 1 position. Changes in fashion mean that hats, once one of the most common lost items, no longer even warrant a separate category, whereas mobile telephones are now lost in increasing numbers. Some 30 per cent of lost property is restored to its owners, rising to 55 per cent of valuable items. Among the stranger items that have been lost in recent years are a skeleton, a box of glass eyes, breast implants, artificial legs and hands, a Yamaha outboard motor, a complete double bed, a theatrical coffin, a wedding dress, a stuffed gorilla and an urn containing human ashes.

TOP 10 LONGEST UNDERGROUND RAILWAY NETWORKS

	CITY	OPENED	STATIONS	TOTAL TRACK LENGTH (KM)	(MILES)
1	**London,** UK	1863	267	392	244
2	**New York,** USA	1904	468	371	231
3	**Moscow,** Russia	1935	160	262	163
4	**Tokyo,** Japan*	1927	241	256	160
5	**Paris,** France#	1900	297	202	126
6	**Mexico City,** Mexico	1969	175	201	125
7	**San Francisco,** USA	1972	42	200	124
8	**Chicago,** USA	1943	140	173	107
9	**Madrid,** Spain	1919	201	1171	107
10	**Washington,** USA	1976	83	166	104

* *Includes Toei, Eidan lines*

\# *Metro and RER*

Source: *Tony Pattison, Centre for Environmental Initiatives Researcher*

▼ **First stop**
London's Baker Street was one of the stations on the world's first ever underground railway system.

Water Ways

TOP 10 LONGEST SHIP CANALS

	CANAL/COUNTRY	DATE	LENGTH (KM)	LENGTH (MILES)
1	**Grand Canal**, China	283*	1,795	1,114
2	**Erie Canal**, USA	1825	584	363
3	**Göta Canal**, Sweden	1832	386	240
4	**St. Lawrence Seaway**, Canada/USA	1959	290	180
5	**Canal du Midi**, France	1692	240	149
6	**Main-Danube**, Germany	1992	171	106
7	**Suez**, Egypt	1869	162	101
8	= **Albert**, Belgium	1939	129	80
	= **Moscow-Volga**, Russia	1937	129	80
10	**Kiel**, Germany	1895	99	62

* Extended from 605–10 and rebuilt between 1958–72

Connecting Hang Zhou in the south to Beijing in the north, China's Grand Canal was largely built by manual labour alone, long before the invention of the mechanized tools and techniques used in the construction of the other major artificial waterways listed above.

TOP 10 LARGEST CRUISE SHIPS

	SHIP	YEAR BUILT	COUNTRY BUILT	PASSENGER CAPACITY	GROSS TONNAGE
1	**Queen Mary 2**	2003	France	2,800	142,200
2	**Navigator of the Seas**	2002	Finland	3,807	138,279
3	**Explorer of the Seas**	2000	Finland	3,840	137,308
4	= **Adventure of the Seas**	2001	Finland	3,840	137,276
	= **Mariner of the Seas**	2003	Finland	3,840	137,276
	= **Voyager of the Seas**	1999	Finland	3,840	137,276
7	**Caribbean Princess**	2004	Italy	3,100	115,000
8	= **Diamond Princess**	2004	Japan	2,600	113,000
	= **Sapphire Princess**	2004	Japan	3,100	113,000
10	**Carnival Conquest**	2002	Italy	3,783	110,239

Source: *Lloyd's Register-Fairplay Ltd. www.lrfairplay.com*

TOP 10 LONGEST CRUISE SHIPS

	SHIP	YEAR BUILT	COUNTRY BUILT	(M)	LENGTH (FT)	(IN)
1	Queen Mary 2	2003	France	345.03	1,131	9
2	Norway (former France)	1961	France	315.53	1,035	2
3	= Adventure of the Seas	2001	Finland	311.12	1,020	7
	= Mariner of the Seas	2003	Finland	311.12	1,020	7
	= Navigator of the Seas	2002	Finland	311.12	1,020	7
6	= Explorer of the Seas	2000	Finland	311.00	1,020	3
	= Voyager of the Seas	1999	Finland	311.00	1,020	3
8	United States	1952	USA	301.75	990	0
9	= Norwegian Dawn	2002	Germany	294.13	965	0
	= Norwegian Star	2001	Germany	294.13	965	0

Source: Lloyd's Register-Fairplay Ltd. www.lrfairplay.com

For comparison, the *Great Eastern* (launched 1858) measured 211 m (692 ft), while the *Titanic*, which sank dramatically on its maiden voyage in 1912, was 269 m (882 ft) long. Former entrant in this list the *Queen Mary* (311 m/1,019 ft) is now a floating museum at Long Beach, California, while the *Queen Elizabeth* (314 m/1,031 ft) was taken out of service and destroyed by fire in 1972.

TOP 10 LARGEST OIL TANKERS*

	TANKER	YEAR BUILT	COUNTRY BUILT	GROSS TONNAGE#	DEADWEIGHT TONNAGE†
1	Jahre Viking	1976	Japan	260,851	564,763
2	= Hellespont Alhambra	2002	South Korea	234,006	441,893
	= Hellespont Metropolis	2002	South Korea	234,006	441,893
	= Hellespont Tara	2002	South Korea	234,006	441,893
5	Hellespont Fairfax	2002	South Korea	234,006	441,585
6	Empress des Mers	1976	Japan	203,110	423,677
7	Hellespont Embassy	1976	Japan	199,210	413,015
8	Marine Pacific	1979	USA	192,707	404,536
9	Marine Atlantic	1979	USA	192,707	404,531
10	= Berge Enterprise	1981	Japan	188,728	360,700
	= Berge Pioneer	1980	Japan	188,728	360,700

* As at October 2003

\# The weight of the ship when empty

† The total weight of the vessel, including its cargo, crew, passengers, and supplies

Source: Lloyd's Register-Fairplay Ltd. www.lrfairplay.com

TOP 10 BUSIEST PORTS

	PORT/COUNTRY	CONTAINER TRAFFIC (2000) (TEUS*)
1	Hong Kong, China	18,098,000
2	Singapore, Singapore	17,090,000
3	Pusan, South Korea	7,540,387
4	Kaohsiung, Taiwan	7,425,832
5	Rotterdam, Netherlands	6,274,000
6	Los Angeles, USA	4,879,429
7	Long Beach, USA	4,600,787
8	Hamburg, Germany	4,248,247
9	Antwerp, Belgium	4,082,334
10	Tanjung Priok, Indonesia	3,368,629

* Twenty-foot Equivalent Units

Source: American Association of Port Authorities

◄ **Med to Red**
Connecting the Mediterranean and Red Sea, the Suez Canal, seen here from space, dramatically reduced the time and cost of transport from Europe to Asia.

TOP 10 COUNTRIES WITH THE LONGEST INLAND WATERWAY NETWORKS*

	COUNTRY	LENGTH (KM)	(MILES)
1	China	110,000	68,351
2	Russia	95,900	59,589
3	Brazil	50,000	31,069
4	USA#	41,009	25,482
5	Indonesia	21,579	13,409
6	Colombia	18,140	11,272
7	Vietnam	17,702	11,000
8	India	16,180	10,054
9	Dem. Rep. of Congo	15,000	9,321
10	France	14,932	9,278
	UK	3,200	1,988

* Canals and navigable rivers

\# Excluding Great Lakes

Source: Central Intelligence Agency

The navigability of the world's waterways varies greatly: only 3,631 km (2,256 miles) of those of India, for example, are navigable by large vessels.

TOP 10 MERCHANT SHIPPING FLEETS (OWNERSHIP)

	COUNTRY OF OWNERSHIP	SHIPS IN FLEET*
1	Japan	3,942
2	Greece	3,039
3	Germany	2,446
4	China	2,089
5	USA	2,015
6	Russia	1,858
7	Norway	1,441
8	Singapore	1,112
9	Netherlands	1,010
10	UK	952
	All countries	35,590

* Ships over 1,000 DWT (deadweight tonnage – total weight of the vessel, including its cargo, crew, passengers, and supplies) in service October 2003

Source: Lloyd's Register-Fairplay Ltd. www.lrfairplay.com

This Top 10 ranks merchant fleets according to the country of ownership, which is not necessarily where the ships are registered. Among the vessels included in a country's merchant fleet are tankers, container ships, passenger ships, and refrigerated cargo ships.

Air Lines

TOP 10 AIRLINES WITH THE MOST PASSENGER TRAFFIC

	AIRLINE/COUNTRY	PASSENGER KMS FLOWN (2001)*
1	United Airlines, USA	187,720,000,000
2	American Airlines, USA	174,388,000,000
3	Delta Airlines, USA	163,765,000,000
4	Northwest Airlines, USA	117,733,000,000
5	British Airways, UK	106,270,000,000
6	Continental Airlines, USA	98,373,000,000
7	Air France, France	94,828,000,000
8	Lufthansa German Airlines, Germany	86,695,000,000
9	Japan Airlines, Japan	79,363,000,000
10	US Airways, USA	74,026,000,000

* Total distance travelled by aircraft of these airlines
  multiplied by number of passengers carried

Source: Airline Business/Air Transport Intelligence
at www.rati.com

TOP 10 COUNTRIES WITH THE MOST AIRPORTS

	COUNTRY	AIRPORTS
1	USA	14,801
2	Brazil	3,590
3	Russia	2,743
4	Mexico	1,823
5	Canada	1,389
6	Argentina	1,342
7	Bolivia	1,081
8	Colombia	1,050
9	Paraguay	879
10	Ukraine	790

Source: Central Intelligence Agency

TOP 10 AIRLINERS IN SERVICE

	AIRCRAFT MODEL	NO. IN SERVICE
1	Boeing B-737-300	985
2	Airbus A-320-200	960
3	Boeing B-757-200	813
4	Boeing B-737-200 Advanced	479
5	Boeing B-737-400	464
6	Boeing B-767-300ER	422
7	Boeing B-747-400	405
8	McDonnell Douglas DC-9-30	308
9	Raytheon Beech 1900D	278
10	Boeing B-727-200 Advanced	270

Source: Air Transport Intelligence at www.rati.com

BUSIEST AIRPORTS IN THE UK

AIRPORT	LOCATION	TOTAL PASSENGERS* (2002)
1 London Heathrow	London	63,338,649
2 London Gatwick	Gatwick, West Sussex	29,628,441
3 Manchester	Manchester	19,038,431
4 London Stansted	Stansted, Essex	16,049,804
5 Birmingham International	Birmingham	8,028,972
6 Glasgow International	Paisley, Renfrewshire	7,806,734
7 Edinburgh	Edinburgh	6,932,123
8 London Luton	Luton, Bedfordshire	6,480,804
9 Belfast International	Belfast, N. Ireland	3,580,030
10 Newcastle International	Newcastle	3,458,845

* Includes international, domestic, and in transit

Source: *Air Transport Intelligence at www.rati.com*

BUSIEST INTERNATIONAL AIRPORTS

AIRPORT	LOCATION	INTERNATIONAL PASSENGERS (2001)
1 London Heathrow	London, UK	53,796,000
2 Charles de Gaulle	Paris, France	43,352,000
3 Frankfurt	Frankfurt, Germany	40,283,000*
4 Schiphol	Amsterdam, Netherlands	39,167,000
5 Hong Kong	Hong Kong, China	32,027,000
6 London Gatwick	Gatwick, UK	28,114,000
7 Singapore Changi	Singapore	26,542,000
8 Narita International	Tokyo, Japan	22,241,000
9 Bangkok International	Bangkok, Thailand	21,394,000
10 Kloten	Zurich, Switzerland	19,698,000

* 2002 data

Source: *Air Transport Intelligence at www.rati.com*

London Heathrow was created 60 years ago when the Great Western Aerodrome, privately owned by the Fairey aircraft company and requisitioned for use as an RAF airfield during wartime, was acquired for civilian use.

AIRLINES WITH THE MOST AIRCRAFT

AIRLINE/COUNTRY*	FLEET SIZE (2001)
1 American Airlines	834
2 United Airlines	554
3 Delta Airlines	551
4 Northwest Airlines	437
5 Continental Airlines	370
6 Southwest Airlines	367
7 US Airways	295
8 Air France, France	247
9 British Airways, UK	236
10 Air Canada, Canada	224

* All from the USA unless otherwise stated

Source: Airline Business/*Air Transport Intelligence at www.rati.com*

◀ Come fly with me
The world's airlines carry over 1.6 billion passengers annually, flying a total of some 3,000 billion passenger kilometres.

Transport Disasters

WORST MARINE DISASTERS

LOCATION/DATE/INCIDENT	NO. KILLED
1 Off Gdansk, Poland, 30 January 1945 The German liner *Wilhelm Gustloff*, laden with refugees, was torpedoed by a Soviet submarine, *S-13*. The precise death toll remains uncertain, but is in the range of 5,348 to 7,800.	up to 7,800
2 Off Cape Rixhöft (Rozeewie), Poland, 16 April 1945 A German ship, *Goya*, carrying evacuees from Gdansk, was torpedoed in the Baltic.	6,800
3 Off Yingkow, China, 3 December 1948 The boilers of an unidentified Chinese troopship carrying Nationalist soldiers from Manchuria exploded, detonating ammunition.	over 6,000
4 Lübeck, Germany, 3 May 1945 The German ship *Cap Arcona*, carrying concentration camp survivors, was bombed and sunk by British Typhoon fighter-bombers.	5,000
5 Off Stolpmünde (Ustka), Poland, 10 February 1945 German war-wounded and refugees were lost when the *General Steuben* was torpedoed by the same Russian submarine that had sunk the *Wilhelm Gustloff* ten days earlier.	3,500
6 Off St. Nazaire, France, 17 June 1940 The British troopship *Lancastria* sank.	3,050
7 Tabias Strait, Philippines, 20 December 1987 The ferry *Dona Paz* was struck by oil tanker *MV Victor*.	up to 3,000
8 Woosung, China, 3 December 1948 The overloaded steamship *Kiangya*, carrying refugees, struck a Japanese mine.	over 2,750
9 Lübeck, Germany, 3 May 1945 The refugee ship *Thielbeck* sank along with the *Cap Arcona* during the British bombardment of Lübeck harbour in the closing weeks of World War II.	2,750
10 South Atlantic, 12 September 1942 The British passenger vessel *Laconia*, carrying Italian prisoners-of-war, was sunk by German U-boat *U-156*.	2,279

Recent re-assessments of the death tolls in some of World War II's marine disasters means that the most famous marine disaster of all, the *Titanic*, the British liner that struck an iceberg in the North Atlantic and sank on 15 April 1912 with the loss of 1,517 lives, no longer ranks in the Top 10. However, the *Titanic* tragedy remains one of the worst ever peacetime disasters, along with such notable incidents as that involving the *General Slocum*, an excursion liner that caught fire in the port of New York on 15 June 1904 with the loss of 1,021. Among other disasters occurring during wartime and resulting in losses of more than 1,000 are the explosion of *Mont Blanc*, a French ammunition ship, following its collision with a Belgian steamer *Imo* off Halifax, Nova Scotia, on 6 December 1917, with 1,635 lost; the sinking of the British cruiser *HMS Hood* by the German battleship *Bismarck* in the Denmark Strait on 24 May 1941, with 1,418 killed; the torpedoing by German submarine *U-20* of the *Lusitania*, a British passenger liner, off the Irish coast on 7 May 1915 with the loss of 1,198 civilians; and the accidental sinking by a US submarine of *Rakuyo Maru*, a Japanese troopship carrying Allied prisoners-of-war, on 12 September 1944, killing some 1,350.

WORST AIR DISASTERS

LOCATION/DATE/INCIDENT	NO. KILLED
1 New York, USA, 11 September 2001 Following a hijacking by terrorists, an American Airlines Boeing 767 was deliberately flown into the North Tower of the World Trade Center, killing all 81 passengers and 11 crew on board and an estimated 1,530 in and around the building, both as a direct result of the crash, and the subsequent fire and collapse of the building.	c.1,622
2 New York, USA, 11 September 2001 As part of the coordinated attack, hijackers commandeered a second Boeing 767 and crashed it into the South Tower, killing all 56 passengers and 9 crew on board and approximately 612 in and around the building.	c.677
3 Tenerife, Canary Islands, 27 March 1977 Two Boeing 747s (PanAm and KLM, carrying 380 passengers and 16 crew and 234 passengers and 14 crew respectively) collided and caught fire on the runway of Los Rodeos airport after the pilots received incorrect control-tower instructions. A total of 61 escaped.	583
4 Mt. Ogura, Japan, 12 August 1985 A JAL Boeing 747 on an internal flight from Tokyo to Osaka crashed, killing all but four of the 509 passengers and all 15 crew on board.	520
5 Charkhi Dadri, India, 12 November 1996 Soon after taking off from New Delhi's Indira Gandhi International Airport, a Saudi Airways Boeing 747 collided with a Kazakh Airlines Ilyushin IL-76 cargo aircraft on its descent and exploded, killing all 312 (289 passengers and 23 crew) on the Boeing and all 37 (27 passengers and 10 crew) on the Ilyushin in the world's worst mid-air crash.	349
6 Paris, France, 3 March 1974 Immediately after take-off for London, a Turkish Airlines DC-10 crashed at Ermenonville, north of Paris, killing all 335 passengers, including many England rugby supporters, and its crew of 11.	346
7 Off the Irish coast, 23 June 1985 An Air India Boeing 747 on a flight from Vancouver to Delhi exploded in mid-air, probably as a result of a terrorist bomb, killing all 307 passengers and 22 crew.	329
8 Riyadh, Saudi Arabia, 19 August 1980 A Saudia (Saudi Arabian) Airlines Lockheed TriStar caught fire during an emergency landing, killing all 287 passengers and 14 crew.	301
9 Off the Iranian coast, 3 July 1988 An Iran Air A300 airbus was shot down in error by a missile fired by the USS *Vincennes*, with 274 passengers and 16 crew killed.	290
10 Chicago, USA, 25 May 1979 An engine fell off an American Airlines DC-10 as it took off from Chicago O'Hare airport, and the plane plunged out of control, killing all 258 passengers and 13 crew on board and two on the ground.	273

THE 10 WORST RAIL DISASTERS

LOCATION/DATE/INCIDENT	NO. KILLED
1 Bagmati River, India, 6 June 1981	c.800

The carriages of a train travelling from Samastipur to Banmukhi in Bihar plunged off a bridge over the river Bagmati near Mansi when the driver braked, apparently to avoid hitting a sacred cow. Although the official death toll was said to have been 268, many authorities have claimed that the train was so massively overcrowded that the actual figure was in excess of 800, making it probably the worst rail disaster of all time.

2 Chelyabinsk, Russia, 3 June 1989	up to 800

Two passenger trains, laden with holidaymakers heading to and from Black Sea resorts, were destroyed when liquid gas from a nearby pipeline exploded.

3 Guadalajara, Mexico, 18 January 1915	over 600

A train derailed on a steep incline, but political strife in the country meant that full details of the disaster were suppressed.

4 Modane, France, 12 December 1917	573

A troop-carrying train ran out of control and was derailed. It has been claimed that it was overloaded and that as many as 1,000 may have died.

5 Balvano, Italy, 2 March 1944	521

A heavily laden train stalled in the Armi Tunnel, and many passengers were asphyxiated. Like the disaster at Torre (No. 6), wartime secrecy prevented full details from being published.

6 Torre, Spain, 3 January 1944	over 500

A double collision and fire in a tunnel resulted in many deaths – some have put the total as high as 800.

7 Awash, Ethiopia, 13 January 1985	428

A derailment hurled a train laden with some 1,000 passengers into a ravine.

8 Cireau, Romania, 7 January 1917	374

An overcrowded passenger train crashed into a military train and was derailed.

9 Reqa al-Gharbiya, Egypt, 20 February 2002	372

A fire on the Cairo-Luxor train engulfed the carriages. The driver was unaware and continued while passengers were burned or leaped from the train to their deaths.

10 Quipungo, Angola, 31 May 1993	355

A trail was derailed by UNITA guerrilla action.

Casualty figures for rail accidents are often extremely imprecise, especially during wartime – and no fewer than half of the 10 worst disasters occurred during the two World Wars. Further vague incidents, such as one at Kalish, Poland, in December 1914, for example, with "400 dead", one in November 1918 at Norrköping, Sweden, alleged to have killed 300, and certain other similarly uncertain cases have been omitted.

▲ Casualty of war

Background picture: designed to carry some 1,500, the *Wilhelm Gustloff* may have had nearly 8,000 on board when she was torpedoed in 1945 – the worst ever loss of life at sea.

THE 10 WORST MOTOR VEHICLE AND ROAD DISASTERS

LOCATION/DATE/INCIDENT	NO. KILLED
1 Afghanistan, 3 November 1982	over 2,000

Following a collision with a Soviet army truck, a petrol tanker exploded in the 2.7-km (1.7-mile) Salang Tunnel. Some authorities have put the death toll from the explosion, fire, and fumes as high as 3,000.

2 Colombia, 7 August 1956	1,200

Seven army ammunition trucks exploded at night in the centre of Cali, destroying eight city blocks, including a barracks where 500 soldiers were sleeping.

3 Spain, 11 July 1978	217

A liquid gas tanker exploded in Los Alfaques, a camping site at San Carlos de la Rapita.

4 Thailand, 15 February 1991	171

A dynamite truck exploded in Phang Nga

5 Nigeria, 4 November 2000	150

A petrol tanker collided with a line of parked cars on the Ile-Ife-Ibadan Expressway, exploding and burning many to death. Some 96 bodies were recovered, but some estimates put the final toll as high as 200.

6 Nepal, 23 November 1974	148

Hindu pilgrims were killed when a suspension bridge over the River Mahahali collapsed.

7 Egypt, 9 August 1973	127

A bus drove into an irrigation canal.

8 Togo, 6 December 1965	over 125

Two lorries collided with dancers during a festival at Sotouboua.

9 South Korea, 28 April 1995	110

An underground explosion destroyed vehicles and caused about 100 cars and buses to plunge into the pit it created.

10 Kenya, early December 1992	106

A bus carrying 112 skidded, hit a bridge, and plunged into a river.

The worst-ever motor racing accident occurred on 13 June 1955, at Le Mans, France, when French driver Pierre Levegh's Mercedes-Benz 300 SLR went out of control, hit a wall, and exploded in mid-air, showering wreckage into the crowd and killing a total of 82. The worst British road accident occurred on 27 May 1975 when a coach crashed near Grassington, North Yorkshire, killing 33. The worst involving pedestrians was an incident when 24 Royal Marine Cadets were run down and killed by a double-decker bus in Gillingham, Kent, on 21 November 1971. It is believed that the worst-ever accident involving a single car occurred on 17 December 1956, when eight adults and four children were killed when the overcrowded car in which they were travelling was hit by a train near Phoenix, Arizona, USA. Although she was injured, 20-month-old Crucita Alires survived after being hurled into a tree by the impact.

World Tourism

⏱TOP10 COUNTRIES OF ORIGIN OF TOURISTS TO THE UK

	COUNTRY	OVERSEAS VISITORS (2002)
1	USA	3,611,000
2	France	3,077,000
3	Germany	2,556,000
4	Ireland	2,439,000
5	Netherlands	1,419,000
6	Spain	1,010,000
7	Italy	977,000
8	Belgium	966,000
9	Australia	702,000
10	Canada	660,000

Source: *Star UK*, International Passenger Survey

Dire predictions of the collapse of world tourism in the wake of 9/11 and the downturn in the global economy that was already evident before this failed to materialize. Visitor figures to the UK are generally up – albeit marginally – and the principal effect of the terrorist threat has been heightened security which, while it does not deter tourists, does ensure that their journey times are longer.

⏱TOP10 TOURIST DESTINATIONS

	COUNTRY	INTERNATIONAL VISITORS (2002)
1	France	77,000,000
2	Spain	51,700,000
3	USA	41,900,000
4	Italy	39,800,000
5	China	36,800,000
6	UK	24,200,000
7	Canada	20,100,000
8	Mexico	19,700,000
9	Austria	18,600,000
10	Germany	18,000,000

Source: *World Tourism Organization*

After a 0.5 per cent decrease in 2001, tourist numbers grew globally by 2.7 per cent in 2002, with the USA and Mexico the only countries in the Top 10 to experience a decline. Worldwide, international (cross-border) tourism was worth a total of some £296 billion ($474 billion), compared with a 1990 figure of £137 billion ($264 billion).

⏱TOP10 COUNTRIES EARNING THE MOST FROM TOURISM

	COUNTRY	INTERNATIONAL TOURISM RECEIPTS (2002) ($)
1	USA	66,500,000,000
2	Spain	33,600,000,000
3	France	32,300,000,000
4	Italy	26,900,000,000
5	China	20,400,000,000
6	Germany	19,200,000,000
7	UK	17,800,000,000
8	Austria	11,200,000,000
9	Hong Kong	10,100,000,000
10	Greece	9,700,000,000

Source: *World Tourism Organization*

⏱TOP10 MOST VISITED NATIONAL TRUST PROPERTIES

	PROPERTY/LOCATION	VISITORS (2002/2003)
1	**Wakehurst Place,** West Sussex	334,487
2	**Stourhead House and Garden,** Wiltshire	311,622
3	**Fountains Abbey and Studley Royal,** North Yorkshire	285,339
4	**Polesden Lacey,** Surrey	254,119
5	**Waddesdon Manor,** Buckinghamshire	219,118
6	**St. Michael's Mount,** Cornwall	215,106
7	**Lanhydrock,** Cornwall	208,433
8	**Sutton Hoo,** Suffolk	202,569
9	**Corfe Castle,** Dorset	178,888
10	**Chartwell,** Kent	178,675

Source: *National Trust*

▼ **French leave**
The cultural and other attractions of Paris and the rest of France have long made the country the world's foremost magnet for tourists.

TOP 10 WORLDWIDE AMUSEMENT AND THEME PARKS

PARK/LOCATION	ATTENDANCE (2003)
1 **The Magic Kingdom at Walt Disney World,** Lake Buena Vista, Florida	14,044,000
2 **Tokyo Disneyland,** Tokyo, Japan	13,188,000
3 **Disneyland,** Anaheim, California	12,720,000
4 **Disneysea,** Tokyo, Japan	12,174,000
5 **Disneyland Paris,** Marne-La-Vallée, France	10,230,000
6 **Universal Studios Japan,** Osaka, Japan	8,811,000
7 **Everland,** Kyonggi-Do, South Korea	8,800,000
8 **Epcot at Walt Disney World,** Lake Buena Vista, Florida	8,620,768
9 **Lotte World,** Seoul, South Korea	8,500,000
10 **Disney-MGM Studios at Walt Disney World,** Lake Buena Vista, Florida	7,870,733

Source: Amusement Business

Most amusement and theme parks have experienced flat or declining entrance numbers in recent years, while the introduction of South Korea's Everland (1976) and Lotte World (1989) and new parks in Japan, such as Tokyo's Disneysea and Universal Studios and Osaka's Universal Studios, which all opened in 2001, has shifted the global balance away from the USA.

TOP 10 TOURIST ATTRACTIONS IN THE UK

ATTRACTION/LOCATION	VISITORS (2003)
1 **Blackpool Pleasure Beach,** Blackpool	5,737,000
2 **British Museum,** London	4,584,000
3 **Tate Modern,** London	3,895,746
4 **Natural History Museum,** London	2,976,738
5 **Science Museum,** London	2,886,859
6 **Victoria & Albert Museum,** London	2,257,325
7 **Tower of London,** London	1,972,263*
8 **Eden Project,** Cornwall	1,404,737*
9 **Legoland,** Windsor, Berkshire	1,321,128*
10 **National Maritime Museum,** Greenwich, London	1,305,150

* Charging admission

Source: Association of Leading Visitor Attractions

SPORT & LEISURE

Olympic Feats

WINTER OLYMPICS MEDAL WINNERS

	MEDALLIST/COUNTRY	SPORT	YEARS	GOLD	MEDALS* SILVER	BRONZE	TOTAL
1	**Bjørn Dählie**, Norway	Nordic skiing	1992–98	8	4	0	12
2	**Raisa Smetanina**, USSR	Nordic skiing	1976–92	4	5	1	10
3 =	**Stefania Belmondo**, Italy	Nordic skiing	1992–2002	2	3	4	9
=	**Sixten Jernberg**, Sweden	Nordic skiing	1956–64	4	3	2	9
=	**Lyubov Egorova**, EUN#/Russia	Nordic skiing	1992–94	6	3	0	9
=	**Larisa Lazutina**, EUN#/Russia	Nordic skiing	1992–2002	5	3	1	9
7 =	**Karin Kania** (née Enke), East Germany	Speed skating	1980–88	3	4	1	8
=	**Galina Kulakova**, USSR	Nordic skiing	1968–80	4	2	2	8
=	**Gunda Neimann-Stirnemann** East Germany/Germany	Speed skating	1992–98	3	4	1	8
10 =	**Kjetil Andre Aamoldt**, Norway	Alpine skiing	1992–2002	3	2	2	7
=	**Peter Angerer**, West Germany/Germany	Biathlon	1984–94	3	2	2	7
=	**Ivar Ballangrud**, Norway	Speed skating	1928–36	4	2	1	7
=	**Andrea Ehrig** (née Mitscherlich; formerly Schöne), East Germany	Speed skating	1976–88	1	5	1	7
=	**Rico Gross**, Germany	Biathlon	1992–2002	3	2	2	7
=	**Veikko Hakulinen**, Finland	Nordic skiing	1952–60	3	3	1	7
=	**Marja-Liisa Kirvesniemi** (née Hämäläinen), Finland	Nordic skiing	1980–98	3	0	4	7
=	**Eero Mäntyranta**, Finland	Nordic skiing	1960–68	3	2	2	7
=	**Bogdan Musiol**, East Germany/Germany	Bobsledding	1986–92	1	5	1	7
=	**Claudia Pechstein**, Germany	Speed skating	1992–2002	4	1	2	7
=	**Clas Thunberg**, Norway	Speed skating	1924–28	5	1	1	7
=	**Elena Valbe**, EUN#/Russia	Nordic skiing	1992–98	3	0	4	7

* All events up to and including the 2002 Salt Lake City Games

\# EUN = Unified Team (Commonwealth of Independent States 1992)

The only person to win gold medals at both the Summer and Winter Games is Eddie Eagan of the United States. After winning the 1920 light-heavyweight boxing title, he then went on to win a gold medal as a member of the USA four-man bobsled team in 1932.

▶ A Bjørn winner

Known as the "Nannestad Express", after his home town in Norway, Bjørn Dählie is the most successful winter Olympic medallist of all time, winning four medals in each of three consecutive Games.

SUMMER OLYMPICS MEDAL WINNERS (WOMEN)

	MEDALLIST/COUNTRY	SPORT	YEARS	GOLD	SILVER	BRONZE	TOTAL
1	**Larissa Latynina**, USSR	Gymnastics	1956–64	9	5	4	18
2	**Vera Cáslavská**, Czechoslovakia	Gymnastics	1960–68	7	4	0	11
3 =	**Polina Astakhova**, USSR	Gymnastics	1956–64	5	2	3	10
=	**Birgit Fischer-Schmidt** East Germany/Germany	Canoeing	1980–2000	7	3	0	10
=	**Agnes Keleti**, Hungary	Gymnastics	1952–56	5	3	2	10
=	**Jenny Thompson**, USA	Swimming	1992–2000	8	1	1	10
7 =	**Nadia Comaneci**, Romania	Gymnastics	1976–80	5	3	1	9
=	**Dara Torres**, USA	Swimming	1984–2000	4	1	4	9
=	**Lyudmila Turishcheva**, USSR	Gymnastics	1968–76	4	3	2	9
10 =	**Shirley Babashoff**, USA	Swimming	1972–76	2	6	0	8
=	**Kornelia Ender**, East Germany	Swimming	1972–76	4	4	0	8
=	**Dawn Fraser**, Australia	Swimming	1956–64	4	4	0	8
=	**Sofia Muratova**, USSR	Gymnastics	1956–60	2	2	4	8

* 1896–2000 inclusive

Larissa Latynina holds the record for total medals won by any athlete in any sport in Olympic history. Vera Cáslavská (1968), along with Daniela Silivas of Romania (1988), are the only gymnasts to obtain medals in all six events at one Olympics. Canoeist Birgit Fischer-Schmidt holds the most Olympic canoeing medals ever.

SUMMER OLYMPICS MEDAL WINNERS (MEN)

	MEDALLIST/COUNTRY	SPORT	YEARS	GOLD	SILVER	BRONZE	TOTAL
1	**Nikolai Andrianov**, USSR	Gymnastics	1972–80	7	5	3	15
2 =	**Edoardo Mangiarotti**, Italy	Fencing	1936–60	6	5	2	13
=	**Takashi Ono**, Japan	Gymnastics	1952–64	5	4	4	13
=	**Boris Shakhlin**, USSR	Gymnastics	1956–64	7	4	2	13
5 =	**Sawao Kato**, Japan	Gymnastics	1968–76	8	3	1	12
=	**Alexei Nemov**, Russia	Gymnastics	1996–2000	4	2	6	12
=	**Paavo Nurmi**, Finland	Athletics	1920–28	9	3	0	12
8 =	**Matt Biondi**, USA	Swimming	1984–92	8	2	1	11
=	**Viktor Chukarin**, USSR	Gymnastics	1952–56	7	3	1	11
=	**Carl Osburn**, USA	Shooting	1912–24	5	4	2	11
=	**Mark Spitz**, USA	Swimming	1968–72	9	1	1	11

* 1896–2000 inclusive

Nikolai Andrianov is married to Olympic gymnast Lyubov Burda, who herself won two Olympic gold medals. Fencer Edoardo Mangiarotti won his first gold at the age of 17, making him the youngest male medallist at the 1936 Berlin Games. Although his overall total relegates him to the bottom of this list, Mark Spitz has the distinction of winning the most gold medals at a single Olympics, with seven in 1972.

SUMMER OLYMPICS MEDAL-WINNING COUNTRIES

	COUNTRY	GOLD	SILVER	BRONZE	TOTAL
1	**USA**	872	658	586	2,116
2	**USSR/Unified Team/Russia**	498	409	371	1,278
3	**Germany/ West Germany**	214	242	280	736
4	**Great Britain**	180	233	225	638
5	**France**	188	193	217	598
6	**Italy**	179	143	157	479
7	**Sweden**	136	156	177	469
8	**East Germany**	159	150	136	445
9	**Hungary**	150	135	158	443
10	**Australia**	102	110	138	350

* 1896–2000 inclusive

There have been 24 Summer Olympics since the 1896 Games in Athens (including the 1906 Intercalated Games, also in Athens). The USSR first entered the Olympics in 1952, but boycotted the 1984 Games. The USA boycotted the 1980 Games.

WINTER OLYMPICS MEDAL-WINNING COUNTRIES

	COUNTRY	GOLD	SILVER	BRONZE	TOTAL
1	**USSR/Unified Team/Russia**	113	82	78	273
2	**Norway**	94	93	73	260
3	**USA**	70	70	51	191
4	**Germany/ West Germany**	68	67	52	187
5	**Austria**	41	57	65	163
6	**Finland**	41	51	49	141
7	**East Germany**	39	37	35	111
8	**Sweden**	36	28	38	102
9	**Switzerland**	32	33	36	101
10	**Canada**	30	28	37	95

* Up to and including the 2002 Lake Placid Games; includes medals won at figure skating and ice hockey, which were included in the Summer Games prior to the launch of the Winter Olympics in 1924

Winter Sports

TOP 10 — SKIERS WITH THE MOST ALPINE SKIING WORLD CUP TITLES (FEMALE)

	SKIIER/COUNTRY		YEARS	OA	S	GS	SG	DH	C*	TOTAL
1	Annemarie Moser–Pröll, Austria		1971–79	6	–	3	–	7	1	16
2	Vreni Schneider, Switzerland		1986–95	3	6	5	–	–	–	14
3	Katia Seizinger, Germany		1992–98	2	–	–	5	4	–	11
4	Erika Hess, Switzerland		1981–84	2	5	1	–	–	1	8
5	= Hanni Wenzel, Liechenstein		1974–80	2	1	2	–	–	3	8
	= Renate Goetschl, Germany		1997–2000	–	–	1	1	4	2	8
7	Michela Figini, Switzerland		1985–89	2	–	–	1	4	–	7
8	= Lise–Marie Morerod, Switzerland		1975–78	1	2	3	–	–	–	6
	= Maria Walliser, Switzerland		1986–87	2	–	–	1	2	1	6
	= Janica Kostelic, Croatia		2001–03	2	2	–	–	–	2	6
	= Anita Wachter, Austria		1990–92	3	1	–	–	–	3	6

* OA = Overall; S = Slalom; GS = Giant slalom; SG = Super-giant slalom; DH = Downhill; C= Combined

The Alpine Skiing World Cup was launched as an annual event in 1967, with the addition of the super–giant slalom in 1986. Points are awarded for performances over a series of selected races during the winter months at meetings worldwide. As well as her 17 titles, Annemarie Moser-Pröll won a record 62 individual events in the period 1970–79, and went on to win gold for the Downhill event in the 1980 Olympic Games, when she achieved a record speed of 99.598 kmph (61.887 mph).

TOP 10 — SKIERS IN THE 2003/04 ALPINE WORLD CUP (FEMALE)

	SKIIER/COUNTRY	OVERALL POINTS*
1	Anja Paerson, Sweden	1,561
2	Renate Goetschl, Austria	1,344
3	Maria Reisch, Germany	977
4	Hilde Gerg, Germany	962
5	Carole Montillet, France	957
6	Michaela Dorfmeister, Austria	943
7	Martina Ertl, Germany	770
8	Alexandra Meissnitzer, Austria	734
9	Tania Poutiainen, Finland	669
10	Elizabeth Georgl, Austria	654

* Awarded for performances in slalom, giant slalom, super giant, downhill, and combination disciplines

Source: *International Ski Federation*

▶ **Downhill racer**
The first Croatian to win an Olympic medal, Janica Kostelic, who won three golds at the 2002 Olympics, has gained more World Cup titles in the 21st century than any other skier.

TOP 10 — SKIERS WITH THE MOST ALPINE SKIING WORLD CUP TITLES (MALE)

	SKIIER/COUNTRY		YEARS	OA	S	GS	SG	DH	C*	TOTAL
1	Ingemar Stenmark, Sweden		1976–84	3	8	7	–	–	–	18
2	= Marc Girardelli, Luxembourg		1984–94	5	3	1	–	2	4	15
	= Pirmin Zurbriggen, Switzerland		1984–90	4	–	3	4	2	2	15
4	Hermann Maier, Austria		1998–2001	4	–	2	5	2	–	13
5	= Phil Mahre, USA		1981–83	3	1	2	–	–	3	9
	= Gustavo Thoeni, Italy		1971–74	4	2	3	–	–	–	9
	= Alberto Tomba, Italy		1988–95	1	4	4	–	–	–	9
8	= Stephan Eberharter, Austria		2002–03	2	–	–	2	3	–	7
9	Jean–Claude Killy, France		1967–68	2	1	2	–	1	–	6
10	= Luc Alphand, France		1997	1	–	–	1	3	–	5
	= Franz Klammer, Austria		1975–83	–	–	–	–	5	–	5
	= Karl Schranz, Austria		1969–70	2	–	2	–	1	–	5
	= Andreas Wenzel, Liechtentein		1979–85	1	–	–	–	–	4	5

* OA = Overall; S = Slalom; GS = Giant slalom; SG = Super-giant slalom; DH = Downhill

TOP 10 — SKIERS IN THE 2003/04 ALPINE WORLD CUP (MALE)

	SKIER/COUNTRY	OVERALL POINTS*
1	Hermann Maier, Austria	1,265
2	Stephan Eberharter, Austria	1,223
3	Benjamin Raich, Austria	1,139
4	Bode Miller, USA	1,134
5	Daron Rahlves, USA	1,004
6	Kalle Palander, Finland	944
7	Michael Walchhofer, Austria	828
8	= Ivica Kostelic, Croatia	796
	= Hans Knauss, Austria	796
10	Rainer Shoenfelder, Austria	727

* Awarded for performances in slalom, giant slalom, super giant, downhill, and combination disciplines

Source: *International Ski Federation*

TOP 10 | OLYMPIC FIGURE SKATING COUNTRIES

| COUNTRY | MEDALS | | | |
---	GOLD	SILVER	BRONZE	TOTAL
1 USA	13	13	16	42
2 USSR*	13	10	6	29
3 Austria	7	9	4	20
4 Canada	3	7	9	19
5 Russia	9	7	0	16
6 UK	5	3	7	15
7 France	3	2	7	12
8 Germany/West Germany	4	4	13	11
9 = East Germany	3	3	4	10
= Sweden	5	3	2	10

* Includes Unified Team of 1992; excludes Russia since

Figure skating was part of the Summer Olympics in 1908 and 1920, becoming part of the Winter programme in 1924.

Track & Field

OLYMPIC TRACK AND FIELD GOLD MEDAL-WINNING COUNTRIES, 1896–2000 (MEN)

	COUNTRY	GOLD MEDALS
1	USA	268
2	Finland	48
3	UK	45
4	USSR*	37
5	Sweden	18
6	Kenya	15
7	East Germany	14
8	= Germany/West Germany	13
	= Italy	13
	= Poland	13

* Includes Unified Team of 1992; does not include Russia since then

The first American Olympic champion was James Connolly, in the Hop, Step and Jump. An undergraduate at Harvard, his dean refused him permission to travel to Athens in 1896, so he dropped out of university in order to compete.

OLYMPIC TRACK AND FIELD GOLD MEDAL-WINNING COUNTRIES, 1896–2000 (WOMEN)

	COUNTRY	GOLD MEDALS
1	USA	44
2	USSR*	34
3	East Germany	24
4	= Australia	18
	= Germany/West Germany	18
6	Romania	10
7	Poland	7
8	= France	6
	= Netherlands	6
	= UK	6

* Includes Unified Team of 1992; does not include Russia since then

FASTEST MILES EVER RUN

	ATHLETE/COUNTRY	YEAR	TIME (MIN:SEC)
1	Hicham El Guerrouj, Morocco	1999	3:43.13
2	Noah Ngeny, Kenya	1999	3:43.40
3	Noureddine Morceli, Algeria	1993	3:44.39
4	Hicham El Guerrouj	1998	3:44.60
5	Hicham El Guerrouj	1997	3:44.90
6	Hicham El Guerrouj	2001	3:44.95
7	Noureddine Morceli	1995	3:45.19
8	Hicham El Guerrouj	1997	3:45.64
9	Hicham El Guerrouj	2000	3:45.96
10	Hicham El Guerrouj	2000	3:46.24

World record holder Hicham El Guerrouj was inspired by his countryman Said Aouita, the 1984 Olympic 5,000-metres champion. Opting instead for the shorter distance, El Guerroj set the current world record in Rome in July 1999. As at 23 March 2004, he holds three world records. The fastest mile by a Briton is 3:46.32 by Steve Cram at Oslo in 1985.

HIGHEST HIGH JUMPS

	ATHLETE/COUNTRY	YEAR	HEIGHT* (M)
1	Javier Sotomayor, Cuba	1993	2.45
2	= Patrik Sjöberg, Sweden	1987	2.42
	= Carlo Thränhardt, West Germany#	1988	2.42
4	Igor Paklin, USSR	1985	2.41
5	= Charles Austin, USA	1991	2.40
	= Hollis Conway, USA#	1991	2.40
	= Sorin Matei, Romania	1990	2.40
	= Rudolf Povarnitsyn, USSR	1985	2.40
	= Vyochaslav Voronin, Russia	2000	2.40
10	= Dietmar Mögenburg, West Germany#	1985	2.39
	= Ralph Sonn, Germany#	1991	2.39
	= Jianhua Zhu, China	1984	2.39

* Highest by each athlete only; as at 1 January 2004

\# Indoor

Javier Sotomayor followed up his Olympic gold in 1992 by winning the 1993 World Indoor title; he then set the world record in Salamanca, followed by gold in the World Championships in Stuttgart.

LONGEST LONG JUMPS

	ATHLETE/COUNTRY	YEAR	DISTANCE* (M)
1	Mike Powell, USA	1991	8.95
2	Bob Beamon, USA	1968	8.90
3	Carl Lewis, USA	1991	8.87
4	Robert Emmiyan, USSR	1987	8.86
5	= Larry Myricks, USA	1988	8.74
	= Erick Walder, USA	1994	8.74
7	Iván Pedroso, Cuba	1995	8.71
8	Kareem Streete-Thompson, USA	1994	8.63
9	James Beckford, Jamaica	1997	8.62
10	Miguel Pate, USA#	2002	8.59

* Longest by each athlete only included; as at 1 January 2004

\# Indoor

The long jump world record has been broken by just four men since 1935, when Jesse Owens set a new world record mark of 8.13 metres. Ralph Boston broke it six times and the Russian Igor Ter-Ovanesyan twice. Their joint record of 8.35 metres was destroyed in Mexico City, when Bob Beamon leapt 8.90 metres. Beamon's record stood for 23 years until it was beaten by Mike Powell.

TOP 10 | FASTEST WOMEN EVER*

	ATHLETE/COUNTRY	YEAR	TIME
1	**Florence Griffith Joyner**, USA	1988	10.49
2	**Marion Jones**, USA	1998	10.65
3	**Christine Arron**, France	1998	10.73
4	**Merlene Ottey**, Jamaica	1996	10.74
5	**Evelyn Ashford**, USA	1984	10.76
6	**Irina Privalova**, Russia	1994	10.77
7	**Dawn Sowell**, USA	1989	10.78
8 =	**Inger Miller**, USA	1999	10.79
=	**Xuemei Li**, China	1997	10.79
10	**Marlies Oelsner-Göhr**, East Germany	1983	10.81

* Based on fastest time for the 100 metres; as at 1 January 2004

◀ **Tim's time**
The world's fastest man, Tim Montgomery of the United States, set a new world record mark of 9.78 seconds for the 100 metres in Paris on 14 September 2002.

TOP 10 | FASTEST MEN EVER*

	ATHLETE/COUNTRY	YEAR	TIME
1	**Tim Montgomery**, USA	2002	9.78
2	**Maurice Greene**, USA	1999	9.79
3 =	**Donovan Bailey**, Canada	1996	9.84
=	**Bruny Surin**, Canada	1999	9.84
5	**Leroy Burrell**, USA	1994	9.85
6 =	**Ato Boldon**, Trinidad	1998	9.86
=	**Frank Fredericks**, Namibia	1996	9.86
=	**Carl Lewis**, USA	1991	9.86
9 =	**Dwain Chambers**, UK	2002	9.87
=	**Linford Christie**, UK	1993	9.87
=	**Obadele Thompson**, Barbados	1998	9.87

* Based on fastest time for the 100 metres; as at 1 January 2004

Some would argue that Michael Johnson (USA) should be in this category with his remarkable 200-metre record of 19.32 seconds in 1996 (equivalent to a 100-metre time of 9.66 seconds), but his best 100-metre time is only 10.09 seconds.

American Football

▼ **A Cowboy catch**
The Dallas Cowboys, winners of a joint record five Super Bowls, have appeared in eight finals – an outright record.

TOP 10 | BIGGEST WINNING MARGINS IN THE SUPER BOWL

	WINNERS	RUNNERS-UP	YEAR	SCORE	MARGIN
1	San Francisco 49ers	Denver Broncos	1990	55–10	45
2	Chicago Bears	New England Patriots	1986	46–10	36
3	Dallas Cowboys	Buffalo Bills	1993	52–17	35
4	Washington Redskins	Denver Broncos	1988	42–10	32
5	Los Angeles Raiders	Washington Redskins	1984	38–9	29
6 =	Baltimore Ravens	New York Giants	2001	34–7	27
=	Tampa Bay Buccaneers	Oakland Raiders	2003	48–21	27
8	Green Bay Packers	Kansas City Chiefs	1967	35–10	25
9	San Francisco 49ers	San Diego Chargers	1995	49–26	23
10	San Francisco 49ers	Miami Dolphins	1985	38–16	22

Source: *National Football League*

The closest Super Bowl was in 1991, when the New York Giants beat the Buffalo Bills 20–19. Scott Norwood missed a 47-yard field goal eight seconds from the end, depriving the Bills of their first-ever Super Bowl win.

TOP 10 MOST SUCCESSFUL SUPER BOWL TEAMS

	TEAM	SUPER BOWL GAMES WINS	RUNNERS-UP	POINTS*
1	Dallas Cowboys	5	3	13
2 =	Pittsburgh Steelers	4	1	10
=	San Francisco 49ers	5	0	10
4 =	Denver Broncos	2	4	8
=	Oakland/Los Angeles Raiders	3	2	8
=	Washington Redskins	3	2	8
7 =	Green Bay Packers	3	1	7
=	Miami Dolphins	2	3	7
9	New England Patriots	2	2	6
10	New York Giants	2	1	5

* Based on two points for a Super Bowl win, and one for runner-up; wins take precedence over runners-up in determining ranking

Source: National Football League

TOP 10 POINTS SCORERS IN AN NFL SEASON

	PLAYER	TEAM	YEAR	POINTS
1	Paul Hornung	Green Bay Packers	1960	176
2	Gary Anderson	Minnesota Vikings	1998	164
3	Jeff Wilkins	St. Louis Rams	2003	163
4	Priest Holmes	Kansas City Chiefs	2003	162
5	Mark Moseley	Washington Redskins	1983	161
6	Marshall Faulk	St. Louis Rams	2000	160
7	Mike Vanderjagt	Indianapolis Colts	1999	157
8	Gino Cappelletti	Boston Patriots	1964	155*
9	Emmitt Smith	Dallas Cowboys	1995	150
10	Chip Lohmiller	Washington Redskins	1991	149

* Including a two-point conversion

Source: National Football League

A winner of the Heisman Trophy (presented to the best college player), Paul Hornung played in the crack Green Bay team of the 1960s. He led the NFL three times in scoring, and was voted MVP (Most Valuable Player) in 1960 and 1961.

TOP 10 PLAYERS WITH THE MOST CAREER POINTS

	PLAYER	POINTS
1	Gary Anderson*	2,346
2	Morten Andersen*	2,259
3	George Blanda	2,002
4	Norm Johnson	1,736
5	Nick Lowery	1,711
6	Jan Stenerud	1,699
7	Eddie Murray	1,594
8	Al Del Greco	1,584
9	Pat Leahy	1,470
10	Jim Turner	1,439

* Still active at end of 2003 season

Source: National Football League

Born in 1959, Gary Anderson started his career with the Steelers in 1982 before two seasons with Philadelphia in 1995–96. He had a year with the 49ers in 1997, moving on to the Minnesota Vikings in 1998 and then to the Tennessee Titans in 2003. He broke George Blanda's points record in 2000.

TOP 10 PLAYERS WITH THE MOST CAREER TOUCHDOWNS

	PLAYER	TOUCHDOWNS
1	Jerry Rice*	205
2	Emmitt Smith*	166
3	Marcus Allen	145
4 =	Cris Carter	131
=	Marshall Faulk*	131
6	Jim Brown	126
7	Walter Payton	125
8	John Riggins	116
9	Lenny Moore	113
10	Barry Sanders	109

* Still active at end of 2003 season

Source: National Football League

A wide receiver, Jerry Rice holds Super Bowl records in touchdowns, receptions, and receiving yards, winning three Super Bowls with the San Francisco 49ers (1989, 1990, 1995). He topped the NFL scoring list in 1987 with 130 points.

TOP 10 PLAYERS WITH THE MOST PASSING YARDS IN AN NFL CAREER

	PLAYER	PASSING YARDS
1	Dan Marino	61,361
2	John Elway	51,475
3	Warren Moon	49,325
4	Fran Tarkenton	47,003
5	Brett Favre*	45,646
6	Dan Fouts	43,040
7	Vinny Testaverde*	40,943
8	Joe Montana	40,551
9	Johnny Unitas	40,239
10	Dave Krieg	38,147

* Still active at end of 2003 season

Source: National Football League

After 17 consecutive seasons with the Dolphins, Dan Marino quit the game in 1999, but left with 20 NFL records to his credit. At the time of his retirement, he led the NFL in touchdown passes, yards passing, pass attempts, and completions.

Basketball Bests

TOP10 TEAMS WITH THE MOST NBA TITLES

	TEAM*	TITLES
1	Boston Celtics	16
2	Minneapolis/Los Angeles Lakers	15
3	Chicago Bulls	6
4	= Philadelphia/Golden State Warriors	3
	= Syracuse Nationals/Philadelphia 76ers	3
6	= Baltimore/Washington Bullets	2
	= Detroit Pistons	2
	= Houston Rockets	2
	= New York Knicks	2
	= San Antonio Spurs	2

* Teams separated by / have changed franchise and won the championship under both names

Source: *National Basketball Association*

Professional basketball in the United States dates to 1898, but the National Basketball Association (NBA) was not formed until 1949, when the National Basketball League and Basketball Association of America merged. The NBA consists of 27 teams split into Eastern and Western Conferences. At the end of an 82-game regular season, the top eight teams in each Conference play off, and the two Conference champions meet in a best-of-seven final.

TOP10 PLAYERS TO HAVE PLAYED MOST GAMES IN THE NBA AND ABA

	PLAYER	GAMES PLAYED*
1	Robert Parish	1,611
2	Kareem Abdul-Jabbar	1,560
3	John Stockton	1,504
4	Karl Malone#	1,476
5	Moses Malone	1,455
6	Kevin Willis#	1,390
7	Buck Williams	1,348
8	Artis Gilmore	1,329
9	Reggie Miller#	1,323
10	Elvin Hayes	1,303

* Regular season games only; up to end of 2003–04 season

 # Still active in the 2003-04 season

Source: *National Basketball Association*

The American Basketball Association (ABA) was established as a rival to the National Basketball Association (NBA) in 1968 and ran until 1976. As many of the sport's top players "defected", its figures are still included above. Robert Parish moved to the top of this list by playing his 1,561st game on 6 April 1996 at the Gateway Arena in Cleveland, between the Charlotte Hornets and the Cleveland Cavaliers.

TOP10 POINT-SCORERS IN AN NBA CAREER

	PLAYER	TOTAL POINTS*
1	Kareem Abdul-Jabbar	38,387
2	Karl Malone#	36,928
3	Michael Jordan	32,292
4	Wilt Chamberlain	31,419
5	Moses Malone	27,409
6	Elvin Hayes	27,313
7	Hakeem Olajuwon	26,946
8	Oscar Robertson	26,710
9	Dominique Wilkins	26,668
10	John Havlicek	26,395

* Regular season games only; up to end of 2003–04 season

 # Still active in the 2003–04 season

Source: *National Basketball Association*

If points from the ABA were also considered, then Abdul-Jabbar would still be No. 1. Born Lew Alcindor, he took a new name when he converted to the Islamic faith in 1969. The following year he turned professional, playing for Milwaukee until he retired in 1989. Despite holding the NBA record, he never scored 100 points in a game, a feat achieved by Wilt Chamberlain for Philadelphia against New York at Hershey, Pennsylvania on 2 March 1962.

TOP10 COACHES WITH THE MOST WINS IN THE NBA

	COACH	YEARS	REGULAR SEASON WINS	PLAY-OFF WINS	TOTAL WINS
1	Lenny Wilkens*	30	1,292	80	1,372
2	Pat Riley*	21	1,110	155	1,265
3	Don Nelson*	25	1,096	69	1,165
4	Red Auerbach	20	938	99	1,037
5	Bill Fitch	25	944	55	999
6	Dick Motta	25	935	56	991
7	Jerry Sloan*	18	875	78	953
8	Larry Brown*	20	879	69	948
9	Phil Jackson*	12	776	162	938
10	Jack Ramsay	21	864	44	908

* Still active in the 2002–03 season

Source: *National Basketball Association*

Pat Riley, coach of the LA Lakers, the New York Knicks, and the Miami Heat, has the best percentage record of those listed above, with 1,110 wins from 1,679 games, representing a 0.608 per cent success rate.

TOP10 HIGHEST SCORES IN THE NBA

	MATCH	DATE	SCORE*
1	Detroit Pistons vs. Denver Nuggets	13 Dec 1983	186(3)
2	Denver Nuggets vs. Detroit Pistons	13 Dec 1983	184(3)
3	= Boston Celtics vs. Minneapolis Lakers	27 Feb 1959	173
	= Phoenix Suns vs. Denver Nuggets	10 Nov 1990	173(3)
5	San Antonio Spurs vs. Milwaukee Bucks	6 Mar 1982	171(3)
6	Philadelphia 76ers vs. New York Knicks#	2 Mar 1962	169
7	Milwaukee Bucks vs. San Antonio Spurs	6 Mar 1982	166(3)
8	Cincinatti Royals vs. San Diego Clippers	12 Mar 1970	165
9	= Denver Nuggets v San Antonio Spurs	11 Jan 1984	163
	= Philadelphia 76ers v San Francisco Warriors	10 Mar 1963	163
	= San Antonio Spurs v San Diego Clippers	8 Nov 1978	163

* Figures in brackets indicate periods of overtime played

 # Game played at Hershey, Pennsylvania

The Denver–Detroit match on 13 December 1983 is the highest-scoring game on aggregate with a total of 370 points scored. The score stood at 145-all at the end of normal play, with Detroit eventually winning after three extra periods of play.

TOP 10 PLAYERS WITH THE HIGHEST POINTS AVERAGE

	PLAYER	GAMES PLAYED	POINTS SCORED	POINTS AVERAGE*
1	= Wilt Chamberlain	1,045	31,419	30.1
	= Michael Jordan	1,072	32,292	30.1
3	Elgin Baylor	846	23,149	27.4
4	Shaquille O'Neal#	809	21,916	27.1
5	= Allen Iverson#	535	14,436	27.0
	= Jerry West	932	25,192	27.0
7	Bob Pettit	792	20,880	26.4
8	George Gervin	791	20,708	26.2
9	Oscar Robertson	1,040	26,710	25.7
10	Karl Malone#	1,476	36,928	25.0

* Regular season games only; up to end of 2003–04 season

\# Still active in the 2003–04 season

Source: National Basketball Association

▶ **West Coast winners**
Along with the Boston Celtics, the Lakers are the most successful team in NBA history. They have won one less title than the Celtics but have appeared in nine more finals than their rivals.

TOP 10 POINT-SCORERS IN THE 2003–04 SEASON

	PLAYER/TEAM	GAMES	FIELD GOALS	FREE THROWS	TOTAL
1	**Kevin Garnett,** Minnesota Timberwolves	82	804	368	1,987
2	**Predrag Stojakovic,** Sacramento Kings	81	665	394	1,964
3	**Tracy McGrady,** Orlando Magic	67	653	398	1,878
4	**Paul Pierce,** Boston Celtics	80	602	517	1,836
5	**Michael Redd,** Milwaukee Bucks	82	633	383	1,776
6	**Carmelo Anthony,** Denver Nuggets	82	624	408	1,725
7	**Dirk Nowitksi,** Dallas Mavericks	77	605	371	1,680
8	**LeBron James,** Cleveland Cavaliers	79	622	347	1,654
9	**Vince Carter,** Toronto Raptors	73	608	336	1,645
10	**Stephon Marbury,** New Orleans Hornets	81	598	356	1,639

Source: National Basketball Association

Cricket Classics

TOP 10 WICKET TAKERS IN TEST CRICKET*

	BOWLER/COUNTRY	YEARS	TESTS	WICKETS*
1	**Courtney Walsh,** West Indies	1984–2001	132	519
2	**Shane Warne,** Australia	1992–2004	110	517
3	**Muttiah Muralitharan,** Sri Lanka	1992–2004	88	513
4	**Kapil Dev,** India	1978–94	131	434
5	**Richard Hadlee,** New Zealand	1973–90	86	431
6	**Glenn McGrath,** Australia	1993–2003	95	430
7	**Wasim Akram,** Pakistan	1985–2002	104	414
8	**Curtly Ambrose,** West Indies	1988–2000	98	405
9	**Anil Kumble,** India	1990–2004	83	392
10	**Ian Botham,** England	1977–92	102	383

* As at 15 April 2004

A right-arm fast bowler, Courtney Walsh was born in Jamaica and made his Test debut for the West Indies against Australia at Perth in 1984–85. He played his 132nd and last Test against South Africa in his home country in 2000–01. In March 2001 he became the first man to take 500 Test wickets, also against South Africa, at Port of Spain, Trinidad.

TOP 10 WICKET TAKERS IN ONE-DAY INTERNATIONALS*

	BOWLER	COUNTRY	MATCHES	WICKETS
1	**Wasim Akram**	Pakistan	356	502
2	**Waqar Younis**	Pakistan	262	416
3	**Muttiah Muralitharan**	Sri Lanka	229	350
4	= **Anil Kumble**	India	251	315
	= **Javagal Srinath**	India	229	315
6	**Shaun Pollock**	South Africa	214	297
7	**Warnakulasuriya Vaas**	Sri Lanka	232	292
8	**Shane Warne**	Australia	193	291
9	**Saqlain Mushtaq**	Pakistan	169	288
10	**Glenn McGrath**	Australia	185	284

* As at 15 April 2004

A left-arm fast bowler, Wasim Akram was the first man to achieve 400 wickets in both Test and One-Day Internationals. He made his One-Day debut against New Zealand at Faisalabad in 1984–85, and took his 500th One-Day wicket in 2003. In October of that year he bowed out of cricket after playing for a Pakistan XI against a World XI. His best One-Day figures were 5–15.

TOP 10 HIGHEST INDIVIDUAL TEST INNINGS

	BATSMAN	MATCH	VENUE	SEASON	RUNS*
1	**Brian Lara**	West Indies v England	St. John's	2003–04	400#
2	**Matthew Hayden**	Australia v Zimbabwe	Perth	2003–04	380
3	**Brian Lara**	West Indies v England	St. John's	1993–94	375
4	**Gary Sobers**	West Indies v Pakistan	Kingston	1957–58	365#
5	**Len Hutton**	England v Australia	The Oval	1938	364
6	**Sanath Jayasuriya**	Sri Lanka v India	Colombo	1997–98	340
7	**Hanif Mohammad**	Pakistan v West Indies	Bridgetown	1957–58	337
8	**Walter Hammond**	England v New Zealand	Auckland	1932–33	336#
9	= **Don Bradman**	Australia v England	Leeds	1930	334
	= **Mark Taylor**	Australia v Pakistan	Peshawar	1998–99	334#

* As at 15 April 2004
 # Not out

Len Hutton's Test record of 364 in 1938 seemed unbeatable until Gary Sobers came along and broke it by one run nearly 20 years later. His record also looked invincible until Brian Lara smashed it with a 375 in 1993–94. The West Indian's record stood for 10 years until October 2003, when Matthew Hayden of Australia scored 380 on the second day of the first Test against Zimbabwe at Perth.

TOP 10 RUN MAKERS IN TEST MATCH CRICKET*

	BATSMAN	COUNTRY	INNINGS	RUNS
1	**Allan Border**	Australia	265	11,174
2	**Steve Waugh**	Australia	260	10,927
3	**Sunil Gavaskar**	India	214	10,122
4	**Brian Lara**	West Indies	187	9,657
5	**Sachin Tendulkar**	India	183	9,469
6	**Graham Gooch**	England	215	8,900
7	**Javed Miandad**	Pakistan	189	8,832
8	**Viv Richards**	West Indies	182	8,540
9	**Alec Stewart**	England	235	8,463
10	**David Gower**	England	204	8,231

* As at 15 April 2004

Allan Border made his Test debut in the 1978–79 series against England. In the final Test he was relegated to drinks waiter. That was the last time he missed a game for Australia, as he went on to play a record 153 consecutive Tests – 47 more than the next best figure of 106 by Sunil Gavaskar. Border's last Test was against South Africa at Durban in the 1993–94 season.

TOP 10 RUN MAKERS IN ONE-DAY INTERNATIONALS*

	BATSMAN	COUNTRY	INNINGS	RUNS
1	Sachin Tendulkar	India	324	13,134
2	Inzamam-ul-Haq	Pakistan	292	9,796
3	Mohammad Azharuddin	India	308	9,378
4	Sourav Ganguly	India	241	9,309
5	Aravinda de Silva	Sri Lanka	296	9,284
6	Sanath Jayasuriya	Sri Lanka	305	9,248
7	Saeed Anwar	Pakistan	244	8,823
8	Desmond Haynes	West Indies	237	8,648
9	Brian Lara	West Indies	224	8,533
10	Mark Waugh	Australia	236	8,500

* As at 15 April 2004

Born in 1973, Sachin Tendulkar made his One-Day International debut for India at Gujranwala against Pakistan in 1989–90 at the age of 16, facing the bowling of Wasim Akram and Waqar Younis. He also made his Test debut at 16. Standing at just 1.6 m (5 ft 4 in), he has played First-Class cricket for Bombay and for Yorkshire. His highest One-Day score is 186 not out.

TOP 10 HIGHEST INDIVIDUAL FIRST-CLASS INNINGS

	BATSMAN	MATCH	VENUE	SEASON	RUNS*
1	Brian Lara	Warwickshire v Durham	Edgbaston	1994	501[#]
2	Hanif Mohammad	Karachi v Bahawalpur	Karachi	1958–59	499
3	Don Bradman	New South Wales v Queensland	Sydney	1929–30	452[#]
4	Bhausahib Nimbalkar	Maharashtra v Kathiawar	Poona	1948–49	443[#]
5	Bill Ponsford	Victoria v Queensland	Melbourne	1927–28	437
6	Bill Ponsford	Victoria v Tasmania	Melbourne	1922–23	429
7	Aftab Baloch	Sind v Baluchistan	Karachi	1973–74	428
8	Archie MacLaren	Lancashire v Somerset	Taunton	1895	424
9	Graeme Hick	Worcestershire v Somerset	Taunton	1988	405[#]
10	Brian Lara	West Indies v England	St John's	2003–04	400[#]

* As at 15 April 2004
[#] Not out

Twenty–four–year–old Hanif Mohammad came agonizingly close to becoming the first man to score 500 runs in a First-Class innings. Playing for Karachi in the semi-final of the Quaid-e-Azam trophy on 8–12 January 1959, he amassed 499 runs in Karachi's first innings total of 772–7 declared. However, having reached 499, he faced the last ball of the day on the third day's play and, keen to take his total to 500, he went for a run but was run out. He batted for 10 hours 35 minutes and hit 64 fours.

TOP 10 WICKET TAKERS IN A FIRST-CLASS CAREER

	BOWLER	CAREER	WICKETS*
1	Wilf Rhodes	1898–1930	4,187
2	Alfred Freeman	1914–36	3,776
3	Charlie Parker	1903–35	3,278
4	Jack Hearne	1888–1923	3,061
5	Tom Goddard	1922–52	2,979
6	W. G. Grace	1865–1908	2,876
7	Alex Kennedy	1907–36	2,874
8	Derek Shackleton	1948–69	2,857
9	Tony Lock	1946–71	2,844
10	Fred Titmus	1949–82	2,830

* As at 15 April 2004

Some sources give Rhodes's total as 4,204 and Grace's as 2,808. This is because of the confusion over what constituted a First-Class match in the late 19th and early 20th centuries. However, even if these second totals were considered, Rhodes would still be No. 1 and Grace would still be in the Top 10 at No. 10.

TOP 10 RUN-MAKERS IN A FIRST-CLASS CAREER

	BATSMAN	YEARS	TOTAL INNINGS	HIGHEST SCORE	RUNS*
1	Jack Hobbs	1905–34	1,325	365[#]	61,760
2	Frank Woolley	1906–38	1,530	305[#]	58,959
3	Patsy Hendren	1907–37	1,300	301[#]	57,611
4	Philip Mead	1905–36	1,340	280[#]	55,061
5	W. G. Grace	1865–1908	1,478	344	54,211
6	Herbert Sutcliffe	1919–45	1,098	313	50,670
7	Walter Hammond	1920–51	1,005	336	50,551
8	Geoff Boycott	1962–86	1,014	261[#]	48,426
9	Tom Graveney	1948–72	1,223	258	47,793
10	Graham Gooch	1973–2000	990	333	44,846

* As at 15 April 2004
[#] Not out

Sir John Berry "Jack" Hobbs was born in Cambridge in 1882. He offered his services to Essex but they turned him down and he played for Surrey instead, making his debut in 1905. Not only is Hobbs the most prolific scorer in First-Class cricket, but his total of 199 centuries is also a record. He was knighted in 1953 and, after retiring, ran a sports shop in Fleet Street.

Football UK

TOP 10 PREMIERSHIP GOALSCORERS

	PLAYER	CLUB(S)	GOALS*
1	Alan Shearer	Blackburn Rovers/Newcastle United	221
2	Andy Cole	Newcastle United/Manchester United/Blackburn Rovers	154
3	Les Ferdinand	Queen's Park Rangers/Newcastle United/Tottenham Hotspur	137
4	Robbie Fowler	Liverpool/Leeds United/Manchester City	136
5	Teddy Sheringham	Nottingham Forest/Tottenham Hotspur/Manchester United	130
6	Dwight Yorke	Aston Villa/Manchester United/Blackburn Rovers	116
7	Ian Wright	Arsenal	113
8	Dion Dublin	Manchester United/Coventry City/Aston Villa	108
9	Michael Owen	Liverpool	102
10	Matt Le Tissier	Southampton	101

* Up to and including the 2002–03 season

Although he started his career at Southampton, Alan Shearer never played for them in the Premiership. His first Premiership goal was for Blackburn Rovers at the start of the 1992–93 season, when he scored two against Crystal Palace on the new league's first day. Despite missing half of the season through injury, he still managed to score 16 goals. In April 1988 Shearer scored a hat trick for Southampton against Arsenal, and in doing so became the youngest scorer of a hat-trick in the top flight, at the age of 17 years and 240 days.

TOP 10 GOALSCORERS IN A FOOTBALL LEAGUE CAREER

	PLAYER	SEASONS	GOALS*
1	Arthur Rowley	1946–65	434
2	Dixie Dean	1923–37	379
3	Jimmy Greaves	1957–71	357
4	Steve Bloomer	1892–1914	352
5	George Camsell	1923–39	346
6	John Aldridge	1978–98	329
7	Vic Watson	1920–36	317
8	John Atyeo	1951–66	315
9	Joe Smith	1908–29	314
10 =	Henry Bedford	1919–34	309
=	Harry Johnson	1919–36	309

* Up to and including the 2002–03 season

Dixie Dean scored 349 goals for Everton, a record for a single club. All John Atyeo's 315 goals were for Bristol City, his only League club. Jimmy Greaves' goals were uniquely all in the First Division.

TOP 10 PLAYERS WITH THE MOST PREMIERSHIP APPEARANCES

	PLAYER	CLUB(S)	APPEARANCES*
1	Gary Speed	Leeds United/Everton/Newcastle United	376
2	Nigel Winterburn	Arsenal/West Ham United	352
3	David James	Liverpool/Aston Villa/West Ham United	345
4	Alan Shearer	Blackburn Rovers/Newcastle United	344
5	Teddy Sheringham	Nottingham Forest/Tottenham Hotspur/Manchester United	343
6	Ryan Giggs	Manchester United	342
7	Gareth Southgate	Crystal Palace/Aston Villa/Middlesbrough	339
8	Tim Sherwood	Blackburn Rovers/Tottenham Hotspur	328
9 =	Gary McAllister	Leeds United/Coventry City/Liverpool	325
=	David Seaman	Arsenal	325

* Up to and including the 2002–03 season

A member of the Leeds United side that was the last to win the old First Division title, Gary Speed has played in the Premiership since its formation in 1992. He moved to Everton in 1996, and from thence to Newcastle United in a £5.5 million deal in 1998. He surpassed Sheffield Wednesday's Peter Atherton as the Premiership's most experienced player in the 2001–02 season. Born in North Wales, Speed is a full Welsh international.

TOP 10 CLUBS TO HAVE WON THE MOST MATCHES IN THE PREMIERSHIP

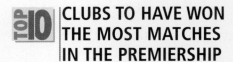

	CLUB	WINS*
1	Manchester United	269
2	Arsenal	218
3	Liverpool	207
4	Leeds United	181
5	Chelsea	178
6	Newcastle United	179
7	Aston Villa	166
8 =	Blackburn Rovers	150
=	Tottenham Hotspur	150
9	Everton	136

* Up to and including the 2002–03 season

Apart from Newcastle United (388 games) and Blackburn Rovers (354), the clubs listed above have played 430 Premiership matches, and have belonged to the league continuously since its inception.

MOST-CAPPED ENGLAND PLAYERS

	PLAYER	YEARS	INTERNATIONAL GOALS	CAPS*
1	Peter Shilton	1970–90	0	125
2	Bobby Moore	1962–73	2	108
3	Bobby Charlton	1958–70	49	106
4	Billy Wright	1946–59	3	105
5	Bryan Robson	1980–91	26	90
6	Kenny Sansom	1979–88	1	86
7	Ray Wilkins	1976–86	3	84
8	Gary Lineker	1984–92	48	80
9	John Barnes	1983–95	11	79
10	Stuart Pearce	1987–2001	5	78

* Up to and including the 2002–03 season

Goalkeeper Peter Shilton made his senior debut for Leicester City in May 1966, and four years later made his first appearance for England, against East Germany. Had Ray Clemence not also been at his peak at the same time, Shilton would surely have added more to his record tally of 125 caps. Third-placed Bobby Charlton's 49 goals scored for England in International matches stands as the all-time scoring record, with eighth-placed Gary Lineker's 48 just behind. Jimmy Greaves's 44-goal tally is remarkable for having been achieved in just 57 matches, while Nat Lofthouse's 30 goals produced from 33 games and Tommy Lawton's 22 from 23 only just miss an average of one goal per game.

PLAYERS WITH THE MOST FOOTBALL LEAGUE APPEARANCES

	PLAYER	YEARS	APPEARANCES*
1	Peter Shilton	1966–97	1,005
2	Tony Ford	1975–2001	914
3	Terry Paine	1957–77	824
4	Tommy Hutchison	1965–91	795
5	Robbie James	1973–94	782
6	Alan Oakes	1959–84	777
7	Dave Beasant	1979–2003	774
8	John Trollope	1960–80	770
9	Jimmy Dickinson	1946–65	764
10	Roy Sproson	1950–72	761

* Up to and including the 2002–03 season

John Trollope's total of 770 is a record for one club: he spent his entire career with Swindon Town. Peter Shilton's career was divided between Leicester City (286 appearances), Stoke City (110), Nottingham Forest (202), Southampton (188), Derby County (175), Plymouth Argyle (34), Bolton Wanderers (1) and Leyton Orient (9). Including cup competitions, he played in a record total of 1,390 senior matches. The record for the Scottish League is held by Graeme Armstrong, who made 879 appearances between 1975 and 1999.

CLUBS WITH THE MOST BRITISH TROPHIES*

	CLUB	LEAGUE TITLES	FA CUP/ SCOTTISH CUP	LEAGUE CUP	TOTAL
1	Glasgow Rangers	50	31	23	104
2	Glasgow Celtic	38	31	12	81
3	Liverpool	18	6	7	31
4	Manchester United	15	10	1	26
5	Arsenal	12	9	2	23
6	Aston Villa	7	7	5	19
7	Aberdeen	4	7	5	16
8	= Everton	9	5	-	14
	= Heart of Midlothian	4	6	4	14
10	Tottenham Hotspur	2	8	3	13

* Up to and including the 2002–03 season

The only club in Europe with 100 major trophies, Glasgow Rangers can also claim to have won more domestic League titles than any other club in the world. Their first honour was in 1890–91 when they won the inaugural Scottish League title, albeit they shared it with Dumbarton.

CLUBS WITH THE MOST FA CUP WINS

	CLUB	YEARS	TOTAL
1	Manchester United	1909–99	10
2	Arsenal	1930–2003	9
3	Tottenham Hotspur	1901–91	8
4	Aston Villa	1887–1957	7
5	= Blackburn Rovers	1884–1928	6
	= Liverpool	1965–2001	6
	= Newcastle United	1910–55	6
8	= Everton	1906–95	5
	= West Bromwich Albion	1888–1968	5
	= The Wanderers	1872–78	5

The first ever FA Cup Final was played in 1872 at the Kennington Oval cricket ground with a crowd of about 2,000, when The Wanderers beat Royal Engineers 1–0. Matches were played at Wembley (except for the 1970 replay, which took place at Old Trafford) from 1923, when Bolton Wanderers met West Ham United in front of a record crowd of 126,047, until the ground's closure in 2001, when the Millennium Stadium in Cardiff became the new home of English football.

International Football

TOP 10 MOST-CAPPED INTERNATIONAL PLAYERS

	PLAYER	COUNTRY	YEARS	CAPS*
1	Claudio Suarez#	Mexico	1992–2003	171
2	Mohamed Al-Deayea#	Saudi Arabia	1990–2004	166
3	Adnan Kh. Al-Talyania	United Arab Republic	1984–1997	164
4	= Hossam Hassan#	Egypt	1985–2004	160
	= Cobi Jones#	USA	1992–2003	160
6	Lothar Matthäus	West Germany/Germany	1980–2000	150
7	= Mohammed Al-Khilaiwi#	Saudi Arabia	1992–2002	143
	= Thomas Ravelli	Sweden	1981–1997	143
9	Majed Abdullah	Saudi Arabia	1978–1994	140
10	Marko Kristal#	Estonia	1992–2004	138

As at 8 March 2004

Still active in 2004

Source: *Roberto Mamrud, Karel Stokkermans, and RSSSF 1998/2004*

The most-capped British Isles footballer is Peter Shilton, with 125 caps won from 25 November 1970 to 7 July 1990. He represented England while with five clubs: Leicester City, Stoke City, Nottingham Forest, Southampton, and Derby County.

TOP 10 HIGHEST-EARNING FOOTBALLERS

	PLAYER/CLUB	ANNUAL INCOME* (£)
1	David Beckham (Real Madrid#)	10,546,000
2	Zinedine Zidane (Real Madrid)	9,842,000
3	Ronaldo (Real Madrid)	8,225,000
4	Rio Ferdinand (Manchester United)	6,763,000
5	Alessandro Del Piero (Juventus)	6,714,000
6	Hidetoshi Nakata (Bologna†)	6,580,000
7	Raul (Real Madrid)	6,538,000
8	Christian Vieri (Inter Milan)	6,524,000
9	Michael Owen (Liverpool)	6,257,000
10	Roy Keane (Manchester United)	6,081,000

As at 6 May 2003

Formerly Manchester United

† *Formerly Parma*

Source: *France Football*

▶ZZ Top

Marseille-born Zinedine Zidane is not only the most expensive footballer ever, but probably the greatest player in the world today as well. When he joined Real Madrid from Juventus in 2001, he cost £47.7 million.

TOP 10 TRANSFERS IN WORLD FOOTBALL

	PLAYER/COUNTRY	FROM	TO	YEAR	FEE (£)*
1	Zinedine Zidane, France	Juventus, Italy	Real Madrid, Spain	2001	47,700,000
2	Luis Figo, Portugal	Barcelona, Spain	Real Madrid, Spain	2000	37,400,000
3	Hernan Crespo, Argentina	Parma, Italy	Lazio, Italy	2000	35,700,000
4	Gianluigi Buffon, Italy	Parma, Italy	Juventus, Italy	2001	32,600,000
5	Rio Ferdinand, UK	Leeds United, England	Manchester United, England	2002	30,000,000
6	Gaizka Mendieta, Spain	Valencia, Spain	Lazio, Italy	2001	28,900,000
7	Ronaldo, Brazil	Inter Milan, Italy	Real Madrid, Spain	2002	28,490,000
8	Juan Sebastian Veron, Argentina	Lazio, Italy	Manchester United, England	2001	28,100,000
9	Rui Costa, Portugal	Fiorentina, Italy	AC Milan, Italy	2001	28,000,000
10	Pavel Nedved, Czech Republic	Lazio, Italy	Juventus, Italy	2001	25,500,000

Figures vary slightly from source to source, depending on whether local taxes, agents' fees, and player's commission are included

The world's first £10 million player was Gianluigi Lentini when he moved from Torino (Italy) to AC Milan (Italy) in June 1992, and the first to be transferred for £20 million was the Brazilian Denilson, when he moved from São Paolo (Brazil) to Real Betis (Spain) in 1998. The world's most expensive footballer, Frenchman Zinedine Zidane, started his professional career with Cannes in 1988 before moving to Bordeaux in 1992. He spent four years there before his move to Juventus. In July 2001 his transfer to Spanish giants Real Madrid made him the world's most expensive footballer.

TOP 10 RICHEST FOOTBALL CLUBS

	CLUB	COUNTRY	TURNOVER (2002/3) (£)
1	Manchester United	England	163,993,248
2	Juventus	Italy	142,401,456
3	AC Milan	Italy	130,594,464
4	Real Madrid	Spain	125,636,832
5	Bayern Munich	Germany	106,132,464
6	Inter Milan	Italy	105,936,768
7	Arsenal	England	97,587,072
8	Liverpool	England	97,456,608
9	Newcastle United	England	90,607,248
10	Chelsea	England	87,280,416

Source: *Sport Business Group at Deloitte*

In August 1989, the sale of Manchester United for £20 million to Isle of Man businessman Michael Knighton was agreed, but the deal fell through after Knighton's backers pulled out, and he duly bought Carlisle United instead. Two years later Manchester United was floated on the Stock Exchange, when it was valued at £18 million. Its subsequent fortunes have gone from strength to strength and the club is now valued at over £160 million.

TOP 10 BIGGEST WINS IN MAJOR INTERNATIONAL TOURNAMENTS

	WINNER/LOSER	TOURNAMENT	SCORE
1	Australia v American Samoa	2002 World Cup Qualifier	31–0
2	Australia v Tonga	2002 World Cup Qualifier	22–0
3	Kuwait v Bhutan	2000 Asian Championship Qualifier	20–0
4 =	China v Guam	2000 Asian Championship Qualifier	19–0
=	Iran v Guam	2002 World Cup Qualifier	19–0
6	Tahiti v American Samoa	2000 Oceanian Championship Qualifier	18–0
7 =	Australia v Cook Islands	2000 Oceanian Championship	17–0
=	China v Maldives	1992 Olympic Games Qualifier	17–0
=	Iran v Maldives	1998 World Cup Qualifier	17–0
10 =	Australia v Cook Islands	1998 Oceanian Championship	16–0
=	Denmark v France	1908 Olympic Games	17–1
=	South Korea v Nepal	2004 Asian Championship	16–0
=	Tajikistan v Guam	2002 World Cup Qualifier	16–0

The record wins for other major tournaments are: Copa America: Argentina v Ecuador, 1942, 12–0; European Championship: Spain v Malta, 1984, 12–1; British Championship: England v Ireland, 1899, 13–2.

TOP 10 GOAL SCORERS IN INTERNATIONAL FOOTBALL

	PLAYER	COUNTRY	YEARS	GOALS*
1	Ali Daei#	Iran	1993–2004	87
2	Ferenc Puskás	Hungary/Spain	1945–56	84
3	Pelé	Brazil	1957–71	77
4	Sándor Kocsis	Hungary	1948–56	75
5	Gerd Müller	West Germany	1966–74	68
6	Majed Abdullah	Saudi Arabia	1978–94	67
7	Jassem Al-Houwaidi#	Kuwait	1992–2004	63
8	Kiatisuk Senamuang#	Thailand	1993–2004	62
9	Hossam Hassan#	Egypt	1985–2004	61
10	Imre Schlosser	Hungary	1906–27	60

* *As at 8 March 2004*

Still active in 2004

Source: *Roberto Mamrud, Karel Stokkermans, and RSSSF 1998/2004*

If amateur appearances were included, Vivian Woodward (England) would figure on the list at No. 5 because he scored 73 goals for both the full and amateur England sides between 1903–14.

Rugby Highlights

MOST-CAPPED RUGBY UNION PLAYERS*

	PLAYER	COUNTRY	YEARS	CAPS
1	Jason Leonard	England/British Lions	1990–2004	119
2	Philippe Sella	France	1982–95	111
3	David Campese	Australia	1982–96	101
4	George Gregan	Australia	1994–2003	95
5	Serge Blanco	France	1980–91	93
6 =	Sean Fitzpatrick	New Zealand	1987–97	92
=	Martin Johnson	England/British Lions	1993–2003	92
8 =	Rory Underwood	England/British Lions	1984–96	91
=	Neil Jenkins	Wales/British Lions	1991–2002	91
=	Fabien Pelous	France	1995–2004	91

* Up to and including the 2003 IRB World Cup

Jason Leonard broke Philippe Sella's world record as the most-capped player when he appeared for England in the 2003 World Cup semi-final against France. After his appearance in England's win over Australia in the final, his tally stood at 118, including his five caps for the Lions. Born in 1968, Leonard has played in three Lions tours and four World Cups. He started his career with his home-town team of Barking before moving to Saracens and then Harlequins. In 2000 Leonard was awarded an MBE for his services to rugby.

POINTS SCORERS IN MAJOR INTERNATIONALS*

	PLAYER/COUNTRY	YEARS	POINTS
1	Neil Jenkins, Wales/British Lions	1991–2002	1,090
2	Diego Dominguez, Italy/Argentina	1989–2003	1,010
3	Andrew Mehrtens, New Zealand	1995–2002	932
4	Michael Lynagh, Australia	1984–95	911
5	Matthew Burke, Australia	1993–2003	866
6	Jonny Wilkinson, England/British Lions	1998–2003	853
7	Gavin Hastings, Scotland/British Lions	1986–95	733
8	Grant Fox, New Zealand	1985–93	645
9	Hugo Porta, Argentina	1971–90	590
10	Nicky Little, Fiji	1976–2003	574

* As at 7 April 2004

Nicknamed "The Ginger Monster", Neil Jenkins became Rugby Union's most prolific points scorer in the World Cup match against Samoa at Cardiff's Millennium Stadium on 14 October 1999. He scored 16 points and took his tally to 925, breaking the record of 911 set four years earlier by Australian Michael Lynagh. Sadly for Jenkins, who was also earning his 72nd cap, the game ended in a shock 38-31 win for the Samoans.

TOP 10 SCORES IN THE 2003 IRB* WORLD CUP

	WINNERS/LOSER	ROUND	SCORE
1	Australia v Namibia	Pool A	142–0
2	England v Uruguay	Pool C	111–13
3	New Zealand v Tonga	Pool D	91–7
4	Australia v Romania	Pool A	90–8
5	England v Georgia	Pool C	84–6
6	South Africa v Uruguay	Pool C	72–6
7	New Zealand v Italy	Pool D	70–7
8	New Zealand v Canada	Pool D	68–6
9	Argentina v Namibia	Pool A	67–14
10	Ireland v Namibia	Pool A	64–7

* International Rugby Board

The World Cup was launched in 1987, when 16 nations competed in the final stages, and New Zealand beat France 29–9 in the final in Auckland. Four years later, Twickenham staged the final, in which England lost 12–6 to Australia. The 1995 tournament was played in South Africa, with the host nation beating New Zealand in a thrilling final by 15 points to 12. Australia beat France 35–12 in the 1999 final at Cardiff, after a tournament was played jointly in Britain, Ireland, and France. The 2003 tournament was hosted by Australia, who were beaten in the final 20–17 by England in the last minute of extra time.

POINTS SCORERS IN THE 2003 IRB* WORLD CUP

	PLAYER	COUNTRY	POINTS
1	Jonny Wilkinson	England	113
2	Frederic Michalak	France	103
3	Elton Flatley	Australia	100
4	Leon MacDonald	New Zealand	75
5	Chris Paterson	Scotland	71
6	Mat Rogers	Australia	57
7	Mike Hercus	USA	51
8	Rima Wakarua	Italy	50
9	Earl Va'a	Samoa	49
10 =	Daniel Carter	New Zealand	48
=	Derick Hougaard	South Africa	48

* International Rugby Board

Jonny Wilkinson went into the 2003 final on 98 points, and passed the 100 mark with a 12th-minute penalty. He scored 15 points in the final, but the one every England fan will remember was his drop goal at the end of extra time to win the Cup. England's next top scorer was fly-half Paul Grayson, who scored 30 points from 15 conversions in his two games.

TOP 10 WORLD CUP POINTS SCORERS*

	PLAYER/COUNTRY	POINTS
1	**Gavin Hastings**, Scotland	227
2	**Michael Lynagh**, Australia	195
3	**Grant Fox**, New Zealand	170
4	**Andrew Mehrtens**, New Zealand	163
5	**Thierry Lacroix**, France	124
6	**Gareth Rees**, Canada	120
7	**Matthew Burke**, Australia	110
8	**Goazlo Quesada**, Argentina	102
9	**Jonathan Webb**, England	99
10	= **Diego Dominguez**, Italy	98
	= **Neil Jenkins**, Wales	98

* In the final stages

Source: *International Rugby Board (IRB)*

Gavin Hastings made his Scotland debut, alongside brother Scott, in the 1986 Five Nations tournament. He played in three World Cups and retired after the 1995 tournament in South Africa.

TOP 10 POINTS SCORERS IN A BRITISH RUGBY LEAGUE MATCH

	PLAYER	MATCH	YEAR	POINTS
1	**George West**	Hull Kingston Rovers v Brookland Rovers	1905	53
2	**Jim Sullivan**	Wigan v Flimby & Fothergill	1925	44
3	**Sammy Lloyd**	Castleford v Millom	1973	43
4	= **Darren Carter**	Barrow v Nottingham City	1994	42
	= **Lestyn Harris**	Leeds Rhinos v Huddersfield Giants	1999	42
	= **Dean Marwood**	Workington Town v Highfield	1992	42
	= **Dean Marwood**	Workington Town v Leigh	1995	42
8	= **Lee Briers**	Warrington Wolves v York	2000	40
	= **Shaun Edwards**	Wigan v Swinton	1992	40
	= **Paul Loughlin**	St. Helens v Carlisle	1986	40
	= **Martin Offiah**	Wigan v Leeds	1992	40
	= **Martin Pearson**	Featherstone Rovers v Whitehaven	1995	40

George Henry "Titch" West re-wrote the Rugby League record books on 4 March 1905. On that day Hull Kingston Rovers were drawn against Cumberland Senior League side Brookland Rovers in the first round of the Northern Union Cup. Hull Kingston Rovers won the match 73–5, with West scoring 11 tries and kicking 10 goals. He scored 180 points in the entire season, but nearly a third of them were in that single match. Hull Kingston Rovers went on to the Challenge Cup final that year, but lost to Warrington.

TOP 10 TEAMS SCORING THE MOST POINTS IN THE BRITISH SUPER LEAGUE

	TEAM	POINTS*
1	**St. Helens**	6,933
2	**Bradford Bulls**	6,843
3	**Wigan Warriors**	6,766
4	**Leeds Rhinos**	5,753
5	**Warrington Wolves**	5,179
6	**London Broncos**	4,690
7	**Halifax Blue Sox**	4,646
8	**Castleford Tigers**	4,554
9	**Hull FC**	3,688
10	**Salford City Reds**	2,892

* Excluding play-offs

The Super League was launched in 1996 after Rupert Murdoch's News Corporation invested £87 million in the European game over five years. The first Super League game was in March of that year, in which Sheffield Eagles played Paris. The first champions were St. Helens, who have won the Super League a record four times. Bradford Bulls (three times) and Wigan Warriors (once) are the only other winners of the title.

TOP 10 TRY SCORERS IN THE 2003 BRITISH SUPER LEAGUE

	PLAYER	CLUB	TRIES*
1	**Dennis Moran**	London Broncos	24
2	**Graham Appo**	Warrington Wolves	23
3	**Lesley Vainikolo**	Bradford Bulls	21
4	= **Colin Best**	Hull FC	19
	= **Mark Calderwood**	Leeds Rhinos	19
	= **Brandon Costin**	Huddersfield Giants	19
7	= **Darren Albert**	St. Helens	17
	= **Leon Pryce**	Bradford Bulls	17
9	**David Hodgson**	Wigan Warriors	16
10	**Tevita Vaikona**	Bradford Bulls	15

* League matches only

Dennis Moran is probably one of the best overseas recruits to the Super League. Australian-born Moran was the League's top try scorer in both 2002 and 2003, largely thanks to his deceptive pace and his ability to spot an opening in his opponents' defence. He stands at just 1.75 m (5 ft 9 in) and weighs just over 610 kg (12 stone) but his size, like his pace, belies his strength.

Tennis Aces

TOP 10 CAREER MONEY WINNERS (WOMEN)

PLAYER/COUNTRY	WINNINGS ($)*
1 **Steffi Graf,** West Germany/Germany	21,895,277
2 **Martina Navratilova,** Czechoslovakia/USA	20,942,793
3 **Martina Hingis,** Switzerland	18,344,660
4 **Arantxa Sanchez Vicario,** Spain	16,917,312
5 **Lindsay Davenport,** USA	16,474,970
6 **Monica Seles,** Yugoslavia/USA	14,891,762
7 **Venus Williams,** USA	13,029,463
8 **Serena Williams,** USA	12,546,863
9 **Jana Novotna,** Czechoslovakia	11,249,284
10 **Conchita Martinez,** Spain	10,613,659

* As at end 2003 season

TOP 10 CAREER MONEY WINNERS (MEN)

PLAYER/COUNTRY	WINNINGS ($)*
1 **Pete Sampras,** USA	43,280,489
2 **Andre Agassi,** USA	28,189,425
3 **Boris Becker,** West Germany/Germany	25,080,956
4 **Yevgeny Kafelnikov,** Russia	23,883,797
5 **Ivan Lendl,** Czechoslovakia/USA	21,262,417
6 **Stefan Edberg,** Sweden	20,630,941
7 **Goran Ivanisevic,** Croatia	19,769,363
8 **Michael Chang,** USA	19,145,632
9 **Gustavo Kuerten,** Brazil	14,224,746
10 **Jim Courier,** USA	14,033,132

* As at end 2003 season

◀ **Volleying to victory**
Germany's Steffi Graf eventually ended Martina Navratilova's five-year reign as the world number one in 1986, going on to win 22 Grand Slam singles titles.

TOP 10 WINNERS OF MEN'S GRAND SLAM TENNIS SINGLES TITLES

	PLAYER/COUNTRY	A	F	W	US	TOTAL*
1	Pete Sampras, USA	2	0	7	5	14
2	Roy Emerson, Australia	6	2	2	2	12
3	= Björn Borg, Sweden	0	6	5	0	11
	= Rod Laver, Australia	3	2	4	2	11
5	Bill Tilden, USA	0	0	3	7	10
6	= Andre Agassi, USA	4	1	1	2	8
	= Jimmy Connors, USA	1	0	2	5	8
	= Ivan Lendl, Czechoslovakia/USA	2	3	0	3	8
	= Fred Perry, Great Britain	1	1	3	3	8
	= Ken Rosewall, Australia	4	2	0	2	8

* Up to and including the 2003 events

A – Australian Open; F – French Open; W – Wimbledon; US – US Open

Australia's Roy Emerson had held the record for the most Grand Slam singles titles since 1968, but Pete Sampras equalled his record of 12 wins when he won Wimbledon in 1999 and the following year. When Sampras beat Pat Rafter to retain his title, it was his 13th – and record-breaking – title.

TOP 10 PLAYERS WITH THE MOST APPEARANCES IN THE DAVIS CUP

	PLAYER	COUNTRY	TIES PLAYED*
1	Nicola Pietrangeli	Italy	66
2	Ilie Nastase	Romania	52
3	= Manuel Santana	Spain	46
	= Orlando Sirola	Italy	46
5	Tomas Koch	Brazil	44
6	= Wilhelm Bungert	Germany	43
	= Ramanathan Krishnan	India	43
	= José-Edison Mandarino	Brazil	43
	= Jaidip Mukerjea	India	43
	= Ion Tiriac	Romania	43

* Number of ties played for one country

Despite playing in a record 66 Davis Cup ties between 1954 and 1972, "Nicky" Pietrangeli was never on the winning team, losing in two finals (1960 and 1961). However, he was the non-playing captain of the winning Italian side in 1976. Born in Tunis, Pietrangeli was the French Open singles champion in 1960 and 1961, and won doubles and mixed doubles titles in the same competition. The most Davis Cup ties played for Great Britain is 34, by Bobby Wilson; for the USA it is 30, by John McEnroe.

TOP 10 COUNTRIES WITH THE MOST WIMBLEDON SINGLES TITLES

	COUNTRY	SINGLES TITLES WOMEN'S	MEN'S	TOTAL
1	USA	47	33	80
2	UK	36	35	71
3	Australia	5	22	27
4	France	6	7	13
5	Germany	8	4	12
6	Sweden	-	7	7
7	Czechoslovakia/Czech Republic	3	2	5
8	New Zealand	-	4	4
9	Brazil	3	-	3
10	Spain	1	1	2

The first of the United States' 80 Wimbledon singles champions was May Sutton, who beat Britain's Dorothea Douglass 6–3 6–4 to win the ladies' title in 1905. The first American to win the men's title was "Big" Bill Tilden, who beat Gerald Patterson of Australia 2–6, 6–2, 6–3, 6–4 to win the first of his three titles in 1920. Tilden was the first American to win back-to-back singles.

TOP 10 WINNERS OF WOMEN'S GRAND SLAM SINGLES TITLES

	PLAYER/COUNTRY	A	F	W	US	TOTAL
1	Margaret Court (née Smith), Australia	11	5	3	5	24
2	Steffi Graf, West Germany/ Germany	4	6	7	5	22
3	Helen Wills-Moody, USA	0	4	8	7	19
4	= Chris Evert, USA	2	7	3	6	18
	= Martina Navratilova, Czechoslovakia/USA	3	2	9	4	18
6	Billie Jean King (née Moffitt), USA	1	1	6	4	12
7	= Maureen Connolly, USA)	1	2	3	3	9
	= Monica Seles, Yugoslavia/USA	4	3	0	2	9
9	= Suzanne Lenglen, France	0	2	6	0	8
	= Molla Mallory (née Bjurstedt), USA	0	0	0	8	8

A – Australian Open; F – French Open; W – Wimbledon; US – US Open

Margaret Court's first Grand Slam singles title was achieved on home soil when she won the 1960 Australian Open. Ten years later she became only the second woman after Maureen Connolly to win all four Grand Slam events in one year. The 1973 US Open was her final Grand Slam singles title.

Golfing Greats

MONEY-WINNING GOLFERS

	GOLFER/COUNTRY*	CAREER WINNINGS# ($)
1	Tiger Woods	41,707,315
2	Vijay Singh, Fiji	28,304,789
3	Davis Love III	28,110,850
4	Phil Mickelson	27,261,706
5	Ernie Els, South Africa	20,381,567
6	Nick Price, Zimbabwe	19,278,428
7	Jim Furyk	19,179,707
8	Scott Hoch	17,456,762
9	David Toms	16,815,009
10	Justin Leonard	16,529,546

* All US unless otherwise stated

\# As at 14 April 2004

MONEY-WINNING GOLFERS ON THE PGA US TOUR, 2003

	GOLFER/COUNTRY*	WINNINGS# ($)
1	Vijay Singh, Fiji	7,573,907
2	Tiger Woods	6,673,413
3	Davis Love III	6,081,896
4	Jim Furyk	5,182,865
5	Mike Weir	4,918,910
6	Kenny Perry	4,400,122
7	Chad Campbell	3,912,064
8	David Toms	3,710,905
9	Ernie Els, South Africa	3,371,237
10	Retief Goosen, South Africa	3,166,373

* All US unless otherwise stated

\# As at 1 January 2004

MONEY-WINNING GOLFERS ON THE PGA EUROPEAN TOUR, 2003

	GOLFER/COUNTRY	WINNINGS* (€)
1	Ernie Els, South Africa	2,975,374
2	Darren Clarke, N. Ireland	2,210,051
3	Padraig Harrington, Ireland	1,555,623
4	Fredrik Jacobsen, Sweden	1,521,303
5	Ian Poulter, England	1,500,855
6	Paul Caey, England	1,360,456
7	Lee Westwood, England	1,330,713
8	Thomas Björn, Denmark	1,327,148
9	Brian Davis, England	1,245,513
10	Phillip Price, Wales	1,234,018

* As at 1 January 2004

WINNERS OF WOMEN'S MAJORS

	GOLFER/COUNTRY*	TITLES#
1	Patty Berg	16
2 =	Louise Suggs	13
=	Mickey Wright	13
4	Babe Zaharias	12
5	Julie Inkster	11
6	Betsy Rawls	8
7	JoAnne Carner	7
8 =	Pat Bradley	6
=	Glenna Collett Vare	6
=	Betsy King	6
=	Patty Sheehan	6
=	Annika Sörenstam, Sweden	6
=	Karrie Webb, Australia	6
=	Kathy Whitworth	6

* All US unless otherwise stated

\# As at 14 April 2004

The present-day Majors are: the US Open, LPGA Championship, Nabisco Championship, British Open, and the amateur championships of both the USA and the UK. Also taken into account in this Top 10 are wins in the former Majors: the Western Open (1937–67), Titleholders Championship (1930–72), and the du Maurier Classic (1977–2000).

▶ **First lady**
Louise Suggs turned professional in 1948 and went on to win 50 LPGA events. She was the first woman elected to the LPGA Hall of Fame.

TOP 10 | GOLFERS TO WIN THE MOST MAJORS

	GOLFER/COUNTRY*	BRITISH OPEN	US OPEN	US MASTERS	US PGA	TOTAL#
1	Jack Nicklaus	3	4	6	5	18
2	Walter Hagen	4	2	0	5	11
3	= Ben Hogan	1	4	2	2	9
	= Gary Player, South Africa	3	1	3	2	9
5	= Tom Watson	5	1	2	0	8
	= Tiger Woods	1	2	3	2	8
7	= Bobby Jones	3	4	0	0	7
	= Arnold Palmer	2	1	4	0	7
	= Gene Sarazen	1	2	1	3	7
	= Sam Snead	1	0	3	3	7
	= Harry Vardon, Great Britain	6	1	0	0	7

* All US unless otherwise indicated

As at 14 April 2004

The four majors are the British Open, the US Open, the US Masters, and the US PGA. No man has won all four Majors in one year. Ben Hogan, in 1953, won three of the four, but did not compete in the PGA Championship. Bobby Jones achieved a unique Grand Slam in 1930 by winning the British Open and US Open, as well as winning the amateur titles in both countries.

TOP 10 | LOWEST FOUR-ROUND TOTALS IN MAJOR CHAMPIONSHIPS

	GOLFER/COUNTRY	VENUE	YEAR	TOTAL
1	David Toms, USA	Atlanta, Georgia*	2001	265
2	Phil Mickelson, USA	Atlanta, Georgia*	2001	266
3	= Greg Norman, Australia	Royal St. George's, Sandwich#	1993	267
	= Steve Elkington, Australia	Riviera, California*	1995	267
	= Colin Montgomerie, UK	Riviera, California*	1995	267
6	= Tom Watson, USA	Turnberry#	1977	268
	= Nick Price, Zimbabwe	Turnberry#	1994	268
	= Steve Lowery, USA	Atlanta, Georgia*	2001	268
9	= Jack Nicklaus, USA	Turnberry#	1977	269
	= Nick Faldo, UK	Royal St. George's, Sandwich#	1993	269
	= Jesper Parnevik, Sweden	Turnberry#	1994	269
	= Nick Price, Zimbabwe	Southern Hills, Oklahoma*	1994	269
	= Davis Love III, USA	Winged Foot, New York*	1997	269
	= Tiger Woods, USA	St. Andrews#	2000	269

* US PGA Championship

British Open Championship

Water Sports

TOP 10 OLYMPIC CANOEING COUNTRIES

	COUNTRY	GOLD	MEDALS SILVER	BRONZE	TOTAL
1	Hungary	14	25	21	60
2 =	Germany*	22	16	15	53
=	USSR#	30	14	9	53
4	Romania	10	10	14	34
5	East Germany	14	7	9	30
6	Sweden	14	11	4	29
7	France	3	7	16	26
8	Bulgaria	4	5	8	17
9	Canada	3	8	5	16
10 =	Poland	0	5	10	15
=	USA	5	4	6	15
	Great Britain	–	2	1	3

* Not including West/East Germany 1968–88

 # Includes Unified Team of 1992; excludes Russia since then

Canoeing has been an official Olympic sport since 1936, although it was first seen as a demonstration sport at the 1924 Paris Olympics.

TOP 10 OLYMPIC SWIMMING COUNTRIES

	COUNTRY	GOLD	MEDALS* SILVER	BRONZE	TOTAL
1	USA	192	138	104	434
2	Australia	45	46	51	142
3	East Germany	38	32	22	92
4	USSR#	18	24	27	69
5	Germany†	12	23	30	65
6	Great Britain	14	22	26	62
7	Hungary	24	20	16	60
8	Japan	15	20	14	49
9	Holland	14	14	16	44
10	Canada	7	13	19	39

* Excluding diving, water polo, and synchronized swimming

 # Includes Unified Team of 1992; excludes Russia since then

† Not including West/East Germany 1968–88

TOP 10 SWIMMERS WITH THE MOST OLYMPIC GOLD MEDALS

	SWIMMER/COUNTRY	YEARS	GOLD MEDALS
1	**Mark Spitz,** USA	1968–72	9
2 =	**Matt Biondi,** USA	1984–92	8
=	**Jenny Thompson,** USA	1992–2000	8
4 =	**Kristin Otto,** East Germany	1988	6
=	**Amy Van Dyken,** USA	1996–2000	6
6 =	**Charles Daniels,** USA	1904–08	5
=	**Krisztina Egerszegi,** Hungary	1988–96	5
=	**Don Schollander,** USA	1964–68	5
=	**Johnny Weissmuller,** USA	1924–28	5
10 =	**Tamus Darnyi,** Hungary	1988–92	4
=	**Kornelia Ender,** East Germany	1976	4
=	**Dawn Fraser,** Australia	1956–64	4
=	**Gary Hall Jr.,** USA	1996-2000	4
=	**Roland Matthes,** East Germany	1968–72	4
=	**John Naber,** USA	1976	4
=	**Alexander Popov,** EUN*/Rus	1992–1996	4
=	**Murray Rose,** Australia	1956–60	4
=	**Vladimir Salnikov,** USSR	1980–88	4
=	**Henry Taylor,** Great Britain	1906–08	4
=	**Dara Torres,** USA	1984–2000	4

* Unified Team representing the Commonwealth of Independent States (former Soviet republics)

Mark Spitz holds the record for winning the most gold medals at one Games – seven in 1972, which is the most by any competitor in any sport. His overall tally of golds is nine, but it should have been much more. He went into the 1968 Mexico Olympics as the holder of several world records and was expecting to win six gold medals, but came away with just two, and they were in relay events. His gold medals haul at the 1972 Munich Games came in the following events and, remarkably, all were won in world record-breaking times:

EVENT	TIME (MIN:SEC)	EVENT	TIME (MIN:SEC)
100 metres freestyle	0:51.22	4 x 100 metres freestyle relay	3:26.42
200 metres freestyle	1:52.78	4 x 200 metres freestyle relay	7:35.78
100 metres butterfly	0:54.27	4 x 100 metres medley relay	3:48.16
200 metres butterfly	2:00.70		

▼ **A team player**
All of Jenny Thompson's gold medals came in relay events. She won an individual silver in 1992 and a bronze in 2000, when she tied with Dara Torres (also from the USA) for third place.

OLYMPIC SAILING* COUNTRIES

	COUNTRY	MEDALS			
		GOLD	SILVER	BRONZE	TOTAL
1	**USA**	17	21	16	54
2	**Great Britain**	18	12	8	38
3	**Sweden**	9	12	10	31
4	**Norway**	16	11	3	30
5	**France**	11	7	9	27
6	**Denmark**	11	8	4	23
7	**Germany/ West Germany**	5	6	7	18
8	= **Australia**	5	3	8	16
	= **Holland**	4	5	7	16
10	**New Zealand**	6	4	5	15

* *Previously named Olympic yachting*

LATEST WINNERS OF THE AMERICA'S CUP

	WINNING BOAT/SKIPPER/COUNTRY	CHALLENGER/COUNTRY	SCORE
2003	**Alinghi,** Russell Coutts, Switzerland	Team New Zealand, New Zealand	5–0
2000	**Black Magic,** Russell Coutts, New Zealand	Prada Luna Rossa, Italy	5–0
1995	**Black Magic,** Russell Coutts, New Zealand	Young America, USA	5–0
1992	**America3,** Bill Koch, USA	Il Moro di Venezia, Italy	4–1
1988	**Stars and Stripes,** Dennis Conner, USA	New Zealand, New Zealand	2–0
1987	**Stars and Stripes,** Dennis Conner, USA	Kookaburra III, Australia	4–0
1983	**Australia II,** John Bertrand, Australia	Liberty, USA	4–3
1980	**Freedom,** Dennis Conner, USA	Australia, Australia	4–1
1977	**Courageous,** Ted Turner, USA	Australia, Australia	4–0
1974	**Courageous,** Ted Hood, USA	Southern Cross, Australia	4–0

The Americans' 132-year domination of the America's Cup came to an end on 26 September 1983 when 37-year-old John Bertrand skippered *Australia II* – a revolutionary boat designed by Ben Lexcen and owned by Alan Bond – to victory. Prior to this the trophy had been in the ownership of the New York Yacht Club – and was held to the floor by a 1.2 m (4 ft) bolt!

Tough Guys

THE 10 | LATEST WINNERS OF THE WORLD'S STRONGEST MAN CONTEST

YEAR	STRONGMAN	COUNTRY
2003	Mariusz Pudzianowski	Poland
2002	Mariusz Pudzianowski	Poland
2001	Svend Karlsen	Norway
2000	Janne Virtanen	Finland
1999	Jouko Ahola	Finland
1998	Magnus Samuelsson	Sweden
1997	Jouko Ahola	Finland
1996	Magnus Ver Magnusson	Iceland
1995	Magnus Ver Magnusson	Iceland
1994	Magnus Ver Magnusson	Iceland

Mariusz Pudzianowski won his second world title in 2003. He was the joint top-scorer with Svend Karlsen of Norway after the opening round, but in the final Pudzianowski destroyed all opposition to win by 20 points from Zydrunas Savickas of Lithuania.

THE 10 | LATEST UNDISPUTED WORLD HEAVYWEIGHT BOXING CHAMPIONS

	BOXER/COUNTRY*	YEAR
1	Lennox Lewis, UK	1999
2	Riddick Bowe	1992
3	Evander Holyfield	1990
4	James Buster Douglas	1990
5	Mike Tyson	1987
6	Leon Spinks	1978
7	Muhammad Ali	1974
8	George Foreman	1973
9	Joe Frazier	1970
10	Muhammad Ali	1967

* All US unless otherwise stated

"Undisputed" champions are those who are recognized by the main governing bodies at the time of winning their world title. The current main governing bodies are: the World Boxing Council (WBC), World Boxing Association (WBA), International Boxing Federation (IBF), and World Boxing Organization (WBO).

TOP 10 | OLYMPIC JUDO COUNTRIES

	COUNTRY	GOLD	MEDALS SILVER	BRONZE	TOTAL
1	Japan	23	12	13	48
2	France	10	5	17	32
3	South Korea	7	10	13	30
4	USSR*	7	5	15	27
5	Cuba	5	7	8	20
6	Germany/ West Germany	2	5	10	17
7	Great Britain	–	7	9	16
8	Netherlands	4	–	7	11
9	= Brazil	2	3	5	10
	= China	4	1	5	10
	= Italy	2	3	5	10

* Includes Unified Team of 1992; excludes Russia since then

Judo made its debut at the 1964 Tokyo Olympics, but for men only, and was not included in the 1968 Mexico City Games. Women's judo was not introduced until the 1992 Barcelona Games.

BOX WITH GLOVES

ALTHOUGH ANCIENT GREEK BOXERS used leather hand coverings, bareknuckle fighting was popular for centuries, and serious injuries and even death were common. Gloves known as "mufflers" had been invented in 1743, but were used only for sparring until the Marquess of Queensberry drew up his rules, under which gloves became mandatory. The first world heavyweight contest under the new rules was fought on 29 August 1885 in Cincinnati, USA, between bareknuckle champion John L. Sullivan and Dominick McCaffrey.

THE FIRST TO....

FIRST BRITISH-BORN BOXING WORLD CHAMPIONS

BOXER	BIRTHPLACE	WEIGHT AT WHICH FIRST TITLE WON	FIRST TITLE WON
1 Ike Weir	Belfast	Featherweight	1889
2 Bob Fitzsimmons	Helston, Cornwall	Middleweight	1891
3 Joe Bowker	Salford	Bantamweight	1904
4 Freddie Welsh	Pontypridd	Lightweight	1914
5 Ted "Kid" Lewis	London	Welterweight	1915
6 Jimmy Wilde	Tylorstown, Wales	Flyweight	1916
7 Jack "Kid" Berg	London	Light-welterweight	1930
8 Jackie Brown	Manchester	Flyweight	1932
9 Benny Lynch	Clydesdale	Flyweight	1935
10 Peter Kane	Golborne, nr. Warrington	Flyweight	1938

Bob Fitzsimmons went on to win world titles at three weights including heavyweight; he is the only British-born boxer to win the sport's premier title. Some sources regard Weir's assertion to be the first world featherweight champion as dubious because he claimed the title following an 80-round draw with Frank Murphy (England) at Kouts, Indiana, on 31 March 1889.

◀ **A heavyweight punch**
Lennox Lewis first hit the headlines when he won the Olympic Super-heavyweight title in 1988, representing Canada. In his first pro bout in June 1989, he beat Al Malcolm with a second round knockout.

LONGEST-REIGNING BOXING WORLD CHAMPIONS*

BOXER/COUNTRY	WEIGHT	YEARS	REIGN# (YRS)	(MTHS)
1 Joe Louis, USA	Heavyweight	1937–49	1	7
2 Johnny Kilbane, USA	Featherweight	1912–23	11	4
3 Ricardo Lopez, Mexico	Strawweight	1990–2000	9	8
4 Archie Moore, USA	Light-heavyweight	1952–62	9	
5 Bernard Hopkins, USA	Middleweight	1995–2004	8	11
6 Felix Trinidad, Puerto Rico	Welterweight	1993–99	8	5
7 Benny Leonard, USA	Lightweight	1917–25	7	8
8 Jimmy Wilde, UK	Flyweight	1916–23	7	4
9 Flash Elorde, Philippines	Junior-lightweight	1960–67	7	3
10 Kaosai Galaxy, Thailand	Junior-bantamweight	1984–91	7	

* Based on longest uninterrupted reign in each weight division
 # As at 14 April 2004

Boxing history was made on 9 May 1988 when Kaokar Galaxy won the WBA bantamweight title, while his twin brother Kaosai was the holder of the WBA junior-bantamweight title at the time – the first time twins had held world titles.

OLYMPIC FREESTYLE WRESTLING COUNTRIES

COUNTRY	GOLD	MEDALS TOTAL
1 USA	44	103
2 USSR*	31	63
3 = Bulgaria	7	33
= Japan	16	33
= Turkey	16	33
6 = Iran	5	26
= Sweden	8	26
8 Finland	8	25
9 South Korea	4	19
10 Great Britain#	3	17

* Includes Unified Team of 1992; excludes Russia since then
 # Great Britain's three gold medals in the freestyle event all date from the 1908 games

Horses for Courses

TOP 10 NATIONAL HUNT JOCKEYS WITH THE MOST CAREER WINS

	JOCKEY	YEARS	WINS*
1	Tony McCoy	1994–2004	2,002
2	Richard Dunwoody	1983–99	1,699
3	Peter Scudamore	1978–95	1,678
4	Richard Johnson	1994–2004	1,141
5	John Francome	1970–85	1,138
6	Stan Mellor	1952–72	1,035
7	Mick Fitzgerald	1988–2004	1,030
8	Adrian Maguire	1991–2002	1,024
9	Peter Niven	1984–2002	1,002
10	Fred Winter	1939–64	923

* As at 18 January 2004

Peter Niven and Adrian Maguire both passed the 1,000 winner mark in 2001 and by coincidence they are the only two members of the "1,000" club never to have won the National Hunt Jockey's title. Niven is the first Scot to ride 1,000 National Hunt winners. Tony McCoy became the first man to ride 2,000 National Hunt winners on *Magical Balliwick* at Wincanton on 17 January 2004.

TOP 10 JOCKEYS IN A FLAT RACING SEASON

	JOCKEY	YEAR	WINS
1	Gordon Richards	1947	269
2	Gordon Richards	1949	261
3	Gordon Richards	1933	259
4	Fred Archer	1885	246
5	Fred Archer	1884	241
6	Frankie Dettori	1994	233
7	Fred Archer	1883	232
8	Gordon Richards	1952	231
9	Fred Archer	1878	229
10	Gordon Richards	1951	227

Richards rode over 200 winners in a season 12 times, while Archer did so on eight occasions. The only other men to reach double centuries are Tommy Loates (1893), Pat Eddery (1990), Michael Roberts (1992), and Kieren Fallon (1997, 1998 and 1999).

TOP 10 JOCKEYS IN THE EPSOM DERBY

	JOCKEY	YEARS	WINS
1	Lester Piggott	1954–83	9
2	= Steve Donoghue	1915–25	6
	= Jem Robinson	1817–36	6
4	= Fred Archer	1877–86	5
	= John Arnull	1784–99	5
	= Frank Buckle	1792–1823	5
	= Bill Clift	1793–1819	5
8	= Sam Arnull	1780–98	4
	= Willie Carson	1979–94	4
	= Tom Goodison	1809–22	4
	= Bill Scott	1832–43	4
	= Charlie Smirke	1934–58	4
	= Jack Watts	1887–96	4

▼ Success breeds success

The leading day in US thoroughbred racing, the Breeders Cup is an end-of-season gathering of the top horses racing in eight featured races. The first Breeders' Cup was held at Hollywood Park, California in 1984.

TOP 10 JOCKEYS IN THE ENGLISH CLASSICS

	JOCKEY	YEARS	1,000 GUINEAS	2,000 GUINEAS	DERBY	OAKS	ST. LEGER	WINS
1	Lester Piggott	1954–92	2	5	9	6	8	30
2	Frank Buckle	1792–1827	6	5	5	9	2	27
3	Jem Robinson	1817–48	5	9	6	2	2	24
4	Fred Archer	1874–86	2	4	5	4	6	21
5 =	Bill Scott	1821–46	0	3	4	3	9	19
=	Jack Watts	1883–97	4	2	4	4	5	19
7	Willie Carson	1972–94	2	4	4	4	3	17
8 =	John Day	1826–41	5	4	0	5	2	16
=	George Fordham	1859–83	7	3	1	5	0	16
10	Joe Childs	1912–33	2	2	3	4	4	15

TOP 10 JOCKEYS IN THE BREEDERS' CUP

	JOCKEY	YEARS	WINS
1	Jerry Bailey	1991–2003	14
2	Pat Day	1984–2001	12
3	Mike Smith	1992–2002	10
4	Chris McCarron	1985–2001	9
5	Gary Stevens	1990–2000	8
6 =	Eddie Delahoussaye	1984–93	7
=	Laffit Pincay Jr.	1985–93	7
=	Jose Santos	1986–2002	7
=	Pat Valenzuela	1986–2003	7
10	Corey Nakatani	1996–99	5

Source: *The Breeders' Cup*

Held at a different venue each year, the Breeders' Cup is an end-of-season gathering culminating in seven races run over one day, with the season's best thoroughbreds competing in each category. Staged in October or November, there is $10 million prize money on offer with $3 million going to the winner of the day's senior race, the Classic. Churchill Downs is the most-used venue, with five Breeders' Cups since the first in 1984. List leader Jerry Bailey, who was born in Dallas, Texas, in 1957, had his first Breeders' Cup success in 1991 when he rode *Black Tie* to victory in the Classic. He has since won the Classic three times more, including in 1995, when his ride was *Cigar*.

TOP 10 FASTEST TIMES IN THE MELBOURNE CUP

	HORSE	YEAR	TIME (MIN:SECS)
1	Kingston Rule	1990	3:16.30
2	Media Puzzle	2002	3:16.97
3	Tawriffic	1989	3:17.10
4	Might and Power	1997	3:18.30
5	Gold and Black	1977	3:18.40
6	Brew	2000	3:18.68
7	Saintly	1996	3:18.80
8 =	Black Knight	1984	3:18.90
=	Empire Rose	1988	3:18.90
=	Kiwi	1983	3:18.90
=	Let's Elope	1991	3:18.90

Held at the Flemington Park racetrack in Victoria, the Melbourne Cup was inaugurated in 1861 and takes place on the first Tuesday in November, when most of Australia comes to a standstill at 3.20 pm to listen to the race. More than 200,000 spectators attend the meeting which, like "Derby Day" and Royal Ascot in England, is a great social event. Originally held over 2 miles, it went metric in 1972 and is now run over 3,200 metres – 18.7 metres shorter than the original distance. The fastest time over two miles was 3 minutes 19.1 seconds by *Rain Lover* in 1968. One of Australasia's greatest race horses, *Phar Lap* (foaled in New Zealand), won the Melbourne Cup in 1930.

TOP 10 FASTEST WINNING TIMES OF THE GRAND NATIONAL

	HORSE	YEAR	TIME* (MIN:SEC)
1	Mr. Frisk	1990	8:47.8
2	Rough Quest	1996	9:00.8
3	Red Rum	1973	9:01.9
4	Royal Athlete	1995	9:04.6
5	Lord Gwyllene	1997	9:05.8
6	Party Politics	1992	9:06.3
7	Bin Daree	2002	9:09.0
8	Papillon	2000	9:09.7
9	Grittar	1982	9:12.6
10	Bobbyjo	1999	9:14.0

* The times of the substitute races held at Gatwick in the years 1916–18 are not included

Mr Frisk became the first horse to win the Grand National in under nine minutes when he won in 1990 with Marcus Armytage in the saddle. A few weeks later the horse went on to win the Whitbread Gold Cup and join a small band of horses to complete the big race double. When *Red Rum* won his first National in 1973 he beat the 38-year-old record for the fastest Grand National, set by *Reynoldstown,* by an amazing 18 seconds.

On Two Wheels

TOP 10 FASTEST ISLE OF MAN SENIOR TTS

	RIDER*/BIKE	YEAR	KM/H	MPH
1	David Jefferies, Suzuki	2002	200.74	124.74
2	Adrian Archibald, Suzuki	2003	200.40	124.53
3	David Jefferies, Yamaha	2000	196.25	121.95
4	Steve Hislop, Norton	1992	195.18	121.28
5	David Jefferies, Yamaha	1999	195.16	121.27
6	Steve Hislop, Honda	1991	194.87	121.09
7	Ian Simpson, Honda	1998	192.78	119.79
8	Philip McCallen, Honda	1996	192.73	119.76
9	Steve Hislop, Honda	1994	191.91	119.25
10	Joey Dunlop, Honda	1995	191.68	119.11

(AVERAGE SPEED over KM/H and MPH columns)

* All from Great Britain and Northern Ireland

The first 100-mph race took place in 1960 when John Surtees won at an average speed of 164.86 km/h (102.44 mph). The first 100-mph lap had been achieved in 1957 by Bob McIntyre riding a Gilera.

TOP 10 RIDERS WITH THE MOST MOTORCYCLE WORLD CHAMPIONSHIP WINS

	RIDER/COUNTRY	CLASSES (CC)	WINS
1	Giacomo Agostini, Italy	350, 500	15
2	Angel Nieto, Spain	50, 125	13
3 =	Mike Hailwood, Great Britain	250, 350, 500	9
=	Carlo Ubbiali, Italy	125, 250	9
5 =	Phil Read, Great Britain	125, 250, 500	7
=	John Surtees, Great Britain	350, 500	7
7 =	Geoff Duke, Great Britain	350, 500	6
=	Jim Redman, Rhodesia	250, 350	6
9 =	Mick Doohan, Australia	500	5
=	Anton Mang, Germany	250, 350	5
=	Valentino Rossi, Italy	125, 250, GP	5

The motorcycle World Championship had its inaugural season in 1949, when it was won by British rider Leslie Graham on an AJS. British riders dominated the event during the 1950s and 1960s, when Italian motorcycles won every Championship, a role consistently overtaken since the mid-1970s by Japanese models. In the 1980s, the title was won on six occasions by two US riders, Freddie Spencer and Eddie Lawson, while Australia's Mick Doohan rode Hondas to win the five races from 1994 to 1998. The 500cc class is now known as the GP class.

TOP 10 MANUFACTURERS WITH THE MOST MOTORCYCLE GRAND PRIX WINS

	MANUFACTURER	FIRST WIN	WINS*
1	Honda	1961	570
2	Yamaha	1963	401
3	MV Agusta	1952	275
4	Aprilia	1987	167
5	Suzuki	1962	153
6	Kawasaki	1969	87
7	Derbi	1970	81
8	Kreidler	1962	65
9	Garelli	1982	51
10	Gilera	1949	47

* As at end of 2003 season

If Superbike wins were also included then Ducati would be No. 4 on the list with a total of 222 Grand Prix and Superbike wins. Japanese manufacturers Yamaha were originally musical instrument makers, and did not make their first motorcycle – a single-cylinder 125cc two-stroke – until 1954. Their first Grand Prix win was at the 1963 Belgian GP at Spa.

TOP 10 MOTOCROSS COUNTRIES

	COUNTRY	125CC	250CC	500CC	TOTAL
1	Belgium	10	14	23	47
2	Sweden	0	6	8	14
3	France	3	5	0	8
4 =	Great Britain	0	1	6	7
=	Italy	5	1	1	7
=	USA	3	3	1	7
7	Finland	1	1	3	5
8 =	Netherlands	3	1	0	4
=	Russia	0	4	0	4
=	South Africa	2	2	0	4

(WORLD CHAMPIONSHIP WINS*)

* As at end of 2003 season

World Moto Cross Championships have been held since 1947 when the five-man Moto Cross des Nations team championship was launched. The first individual championship was in 1957 when the 500cc class was launched, since when 250cc (1962), 125cc (1975), and sidecar (1980) have been introduced. From the 2003 season the 250cc was replaced with a new 650 class and the 500cc became the MXGP.

▶ **Valentino's victories**
The most successful rider of the modern era, Valentino Rossi won his first world title (125cc) in 1997, aged 18, and has since won the 250cc and MXGP (formerly 500cc) titles.

RACE MOTORCYCLES

THE FIRST TO...

RACES ON THREE-WHEELED VEHICLES had taken place in France the previous year, but on 29 November 1897 Charles Jarrott organized the first-ever race for two-wheelers at Sheen House, Richmond, UK, as part of an event to celebrate the first anniversary of the "Emancipation Act" that permitted motorists to drive on public roads without being preceded by a man waving a red flag. Jarrott himself won the race on a Fournier motorcycle on a 1-mile oval track in 2 minutes 8 seconds, an average speed of 45 km/h (28 mph).

RIDERS WITH THE MOST GRAND PRIX RACE WINS

	RIDER/COUNTRY	YEARS	RACE WINS*
1	**Giacomo Agostini**, Italy	1965–76	122
2	**Angel Nieto**, Spain	1969–85	90
3	**Mike Hailwood**, Great Britain	1959–67	76
4	**Valentino Rossi**, Italy	1996–2003	59
5	**Rolf Biland**, Switzerland	1975–90	56
6	**Mick Doohan**, Australia	1990–98	54
7	**Phil Read**, Great Britain	1961–75	52
8	**Jim Redman**, Southern Rhodesia	1961–66	45
9	**Anton Mang**, West Germany	1976–88	42
10	**Max Biaggi**, Italy	1992–2003	41

* As at end of 2003 season

All except Rolf Biland were solo machine riders. Great Britain's Barry Sheene won 23 races during his career and, despite not making the Top 10, is the only man to win Grands Prix at 750 and 500cc.

FASTEST AVERAGE WINNING SPEEDS IN THE TOUR DE FRANCE

	WINNER/COUNTRY	YEAR	AVERAGE SPEED (KM/H)	(MPH)
1	**Lance Armstrong**, USA	2003	40.956	25.448
2	**Lance Armstrong**	1999	40.276	25.026
3	**Lance Armstrong**	2001	40.070	24.898
4	**Marco Pantani**, Italy	1998	39.983	24.844
5	**Lance Armstrong**	2002	39.919	24.804
6	**Lance Armstrong**	2000	39.570	24.587
7	**Miguel Indurain**, Spain	1992	39.504	24.546
8	**Jan Ullrich**, Germany	1997	39.237	24.380
9	**Bjarne Rijs**, Denmark	1996	39.227	24.374
10	**Miguel Indurain**, Spain	1995	39.193	24.353

The first Tour de France in 1903 was won by Maurice Garin of France at an average speed of 25.679 km/h (15.956 mph). The race was over 2,428 km (1,509 miles) and consisted of just six stages.

Motor Sports

DRIVERS WITH THE MOST FORMULA ONE WORLD TITLES

	DRIVER/COUNTRY	WORLD TITLES YEARS	RACES WON	WORLD TITLES
1	Michael Schumacher (Germany)	1994–2003	70	6
2	Juan Manuel Fangio (Argentina)	1951–57	24	5
3	Alain Prost (France)	1985–93	51	4
4	= Jack Brabbham (Australia)	1959–60	14	3
	= Niki Lauda (Austria)	1975–84	25	3
	= Nelson Piquet (Brazil)	1981–87	23	3
	= Ayrton Senna (Brazil)	1988–91	41	3
	= Jackie Stewart (UK)	1969–71	27	3
9	= Alberto Ascari (Italy)	1952–53	13	2
	= Jim Clark (UK)	1963–65	25	2
	= Emerson Fittipaldi (Brazil)	1972–74	14	2
	= Graham Hill (UK)	1962–68	14	2

FORMULA ONE DRIVERS WITH THE MOST GRAND PRIX WINS

	DRIVER/COUNTRY	CAREER	WINS*
1	Michael Schumacher (Germany)	1991–2003	70
2	Alain Prost (France)	1980–93	51
3	Ayrton Senna (Brazil)	1984–94	41
4	Nigel Mansell (UK)	1980–95	31
5	Jackie Stewart (UK)	1965–73	27
6	= Jim Clark (UK)	1960–68	25
	= Niki Lauda (Austria)	1971–85	25
8	Juan Manuel Fangio (Argentina)	1950–58	24
9	Nelson Piquet (Brazil)	1978–91	23
10	Damon Hill (UK)	1992–99	22

* As at end of 2003 season

Michael Schumacher's first Formula One drive was for Jordan in the 1991 Belgian Grand Prix. His first win was in Belgium too, a year later with Benetton. It was also in Belgium, in a Ferrari, that he beat Alain Prost's record of 51 wins in 2001.

FASTEST WINNING SPEEDS OF THE INDIANAPOLIS 500

	DRIVER/COUNTRY	CAR	YEAR	SPEED (KM/H)	(MPH)
1	Arie Luyendyk (Netherlands)	Lola-Chevrolet	1990	299.307	185.981
2	Rick Mears (USA)	Chevrolet-Lumina	1991	283.980	176.457
3	Bobby Rahal (USA)	March-Cosworth	1986	274.750	170.722
4	Juan Pablo Montoya (Colombia)	G Force–Aurora	2000	269.730	167.607
5	Emerson Fittipaldi (Brazil)	Penske-Chevrolet	1989	269.695	167.581
6	Helio Castroneves (Brazil)	Dallara-Chevrolet	2002	267.954	166.499
7	Rick Mears (USA)	March-Cosworth	1984	263.308	163.612
8	Mark Donohue (USA)	McLaren-Offenhauser	1972	262.619	162.962
9	Al Unser (USA)	March-Cosworth	1987	260.995	162.175
10	Tom Sneva (USA)	March-Cosworth	1983	260.902	162.117

American drivers start on the run and race round oval circuits, and so consistently higher average lap speeds are achieved than in Formula One. Car racing in the United States on purpose-built circuits dates back to 1909, when Indianapolis Speedway opened. CART (Championship Auto Racing Teams, Inc.) was formed in 1978, and in 1996 the Indy Racing League was established in response to disputes over regulations governing the Indy 500. Indy 500 races have counted for CART points in 1979, 1980, and 1983–95.

CONSTRUCTORS WITH THE MOST FORMULA ONE WORLD TITLES

	CONSTRUCTOR/COUNTRY	YEARS	TITLES*
1	Ferrari (Italy)	1961–2003	13
2	Williams (UK)	1980–97	9
3	McLaren (UK)	1974–98	8
4	Lotus (UK)	1963–78	7
5	= Brabham (UK)	1966–67	2
	= Cooper (UK)	1959–60	2
7	= Benetton (Italy)	1995	1
	= BRM (UK)	1962	1
	= Matra (France)	1969	1
	= Tyrrell (UK)	1971	1
	= Vanwall (UK)	1958	1

* As at end of 2003 season

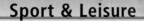

TOP 10 NASCAR DRIVERS WITH THE MOST RACE WINS

	DRIVER*	CAREER	WINS#
1	Richard Petty	1958–92	200
2	David Pearson	1960–86	105
3 =	Bobby Allison	1975–88	84
=	Darrell Waltrip	1975–92	84
5	Cale Yarborough	1957–88	83
6	Dale Earnhardt	1979–2000	76
7	Jeff Gordon	1994–2003	64
8 =	Lee Petty	1949–64	54
=	Rusty Wallace	1986–2001	54
10 =	Ned Jarrett	1953–66	50
=	Junior Johnson	1953–66	50

* All from the USA

As at 15 March 2004

◄ **Six up for Schumacher**

When Michael Schumacher won his fourth consecutive world title in 2003, it was his record-breaking sixth title – one more than the great Juan-Manuel Fangio of Argentina.

TOP 10 CONSTRUCTORS WITH THE MOST FORMULA ONE GRAND PRIX WINS

	CONSTRUCTOR/COUNTRY	YEARS	WINS*
1	Ferrari (Italy)	1951–2003	169
2	McLaren (UK)	1968–2003	137
3	Williams (UK)	1979–2003	112
4	Lotus (UK)	1960–87	79
5	Brabham (UK)	1964–85	35
6	Benetton (Italy)	1986–97	27
7	Tyrrell (UK)	1971–83	23
8	BRM (UK)	1959–72	17
9 =	Cooper (UK)	1958–67	16
=	Renault (France)	1979–2003	16

* As at end of 2003 season

Sports Media & Miscellany

TOP 10 | LARGEST SPORTS STADIUMS

	STADIUM*	LOCATION	CURRENT CAPACITY
1	Strahov Stadium	Prague, Czech Republic	250,000
2	Beaver Stadium	Pennsylvania, USA	197,282
3	May Day Stadium	Pyŏngyang, North Korea	150,000
4	Yuba Bharati Krirangan	Kolkata, India	120,000
5	Estádio Azteca	Mexico City	114,465
6	Michigan Stadium	Ann Arbor, USA	107,501
7	Neyland Stadium	Tennessee, USA	104,079
8	Jornalista Mário Filho	Rio de Janeiro, Brazil	103,045
9	Ohio Stadium	Columbus, USA	101,568
10 =	Azadi Stadium	Tehran, Iran	100,000
=	Kim Il-Sung Stadium	Pyŏngyang, North Korea	100,000
=	National Stadium Bukit Jal	Kuala Lumpur, Malaysia	100,000
=	Utama Senayan	Jakarta, Indonesia	100,000

* Excluding speedway and motor racing circuits, and horse race tracks

The Strahov Stadium, a wooden structure built in 1926 and since much modified, covers a total area of 6.3 sq km (2.4 sq miles).

▶ Stadium of dreams
Brazil's Estádio Jornalista Mário Filho (formerly Maracaña Stadium) hosted a record crowd of over 200,000 for the 1950 World Cup final.

TOP 10 | SPORT FILMS

	FILM	YEAR	SPORT
1	Rocky IV	1985	Boxing
2	Seabiscuit	2003	Horse racing
3	Space Jam	1996	Basketball
4	The Waterboy	1998	American football
5	Days of Thunder	1990	Stock car racing
6	Cool Runnings	1993	Bobsleighing
7	A League of Their Own	1992	Baseball
8	Remember the Titans	2000	American football
9	Rocky III	1982	Boxing
10	Rocky V	1990	Boxing

TOP 10 | SPORTS VIDEOS IN THE UK

	VIDEO	SPORT
1	Torvill & Dean: Face the Music	Ice skating
2	Nick Hancock: Football Nightmares	Football
3	Manchester United: The Treble	Football
4	Rugby World Cup 2003 – Official Review	Rugby
5	Murray's Magic Moments	Formula One
6	Danny Baker's Own Goals and Gaffs	Football
7	Jeremy Clarkson's Motorsport Mayhem	Motorsport
8	England Rugby – Sweet Chariot	Rugby
9	The Very Best of Torvill & Dean	Ice skating
10	Nick Faldo's Golf Course	Golf

Source: *British Video Association*

TOP 10 SPORTS PROGRAMMES WITH THE LARGEST TV AUDIENCES IN THE UK, 2003

	PROGRAMME/MATCH	DATE	AVERAGE CHANNEL	AUDIENCE
1	Rugby World Cup Final: Australia v England	22 Nov	ITV1	12,661,000
2	UEFA Champions League Live: Manchester United v Real Madrid	23 Apr	ITV1	10,490,000
3	Match of the Day Live – Euro 2004 Qualifier: England v Turkey	2 Apr	BBC1	9,327,000
4	Grand National	5 Apr	BBC1	7,600,000
5	Formula One: Brazilian Grand Prix	6 Apr	ITV1	7,083,000
6	Wimbledon 2003 – Mens Singles Quaterfinals: Tim Henman v Sebastien Grosjean	2 July	BBC1	6,176,000
7	Rugby Six Nations: Wales v England	22 Feb	BBC1	6,002,000
8	Snooker: Embassy World Championship Final	5 May	BBC2	5,281,000
9	The Boat Race	6 Apr	BBC1	5,060,000
10	The Premiership	3 May	ITV1	4,599,000

Source: *BARB/TNS*

THE 10 LATEST WINNERS OF THE BBC SPORTS PERSONALITY OF THE YEAR AWARD

YEAR	WINNER	SPORT
2003	Jonny Wilkinson	Rugby
2002	Paula Radcliffe	Athletics
2001	David Beckham	Football
2000	Steve Redgrave	Rowing
1999	Lennox Lewis	Boxing
1998	Michael Owen	Football
1997	Greg Rusedski	Tennis
1996	Damon Hill	Motor racing
1995	Jonathan Edwards	Athletics
1994	Damon Hill	Motor racing

First presented in 1954, when it was won by athlete Chris Chataway, the annual award is based on a poll of BBC television viewers. At the end of the 20th century, Muhammed Ali was voted the Sports Personality of the Century. Jonny Wilkinson's prowess during the Rugby World Cup led to his 2003 win – the first ever for a rugby player. With 16 winners, athletics is the most represented sport, followed by motor racing with seven: two of these, Nigel Mansell and Damon Hill, have won twice. Boxer Henry Cooper is the only other double winner.

TOP 10 THEMES OF SPORT FILMS

	SPORT	FILMS
1	Boxing	204
2	Horse racing	139
3	American football	123
4 =	Baseball	85
=	Motor racing	85
6	Basketball	41
7	Athletics	33
8	Golf	24
9	Wrestling	20
10	Motorcycle racing	15

A survey of feature films with competitive sports as their principal themes produced in Hollywood from 1910 to 2000 identified a total of 891 films, with boxing accounting for 22.9 per cent of the total.

Leisure Pursuits

TOP 10 PARTICIPATION ACTIVITIES AMONG ADULTS IN THE UK

	MEN ACTIVITY	PERCENTAGE*	PERCENTAGE*	WOMEN ACTIVITY	
1	Walking/hiking	19	23	Walking/hiking	1
2	Snooker	15	18	Keep fit	2
3	Swimming	13	17	Swimming	3
4	Cycling	12	7	Cycling	4
5	Football	10	4	Racket sports =	5
6	Golf	9	4	Snooker =	
7 =	Keep fit	8	4	Weights =	
=	Weights	8	3	Running/athletics	8
9	Running/athletics	7	2	Bowls =	9
10	Racket sports	6	2	Darts =	

* Based on the percentage of people over age 16 participating in each activity in the four weeks before interview

Source: *Office for National Statistics*, UK 2000 Time Use Survey

▼ In the swim
Swimming is one of the UK's most popular leisure activities, while competitive swimming and diving attract more lottery funding than any other sport.

TOP 10 LEISURE ACTIVITIES AMONG ADULTS IN THE UK

	ACTIVITY	PERCENTAGE OF ADULTS*
1	Watching television	99
2	Visiting/entertaining	96
3	Listening to the radio	88
4	Listening to records/tapes/CDs	78
5 =	Reading books	65
=	Visiting a pub	65
7	Meal in a restaurant (not fast food)	62
8	Gardening	49
9	Driving for pleasure	47
10	Walking	45

* Based on the percentage of people over age 16 participating in each activity in the three months prior to interview for leisure activities away from the home, or in the four weeks prior to interview for leisure activities in the home.

Pub visiting habits vary countrywide: in the north, most people had visited a pub in the previous three months, whereas in London only half had done so.

TOP 10 COUNTRIES SPENDING THE MOST ON CONSOLE AND COMPUTER GAMES

	COUNTRY	PER CAPITA	SALES (2003) TOTAL($)
1	USA	37.4	10,866,000,000
2	Japan	33.5	4,267,250,000
3	UK	57.1	3,432,020,000
4	Germany	31.4	2,584,430,000
5	France	22.7	1,365,870,000
6	South Korea	26.3	1,269,850,000
7	Spain	23.9	960,880,000
8	Canada	22.2	713,650,000
9	Australia	34.8	687,550,000
10	Italy	11.3	653,660,000

Source: *Euromonitor*

TOP 10 BESTSELLING COMPUTER GAMES AT W.H. SMITH*

	GAME	PUBLISHER
1	Medal of Honor: Rising Sun	Electronic Arts
2	FIFA 2004	Electronic Arts
3	Disney Monsters Inc: Scream Arena	THQ
4	Lord of the Rings: Return of the King	Electronic Arts
5	Championship Manager 4	Eidos
6	The Simpsons Hit and Run	Vivendi
7	Need for Speed Underground	Electronic Arts
8	Grand Theft Auto Vice City	Rockstar
9	True Crimes: Streets of LA	Activision
10	The Sims	Electronic Arts

* During 2003

Medal of Honor: Rising Sun was a huge success in the UK, despite its focus on the American role in the World War II Pacific theatre, outselling *FIFA 2004*.

MONOPOLY® MAN

MONOPOLY WAS DEVISED in Philadelphia in 1934 by Charles Darrow and patented on 7 February 1936. Darrow's streets were those of the New Jersey resort, Atlantic City – it is said because he dreamed of going there, but, being unemployed during the Depression, could not afford the fare. Building on earlier property games, Monopoly, with its subtle balance of skill and luck, enjoyed rapidly growing sales. It was the bestselling board game in the USA in 1935 – and national versions were introduced worldwide. Darrow became a millionaire, devoting the rest of his life to travel and the cultivation of rare orchids.

IT'S A FACT

TOP 10 TOY-BUYING COUNTRIES

	COUNTRY	PER CAPITA	SALES (2003) TOTAL($)
1	USA	120.9	35,115,300,000
2	Japan	69.3	8,811,570,000
3	UK	112.5	6,758,620,000
4	Germany	63.3	5,213,810,000
5	France	70.8	4,259,480,000
6	Italy	46.8	2,714,230,000
7	China	1.9	2,384,270,000
8	Spain	48.7	1,957,960,000
9	Canada	54.1	1,743,950,000
10	Mexico	16.4	1,704,260,000

Source: *Euromonitor*

As the 21st century dawned, world toy industry sales were reported to have totalled $69.493 billion. This is equivalent to $11 for every person on the planet. Taking age into account, this figure represents an average of $32 for every child, and reflects an average expenditure of $328 in North America and $100 in Europe, but just $2 in Africa.

TOP 10 MOST POPULAR TYPES OF TOY

	TYPE OF TOY	MARKET SHARE PERCENTAGE (2002)
1	Video games	27.7
2	Infant/pre-school toys	12.0
3	Activity toys	11.4
4	Dolls	10.5
5	Other toys	9.8
6	Games/puzzles	9.6
7	Toy vehicles	8.6
8	Soft toys	4.2
9	Action figures	3.4
10	Ride-on toys	2.8

Source: *Eurotoys/The NPD Group Worldwide*

This list is based on a survey of toy consumption in the European Union, and can be taken as a reliable guide to the most popular types of toy in the developed world. Taken as a whole, a worldwide survey conducted in 2000 valued video games sales at $14.752 billion compared with a cumulative total for "traditional" toy sales of $54.742 billion.

TOP 10 BESTSELLING BOARD GAMES AT W.H. SMITH*

	GAME	PUBLISHER
1	Simpsons Monopoly	Hasbro Games
2	Scrabble	Mattel UK Ltd.
3	Monopoly	Hasbro Games
4	Bop It Extreme	Hasbro Games
5	Pass the Bomb	HP Gibson and Sons Ltd.
6	Cranium	Cranium Inc.
7	Simpsons Cluedo	Hasbro Games
8	Articulate	Drummond Park Ltd.
9	Rummikub Numbers	Tomy UK Ltd.
10	Risk	Hasbro Games

* During 2003

If any pattern can be discerned in board game sales it is that while those linked to popular TV programmes, such as the Simpsons, and newly-introduced products, often supported by extensive TV advertising, may dominate the charts, long-established games such as Monopoly, Scrabble, and Risk continue to hold their own as they are introduced to new generations of players.

Further Information

THE UNIVERSE & THE EARTH

BBC Weather
http://www.bbc.co.uk/weather/
Weather updates for the UK and abroad

Encyclopedia Astronautica
http://www.astronautix.com/
Spaceflight news and reference

NASA
http://www.nasa.gov/
The principal website for the American space programme

The Nine Planets
http://www.nineplanets.org/
A multimedia tour of the Solar System

Peaklist
http://www.highalpex.com/Peaklist/peaklist.html
Lists of the world's tallest mountains

Space.com
http://www.space.com/
Reports on events in space exploration

United Nations Atlas of the Oceans
http://www.oceansatlas.org/index.jsp
An information resource on oceanographic issues

Volcano Live
http://www.volcanolive.com/
World volcano news and information

WebElements
http://www.webelements.com/
A guide to all the elements in the periodic table

World Space Flight
http://www.worldspaceflight.com/
Astronaut biographies and other data on human space flight

LIFE ON EARTH

Animal Diversity Web
http://animaldiversity.ummz.umich.edu/site/index.html
Animal data from the University of Michigan

Convention on International Trade in Endangered Species of Wild Fauna and Flora (CITES)
http://www.cites.org/
Lists endangered species of flora and fauna

The Electronic Zoo
http://netvet.wustl.edu/e-zoo.htm
Links to sites devoted to animals

FishBase
http://www.fishbase.org/home.htm
Global information on fishes

Food and Agriculture Organization of the United Nations
http://www.fao.org/
FAO statistics on agriculture, fisheries, and forestry

Ichthylogy at the Florida Museum of Natural History
http://www.flmnh.ufl.edu/fish/default.htm
Fish and shark data

International Union for the Conservation of Nature
http://iucn.org/
The leading nature conservation site

PetForum
http://petsforum.com/
Information about cats, dogs, and other pets

United Nations Environment Programme
http://www.unep.ch/
Includes the UN's System-wide Earthwatch and its Global Resource Information Database

University of Florida Book of Insect Records
http://ufbir.ifas.ufl.edu/
Insect champions in many categories

THE HUMAN WORLD

Amnesty International
http://www.amnesty.org/
The foremost human rights organization

Babies' Names
http://www.statistics.gov.uk/
Annual updates from the National Statistics site

Department of Health
http://www.doh.gov.uk/
UK-specific health information

The Home Office
http://www.homeoffice.gov.uk/
Crime data and prison population statistics

Inter-Parliamentary Union
http://www.ipu.org/
Including data on women in parliaments

Interpol
http://www.interpol.int/
Worldwide crime statistics

Rulers
http://rulers.org/
Database of the world's rulers and political leaders

United Nations
http://www.un.org/
The launch site for the UN's many bodies

World Health Organization
http://www.who.int/en/
World health information and advice

TOWN & COUNTRY

CIA World Factbook
http://www.odci.gov/cia/publications/factbook/
Detailed country-by-country data and rankings

National Statistics Online
http://www.statistics.gov.uk/
Official UK figures on population, births, etc

Population Reference Bureau
http://www.prb.org/
US and international population issues

Skyscrapers.com
http://www.skyscrapers.com/re/en/
Searchable guide to the world's tallest buildings

United Nations City Data
http://www.photius.com/wfb1999/rankings/cities.html
City information for capitals and those with 100,000-plus populations

United Nations Population Division
http://www.un.org/esa/population/unpop.htm
Worldwide data on population issues

US Census Bureau
http://www.census.gov/
US and international population statistics

World Bank
http://www.worldbank.org/
Development and other statistics from around the world

World's Largest Bridges
http://www.struct.kth.se/research/bridges/Bridges.htm
The world's longest bridges listed by type

The World's Longest Tunnel Page
http://home.no.net/lotsberg/
A database of the longest rail, road, and canal tunnels

CULTURE & LEARNING

24 Hour Museum
http://www.24hourmuseum.org.uk/index.html
A guide to exhibitions and events at the UK's museums and galleries

The Art Newspaper
http://www.theartnewspaper.com/
News and views on the art world

The British Library
http://www.bl.uk/
A portal to the catalogues and exhibitions in Britain's national library

Department for Education and Skills
http://www.dfes.gov.uk/statistics/
A wide-ranging collection of statistics relating to education in the UK

The Bookseller
http://www.thebookseller.com/
The organ of the British book trade

Dorling Kindersley
http://uk.dk.com/
The website of the publishers of this book

Global Reach
http://www.global-reach.biz/globstats/index.php3
Facts and figures on online languages

The Man Booker Prize
http://www.bookerprize.co.uk/
Britain's most prestigious literary prize

Nobel Prizes
http://www.nobel.se/
A searchable database of all Nobel Prizewinners

United Nations Educational, Scientific and Cultural Organization (UNESCO)
http://www.unesco.org/
Comparative international statistics on all aspects of education and culture

Index

Acknowledgments

Special US research: Dafydd Rees
Sport consultant: Ian Morrison

Alexander Ash; Caroline Ash; Nicholas Ash; Emma Beatty; Peter Bond; Phil Borge; Richard Braddish; Thomas Brinkoff; Richard Chapman; Pete Compton; Dr. Chris Corrigan; Kaylee Coxall; Luke Crampton; David Crystal; Sidney S. Culbert; Philip Eden; Raymond Fletcher; Christopher Forbes; Cullen Geiselman; Russell E. Gough; Monica Grady; Stan Greenberg; Barry Gromett; Angela Hayes; Duncan Hislop; Andreas Hörstemeier; Murray Hughes; Richard Hurley; Alan Jeffreys; Todd M. Johnson; Rex King; Dr. Benjamin Lucas; Roberto Mamrud; Chris Mead; Roberto Ortiz de Zarate; Jim Osborne; Sarah Owen; Matthew Paton; Tony Pattison; Gillian Payne; Adrian Room; Robert Senior; Karel Stockkermans; Mitchell Symons; Thomas Tranter; Lucy T. Verma; Peter Wynne-Thomas

Absolut Elephant; Academy of Motion Picture Arts and Sciences (AMPAS) – Oscar statuette is the registered trademark and copyrighted property of the Academy of Motion Picture Arts and Sciences; *Ad Age Global*; The Advertising Association; Aintree Racecourse; *Airline Business*; Air Transport Intelligence; Allergy Clinic, Guy's Hospital, London; American Association of Port Authorities; American Forests; American Wind Energy Association; Amnesty International; *Amusement Business*; Argos Insurance Services; *The Art Newspaper*; Art Sales Index; Association of Leading Visitor Attractions; Atlantic Oceanographic and Meteorological Laboratory/National Oceanic and Atmospheric Administration; Audit Bureau of Circulations Ltd.; Bat Conservation International; BBC Radio 4; *BP Statistical Review of World Energy 2003*; British Academy of Film and Television Arts (BAFTA); British Broadcasting Corporation (BBC); *British Crime Survey*; British Library; British Museum; British Phonographic Industry (BPI); British Video Association

(BVA); Broadcasters Audience Research Board Ltd (BARB); *Business Week*; Cameron Mackintosh Ltd; Central Intelligence Agency (CIA); Channel Swimming Association; Charities Aid Foundation; Christian Research; Christie's; Comité Interprofessionel du Vin de Champagne (CIVC); Commission for Distilled Spirits; Cremation Society; CricInfo; CRC Handbook of Chemistry and Physics; *Criminal Statistics England & Wales*; CyberAtlas; De Beers; Department for Environment, Food and Rural Affairs (DEFRA); Department of Health; *The Economist*; EM-DAT, CRED, University of Louvain, Belgium; Energy Information Administration (EIA); Euromonitor; European Wind Energy Association; Eurotoys; Fédération Internationale de Football Association (FIFA); Feline Advisory Bureau/Felix; The Financial Times Ltd.; Food and Agriculture Organization of the United Nations (FAO); *Forbes*; Forestry Commission; *Fortune*; *France Football*; Gallup Organization; Gemstone Publishing, Inc.; Global Reach; Gold Fields Mineral Services; Governing Council of the Cat Fancy; Halifax; Health and Safety Executive (HSE); Hitwise.com; HM Treasury; Home Accident Surveillance System (HASS); Home Office; Imperial War Museum; Interbrand; International Atomic Energy Agency; International Bulletin of Missionary Research; International Coffee Organisation; International Olympic Committee (IOC); International Rugby Board (IRB); International Shark Attack File/American Elasmobranch Society/Florida Museum of Natural History; International Ski Federation (FIS); International Tea Committee Ltd.; International Telecommunication Union (ITU); International Union for the Conservation of Nature (IUCN); Interpol; Joint United Nations Programme on HIV/AIDS (UNAIDS); Kennel Club; Kuoni Travel; Leisure Accident Surveillance System (LASS); Lloyds Register-Fairplay Ltd.; London Transport; Lycos; Mars; McDonald's; *Melody Maker*; Met Office; MRIB; Music Information Database; National Academy of Recording Arts and Sciences, USA (NARAS) (Grammy Awards);

National Aeronautics and Space Administration, USA (NASA); National Basketball Association, USA (NBA); National Football League, USA (NFL); National Fraud Information Center, National Consumers League, USA; National Phobics Society; National Trust; Natural History Museum; *New Musical Express (NME)*; Niagara Falls Museum; Nielsen; Nielsen BookScan; Nielsen/NetRatings; The NPD Group Worldwide; Office for National Statistics (ONS); Official UK Charts Company; Organisation for Economic Co-operation and Development (OECD); Organisation Internationale des Constructeurs d'Automobiles (OICA); *The Overstreet Comic Book Price Guide*; Patent Office; Professional Golfers' Association (PGA); Public Lending Right; Radio Joint Audience Research Ltd (RAJAR); *Railway Gazette International*; Relate National Marriage Guidance; Royal Academy of Arts; Royal Astronomical Society; Royal Opera House, Covent Garden; RSSSF; *Screen Digest*; SearchEngineWatch.com; Shakespeare Centre; Society of London Theatre (SOLT) (Olivier Awards); Society of Motor Manufacturers and Traders Ltd; Sony Radio Academy Awards; Sotheby's; Sport Business Group at Deloitte; Star UK; *Stores*; Swiss Re; TNS; Tour de France; Tree Register of the British Isles; TUC Certification Office; Union Cycliste Internationale (UCI); United Nations (UN); United Nations Children's Fund (UNICEF); United Nations Economic Commission for Europe; United Nations Educational, Scientific and Cultural Organization (UNESCO); United Nations Population Division (UNPD); Universal Postal Union (UPU); US Census Bureau ; *Variety*; WebElements; W.H. Smith; World Association of Newspapers (WAN); World Bank; *World Christian Database*; World Christian Encyclopedia; World Gold Council; World Health Organization (WHO); World Intellectual Property Organization (WIPO); World Motocross Championships; *World of Learning*; World's Strongest Man Contest; World Tourism Organization (WTO); Zenith Optimedia

Acknowledgments

Publisher's acknowledgments
Dorling Kindersley would like to thank the following for their
contributions: Editorial Sharon Lucas; Design Marianne Markham;
Picture Library Hayley Smith, Richard Dabb, Claire Bowers.

Index
Patricia Coward

Packager's acknowledgments
The Bridgewater Book Company would like to thank Alison Bolus,
Julia Greenwood, Nicky Gyopari, Tom Kitch, Philippa Smith and
Hazel Songhurst for editorial assistance, and Richard Constable,
Chris Morris and Roger Wheeler for their design work.

Picture Credits

**The publisher would like to thank the following for
their kind permission to reproduce their photographs:**
(Abbreviations key: t = top, b = bottom, r = right, l = left,
c = centre)

1: Science Photo Library/David Nunuk (t); Science Photo Library/
Alexis Rosenfeld (b); 2-3: Corbis/Mark A Johnson (t); Alamy/
Redferns Music Picture Library (b); 4: Empics (bc); 5: Rex/ Everett
(tl); Corbis/Galen Rowell (b); 6-7: Corbis/Bill Ross; 7: Corbis/Jerry
Cooke (bc); 8-9: Science Photo Library/Alexis Rosenfeld (t);
11: Robert Gendler/NASA (b); 13: NASA (b); 15: Galaxy Picture
Library/NASA (l); 16: Corbis/Ralph A Clevenger (b); 17: Corbis
1996/Original image courtesy of NASA/Corbis (tr); 18-19: Corbis/
Galen Rowell (b); 21: Naturepl.com/Hanne & Jens Eriksen (b);
22: Corbis/James Marshall; 24: Corbis/Paul Hardy (b); 26-27:
Rex/Sipa (bc); 28-29: Naturepl.com/Anup Shah (t); 32: Alamy/
Stefan Binkert (bl); 33: Naturepl.com/Jeff Rotman & Avi Klapfer (t);
42-43: Corbis/Macduff Everton (b); 44-45: Corbis/
Bill Ross; 46-47: Corbis/Erik Svensson (t); 48:
Getty Images/Sally Ullman (tr); 50: Rex/Sipa (b);
52: Corbis SABA/ Louise Gubb (r); 54-55: Getty
Images/Mark Douet (c); 56: Corbis/Lynsey
Addario (b); 58-59: Corbis/Larry Williams (b);
61: *Louis XIV (1638-1715)*, (oil on canvas) by
Hyacinthe Rigaud (1659-1743): Bridgeman
Art Library, London/New York, Museu do
Caramulo, Portugal/ www.bridgeman.co.uk
(l); 64-65: Getty Images/Keystone (bc); 70:
Getty Images/Paul Buck/AFP (b); 72-73: Getty
Images/Hulton Archive (b); 74-75: Corbis
Sygma/China Features (t); 78-79: Mark A
Johnson/Corbis (t); 82-83: Corbis/Brian A
Vikander (b); 86-87: Corbis SABA/David
Butow (b); 88: Panos Pictures (r); 92-93:
Axiom/Jim Homes (bc); 94-95: Alamy/
Oxford Picture Library (t); 96: Getty
Images/China Tourism Press (b);

99: Corbis/ Lindsay Hebberd (b); 100: TopFoto (t); 102-103: Corbis/
Barry Lewis (b); 105: Alamy/Leslie Garland Picture Library (r);
106: *The Massacre of the Innocents* (1609-1611) by Sir Peter Paul
Rubens (1577-1640): PA Photos, Sotheby's, London (b); 108-109:
Anatomical studies by Leonardo da Vinci (1452-1519): Bridgeman
Art Library, London/New York, Galleria dell' Accademia, Venice,
Italy/www.bridgeman.co.uk (c); 111: *Noir et Blanche* (1926) by
Man Ray (1890-1976): Corbis/Christie's Images/© Man Ray Trust
/ADAGP, Paris and DACS, London 2004 (b); 112-113:
Alamy/Redferns Music Picture Library (t); 115: Rex/Terry O' Neill (b);
116: Rex/Crollalanza (b); 118: Rex/Kern Mackay (r); 120-121:
Rex/Hoffman (b); 127: PA Photos (l); 128: Retna/Kelly
A Swift (r); 130-131: Redferns/Hayley Madden (c); 132-133: Getty
Images/Phil Hunt (t); 135: ArenaPAL/Michael Le Poer Trench/
Cameron Mackintosh Ltd. (b); 136-137: The Kobal Collection (b);
138-139: TopFoto/New Line Productions (c); 141: Corbis/
Underwood & Underwood; 142: Getty Images/Variety (b);
145: Getty Images/Variety (t); 147: Rex/Lucas Films, Everett (b);
148-149: TopFoto/Warner Bros (t); 150: The Kobal Collection/
Columbia/Darren Michaels (l); 152-153: Rex/Everett (b); 154: The
Kobal Collection/Paramount 1978 (b); 156: Getty Images/Don
Smetzer (b); 159: Corbis/Jose Luis Pelaez, Inc. (t); 161: The Kobal
Collection/Touchstone (b); 162-163: Alamy/Mark Lewis (t); 164-
165: Getty Images/Yellow Dog Productions (b); 167: Rex/Cameron;
168-169: Corbis/Alan Schein Photography (b); 170: Corbis
SABA/Keith Dannemiller (b); 175: The Australian Museum (tr);
176-177: Alamy/Chuck Pefley (t); 183: Alamy (r); 184: Corbis/
Owaki-Kulla (b); 186: Rex/Nils Jorgsen (b); 188: Alamy/Leslie
Garland Picture Library (b); 190-191: Alamy/Joe Sohm (b);
192: Robert Harding Picture Library (t); 194-195: Science Photo
Library/David Nunuk (t); 197: Alamy/Chuck Pefley; 198: PA Photos
(t); 200: Corbis (b); 202-203: Rex/Jian Chen (b); 204-205:
akg-images; 208-209: Empics (t); 210: Getty Images
(r); 213: Corbis/Reuters; 215: Empics (l); 216:
Empics; 219: Empics (r); 224: Empics (r); 228:
Empics (l); 230: Corbis/Bettmann (bl); 231:
Alamy/Popperfoto (r); 233: Empics (t); 234-235:
Empics (bc); 236: Corbis/Jerry Cooke (b); 239:
Empics (t); 241: Empics (l); 242-243: Empics (bc);
256: Galaxy Picture Library/NASA (bc).

All other images © Dorling Kindersley.
Additional Photography by Geoff Dann,
Frank Greenaway, Dave King, Steve Shott,
Max Alexander, Matthew Ward,
Demetrio Carrasco, Alan Keohane,
Peter Wilson, Karl Shone, Harry Taylor,
Ian O'Leary, Andrew Whittuck, Nick
Wright, Reuben Paris.

For further information see:
ww.dkimages.com

"In her debut cookbook, Samah Dada brings the fun, warm spirit we've come to love on social media and television to the page. Filled with creative, irresistible recipes, *Dada Eats Love to Cook It* will bring new energy into your kitchen."

—JULIA TURSHEN, bestselling author of *Now & Again* and founder of Equity at the Table (EATT)

"Samah's story and food will uplift and inspire. So bright, passionate, and approachable, this cookbook is not just a series of beautiful recipes but a life story that will inspire and encourage anyone who is obsessed with food and looking to make it their career. Samah's food is healthy, happy, and totally welcoming. I love it, and I just know I will be going back to this book over and over again. Congrats, Samah!"

—EDEN GRINSHPAN, author of *Eating Out Loud*

"Samah Dada is a star. Her recipes rock, and her mind-set about cooking is just where you want to be. You will especially love 'eating your vegetables' Samah's way."

—MICHAEL SOLOMONOV, author of *Zahav: A World of Israeli Cooking*

"Plant-based treats never looked so good. Samah makes it easy to take the guilt out of guilty pleasure."

—CAMILA ALVES McCONAUGHEY, founder of Women of Today

RODALE

RODALE BOOKS
NEW YORK

100 Plant-Based Recipes
for Everyone at Your Table

DADA eats

LOVE TO COOK IT

Samah Dada

Photography by Julia Gartland

To Mama, Papa,
and Suhaa:

I do what I do
because of and for you.

Contents

around the NBC studios for hours a day, work the *Tonight Show*, and come home to bake brownies. I'd wake up at 3:30 a.m. to get to work at 4 a.m. for my assignment at the *Today* show, change into my stiff Page uniform (you'd love to see it), and head to my wobbly desk in the studio's greenroom. I would book cars for our talent and escort guests from their dressing rooms to the set and proceed to come home in the afternoon to immediately blitz spinach and basil in my blender to make a five-minute pesto.

With a new set of best friends in my Page cohort to feed, I had accidentally acquired a second job that I enjoyed just as much as the dream one I had at the network. Beyond that, I became someone in my class who was known for something. I had never felt a sense of belonging like I did in this program. And while that could very well have been because I brought cookies to work every other day, I think it ran deeper than that. Cooking for others without occasion or reason gave me a sense of confidence that finally allowed me to feel seen.

Funnily enough, it was never my aim to make my recipes fall into a specific diet or lifestyle. But a lot of my dishes happen to be vegetarian, vegan, gluten-free, and dairy-free. I don't lead with these labels because they can seem clinical or trendy—I mean, no one is calling broccoli "vegan broccoli." The truth is, by using minimally processed and real ingredients, the results often come with the potential to satisfy a wider audience, including those who battle with dietary restrictions or simply want to follow their preferences.

The accidental plant-based energy of this book, and of my style of cooking, has been just that, an accident—but I couldn't be more thrilled about it. These recipes represent all the ways you can be creative with a short list of ingredients. It's about doing more with less. Sure, I love boasting that the ridiculously soft and chewy cookie you ate was mainly made up of almonds, coconut, and maple syrup. Or that the creamy pasta had no cream in it at all, but was created using just ripe avocados, fresh basil, and olive oil. It can be a flex, definitely, but it's more than that. The fact that my recipes can be relished by individuals who never thought they could enjoy a gluten-free brownie or a slice of dairy-free carrot cake represents the inclusivity that I both chase and seek to shine on every aspect of my work. This is something that I am extremely proud of.

I've noticed that my friends of all ages, those with kids and without, both in real life and on social media, can sometimes feel daunted by the idea of cooking or baking. And even if they love to be in the kitchen, they have busy lives and understandably feel constrained by the limited time they do have to cook for themselves and their loved ones. It's a lot easier to tap a button on your phone and track the journey of your meal on a map than it is to track it from your fridge to a dinner plate. I don't subscribe to everything of the millennial persuasion, but when it comes to food, I get it. Sometimes you want at least near-instant gratification. I mean, you're hungry! You're tired! Maybe you have plans tonight, or this afternoon! Even if those plans are to give your couch some attention with the help of a movie and some popcorn, I know that often the absolute last thing you want to do after a long day at work is to gaze blankly into your fridge waiting for your kale to tell you what to do with it or to stand at your counter, laboriously dicing up onions so fine that you start to cry.

That's the whole idea of this book: recipes that make even the most reluctant and busiest of people want to cook. Whether you're a college student, a young person starting their first job, a mom, a dad, with kids or without, this is where I show you that you can do it. When you want a bright and gorgeous pasta but have only five minutes to make it, I've got you covered with a creamy sauce that you can throw together in your blender. If you just got invited to a potluck and need to bring a dessert and an appetizer, allow me to show you how to skip store-bought hummus and make it quicker (and cheaper) at home, all while whipping up some banana bread muffin tops with that sad and lonely nearly perished banana you have left on your counter from last week. But I also want you to be adventurous, experimenting with spices and recipes that showcase the ingredients I grew up with and the foods I've experienced while living in Europe and traveling to India to visit my family.

Confidence in the kitchen is what has allowed me to exhibit it in every other aspect of my life. It has given me the courage to show off my heritage and the colorful flavors that come with it, instead of hiding it in fear that I won't be accepted. And perhaps most importantly, it has booked me a direct flight to helping people—which is all I ever want to do. Whether it's making your life more fulfilling, tastier, easier, or sweeter, I hope that you'll discover parts of yourself on the pages before you, just as I have. I want you to learn to trust your instincts like I've learned to trust mine. I hope that you will see cooking as a beautiful and messy process, and not as a means to a perfect end result because—plot twist—that perfect result doesn't exist. All it is, is *your* result.

And at the end of the day, I'm not trying to give you recipes that are so complicated you'll flip the page immediately. I want you to look at these little pieces of my heart and soul, use only one bowl to make brownies, and go about your day with plenty of daylight to spare. I revel in the idea of you eating more vegetables than you did before reading this book, because who knew you could even make a tangy, spicy masala with the can of chickpeas hiding in the back of your pantry? I smile at the thought of you telling your friend that you're bringing a lemon olive oil cake to their house, because doesn't that sound chic? It doesn't matter whether you're cooking for one, for two, for kids, or for yourself. We're in it together, and I couldn't be more honored to have you here.

PANTRY ESSENTIALS

Is grocery shopping a hobby? Should I put "expert obsessive grocery shopper" as a skill on my résumé? I'm mildly obsessed with grocery shopping. And when I say mildly, I mean wholeheartedly, absolutely, irrevocably in love with grocery shopping. I find myself in a store at least once a day. I may not even need anything, but you bet walking through those aisles gives me an unparalleled sense of calm and tranquility.

I acquired the grocery shopping gene from my dad, who, like me, also finds strolling through the aisles therapeutic, though I'm sure he'd never admit it. When our family was living in London for a few years, he would frequently make the forty-minute tube trip out to Alperton to visit the many Indian grocery stores there—and would always come home with more spices than we would ever need in one hand and a bag of biryani from a local restaurant in the other.

Even when I'm traveling, I always make it a point to visit a grocery store or four, basically just to see what's up. It's a ritualistic activity that makes me feel a little more at home wherever I am. On the trip home, my carry-on bag is always filled with the fruits of my labor, like crunchy, spicy, savory snacks from India, different types of granola bars and cookies from the UK, or argan oil from Morocco.

When I'm home and operating in my own kitchen, there are some staples you'll never find my pantry without. Tahini, for sauces, dips, and dessert. Nut butters and nuts, for snacking and baking. Legumes and legume-based pastas. Canned crushed tomatoes for pasta sauce and *chana masala*. Some of these ingredients you may already have in your pantry. Some you may need to make a quick trip to the store to buy, or a quick search on the internet to find. Once you have the ingredients listed on the following pages, you can make most everything in this book.

INDIAN SPICES AND MY SPICE BOX

Growing up, I didn't know of any other way to store spices but in these spice boxes. I'd only ever seen my mom cook with spices that lived in these metal tins, tins that we'd shuttle back from India at the bottom of our suitcases whenever we would make a trip. My mom, and consequently now I, have two separate boxes. One is dedicated to ground spices like turmeric, cayenne, salt, garam masala, coriander, and cumin, while the other is for seeds and other crunchy, sizzling objects of my affection. Think: whole black peppercorns, cumin seeds, fennel seeds, cardamom pods, whole cloves. Even if you don't have these slightly insane spice tins, you can take note of the spices you see inside of them. The ones I use daily are my pantry spice essentials like turmeric, cumin, and cayenne, while others I use more sparingly. Whatever the case, these spices are nice to have around in your kitchen as they amplify flavor and are indispensable in Indian cooking. You can find them at your local grocery store, in international grocery stores, or on the World Wide Web. Make sure you replace your ground spices especially at least every six months (whole spices have a longer shelf life), as spices do lose their aromatics, potency, and flavor over time. If your spices have lost their fragrant smell or don't taste like anything, it's time to say goodbye!

Turmeric

Ground Cumin

Cumin Seeds

Ground Coriander

Cardamom, Cinnamon, Cloves, Whole Black Peppercorns

Mustard Seeds

Cayenne Pepper

CINNAMON

Whether I'm sprinkling it on yogurt, toast with peanut butter and banana, rice cakes, or fruit, cinnamon is a part of my daily routine. Except for when I accidentally mistake my bottle of cumin for cinnamon and start shaking that over my toast. That, I can definitely do without. Cinnamon is a nice addition in pancakes, banana breads, granola, and wherever else you'd like a little kick of spice.

CUMIN // CORIANDER // CAYENNE // TURMERIC // GARAM MASALA

I am grouping these together like a cute little family because these are the spices I grew up with and that will make countless appearances within these pages. Thanks to watching my mom cook with them, I have been accustomed to seeing these spices in her metal spice box, made for heaping up spices and storing them in these ridiculously precious silver bowls. Cumin is one of my favorite spices—I suggest you get both the whole cumin seeds and the ground powder. With coriander, I tend to stick with just the ground powder (and the fresh leaves of course, known as, yep, cilantro!). Cayenne for spice, and turmeric for basically everything else—color, taste, and some gorgeous anti-inflammatory benefits. Garam masala, a quintessential staple in Indian cooking, blends many spices—coriander, cumin, cloves, cinnamon, and cardamom—together. The word *garam* means "heat," though these spices aren't necessarily *spicy*. Rather, in ancient Ayurvedic Indian medicine, they are said to heat up the body and the metabolism.

CURRY LEAVES

Sometimes I think that my mom loves curry leaves more than me. Okay I'm kidding, of course—but they definitely come as a close second. Curry leaves are an irreplaceable feature in any Indian kitchen, and their unique, citrusy flavor and aroma brings life to many dishes. My parents have a plant in their garden, so we feel pretty spoiled, but I do recognize that curry leaves can sometimes be a challenge to track down. You can find them at Indian markets or online either fresh or dried—and if you buy them fresh, you can freeze them to keep for longer. If you're unable to find curry leaves, don't sweat—you can omit in any recipe I call for them. Or you can just come pay a visit to my family's garden, we're happy to share.

SALT

Flaky sea salt is a lifestyle and I am confident that I use it more aggressively than most. Whether it's finishing cookies, pastas, roasted vegetables, my entire life . . . flaky sea salt elevates basically anything you add it to.

Another type of salt I love is pink Himalayan sea salt. This stuff is saltier than the OG and I grind it on top of salads and avocado toast with some pepper and lemon juice on the regular.

And for everything else, I use kosher salt. From seasoning while I'm cooking, adding extra salt to food, to salting pasta water, kosher salt is my go-to.

PASTA

I am super intrigued by alternative-ingredient anythings, so I love a good bean-based pasta. My favorites are chickpea and lentil pastas, however if the bean life is not for you, but you're still in the market for a gluten-free pasta, I also recommend reaching for brown rice or quinoa pasta, which are both delicious, too. When it comes to cooking gluten-free pasta specifically, my main tip is to be a helicopter pasta parent and keep checking it (fish for a piece of pasta and bite into it) until you know it's at your desired consistency. For me, that's al dente. If you leave it in the boiling water for too long, it might get gummy and not hold up. So let's avoid that. And of course it goes without saying that if you are not about the gluten-free pasta life, then choose your favorite type of pasta.

CHICKPEAS

I think I might be chickpeas' number one fan. Whether I'm blending up some hummus, making chana masala, throwing chickpeas in a dessert (please see page 199 if you just raised your eyebrow), or simply pan-frying them in some olive oil and spices so they get golden and crispy, chickpeas are one of my secret weapons. There are so many options of what you can become if you are a chickpea, and for that reason, I always keep a few cans in my pantry. And if I've run out, then someone, anyone, please come find me because something is seriously wrong.

TAHINI

I could probably devote an entire section of this book to tahini (please see my note on it on page 29). At this point it is basically my love language. From salad dressings to cake (yep, that's right), tahini is the savory, grounding flavor you never knew you needed in your pantry. You can typically find tahini next to the nut and seed butters in your local grocery store. If not, the internet is a gorgeous place!

EXTRA-VIRGIN OLIVE OIL

It's worth it to invest in a good bottle of extra-virgin olive oil for a number of reasons. For one, there is a lot of phony extra-virgin olive oil business out there, and often the "extra-virgin" olive oil we see in the stores doesn't actually meet industry EVOO requirements. Yet it can be marketed this way, even if it's diluted with cheaper oils, a bunch of other additives, or chemicals. Good olive oil is different—it should taste fresh, almost grassy, with peppery afternotes. Do some research on the brand of olive oil you're looking at to determine where it's sourced from, and stay away from any olive oil that is kept in a clear bottle. Exposure to light will change the quality of the olive oil for the worse.

CANNED TOMATOES

I'm all for picking up fresh, ripe tomatoes at the store or farmers' market, but it is hard to ignore the convenience that canned crushed tomatoes provide. I use them frequently, if not more than fresh tomatoes, because they are consistent, reliable, and always there for you. Ultimately you can buy them, store them in your pantry, forget about them for a little while, and they'll still be alive. I love to use canned crushed tomatoes for soups, tomato-based pasta sauces, and in Indian dishes like *chana masala* and *baingan bharta*.

ROLLED OATS

When I first started my blog in college, I'd food-style oatmeal like there was no tomorrow. I was like Picasso with those chia seeds. Monet with the berries. Peanut butter was my paint. Flash forward to today, whether it's to make oatmeal, homemade clustery granola, or to blitz in my blender for oat flour, rolled oats are something I always have in my pantry. If you are gluten-intolerant or -sensitive, make sure to buy oats that explicitly say "gluten-free" on the package. While naturally occurring oats are gluten-free, they are sometimes processed in a facility that is not.

HONEY

In addition to being one of my favorite terms of endearment, honey is, in fact, truly my honey. It's a sweetener I turn to for homemade granola and desserts, and even just to drizzle on my daily peanut butter and banana toast. My favorite variety is manuka honey, which is native to New Zealand and sourced from the manuka plant. I love it not just because it has a purer flavor than any other honey I've ever had, but also because it has major antiviral and antibacterial benefits—which for me, makes its higher price point worth it. If you don't have access to manuka honey, I suggest buying honey that only has one ingredient: honey. It's common that some commercial brands will cut their honey products with other sweeteners, which is why I will always recommend local honey if that option is available to you. Additionally, honey won't be as stable in plastic containers, so look to buy it in glass containers when you can.

SEEDS

Chia seeds, hemp seeds, sunflower seeds, sesame seeds, flaxseeds, and pumpkin seeds. These are the seeds I keep in my pantry for snacking, baking, or topping. Seeds add texture, some excitement, and some crunch (what a thrill!), and they are a good way to get in some fiber. We love fiber.

BAKING (AND NO-BAKING)

NUT AND SEED BUTTERS

Peanut, almond, cashew, sunflower seed butter. I cannot emphasize this enough. Nut butter is my life blood. From baking cakes and cookies, to topping rice cakes, to eating with fruit or even a spoon, nut butters are one of those shelf staples that I can't live without. Peanut and almond butter are my two favorites, but I also recommend cashew butter if you prefer a more neutral taste. For my nut-free friends, sunflower seed butter is a great option. If you're baking with it, be warned that the chlorophyll content in sunflower seed butter reacts with baking agents and will cause your cookie or cake to turn green. This is totally harmless and safe to eat. It's mostly hilarious.

ALMOND FLOUR

If I can entice you to buy any alternative flour, let it be this one. Almond flour is my absolute favorite to use in the kitchen. Its uncanny ability to make everything taste cakey and moist, dense yet airy, wholesome yet decadent, is one that I've found to be unmatched with any other flour. You'll see it frequently in my desserts because I simply can't get enough of it. It is pricier than regular flour, but remember that the only ingredient is *almonds*, so it also happens to be grain-free and gluten-free. It makes me happy to see that it's widely available in most stores.

COCONUT FLOUR

Coconut flour was maybe wronged in another life because she soaks up three times as much liquid as regular flour. This makes coconut flour kind of a pain to bake with on its own, because it has a pretty high tendency to absorb everything up and leave you with a mildly dry finished product. A little goes a long way! This is why I frequently use it in conjunction with almond flour, because I've found that alongside almond, coconut flour's properties aid in creating a light sponginess that is actually delightful.

MAPLE SYRUP

Taking my pancakes for a swim is just one of the many reasons why I keep maple syrup around. Along with coconut sugar, it's one of my favorite unrefined sweeteners to bake with, and it adds a full-bodied, rich taste to anything it's used in. Maple syrup and pancake syrup, however, are two very different things, with the latter containing a slew of other

JUST SO YOU KNOW

I also recommend keeping a bag of almond meal in your pantry. Almond meal is made from raw, unpeeled almonds, giving it a coarser consistency than almond flour. Almond flour is made from blanched almonds, which lends itself to a much finer consistency, more similar to regular flour. I turn to almond meal for crusts (like in my Spicy Turmeric Quiche, page 75) for a heartier texture.

sketchy ingredients (high-fructose corn syrup, I am looking at you) that I don't love to welcome to the party. Choose pure maple syrup, in the intensity you prefer—whether that's golden (lighter), amber (rich), or dark (robust).

FLAXSEED MEAL

Not all heroes wear capes, and flaxseed meal is definitely one of these capeless heroes. Flaxseed meal is just a more sophisticated term for straight ground-up flaxseed. While flaxseed meal isn't something I'm actively consuming by the spoonful every day (that journey probably would not bode well), it's an amazing kitchen hack to work as an egg replacer when you're baking.

If you're allergic, vegan, or simply have some sort of aversion to eggs, what we call "flax eggs" generally serve as a good replacement. To make a flax egg, combine 1 tablespoon of flaxseed meal with 2½ tablespoons warm water. Set it aside to thicken for about 5 minutes. You should be left with a gelatinous mixture that can be subbed into recipes that call for 1 egg. If a recipe calls for 2 eggs, bump it up to 2 tablespoons flaxseed meal and 5 tablespoons warm water. I've found that using any more than 2 flax eggs tends to compromise the integrity of the recipe as it's written.

NON-DAIRY MILK (ALMOND, CANNED COCONUT, HEMP, OAT, FLAX, I COULD GO ON . . .)

The degree to which the body can process lactose and milk products varies from person to person. What I do stand by is the fact that everyone is just a little bit on the spectrum of lactose intolerance. The good news is that non-dairy milks abound, and it's more a question of what people are *not* milking these days. Cashews, oats, flaxseeds . . . there are a lot of options for non-dairy humans out there. I recommend keeping canned coconut milk (full-fat!) around as well, to make soups and dals, as a substitute for heavy cream in baked goods, and for a no-bake cheesecake filling.

COCONUT SUGAR

Coconut sugar is typically the only type of sugar I keep in my pantry. Also called "coconut palm sugar," it's a natural sugar made from the sap of coconut palms, and is lower in sucrose, making it a good choice for people who are interested in a low glycemic sweetener or just something that's a little better for you than regular cane sugar. While I appreciate the fact that coconut sugar is touted as a better-for-you sugar, that's not the only reason why I use it. My love affair with coconut sugar is due largely in part to the warm, golden taste it brings to baked goods—from cookies to loaf cakes, I lay awake at night thinking about the subtle yet rich sweetness it brings to everything I put it in. In summary, it is something my kitchen and body cannot live without.

COCONUT OIL

Coconut oil is like the friend we all have who's good at everything and it's kind of annoying to watch, but we still love that energy for them. Coconut oil is incredibly versatile—from baking with it, popping popcorn in it, making coconut rice using it, to even lathering your body with it so we can all be moisturized humans, there are no bounds to what coconut oil can do. Note that coconut oil is solid at room temperature and becomes liquid when it has been heated or warmed (a melting point of 78°F to be exact). Many sweet recipes will call for your coconut oil to be melted and then cooled so that it won't coagulate when you're combining it with other ingredients. However, in cases where your coconut oil needs to be "scoopable" but is at a liquid state in its jar, all you have to do is chill it in the fridge, stir it, and then let it rest at room temperature to get it to the consistency you need.

CHOCOLATE CHIPS

Need I say more? Need I? I will anyway. What is life without chocolate chips? Most of the time I even hesitate to note specific amounts for chocolate chips in recipes because we all know that those proportions are rightly measured with the soul. But I humor myself sometimes. There is hardly any more real estate for chocolate in my pantry because I like to stock it with everything: whether that's dark chocolate chips, semisweet chips (some of these are actually dairy-free, so keep your eyes peeled on the ingredients list), bars made purely from 100% cacao, and even some really great sugar-free varieties. I always suggest keeping some of your favorite chocolate bars on hand as well, as these can easily be chopped up for use in any recipe in lieu of chips. And, if you are one of those people who couldn't care less about chocolate, then don't stress, there is still plenty of room for you in this book, too.

CACAO // COCOA POWDER

From brownies to smoothies, cacao and cocoa powder both make many cameos in my place of work. The beans used to make cacao products are raw and in their unprocessed, unroasted form, while in cocoa products, the bean has been roasted at a high temperature and is sometimes cut with other additives or sugar. Cocoa is likely the chocolate taste you're used to—a little sweeter and less bitter than straight up cacao. I typically choose cacao over cocoa because I like that kind of drama and intensity in my life, but they are interchangeable in any recipe you see them in throughout this book. Always reach for unsweetened cocoa powder when baking (we're going to be adding sugar to the recipe anyway!), and check the ingredients to make sure you're only seeing either "cacao" or "cocoa powder" on the list.

RAW CASHEWS

Raw cashews are the ultimate shapeshifter. Because of their lightly sweet, buttery, yet neutral taste, cashews can really be anything that they, or I guess we, want them to be. Soaking cashews in particular softens them and makes them pliable enough to be used in sauces, cheesecake fillings, and dips.

You can either soak cashews overnight in room-temperature water or, if you're impatient like me, you can use the flash-soaking method. This saves us basically . . . a whole night. All you do is boil some water and pour it over the cashews. Let them sit in the hot water off the heat for one to two hours. By the end, they will be soft enough to blend and subsequently transform into whatever you'd like them to be.

Make sure you buy the "raw" variety of cashews—they aren't roasted or salted, and because of this, work well as a neutral base for savory recipes like my Roasted Jalapeño Queso (page 32), or sweet ones like my No-Bake Raspberry Cheesecake (page 207).

RAW ALMONDS

When I was growing up, my mom used to buy raw almonds, soak them in water, and laboriously peel the skin off of each almond for us to eat. I found out later that she did this because our grandma thought that the sweeter, tender taste

TIP

If you've stored your dates in the fridge and they've consequently become a little tough or stale, revive them by boiling some water and pouring it over the dates, allowing them to soak in the water off the heat for 5 to 10 minutes and soften them (but don't leave them soaking for too long as it breaks down the sugars). And if you're looking for an alternative to jam or a sweet spread to have on toast, soak your dates, pit them, and blend them with a little bit of water until a paste is achieved. Add in some vanilla or cinnamon and you have a perfect homemade date spread.

that results from this soaking method would entice us all to eat more almonds. It worked.

In addition to enjoying them as a really reliable snack on their own, I like to transform raw almonds into cheesecake crust, sweet and salty energy bites, and granola. I prefer to buy raw almonds because they're easy to find in bulk and aren't roasted with sketchy oils or additives.

MEDJOOL DATES

There is an extremely high likelihood that by the day's end, I've snacked on a few dates stuffed with peanut butter and finished with some flaky sea salt. Dates are naturally extremely sweet, with caramel and brown sugar undertones that work well whether baked into a dessert (see page 210 for a salted toffee date cake) or simply stuffed with nut butter and coated in chocolate (see page 238). My favorite variety to eat and bake with is the Medjool date, because of its fleshy, chewy texture and unmatchable sweet taste. I always recommend buying the Medjool variety (unpitted) over the more common Deglet Noor dates, as the latter is firmer and drier, making it tougher to work with.

SHREDDED COCONUT AND COCONUT CHIPS, UNSWEETENED

And . . . you thought that there couldn't possibly be another form of coconut in my pantry. Well, look what we have here. Though it probably doesn't cross your mind too often to buy shredded coconut or coconut chips, they are incredibly versatile additions for topping smoothies, adding to homemade granola, or using as a component in baking (and no-baking). Look for the unsweetened kind, as we'll likely be sweetening any recipe we add it to anyway.

Spicy
White Bean
Dip

Tahini
Beet Dip

Any Occasion Crackers

(READ: A LOT OF DIPS)

sides + apps

Creamy Sweet Potato & Garlic Dip

OG Hummus

Serves 6—8

Hummus is a key component of my personality. Give me your hummus puns, your hummus-centric restaurants, your hummus skepticism (and I'll turn it into adoration). While hummus is traditionally made using dried chickpeas that are soaked and then cooked until they break down, I recognize that canned chickpeas are a lot more accessible and convenient for most of us. I, for one, make hummus using canned chickpeas, and know that this method yields great results. The trick is (1) blending until you literally cannot blend anymore so the tahini and chickpeas really marry each other and become extremely, velvety smooth and (2) not rinsing the chickpeas beforehand so they hang onto the aquafaba (the chickpea brine in the can), which will actually allow for fluffier hummus.

It's also important to pay attention to the tahini. The best, highest-quality sesame seeds are called Humera seeds, and they're sourced from a specific region in Ethiopia. Buy a brand of tahini made with Humera seeds and you're on your way to an obscenely delicious hummus. Whether you're using dried chickpeas or canned, the only thing I urge you to do is to break up with store-bought hummus. Homemade hummus is far fresher and tastier than its store-dwelling counterparts.

¾ cup tahini

Juice of 1 lemon

4 garlic cloves

1 (15.5-ounce) can chickpeas, drained but not rinsed

1 teaspoon ground cumin

¼ teaspoon paprika, plus extra for dusting

Kosher salt to taste

Extra-virgin olive oil for drizzling

Za'atar for dusting

In a food processor or high-speed blender, combine the tahini, lemon juice, and garlic and pulse 4 or 5 times. The mixture will seize and not look too cute at first, but that's normal!

Now add the chickpeas and ¼ cup cold water. Blend until the mixture begins to become smooth.

Now add another 3 to 4 tablespoons of cold water and blend until it is completely smooth. Feel free to add more cold water to reach your desired consistency.

Add the cumin, paprika, and salt. Blend 2 or 3 more times, until the hummus is extremely, velvety smooth.

Season to taste. Transfer the hummus to a bowl, top it with a generous drizzle of olive oil, and dust with paprika and za'atar before serving.

Pesto Hummus

Serves 6—8

When I find a song that I like, I play it on "repeat" until I can't hear it for one second more. I've taken a similar approach to hummus, in that I eat it over and over again, but in this case, I *never* get sick of it. While I hope to grow as a human in general, I really hope that my inherent ability to always hold a space in my soul for hummus is a character trait that is here to stay.

I created this particular recipe in an effort to bring the brightness of pesto to hummus, and the creaminess of hummus to pesto. It's zesty, fresh, and light, and sneaks a ton of greens in without you even registering what's happening (hear that, parents?). Chickpeas, tahini, basil, and spinach are all key players, but don't forget the cumin and smoked paprika. I also live for the act of adding za'atar (a Middle Eastern blend of herbs, commonly oregano, marjoram, cumin, coriander, sesame seeds, and sumac) on top of my hummus—find it on the internet or in the international section at your grocery store.

1 (15.5-ounce) can chickpeas, drained, reserving 1 tablespoon aquafaba (that liquid in the can), but not rinsed

⅓ cup plus 1 tablespoon tahini

3 tablespoons extra-virgin olive oil, plus extra for drizzling

Juice of 1 lemon

3 garlic cloves

⅓ cup (packed) fresh basil leaves

¾ cup (packed) fresh baby spinach

½ teaspoon ground cumin

¼ teaspoon smoked paprika, plus extra for dusting

Kosher salt to taste

Freshly ground black pepper to taste

Za'atar for dusting

In a food processor or high-speed blender, combine the chickpeas with the reserved aquafaba and the tahini, olive oil, lemon juice, garlic, basil, spinach, cumin, and paprika. Blend 3 to 4 times until completely smooth. Season with salt and freshly ground black pepper.

Transfer the hummus to a shallow bowl. Finish with a drizzle of olive oil and garnish with a dusting of za'atar and paprika before serving.

Tahini Beet Dip

Serves 6—8

You're probably wondering, WOW, Samah, are you . . . obsessed with dips? And I can confidently say: YES. Yes, I am obsessed with dips. Do you blame me, though? You can throw everything into a food processor or blender and, with the push of a button, it's done. All of my dip recipes require minimal time and equally minimal ingredients. Yet once you spoon them into a nice bowl and add a garnish, they look so sophisticated and almost like you've spent your entire life in the kitchen making them. And listen, sometimes it really is about less time in the kitchen and more time to enjoy with friends or even just with yourself. A party of one is still a party.

The deep pink color of this dip, created by the beets, objectively makes it pretty, well, pretty to look at. The sweetness from the beets is undercut by the savory tahini, creating a divine depth of flavor. With the addition of lemon and garlic, it's tangy, flavorful, not too sweet, and a little addicting if I'm real with you (and I always will be).

1 cup chopped cooked beets (about 5 baby beets—I often use the vacuum-packed cooked beets in the produce section of the grocery store)

¾ cup tahini

Juice of 1 lemon

3 garlic cloves

1 tablespoon extra-virgin olive oil

¼ teaspoon smoked paprika

Kosher salt to taste

Freshly ground black pepper to taste, plus more for garnish

Flaky sea salt for garnish

Handful of fresh cilantro or parsley leaves, roughly chopped, for garnish

In a high-speed blender or food processor, combine the beets, tahini, lemon juice, garlic, olive oil, paprika, kosher salt, and ground black pepper.

Blend or process on high until completely smooth. You may have to scrape down the sides of your blender to ensure everything is thoroughly combined.

Transfer the dip to a serving bowl and garnish it with sea salt, freshly ground black pepper, and the cilantro.

A NOTE ON TAHINI

I am overwhelmed. Where do I begin? I guess I could start by saying that I have loved tahini for as long as I can remember. Somehow, some way, many people have even told me that I was the one who first introduced them to tahini. I cannot fathom a higher compliment than that.

Though I've eaten tahini for years, I first bought the sesame substance of my dreams to make hummus at home—but let's just say that my foray did not end with hummus. I started baking with tahini, putting it into energy bites, into cookies, and more famously, into my Chocolate Chip Tahini Cake with Chocolate Frosting (page 187), which has become one of the most popular recipes I've ever written.

So what's the deal with tahini, anyway? Tahini, which comes from the Arabic word *tahana* meaning "to grind," is made from sesame seeds that are ground into a paste. It can be made from hulled or unhulled sesame seeds, often toasted to expel a nuttier flavor, and made into a consistency that sort of resembles peanut butter. Sesame seeds have been cultivated in India since 5000 BCE (what's up, ancestors), and today they're grown in many different regions. It's thought that tahini itself originated in what is present-day Iran, but it

has since spread throughout the eastern Mediterranean and many other parts of the world.

Tahini is my kitchen's MVPP (Most Valuable Pantry Player). It is one of the ingredients I use the most for its versatility in lending itself well to both taste and texture. In baked goods it undercuts the sugar and balances out the chocolate. The buttery notes make it perfect for cookies or cakes, but equally as great in salad dressings and hummus. I often use it in pasta, or combine it with spices and herbs to make a sauce for roasted vegetables. Tahini is widely available, but it's crucial to look for the ones with minimal oil separation and where the ingredients are just "sesame seeds." The best tahini is made with Humera sesame seeds, which are sourced from a particular region in Ethiopia, so if you can do some research on the brand of tahini you're using, all the better.

Spicy White Bean Dip

Makes about 2½ cups

In my family, going to a restaurant means asking the servers, "Do you have any chili sauce?" This question may vary depending on the type of cuisine; maybe "red pepper flakes?" or simply "anything spicy?" For us, pizza should come with jalapeños, onions, and green peppers—all controversial, questionable toppings that we will always still top with red pepper flakes. Let me be clear, we are never adding chile to stifle the taste of the food itself, but rather to please our very-much-accustomed-to-spicy-Indian-food palates.

As a result, I always like to have a bit of spice in everything—not to the point where you feel like you can't enjoy what you're eating, but enough so that your taste buds are a little surprised and awakened every time you take a bite. This roasted jalapeño dip will not let you down in that department.

1 jalapeño

Extra-virgin olive oil

1 (15.5-ounce) can white beans, drained and rinsed

¾ cup tahini

4 garlic cloves

Juice of 1 lemon

½ teaspoon ground cumin

Kosher salt to taste

Za'atar for dusting

Paprika for dusting

Preheat the oven to 400°F. Place the jalapeño on a small parchment-lined baking sheet and drizzle it with olive oil so that it is nicely and lightly coated all around. Roast in the oven for 10 to 15 minutes, until the skin starts to peel and blacken and the jalapeño becomes tender. Remove the jalapeño from the oven, remove the stem, and set it aside to cool. If you'd like this dip to be less spicy, you can slice the jalapeño open and remove the seeds.

In a food processor or high-speed blender, combine the cooled jalapeño with the beans, tahini, garlic, lemon juice, cumin, and salt. Process or blend until incorporated.

Tablespoon by tablespoon, add cold water until the mixture thins to your desired consistency. I typically use 4 to 5 tablespoons, but I encourage you to use more or less depending on the consistency you like! Blend until the dip is extremely smooth. Season to taste with salt.

Transfer the dip to a bowl. Before serving, drizzle generously with olive oil, and top with a dusting of za'atar and paprika.

Creamy Sweet Potato & Garlic Dip

Serves 6—8

Every day, and this is a fact, I ask myself, how can I consume sweet potatoes today? Should I bake them? Cut them into cute triangles and sauté them with masala? Or should I boil them, and allow the little beta-carotene wonders to start a friendship with tahini, fresh garlic, and spices, for a dip? If a dip calls to you today, then you're in luck. This one pulls in sweetness from the potatoes but is also smooth and savory with the grounding addition of tahini. It's the type of dip that will make you rethink your "sweet-potato-dip-is-only-for-Thanksgiving policy."

2 medium sweet potatoes

¼ cup tahini

3 tablespoons extra-virgin olive oil, plus extra for drizzling

4 garlic cloves, smashed

Juice of 1 lemon

½ teaspoon paprika, plus extra for dusting

¾ teaspoon ground cumin

Kosher salt and freshly ground black pepper to taste

Handful of chopped fresh parsley for garnish

Sesame seeds for garnish

Bring a large pot of water to a rolling boil. Add the sweet potatoes and boil until they are completely soft and cooked through, 20 to 30 minutes. Drain the sweet potatoes and let them cool completely.

Once cooled, peel the sweet potatoes, discard the skins, and place the peeled potatoes in a food processor or high-speed blender. Add the tahini, olive oil, garlic, lemon juice, paprika, cumin, and salt and pepper. Process or blend until completely smooth.

Season the dip to taste. If you want more of a kick, add extra paprika. If you think it needs some more tang, add an extra squeeze of lemon! Make sure that you're both tasting and adjusting the flavor to your liking—at every step of the way! Season to taste with salt and pepper as well. Transfer it to a bowl and drizzle with olive oil. Garnish with the parsley, sesame seeds, and a dash of paprika (aesthetics, we love it).

Roasted Jalapeño Queso

Makes about 1½ cups

I love the idea of creating flavors with ingredients that you don't necessarily think belong at the party. Cashews are probably the last thing you think of when you're craving queso. But the creamy, buttery consistency created by the cashews, the fiery kick from a roasted jalapeño, and the "cheesy" taste thanks to nutritional yeast all work together here to create a velvety, luxurious dip that you may want to bathe in, but should probably just eat with some tortilla chips.

I want to touch on nutritional yeast because while it doesn't have the cutest name, it does work wonders in creating a cheesy flavor, minus the cheese. It is a deactivated yeast, a form of the same strain used to leaven bread, but it's been dried out to extract its gorgeous nutritious benefits. It's really high in B-complex vitamins and other minerals. You can find it in health food stores or in grocery bulk bins. It's also great in popcorn (check it out with my Masala Popcorn on page 242) or on top of avocado toast for a unique savory kick.

1 jalapeño

Extra-virgin olive oil

1 cup raw cashews, soaked overnight or "flash-soaked" (see page 21)

2 garlic cloves, smashed

½ cup nutritional yeast

½ cup vegetable broth, plus extra if needed

Kosher salt and freshly ground black pepper to taste

Tortilla chips or Any Occasion Crackers (page 47; optional)

Preheat the oven to 400°F. Place the jalapeño on a small parchment-lined baking sheet and drizzle it with olive oil so that it is completely coated. Roast the jalapeño in the oven for 10 to 15 minutes, until it is tender and the skin begins to blacken. Remove the baking sheet from the oven, remove the jalapeño's stem, and set the jalapeño aside to cool. For a less spicy queso, slice the jalapeño open and remove the seeds.

Drain the soaked cashews and place them in a high-speed blender or a food processor. Add the garlic, nutritional yeast, vegetable broth, and roasted jalapeño. Blend until the mixture is completely smooth and velvety. I live for a thick queso but if yours is coming out too creamy for your liking, blend in a couple extra splashes of vegetable broth.

Season the queso with salt and pepper to taste, and transfer it to a bowl.

Serve immediately, with tortilla chips or homemade Any Occasion Crackers!

Cucumber Ribbon Kachumber

In Indian cuisine, *kachumber* is simply always on the table. It's like that one friend who you can't *not* invite to your party. A medley of diced tomatoes, onions, cucumbers, lemon juice, and often green chiles, kachumber serves as a refreshing complement and palate cleanser to all the deliciously spicy Indian food it is often served with. I decided to take traditional Indian kachumber and instead shave the cucumber into ribbons for some extra glamour. You can do this with a simple vegetable peeler, shaving down on one side of the cucumber until you reach the seeds, then flipping it over to shave the other side. This is perfect as an accompaniment to your mains, or as a great light snack when you need something to keep you and your palate cool and refreshed.

½ red onion, diced

1 cup fresh cilantro leaves and tender stems, roughly chopped, plus extra for garnish

½ cup grape tomatoes, halved

1 green chile, thinly sliced (seeds removed if you don't want it to be too spicy), or ½ to 1 whole jalapeño, thinly sliced

1 large hothouse cucumber, or 5 Persian cucumbers

Juice of 1 lemon

Kosher salt and freshly ground black pepper to taste

In a medium bowl, combine the red onion, cilantro, grape tomatoes, and sliced chile.

Start by peeling the cucumber and discarding the skin. Now, use the vegetable peeler to shave the cucumber until you reach the seeds, rotating the cucumber around to each side so that all you are basically left with is a cucumber-seed carcass. Transfer the cucumber ribbons to the bowl.

Add the lemon juice and season to taste with salt and pepper. Garnish with cilantro. Serve immediately!

Masala Sweet Potatoes

Makes about 2 cups

If you've ever had a *dosa* (a South Indian savory crepe), it was probably served with masala-spiced potatoes, bright yellow in their turmeric glory, with mustard seeds and cilantro. The potatoes practically beg dosa eaters to use the thin, crispy crepe as a vehicle to scoop them all up. The only issue I have with those potatoes is that they often serve as a sidekick, usually hidden inside the dosa itself. They're arguably not essential to dosa consumption and you can order a dosa without, but they come simply as just . . . a welcome addition.

I devised this recipe solely to seek justice for masala potatoes. Dramatic much? Okay, maybe a little bit. Nonetheless, I was inspired by those South Indian–style potatoes to create my own version using sweet potatoes. And they don't need a dosa to shine! They're perfect on their own, as a dish to bring to a potluck, or to eat alongside your favorite savory breakfast.

1 tablespoon extra-virgin olive oil

½ teaspoon mustard seeds

1 small yellow onion, sliced

Kosher salt and freshly ground black pepper to taste

½ teaspoon ground turmeric

½ teaspoon ground cumin

⅛ teaspoon cayenne pepper (you can use ¼ teaspoon if you like it spicier!)

1 sweet potato, cut into small wedges

Handful of fresh cilantro leaves, roughly chopped, for garnish

Heat a medium skillet over medium heat and add the olive oil.

When the olive oil starts to shimmer, add the mustard seeds. After a few seconds, when the mustard seeds start to sizzle, add the onions and cook until they are translucent and starting to brown around the edges, 3 to 5 minutes.

Season the onions with salt, black pepper, and the turmeric, cumin, and cayenne. Cook for a few minutes, until the masala smells aromatic. The "raw" masala smell should have dissipated at this point. Then, add the sweet potatoes.

Cover the skillet and cook over medium heat for 10 to 15 minutes, or until the sweet potatoes are tender, making sure to stir them intermittently. Season with salt to taste. Garnish with the cilantro and serve!

Snacking Bread

Makes 1 loaf, 10—12 slices

Bread is an integral part of Indian cuisine. While many are used to prodding and spearing veggies with a fork, Indians are scooping them up with fluffy naan, some thin golden-brown roti, or a crisp, flaky paratha. I can say with confidence that I was conditioned in my youth to have a deep appreciation for bread in all its forms. It was always there to supplement the food on our table.

Given my history with bread, it felt wrong not to have a go-to recipe in this book. The best part about this one is that it is completely customizable to your taste, whether you want to add garlic and rosemary, some scallions, or keep it simple with sea salt and freshly ground pepper. Go off and get creative; just stick with the ingredients you see here as your base and you'll be well on your way to the bread of your dreams. Note that this is a snacking, shorter stacked bread rather than one that rises higher, allowing it to be fluffy while still remaining perfectly dense, satisfying, and hearty.

2 tablespoons coconut oil, melted and cooled, plus extra for greasing the pan

1¼ cups almond flour

3 tablespoons coconut flour

2 tablespoons psyllium husk powder

2 tablespoons flaxseed meal

2 teaspoons baking powder

1 teaspoon garlic powder

1 teaspoon kosher salt

4 eggs

1 tablespoon apple cider vinegar

Preheat the oven to 350°F. Either grease a 9 × 5-inch loaf pan well with coconut oil or line the bottom and sides with parchment paper and lightly grease the parchment with coconut oil.

In a medium bowl, whisk together the almond flour, coconut flour, psyllium husk powder, flaxseed meal, baking powder, garlic powder, and salt.

In a separate medium bowl, beat the eggs with the apple cider vinegar. Stir the 2 tablespoons coconut oil into the egg mixture.

Combine the wet and dry mixtures and transfer the batter to the prepared loaf pan. Bake for 35 minutes or until the edges are golden brown and start to pull away from the sides of the pan. Cool in the pan completely before enjoying. Slice and store in an airtight container for up to 4 days on the counter, or a week in the fridge!

Hummucado Toast

Serves 2—4

I started making *hummucado* (a word I fully made up, I am aware) toast several years ago, around the peak of the avocado toast craze. At the time, I had yet to see anyone combine my two love languages and slap it on my third love language, so ultimately it was up to me to make my dreams come true. I actively enjoy making this for myself at any time of the day (maybe with a side salad or topped with an egg), but it also makes for a great light bite when you have guests over. So when I'm not smashing some avocado, hummus, lemon, and spices onto a piece of fresh sourdough or my homemade snacking bread to eat myself, I'm slicing this toast up into slivers for my dinner guests to enjoy pre-entrée.

2 slices sourdough bread or your favorite bread

1 avocado, halved and pitted

2 tablespoons hummus (check out page 25 for a homemade option)

1 lemon wedge

Kosher salt

Freshly ground black pepper

Red pepper flakes

Fresh basil, sliced tomatoes, sliced radishes, za'atar, and/or extra-virgin olive oil for garnish

Toast the slices of bread.

Scoop the avocado flesh out of one half and smash it onto one of the slices of toast. Repeat with the remaining half avocado and toast. Then, spread the hummus on top of the smashed avocado.

Squeeze the lemon wedge over the hummus, and season with salt, black pepper, and red pepper flakes.

Garnish the toasts with basil, tomatoes, radishes, za'atar, a drizzle of extra-virgin olive oil, or any additional toppings. The choice is yours!

Turmeric Cornbread

Makes
16 pieces

I didn't discover cornbread until I went to college. Right near the campus, there was a salad and sandwich place called Smart Alec's (that has since closed down! cue single sad tear!) that would bestow a complimentary plate of fries upon you if you brought them a paper that you got an A on. While I don't think that Berkeley students needed the added stress of missed potato opportunities every time a B showed up on their papers, I do know that even better than the fries was the cornbread that arrived as a side with every salad. It was unbelievably buttery and sweet and delicious, and though I told myself I went to Smart Alec's to get the salad, it was really the cornbread I was aiming for. My version here is a turmeric cornbread that uses coconut oil instead of butter and turmeric for spice and color. It is crumbly and light, yet decadent enough to transport me back to the one I fell in love with at Smart Alec's.

1 egg

⅓ cup coconut oil, melted and cooled, plus extra for greasing the pan

1½ tablespoons honey

1 cup unsweetened almond milk

¼ cup coconut sugar

¾ teaspoon ground turmeric

1 cup almond flour

1 cup medium-grind cornmeal

2 teaspoons baking powder

¼ teaspoon kosher salt

Preheat the oven to 400°F and grease a 9-inch round cake pan with coconut oil.

In a medium bowl, beat the egg and then mix it with the coconut oil, honey, almond milk, and coconut sugar. Whisk in the turmeric. Set aside.

In a separate medium bowl, whisk together the almond flour, cornmeal, baking powder, and salt.

Combine the wet and dry ingredients. Transfer the batter to the prepared cake pan.

Bake for 15 to 20 minutes, until the top is golden brown. Let the cornbread cool *completely* in the pan before cutting it into pieces; otherwise it will crumble (though please note, this is supposed to be a crumbly cornbread).

Sweet Potato Aloo Tikki
with Spiced Coconut Yogurt

Serves 4—6

1 medium sweet potato

½ teaspoon garam masala

1 teaspoon ground cumin

½ teaspoon ground turmeric

¼ teaspoon cayenne pepper

Kosher salt to taste

¼ cup plus 1 tablespoon oat flour

1 tablespoon coconut flour

1 tablespoon extra-virgin olive oil, plus 2 to 3 tablespoons for pan-frying

½ teaspoon fennel seeds

½ teaspoon cumin seeds

Handful of fresh cilantro leaves, roughly chopped, for garnish

Flaky salt, for garnish

Spiced Coconut Yogurt

1½ cups coconut yogurt

⅛ teaspoon cayenne pepper

½ teaspoon chaat masala

½ red onion, diced

¼ teaspoon ground cumin

Juice of ½ lemon

Handful of chopped fresh cilantro leaves

Kosher salt and freshly ground black pepper to taste

The culture of street food in India is unlike anything I've seen elsewhere in the world. *Chaat*, as it's called, is the all-encompassing word for Indian street food, which consists of a variety of deliciously crunchy, mostly fried snacks made complete with different chutneys, spices, and vegetables. Chaat is food, but it is much more than that. For Indians, it is truly a lifestyle. This is apparent the second you get a glimpse of the hundreds of food carts found at every corner on the streets of India, serving as a pause for all who sidle up and eat their chaat standing next to the stall. It is an appetizer. It is a full meal. It is a break from life.

In Hindi, *aloo* translates to "potato," and *tikki* to "patty" or "cutlet." These are a recurring pair in Indian chaat, typically deep-fried and served with an amalgam of spices, yogurt, and other crunchy textural elements. My version of aloo tikki uses sweet potatoes and is pan-fried instead of deep-fried. I include all the usual suspects in the spice department, with the addition of olive oil–sizzled cumin and fennel seeds. With a topping of fresh herbs and a side of spiced coconut yogurt, they're my ode to chaat, made to eat at any time of your day.

Bring a small pot of water to a boil, add the sweet potato, and boil until it's completely tender and soft, 20 to 30 minutes. Set it aside to cool for about 10 minutes, and then peel the skin off.

Make the Spiced Coconut Yogurt: In a medium bowl, combine the yogurt with the cayenne, chaat masala, onion, cumin, lemon juice, cilantro, and salt and pepper. Adjust with spices to taste. Mix until fully incorporated. Store in the fridge while you finish preparing the aloo tikki.

Make the Sweet Potato Aloo Tikki: Once the potato has cooled and the skin has been discarded, mash the potatoes using a potato masher or a fork. Add the garam masala, ground cumin, turmeric, cayenne, kosher salt, oat flour, and coconut flour and mix everything together.

Heat the 1 tablespoon olive oil in a small skillet. Once it begins to shimmer, add the fennel and cumin seeds. Let them sizzle for about 1 minute and become fragrant. Now, add these toasty seeds and oil to your mashed sweet potato mixture, and mix to combine. Stir until thoroughly incorporated.

Form the sweet potato mixture into patties using about 2 tablespoons each. Heat a couple tablespoons of olive oil in a skillet and pan-fry the patties until they are golden brown and crisp on each side, 4 to 6 minutes per side on medium-low heat.

Garnish the patties with the chopped cilantro and flaky salt. Serve immediately, and with the Spiced Coconut Yogurt.

Any Occasion Crackers

Serves 4–6

I've always been a huge snacker, especially when it comes to savory goods like popcorn, crackers, and chips. I love a nice crunch and need texture with pretty much everything I eat. I also love eating what I like to call "vehicles," and by this I mean vehicles for toppings like hummus, guacamole, my creamy vegan queso (page 32) . . . you get the point. These Any Occasion Crackers (or as my family likes to call them, "Suhaa's Crackers" because my sister Suhaa can't survive a week without them) really do live up to the name—they're perfect for, yes, any occasion, by themselves or as a vehicle. I find a great amount of joy when adding some za'atar, garlic, and cumin seeds to the flour, or even just keeping it salty and simple with some freshly ground black pepper and sea salt. You could also toss in some oregano and red pepper flakes for a pizza vibe, or nutritional yeast for a cheesy (albeit, cheeseless!) crunch. See more flavor ideas (page 48) and choose your adventure.

Cracker Dough

- 1½ cups blanched almond flour
- 1½ teaspoons garlic powder
- ½ teaspoon ground cumin
- 1 teaspoon salt (I like fine sea salt here)
- Freshly ground black pepper to taste
- Spice mix (see Flavor Options, page 48)
- 1 egg

Egg Wash

- 1 egg
- 1 tablespoon unsweetened almond milk
- Pinch of flaky sea salt, plus extra (optional) for sprinkling

Preheat the oven to 350°F.

Make the cracker dough: In a medium bowl, combine the almond flour, garlic powder, cumin, salt, and black pepper. You can bake as is, with just these spices, or use this base plus your spice mix of choice on page 48. Stir well.

Beat the egg in a small bowl, and add it to the almond flour mixture. The cracker dough will be pretty thick, and feel dry at first, but keep mixing so that everything is well incorporated. It helps to use your hands here to knead it together. After a few minutes of kneading, it should feel like it can stick together.

Place the dough on a piece of parchment paper about the size of a large baking sheet, ensuring that it is on a flat surface. Place another piece of parchment paper on top of the dough, and use a rolling pin or a bottle to roll the dough between the two pieces of parchment. Roll until the cracker dough is spread out and quite thin. (If you'd like thinner crackers, you can divide the dough in half, roll both portions of the dough out super-thin, and bake the crackers in two batches.)

(recipe continues)

Peel the top layer of parchment off the cracker dough. Using a large knife or pastry/ravioli wheel, cut the cracker dough into 1- to 2-inch squares. You don't need to separate each cracker piece, but make sure you've fully cut through the dough so it will be easy to break off into pieces after emerging from a journey in the oven. Transfer the parchment paper with the dough pieces to a baking sheet.

Make your egg wash: In a small bowl, beat the egg, almond milk, and pinch of salt together. Very lightly brush the tops of the crackers with the egg wash. Note that you won't use all of the egg wash—save the rest for your next batch!

Sprinkle the crackers with salt if desired, and place the baking sheet in the oven. Bake for 15 to 20 minutes, rotating the pan halfway through baking, until the crackers are golden brown around the edges. Remove them from the oven and let them cool on the baking sheet completely before breaking them into the pieces. Enjoy with dips or solo! Store in an airtight container on your counter for 4 to 5 days (if they last that long . . .).

FLAVOR ADVENTURES

ZA'ATAR & CUMIN SEEDS
½ teaspoon za'atar + 1 tablespoon cumin seeds

TURMERIC & SPICE
½ teaspoon ground turmeric + ¼ teaspoon cayenne pepper + ½ teaspoon garam masala

PIZZA
1 teaspoon dried oregano + ½ teaspoon red pepper flakes + ½ teaspoon ground cumin

CHILI CHEESE
¼ teaspoon smoked paprika + ¼ teaspoon ground cumin + 1 tablespoon nutritional yeast

lates to your own style and estimation. And that, to me, is one of the best parts of cooking—you iterate and change until you surprise even yourself.

Though my mom would cook multiple dishes a night, she was never in the kitchen for hours. She has always had a particular style of Indian cooking; her dishes are a little lighter and brighter, without using any dairy or exorbitant amounts of oil. She would swap cream for fresh tomatoes to change what would normally be a cream-based masala into one that was tomato-based. In a similar way, I have found myself intrigued by alternative ingredients, baking with almond flour instead of all-purpose, using coconut oil instead of butter, challenging myself to create in a way that is different from what is considered the norm but has my own stamp on it. My version, my take.

At the time it never occurred to me that my friends might never have had this type of food, nor this ritualistic dinner experience with their whole family every night—using your hands as utensils, tearing into pieces of roti, scooping up rice, all together. Nearly every night it was my mom's home-cooked food, sometimes pre-gamed by *bhel puri* (my dad's favorite snack).

At the dinner table, I no longer felt the pressure of my cultural balancing act. It didn't matter that Indian people my age were living across the world—they were likely also eating dal and rice with their hands, next to their own siblings and probably all of the aunties, too. It also didn't make a difference that I felt like an outsider in my school and even among my own friends. I felt comfortable here, in this routine of eating as a unit, with intention.

To revel in sitting down at the table across from family instead of the TV was something I learned from my culture and my home. Regardless of where you come from and where you've been brought up, who you are, who you'll become, food has and will always be our common denominator of connection, conversation, and love. I didn't register any of this at the time because I didn't have to. Unlike my place in other aspects of my life, this part just felt right.

Carrot Cake
Muffin Tops

breakfasts to dream about

One Banana Only Muffin Tops

Carrot Cake Muffin Tops

Makes 8–10 muffin tops

When I was in high school and still living under the same roof as my sister, mom, and dad, all four of us would go for morning walks into Newport Beach.

When my dad was feeling indulgent, he would buy his favorite carrot coconut cashew muffin from a café on the way back. He'd wait until we got home, pop it in the toaster to warm it up (there are few things we don't toast), and then finally eat it. These Carrot Cake Muffin Tops are an ode to him.

When it comes to muffins in general, I feel confident that all of us (or at the very least, *most* of us) can agree that we are in the game solely for the tops. There's something about that golden crispness from the caramelization of the sugars (and Maillard reaction!) that, in my opinion, gives muffin tops the lead over their fluffy inside. Since muffin tops are made on a baking sheet rather than in a tin, we maximize the esteemed opportunity for sugar caramelization by allowing heat to hit more surface area of the muffin top. I always gravitate toward making muffin tops for this reason. But it should go without saying that if you're eating muffins just for the inside, I respect your journey, too. *Pictured in chapter opener photo, page 52.*

2 eggs

3 tablespoons coconut oil, softened until scoopable

1 teaspoon vanilla extract

¾ cup coconut sugar, plus extra for topping

1 cup (packed) grated carrots

1 cup almond flour

1 cup oat flour

1 teaspoon baking powder

1 teaspoon ground cinnamon

½ teaspoon ground ginger

¼ teaspoon kosher salt

½ cup unsweetened shredded coconut

Crushed raw, unsalted nuts (optional; I like crushed almonds and pistachios here)

Preheat the oven to 350°F and line a baking sheet with parchment paper.

In a large bowl, beat the eggs. Add the coconut oil, vanilla, and coconut sugar. Mix until completely smooth. Add the carrots to the mixture and stir to combine.

In a separate medium bowl, whisk together the almond flour, oat flour, baking powder, cinnamon, ginger, and salt.

Add the flour mixture to the carrot mixture. Fold to combine so that everything is thoroughly incorporated. Now add the shredded coconut to the muffin batter. You can even add some crushed nuts if you're feeling like you want a little extra texture (and we love texture!). The batter should be fairly wet.

Scoop 3- to 4-tablespoon amounts of the batter onto your lined baking sheet. Sprinkle about 1 teaspoon of coconut sugar over each of the muffin tops.

Bake 25 to 30 minutes, until the edges are crisp and the muffin tops are golden brown.

Let cool slightly on a wire rack before enjoying.

Rice Crispy Granola

Makes 3–4 cups

One of my deepest darkest secrets when making granola at home is to use brown rice crisps in addition to the traditional rolled oats. Not only does it take the crunch factor up intensely, but it also adds a lot more texture and makes the granola simply more interesting to eat. What will I get in this bite? Oats? Rice crisps? Nuts? All of the above? That, in essence, is the multi-layered experience of eating this granola. I like to crush the almonds and cashews slightly so that they catch more of the nut butter and honey—you can do this by placing them in a ziplock bag and hitting them with the bottom of a measuring cup, simultaneously getting out any of your aggression.

⅓ cup creamy almond butter

¼ cup honey (you can sub maple syrup, but I love the way honey works with the rice crisps)

2 tablespoons coconut oil, melted and cooled

1 cup raw almonds and cashews (or raw mixed nuts), slightly crushed

¾ cup unsweetened coconut chips

1 cup rolled oats

1 cup brown rice crisps cereal

1 tablespoon hemp seeds

1 tablespoon chia seeds

1 tablespoon flaxseed meal

½ teaspoon kosher salt

½ teaspoon ground cinnamon

Preheat the oven to 325°F and line a baking sheet with parchment paper.

In a medium bowl, combine the almond butter, honey, and coconut oil, and mix until smooth.

In another medium bowl, combine the nuts, coconut chips, rolled oats, brown rice crisps, hemp seeds, chia seeds, flaxseed, salt, and cinnamon. Add this to the almond butter mixture.

Stir to combine so that all of the dry ingredients are well coated in the almond butter mixture. At this time resist the temptation to snack.

Transfer the granola mixture to your parchment paper–lined baking sheet. Spread it out evenly so that everyone has some personal space and you can ensure an even crispness.

Bake for 30 to 40 minutes, tossing the granola every 10 minutes or so to ensure that everything becomes golden and toasty.

Once you remove the granola from the oven, do not stir it! This is how we achieve clusters (our granola goal), so let the granola sit until it is completely cool before breaking it apart and enjoying. Store in an airtight container or sealed mason jar on your counter or pantry for up to 2 weeks.

One Banana Only Muffin Tops

Makes 4–6 muffin tops

Do you have a lone banana sitting on your counter? Just one? That has maybe been sitting there for a few days, just staring at you, wondering what will become of its existence? Every time I would see one sad banana on my counter, it always served as a reminder that I couldn't whip up a full banana bread, which typically calls for more than one banana. And that realization is the exact reason why this recipe was born. This is the recipe to make if you're craving banana bread but have only one banana to work with.

This is a small-batch recipe, meaning it makes only four to six muffin tops, depending on how large or small you'd like them, which I find to be perfect if I'm just craving a little something sweet at the end of the day or to pair with my morning coffee. I sweeten these with just a touch of maple syrup, which you can totally swap out for honey if that's more your speed. You can omit the chocolate chips if you'd like, but do you like happiness? Then don't skip them. *Pictured in chapter opener photo, page 53.*

1 egg

1 ripe banana

2 tablespoons creamy almond butter or peanut butter

2 tablespoons maple syrup

½ tablespoon coconut oil, melted and cooled

¼ cup almond flour

¼ cup coconut flour

¼ teaspoon baking powder

½ teaspoon baking soda

⅛ teaspoon kosher salt

⅓ cup chocolate chips (I usually measure this with my soul), plus extra for topping

Preheat the oven to 350°F and line a baking sheet with parchment paper.

In a small bowl, beat the egg.

In a medium bowl, mash your one banana. Add the beaten egg, almond butter, maple syrup, and coconut oil and stir the mixture together until it's smooth.

In a separate medium bowl, whisk together the almond flour, coconut flour, baking powder, baking soda, and salt.

Combine the wet and dry ingredients and fold in the chocolate chips.

Scoop 3- to 4-tablespoon amounts of the batter onto your lined baking sheet. Place extra chocolate chips on top, if desired (this is something I always desire).

Bake for 15 to 20 minutes, until the edges are golden brown. Let the muffin tops cool slightly before removing them from the baking sheet. Transfer to a wire rack to cool further before serving or enjoy warm straight out of the oven.

Fluffy Pillow Pancakes

Makes 6–8 pancakes

I basically go to sleep thinking about what I'll eat for breakfast the next morning. And the thought of eating these Fluffy Pillow Pancakes in the morning? Chief among those dreams.

Let me run it back for a second. Once upon a time, I was a pancake mix kind of gal. My family and I used to be all about them. Now, let me be clear—there's absolutely nothing wrong with pancake mixes. But when I realized how simple it is to make a pancake batter from scratch, I was forever changed. (And my alarm clock was also changed. To an hour earlier. So I could eat sooner.)

The name of these Fluffy Pillow Pancakes speaks for itself—they are truly little clouds of heaven, made even more delicious and customizable by the toppings of your choice. I want you to use them as a perfect canvas for anything sweet and extra; choose your add-in adventure below, and top with maple syrup or honey to seal the deal.

¾ cup almond flour

2 tablespoons coconut flour

½ teaspoon baking powder

⅛ teaspoon kosher salt

Dash of ground cinnamon to taste

2 eggs

2 tablespoons coconut sugar

½ teaspoon vanilla extract

½ cup almond milk

Optional add-ins of choice (below)

Coconut oil, for greasing the skillet

Maple syrup, honey, or other topping of choice

In a large bowl, whisk together the almond and coconut flours, baking powder, salt, and cinnamon.

In a separate medium bowl, beat the eggs, then stir in the coconut sugar, vanilla, and almond milk.

Combine the wet and dry ingredients, mixing well. Fold in your choice of add-ins (or leave the batter as is).

Grease a large skillet with coconut oil and set it over medium heat. Spoon 2- to 3-tablespoon amounts of the batter onto the hot skillet. Let the pancakes cook until the edges start to curl up and the pancakes become golden and fluffy, 3 to 5 minutes. Then flip them over and cook until the other side is golden, another 3 to 5 minutes.

To serve, top the pancakes with maple syrup, honey, or your choice of toppings. (I like fresh berries, nuts, cinnamon, and coconut flakes.)

CHOOSE YOUR ADVENTURE:

BANANA
Mash half a ripe banana and fold it into the pancake batter until thoroughly incorporated. Slice the other half of the banana into coins and sauté them in ½ tablespoon coconut oil over medium heat until golden brown on both sides, 3 to 5 minutes per side. Serve on top of the banana pancakes.

BLUEBERRY
Stir ⅓ cup fresh or frozen blueberries into the pancake batter.

CHOCOLATE CHIP
Stir ¼ cup mini chocolate chips into the pancake batter.

The OG Green Smoothie

Serves 1

Green smoothies are obviously not a novelty. There is a lot of "green smoothie noise" out there, in the sense that everyone has a version that they like to make. This is mine.

I have been making this combination for years, and even people who aren't into green smoothies like it. Because, first of all, it doesn't taste green. Oh, and you just *know* when something tastes green. Grass is something I prefer to look at rather than taste, thank you very much. (And maybe not even look at it for too long. I'm mildly allergic to grass.) Make sure your bananas and spinach are both frozen, as this will help to create a thicker, creamier smoothie—a watery smoothie is not cute. We don't want to wake up to that.

1 or 2 frozen bananas (see Note)

½ cup frozen spinach

1 cup unsweetened almond milk

1 tablespoon chia seeds, plus (optional) extra for garnish

1 tablespoon almond butter or peanut butter, creamy or crunchy, plus (optional) extra for garnish

1 teaspoon cacao nibs (optional)

¼ teaspoon vanilla extract

Dash of ground cinnamon

Granola, homemade (page 55) or store-bought, for garnish (optional)

To make the smoothie, combine the bananas, spinach, almond milk, chia seeds, nut butter, cacao nibs (if using), vanilla, and cinnamon in a blender. Blend it up!

If you want to make a thicker smoothie bowl, add 1 more frozen banana and use just enough almond milk for the smoothie to blend. Garnish the smoothie or bowl with your favorite toppings—I turn to granola, more chia seeds, and more nut butter (always).

NOTE

Freeze your ripe bananas by removing the peel, slicing, and storing the chunks in a reusable container or bag in your freezer!

Peanut Butter & Jelly Smoothie

Serves 1

I spent at least eight years of my youth eating a peanut butter and jelly sandwich every day. It would appear that for me, the PB&J transcended its personality as a cute, easy, kid-friendly school lunch to become, well, an inherent part of *my* personality. It felt only right to transform this iconic combo into a smoothie. The frozen banana works here as the sweet and creamy base, and I like to add both blueberries and strawberries as the "jelly." Feel free to use all blueberries or all strawberries if that feels more true to your jelly journey. It goes without saying that you don't need to be shy with the peanut butter here, it's probably why we're all on this page in the first place.

1 or 2 frozen bananas (see Note, opposite)

1 cup unsweetened almond milk, or more to taste

½ cup frozen blueberries

⅓ cup frozen strawberries, plus (optional) extra for garnish

½ cup frozen spinach (optional)

2 tablespoons peanut butter, creamy or crunchy, plus (optional) extra for garnish

½ tablespoon chia seeds

½ tablespoon cacao powder or unsweetened cocoa powder

Chopped roasted peanuts (optional)

Granola, homemade (page 55) or store-bought, for garnish (optional)

In a blender, combine the banana, almond milk, blueberries and strawberries, spinach (if using), peanut butter, chia seeds, and cacao powder. If you want a more drinkable versus spoonable consistency, add a little more almond milk. Blend it up!

If you want to make a thicker smoothie bowl, add 1 more frozen banana and use just enough almond milk for the smoothie to blend. Top the smoothie or bowl with your toppings of choice—in this smoothie I like to add roasted peanuts, granola, and strawberries.

Pancake Bread

Makes 1 loaf,
10–12 slices

Imagine. Imagine a world in which you can eat pancakes in a bread form with a sweet and golden cinnamon sugar topping. Well, all I have to say is that it's a good thing that you're here because this is a world in which you can now live.

If you want a good laugh, just envision me sitting on the floor of my sub-500-square-foot apartment in New York, thinking about all the ways in which I can make pancakes happen in other forms. I'm thrilled to announce that this pancake bread is a product of that thought spiral. It's somehow perfect for breakfast with a drizzle of maple syrup, but also makes complete logical sense as a dessert or midday sweet treat. I put it here, alongside my breakfast staples, because there's really nothing better than knowing you have another form of pancake to guide you out of bed in the morning.

Batter

⅓ cup coconut oil, melted and cooled, plus extra for greasing the pan

2 eggs, beaten

⅓ cup maple syrup

1 teaspoon vanilla extract

½ cup full-fat coconut milk

⅔ cup coconut sugar

1¼ cups oat flour

1¼ cups almond flour

½ teaspoon baking soda

½ teaspoon baking powder

⅛ teaspoon kosher salt

¼ teaspoon ground cinnamon

Cinnamon Sugar Topping

⅓ cup coconut oil, softened

¼ cup coconut sugar

1 cup oat flour

½ teaspoon ground cinnamon

Preheat the oven to 350°F and grease a 9 × 5-inch loaf pan well with coconut oil.

Make the batter: In a medium bowl, mix together the eggs, ⅓ cup coconut oil, maple syrup, vanilla, and coconut milk until smooth.

Add in the coconut sugar and mix until everything is well incorporated.

In a separate medium bowl, whisk together the oat flour, almond flour, baking soda, baking powder, salt, and cinnamon.

Combine the wet and dry ingredients, mixing well. Transfer the pancake bread batter to the prepared loaf pan, tapping the pan on the counter and smoothing out the top to make sure it is even.

Make the Cinnamon Sugar Topping: In a small bowl, combine the coconut oil, coconut sugar, oat flour, and cinnamon. Sprinkle the cinnamon sugar topping over the batter in the loaf pan.

Bake for 15 minutes. Then reduce the heat to 325°F and bake for an additional 30 to 35 minutes, until the edges of the loaf are nice and golden brown, and a knife inserted in the center comes out clean.

Let cool completely in the pan before slicing and serving.

Maple & Olive Oil Tahini Granola

Makes 3–4 cups

When I'm stressed, I make granola. So in periods of high anxiety, my apartment is filled to the brim with crunchy, lightly sweet, golden clusters of oats, nuts, and seeds. I guess it's not such a bad coping mechanism.

There's something very satisfying about making granola at home. I can't figure out whether it's because it's so easy to make, or because you end up saving some funds by making a fresher and crunchier version than store-bought. Whatever the case, I'm addicted to the instant gratification that homemade granola gives me. Not to mention it's super portable as a snack or even as a gift for someone because it travels well, especially when you throw it into a cute mason jar.

The base of this granola is made with tahini, maple syrup, and a touch of olive oil. These three factors create a rich sweet-and-savory flavor profile and also some pretty intense clusters, which is the primary reason we're eating granola in the first place, right?

⅓ cup tahini

¼ cup maple syrup

2 tablespoons extra-virgin olive oil

1½ cups whole, skin-on, unsalted almonds or mixed nuts of choice, slightly crushed or chopped

¾ cup unsweetened coconut chips

2 cups rolled oats

1 tablespoon hemp seeds

1 tablespoon chia seeds

1 tablespoon flaxseed meal

½ teaspoon kosher salt

½ teaspoon ground cinnamon

Preheat the oven to 325°F and line a baking sheet with parchment paper.

In a medium bowl, combine the tahini, maple syrup, and olive oil, and mix until smooth.

In another medium bowl, combine the nuts, coconut chips, rolled oats, hemp seeds, chia seeds, flaxseed, salt, and cinnamon. Once they're mixed, add these dry ingredients to the tahini-maple syrup mixture. Stir to combine so that the tahini mixture thoroughly coats the nuts, seeds, and oats.

Spoon the granola onto your parchment paper–lined baking sheet. Spread the mixture out so that everything has room to breathe and some personal space—this will ensure an even, crisp bake.

Bake for 30 to 40 minutes, tossing the granola every 10 minutes or so to ensure that everything becomes golden and toasty.

Once you remove the baking sheet from the oven, do not stir the granola! This is how we achieve clusters, so let it sit until it has cooled completely before breaking it apart into clusters. Store in an airtight container or sealed mason jar on your counter or pantry for up to 2 weeks.

Maple
& Olive Oil
Tahini Granola

Rice Crispy
Granola

Cinnamon Pain Perdu
with Almond Butter Caramel

Serves 2

While I was in college, each year when my birthday rolled around (November 18th for all of you who would like to send me almond butter jars or tahini in celebration), I knew where I needed to go for breakfast: La Note on Shattuck Avenue. I was never interested in any of the savory options but instead went straight for the Brioche Pain Perdu. This true state-of-the-art French toast was soaked in an orange flower water batter and sprinkled with confectioners' sugar and lavender honey. Soft, light, but impossibly decadent, the La Note French toast reminds me of a celebration, and so does my own Cinnamon Pain Perdu. You can use brioche here, your leftover French bread from last night, or my personal favorite, sourdough. And don't blame me if you want to carry this Almond Butter Caramel everywhere you go. I do it, too.

Almond Butter Caramel

3 large Medjool dates, pitted

3 tablespoons creamy almond butter

2 tablespoons coconut sugar

½ cup unsweetened vanilla almond milk

French Toast

2 eggs

1 teaspoon vanilla extract

1 teaspoon ground cinnamon

2 tablespoons unsweetened vanilla non-dairy milk

Coconut oil for pan-frying

2 large slices sourdough bread

Coconut sugar for sprinkling

Confectioners' sugar (optional)

Fresh berries (optional)

Prepare the Almond Butter Caramel: In a high-speed blender, combine the dates, almond butter, coconut sugar, and almond milk. Blend until smooth and set aside.

Make the French Toast: In a shallow dish, beat together the eggs, vanilla, cinnamon, and non-dairy milk.

Heat a medium skillet over medium heat. Once the skillet is hot, add coconut oil (I use about ½ tablespoon per slice). Submerge one piece of bread into the egg mixture, flipping to make sure it's evenly soaked. Sprinkle each side of the soaked bread with a bit of coconut sugar and place the bread in the pan. Pan-fry 3 to 5 minutes per side, or until the French toast is cooked through and golden brown on both sides.

Drizzle the Almond Butter Caramel over the slices of French toast and top them with confectioners' sugar and berries, if desired. Serve immediately.

Blueberry Muffin Loaf Cake

Wouldn't it be nice if your bowl of oatmeal and favorite blueberry muffin decided to get together and form one gorgeous breakfast? Or so I caught myself thinking while staring maybe just a little too long at the blueberry muffin behind the glass at my local coffee shop. Once I got my coffee and my act together, I decided to create this blueberry muffin loaf cake situation.

Teaching myself how to bake has been both a blessing and a curse, because the ability to make whatever I want whenever I want is a mildly dangerous skill to have. Another realization I've had about myself, other than my treacherous ability to bake at all hours, is that I have a tendency to turn everything into a loaf. This is my case in point. Muffins are great and all, but that ratio of fluffy middle to crunchy crust in a loaf? It cannot be beat.

¼ cup coconut oil, melted and cooled, plus extra for greasing the pan

1 egg

⅓ cup creamy almond butter

1 teaspoon vanilla extract

2 tablespoons maple syrup

2 tablespoons fresh lemon juice

½ teaspoon grated lemon zest

¾ cup coconut sugar, plus 1 tablespoon for topping

1¼ cups almond flour

1¼ cups oat flour

1½ teaspoons baking powder

¼ teaspoon kosher salt

1 teaspoon ground cinnamon

¼ cup unsweetened almond milk

1 cup fresh blueberries

Preheat the oven to 350°F and grease the bottom and sides of a 9 × 5-inch loaf pan with coconut oil.

In a medium bowl, beat the egg. Then add the almond butter, ¼ cup coconut oil, vanilla, maple syrup, lemon juice, and lemon zest. Mix until smooth. Add the coconut sugar and stir together until everything is well incorporated.

In a separate medium bowl, whisk together the almond flour, oat flour, baking powder, salt, and cinnamon.

Combine the almond butter mixture with the dry ingredients and stir well to incorporate. Add the almond milk to help everything come together. Gently fold in the blueberries.

Transfer the batter to the prepared loaf pan, tapping the pan on the counter and smoothing out the top to make sure it is evenly distributed. Sprinkle the 1 tablespoon coconut sugar on top, and bake for 30 to 35 minutes, until the edges are golden crispy brown and a knife inserted in the center comes out clean.

Once completely cool, run a non-serrated knife alongside the edges of the loaf. Place an upside-down plate on top of the loaf and invert it onto the plate.

RASPBERRY LEMON JOURNEY

Substitute the 1 cup blueberries for 1 cup raspberries and add 1 extra tablespoon of lemon juice and ½ teaspoon extra lemon zest.

Honey-Tahini Scones

Makes 8 scones

If I were to conjure up the scones of my dreams, well, you're looking at them right here. They're lightly sweetened with honey and just a tiny touch of coconut sugar. Thanks to the tahini, these are creamy and earthy, and they maintain a stunning crumbly texture that ruins all of your clothing because you won't be able to stop eating them and you'll find crumbs on your sleeves for the rest of the day. Not from personal experience or anything.

I suggest making these with store-bought oat flour because it is finer in texture than the oat flour you can create at home. However, if that's inaccessible, you can most definitely use rolled oats that you've ground into flour in your food processor or blender. Try to get it as fine as possible, but it's no big deal if it's not crazy pulverized because it will give these a really hearty, wholesome, oaty texture.

2 flax eggs (see Note on page 72)

⅓ cup tahini

5 tablespoons coconut oil, softened until scoopable, plus extra for greasing the baking sheet

¼ cup honey, plus extra (optional) for drizzling

1 teaspoon vanilla extract

1 tablespoon fresh lemon juice

2 tablespoons coconut sugar

2 cups oat flour, plus extra for dusting

¼ teaspoon sea salt

2 teaspoons baking powder

3 tablespoons non-dairy milk (perhaps hemp, almond, or oat)

Prepare the flax eggs and set aside. In a medium bowl, mix together the tahini, coconut oil, and honey. Add the vanilla, lemon juice, and 1 tablespoon of the coconut sugar. Stir to combine.

At this point your flax egg should have thickened up. Add it to the tahini mixture and stir to combine.

Add the oat flour and salt to the tahini mixture. Now, add the baking powder on top, sprinkling it over the entire surface area of the flour and salt. Fold everything together thoroughly. Once you've mixed everything so it's as fully incorporated as it can be, add the non-dairy milk to help pull it all together.

Form the dough into a ball and transfer it to a floured surface. Flatten it into a disk that's about 1½ inches thick. Use a large knife to cut the disk into 8 wedges.

Lightly grease a baking sheet with coconut oil or line it with parchment paper. Transfer the separated wedges to the prepared baking sheet. Sprinkle the tops with the remaining 1 tablespoon coconut sugar.

Place the baking sheet in your refrigerator to chill for at least 15 minutes or as long as 30 minutes.

(recipe continues)

Preheat the oven to 400°F.

Once the oven is heated, remove the baking sheet from the fridge and bake the scones for about 15 minutes. The scones should be golden and crisp around the tops and sides.

Remove the baking sheet from the oven and let the scones cool on the baking sheet. Enjoy the scones by themselves or with a drizzle of honey, and especially with your coffee or tea.

WHAT IS A FLAX EGG?

There is probably nothing that sounds less cute than a "flax egg." But the thing about flax eggs is that they make all the difference for people who can't tolerate eggs or who follow a vegan diet. A flax egg is a combination of water and flaxseed meal (a.k.a. ground-up flaxseed) that yields a thick, gelatinous (are you cringing, because same) substance. When added to recipes in the place of eggs, it works as a binder and a replacement for eggs with a nice little dose of fiber to boot. I actually really love the way flax eggs work in recipes; they make the texture a little denser than eggs would, while allowing the recipe to remain light. And I appreciate the fact that it makes recipes a lot more accessible for different dietary preferences or needs. Here is the formula for a flax egg; it can be substituted in most recipes that call for eggs, but where more than two eggs are called for, I stick with regular eggs, as the recipe may be compromised.

1 tablespoon flaxseed meal + 2½ tablespoons warm water

Let sit for 5 minutes until a gel-like texture is achieved.

Masala Scrambled Eggs

This recipe was *the* Sunday breakfast in my house when I was growing up. We'd pair these masala scrambled eggs with some extra-toasted sourdough bread and use the delightfully, and very audibly, crunchy toast (arguably a cracker at this point) to scoop up the eggs, *sans* forks. The utensil simply wasn't necessary.

Turmeric, cayenne, and cumin are all major players here, and along with onions, green chiles, and cilantro, this is a pretty zesty, herby, spicy way to wake up in the morning. It's also a very easy throw-it-together meal to double when you invited guests over for breakfast and sort of forgot they were coming.

5 eggs

½ teaspoon ground turmeric

Freshly ground black pepper

1 tablespoon extra-virgin olive oil

1 medium red onion, diced

½ teaspoon ground cumin

¼ teaspoon cayenne pepper

Kosher salt

Handful of fresh cilantro, stems removed, roughly chopped, plus more for garnish

2 green chiles

Handful fresh spinach, roughly chopped

Toast for serving

In a medium bowl, beat the eggs with ¼ teaspoon of the turmeric and a dash of black pepper. Whisk until the eggs are well beaten and frothy and the spices are nicely incorporated. Set the eggs aside.

Heat a medium skillet over medium heat and add the olive oil. Once the oil is shimmering, add the onions to the pan and cook until they become translucent and are a little golden around the edges, 5 to 6 minutes.

Add the cumin, the remaining ¼ teaspoon turmeric, the cayenne, and salt to taste, and cook until the spices smell aromatic and have roasted, darkening slightly in color, about 2 minutes. Add the cilantro and green chiles. Cook for another minute.

Now add the beaten eggs to the onions. Cook, scrambling the eggs until they are completely cooked through. Add the spinach and cook until it wilts, 2 to 3 minutes.

Garnish with cilantro and enjoy with toast!

Spicy Turmeric Quiche

Serves 6

I've never understood quiche. Are you a breakfast item? Are you made for brunch? Are you there as the savory component for an afternoon tea? Literally *what are you*? And then I realized I don't need to put quiche in a corner. Quiche can be whatever it wants to be. And so I made it spicy and added turmeric.

The crust of this quiche is made with a blend of spices, garlic, herbs, and almond meal. I didn't want the crust to just be a place for the filling to live, but rather a star in its own right! As for the filling, I adore the combination of spinach and onions but you're more than welcome to switch it up to your liking. Add some arugula! Maybe some bell peppers! Even some mushrooms! Moral of the story is that quiche is a versatile, excellent thing and I really have to apologize to quiche everywhere for my previous oversights.

Crust

½ cup extra-virgin olive oil, plus extra for greasing the pie dish

2 cups almond meal

2 tablespoons coconut flour

1 teaspoon garlic powder

¼ teaspoon ground cumin

½ teaspoon dried oregano

½ teaspoon kosher salt

½ teaspoon cracked black pepper

¼ teaspoon red pepper flakes

1 tablespoon nutritional yeast

3 tablespoons unsweetened almond milk

Filling

1 tablespoon extra-virgin olive oil

½ white onion, chopped

Kosher salt

1 cup (packed) fresh spinach

5 eggs

½ teaspoon freshly ground black pepper

1 teaspoon ground cumin

¼ teaspoon cayenne pepper

¼ teaspoon ground turmeric

¼ cup unsweetened almond milk

Preheat the oven to 400°F. Grease an 8-inch pie dish with extra-virgin olive oil and set it aside.

Make the crust: In a medium bowl, combine the almond meal, coconut flour, garlic powder, cumin, oregano, salt, black pepper, red pepper flakes, and nutritional yeast. Stir together well. Then add the ½ cup olive oil and almond milk, and mix thoroughly. Press the crust mixture into the pie dish, covering the bottom and up the sides. Bake the crust for 15 to 20 minutes, until the edges are lightly golden.

Prepare the filling: Heat the olive oil in a small skillet over medium heat. Add the onions and a pinch of salt, and sauté until they are translucent, tender, and starting to brown, 5 to 6 minutes. Then add the spinach and cook with the onions until it has wilted. Set the mixture aside to let cool.

In a medium bowl, whisk the eggs with the black pepper, cumin, cayenne, turmeric, and salt (I use ½ teaspoon). Then add the cooled sautéed onions and spinach. Finally, stir in the almond milk.

Pour the filling into the baked crust and bake for 20 to 25 minutes, until a knife or toothpick inserted in the center comes out clean and the crust has darkened in color. The egg filling will have risen but will fall once it cools slightly. Let the quiche cool for about 10 minutes. Then cut it into slices and serve immediately.

Tomato Egg Curry

Serves 3–4

This is a dish to make if you want the glitz and glam of baked eggs in tomato sauce but don't feel like baking eggs in tomato sauce. I was inspired by a traditional Punjabi egg curry, a North Indian dish that is cooked in this way, adding boiled eggs to a punchy tomato-based sauce made with garlic, ginger, onions, and masala. I like leaving the boiled eggs whole and scoring them so that the sauce finds its way in, but you are also welcome to halve the eggs and let the sauce get *really* all up in there. My mom used to eat this dish as a kid growing up in India, so it always reminds me of her. Note: this transitions beautifully to lunch or dinner, too!

6 eggs

2 tablespoons extra-virgin olive oil

7 fresh curry leaves (omit if you're unable to locate some!)

½ teaspoon mustard seeds

1 yellow onion, diced

3 garlic cloves, halved

½ teaspoon ground turmeric

¼ teaspoon cayenne pepper (or ½ teaspoon if you want it spicier)

1 teaspoon ground cumin

1 (28-ounce) can crushed tomatoes

Kosher salt

Handful of roughly chopped fresh cilantro, plus extra for serving

2 green chiles, stem removed, trimmed, and slit open lengthwise

Toasted bread, rice, or roti for serving

Bring a medium saucepan of water to a boil. Once the water has come to a rolling boil, lower the eggs into the water one by one, using a slotted spoon. Boil for 8 minutes. Pour the water out of the pot and transfer the eggs to a colander. Transfer the eggs to a bowl of ice water and let them cool in this cute little bath for 2 to 3 minutes to stop them from cooking further.

Peel and score the eggs (make shallow slashes using a paring knife) or cut them in half so when we add them to the masala, the sauce will find its way in. Set the eggs aside.

Heat the olive oil in a deep medium saucepan over medium heat. Once the oil starts to shimmer, add the curry leaves (if using) and the mustard seeds. Cook for a few seconds, until the mustard seeds start to sizzle, then add the onions. Cook the onions for 5 to 7 minutes, or until they become lightly browned. Then, add the garlic.

Cook the onions and the garlic together in the oil until they start to brown around the edges, after 2 to 3 minutes. Now add the turmeric, cayenne, and cumin. Cook and brown the spices for 2 to 3 minutes until fragrant. You can add a splash of water if the mixture starts to burn.

Add the tomatoes, cover the pan, and cook over medium heat for 20 minutes so the masala infuses with the sauce, stirring often. Then season with salt to taste.

Add the handful of cilantro and the green chiles to the sauce. Cook for about 5 more minutes, then add the scored or halved boiled eggs.

Cook on low heat for another 3 to 4 minutes, stirring gently so that the sauce coats the eggs well. Garnish with cilantro, and serve with your favorite toasted bread, rice, or roti.

Caramelized Onion Savory Oatmeal

Serves 1

I really discovered oatmeal in college, where I would get it from the dining hall (thank you for your service, Crossroads dining hall of UC Berkeley), mash half a banana into it, slice the other half into coins to gingerly lay on top, and finish it all off with a huge scoop of peanut butter and a sprinkle of cinnamon. As I matured, my oatmeal creations followed suit. However, it wasn't until recently that I dabbled in the world of savory oatmeal.

Savory oats sort of freaked me out at first, mostly because I am a creature of habit. But this dish has really changed the game for me. It's hearty, comforting, and warming straight down to your soul. Caramelizing the onions allows for a bit of sweetness to come through, which balances out the spices and the earthy, grounding oats. While you could most certainly exercise your freedom of topping rights, I highly recommend the choices here: a crispy fried egg, creamy avocado, and cilantro.

½ cup rolled oats

1 cup vegetable broth

1 tablespoon extra-virgin olive oil, plus extra for the skillet and for drizzling

¼ yellow onion, diced

Kosher salt and freshly ground black pepper to taste

½ teaspoon ground turmeric

½ teaspoon ground cumin

½ cup (packed) fresh arugula

1 egg

½ avocado, sliced

Fresh cilantro leaves or other herbs, roughly chopped, for garnish

In a medium pot, bring your oats and vegetable broth to a boil. Cook, stirring frequently, until the oats become soft, creamy, and have absorbed almost all of the broth.

While the oats are cooking, heat the olive oil in a medium saucepan over medium heat. Once it shimmers, add the onions and sauté until they become tender and start to caramelize, 15 to 20 minutes, reducing to medium-low heat if the onions start to darken too quickly. Season the onions with salt and black pepper.

Add the turmeric and cumin to the onions and roast the spices with the onions for 2 to 3 minutes. The spices should smell fragrant and toasty.

When the oats are mostly cooked but have just a little vegetable broth left to absorb, add them to the onions. Stir to combine.

Stir the arugula into the oats until it wilts. Season to taste with salt and pepper.

In a small skillet, heat a dash of olive oil. When it shimmers, crack the egg into the pan and fry until it is done to your liking.

Transfer the oatmeal to a shallow bowl, top it with the fried egg, and add the sliced avocado. Drizzle a bit of olive oil on top and add some freshly ground black pepper and salt. Garnish with cilantro or fresh herbs of your choosing.

Morning Soft-Serve

Serves 1

I know myself well enough to know that I mostly go for a sweet breakfast over a savory one. This Morning Soft-Serve is mostly to blame for this life choice. It's hard to go back to simple eggs after starting my day with something reminiscent of dessert.

I like to pretend that I am Picasso with this breakfast soft-serve, using the base ingredients you see below as a blank canvas for adding whatever toppings I please. Some of my favorites are berries, granola, nuts, or more almond/ peanut butter (always).

It's incredible how this gives me Frosty vibes (if you know, you know), yet is just made with a base of frozen bananas. So, the next time you find yourself with many bananas that have all decided to ripen at the same time, it's a good move to freeze a few to make this for breakfast and bake banana bread with the rest.

2 frozen bananas (see Note on page 60)

1 heaping tablespoon crunchy almond butter or peanut butter

1 tablespoon hemp seeds

½ teaspoon ground cinnamon

5 tablespoons unsweetened vanilla non-dairy milk

Toppings of choice

In a food processor or high-speed blender, combine the bananas, nut butter, hemp seeds, and cinnamon. Add the non-dairy milk and pulse to blend. It will seem like it's not blending easily, and that's okay. You can add a couple more tablespoons of the milk, but know that adding too much liquid will compromise the thick soft-serve consistency we want, so I recommend using a utensil to scrape down the sides of your processor or blender and keep blending until smooth.

Transfer the soft-serve to a bowl and serve it immediately with your toppings of choice.

Khichdi

Khichdi has been around since the dawn of Indian time. It's a comfort food that appears in slightly altered forms depending on which region of India you come from, and is considered within Ayurveda to be one of the most healing dishes because it balances all three *doshas*. I will save you a detailed explanation about Ayurvedic principles—partially because I am by no means an expert, but mostly because Google is a precious gift. Instead I'll give you what you're here for.

Khichdi (pronounced khitch-dee) typically consists of lentils and basmati rice, stewed together with seasonings like turmeric, ginger, and garlic, with the addition of some vegetables. It's simple to prepare and serves as a nice base for any vegetables you feel are particularly worthy to hang out with the dal and rice, whether that be cauliflower, potatoes, green beans, or carrots. I enjoy any opportunity to use carrots and sweet potatoes, but I also enjoy a good toss of spinach in there for some greens. This is an amazing breakfast, lunch, or dinner option for when you want to be literally hugged in the form of a porridge.

½ cup brown or white basmati rice

1 cup *moong dal* (yellow lentils)

2 carrots, chopped

1 sweet potato, diced

½ zucchini, diced

1½ teaspoons ground turmeric

1 tablespoon coconut oil

1 tablespoon cumin seeds

1 yellow onion, chopped

1 (1-inch) knob fresh ginger, grated

Kosher salt and freshly ground black pepper to taste

½ cup fresh cilantro, roughly chopped

Wash the rice and moong dal very well until the water runs clear. Put the rice and the moong dal in a large bowl and add water to cover. Soak the rice and lentils in this bowl for at least an hour, or for as long as overnight (you can set them to soak right before you go to sleep).

Drain the soaked rice and lentils.

Using a steamer, steam the carrots, sweet potatoes, zucchini, and any other vegetables you plan to use until just crisp-tender. Set the vegetables aside.

In a medium pot, combine the rice and lentils with the turmeric. Add 4 to 5 cups of water (enough to cover the mixture). Cook over medium heat until the texture is mushy, 30 to 35 minutes.

Heat the coconut oil in a medium saucepan over medium heat, and add the cumin seeds. When they start to sizzle after a few seconds, add the onions and sauté for 3 to 4 minutes until the onions start to become tender and translucent. Add the ginger and cook with the onions for an additional 2 to 3 minutes. Season the onions and ginger with salt and pepper.

Add the cooked lentils and rice to the saucepan with the onions and cook together for about 2 minutes. Add the steamed vegetables and simmer for a few minutes so that everyone starts to become friendly. Add water if needed to adjust the consistency so that it's thick and soupy and kind of mushy. It's okay, it's cute and we want it that way. Season with salt and pepper to taste, garnish with chopped cilantro, and serve.

LONDON

I have never been consistent about keeping a diary, but like most people, I've gone through some short-lived but pretty committed phases. I must have been in one of those phases at the start of seventh grade, because I wrote in my journal right when I got the news that my dad's company was moving him—and consequently my sister, mom, and me—to London. My tear-stained, scribbled words "I can't believe this is happening, I just started seventh grade!" and "I'm crying," sum it up pretty well.

Today I can talk to a wall, but I was the complete opposite growing up. I was very reserved, with major people-pleasing tendencies. I couldn't stand the thought of someone not liking me, so I did everything in my power to make sure that didn't happen. Paired with feeling different from my classmates in California, this move was my ultimate nightmare, especially at the height of such a formative (okay, awkward) stage of life. Read: simultaneous braces, glasses, and a middle part. In short, I was terrified.

Despite my initial fears, moving to London became one of the most transformative experiences of my life. While I had the privilege of traveling to India to visit my relatives and experience my own culture in a broader sense, I had hardly been exposed to any diversity in my day-to-day life in California.

Living in London forced me to open my eyes, and lift my head up. Life in a city made me smarter—not in the book-smart way, but street-smart—and fiercely independent at a young age. And aside from becoming more certain of who I was, in London I discovered my passion for all types of food—food that now informs and inspires everything you see on these pages.

I had *fattoush* salad and *shish taouk* for the first time at a casual restaurant in South Kensington called Beirut Express. I ate the most heavenly dal tadka, biryani, and naan at Lahore Kebab House, the type of meal after which you rolled yourself home on the tube, mildly in pain but mostly in glee. My friends (yes, I made them!) and I would walk off campus for lunch to pick up pad thai and green curry at a tiny spot called Baan Thai, quickly sprinting back to school to shovel in the spicy, rich, peanutty noodles before class started. Or, when we had some extra time, trek to an Italian deli called Ambra to get piping-hot, spicy *penne arrabbiata*. The grocery stores were chock-full of international food—the lemon rice, samosas, and packaged papadums at Waitrose were all staples in our apartment. I had never seen such variety in anything, anywhere. Absorbing all of this gave me something I'll never be able to let go of: joy in the diversity of food, just as much as in people.

Just as I was getting settled into high school in London, my dad's work called us back to California. This was right before my junior year of high school, so you can imagine that I genuinely thought it was a joke. I was gutted. For the first time in my entire life, I was starting to feel like I belonged somewhere. But I also felt at peace, knowing that the experience was something I was lucky to have had. London's beautiful mosaics of culture and food allowed me to discover myself. I left London accepting my difference and translating that feeling, ever so slightly, to confidence. When we left, I knew that I would come back again one day. I fell in love with London because it was the first place where I started to realize that I didn't need to dilute my existence for the sake of others. It felt like home.

not
just
a
salad

Cabbage Is Cool! Salad

Serves 2–3

I know what you're thinking. It's *just* cabbage. Well, *think again*. Might I be so bold as to state that this salad transcends the level of the common cabbage. I gravitate toward the cabbage selections in any salad bar or menu because I love the texture, and while it can sometimes be unremarkable on its own, cabbage has a satisfying crunch that makes it adaptable to whatever flavors it's paired with. I wanted to take this character trait and contrast it with the ultimate thick and creamy zesty avocado dressing, which you may have to try your best not to lather over your entire body in addition to the salad. I'm sorry if that was too graphic.

The sweet potatoes provide us with some creaminess here, while the cumin-spiced chickpeas add spice and texture. Tied all together with some fresh grape tomatoes, this is a game changer for all of you cabbage skeptics out there.

Salad

- 1 sweet potato, cut into 1-inch wedges
- 1 tablespoon extra-virgin olive oil
- Kosher salt and freshly ground black pepper to taste
- 9 ounces cabbage (I like to use a combo of green and red), thinly sliced
- ½ cup grape tomatoes, halved

Chickpeas

- 1 tablespoon extra-virgin olive oil
- 1 (15.5-ounce) can chickpeas, drained, rinsed, and patted dry
- 1 teaspoon ground cumin
- Kosher salt and freshly ground black pepper

Dressing

- 1 avocado
- 2 tablespoons extra-virgin olive oil
- 2 garlic cloves
- ½ cup (packed) fresh cilantro
- Juice of 2 limes
- Kosher salt and freshly ground black pepper to taste

Preheat the oven to 425°F.

On a rimmed baking sheet, toss the sweet potato pieces in the olive oil. Season them with salt and pepper, and roast, turning over halfway through roasting, until they are tender and browned, about 40 minutes.

While the sweet potatoes are roasting, cook the chickpeas. Heat the olive oil in a medium skillet over medium-high heat. Once it shimmers, add the chickpeas and cook for 2 to 3 minutes so that the oil coats them nicely. Then add the cumin and salt and pepper to taste. Toss to coat the chickpeas. Then cook, tossing the chickpeas frequently, for about 15 minutes, or until they start to brown and crisp on the outside but are still tender on the inside.

While the chickpeas and sweet potatoes are cooking, you can make the dressing! In a high-speed blender or food processor, combine the avocado flesh with the olive oil, garlic, cilantro, and lime juice, and blend well. Add 3 to 4 tablespoons of water to the dressing to thin it out slightly. Feel free to add a couple extra tablespoons of water to thin to your desired consistency. Season the dressing with salt and pepper to taste.

To make the salad, toss the cabbage, roasted sweet potatoes, and grape tomatoes in a large serving bowl. Add the dressing and toss to coat. Sprinkle some of the chickpeas on top, and serve the rest on the side for easy access.

Kale & Romaine Za'atar Caesar Salad

Serves 3–4

Croutons

3 slices sourdough bread

2 tablespoons extra-virgin olive oil

Kosher salt and freshly ground black pepper

Red pepper flakes

Dressing

3 tablespoons tahini

1 tablespoon extra-virgin olive oil

Juice of 1 lemon

1 teaspoon za'atar

Kosher salt and freshly ground black pepper

Red pepper flakes

Salad

6 ounces romaine lettuce, chopped

6 ounces Tuscan kale, tough stems removed, chopped

1 cup grape tomatoes, halved

Freshly ground black pepper for finishing

Vegan Parmesan

½ cup raw cashews

3 tablespoons nutritional yeast

½ teaspoon garlic powder

½ teaspoon kosher salt, plus more to taste

You know those packaged "make-it-yourself" salads at the grocery store, where they have the lettuce in one bag, then the dressing in a second little bag, and then the croutons (always approximately six pieces and half a crushed one) in another bag? Well, my family used to be all about these, especially the Caesar salad ones. Little did we know that whipping up a homemade Caesar salad and dressing is far superior to its plastic-imprisoned counterpart.

This za'atar tahini dressing is something I want to put over literally everything, and the kale is perfectly complemented by the crunchy sweetness of romaine lettuce and grape tomatoes. Though I could snack on these croutons solo, I'll admit that this salad makes a very comfortable home for them.

Make the croutons: Preheat the oven to 425°F. Line a baking sheet with parchment paper.

Cut the slices of sourdough bread into cubes. In a medium bowl, combine the olive oil with salt, black pepper, and red pepper flakes to taste. Toss the bread cubes in the oil to coat. Spread the cubes out in a single layer on the baking sheet and bake for 10 to 15 minutes, rotating the sheet and tossing the croutons halfway through. Remove from the oven and let cool on the baking sheet. They will crisp up more as they cool!

Make the dressing: In a small bowl, whisk together the tahini, olive oil, lemon juice, and za'atar with salt, black pepper, and red pepper flakes to taste. If the mixture starts to seize, add in a few tablespoons of water to thin it and help the dressing come together smoothly.

Toss the salad: In a large bowl, toss the romaine, kale, and grape tomatoes together with the dressing, ensuring that the salad is coated evenly.

Make the Vegan Parmesan: In a high-speed blender, combine the cashews, nutritional yeast, garlic powder, and salt, and blend just until a fine powder is achieved—this should take under 10 seconds. You don't want to over-blend or else it will become sticky from the cashews' natural oils. Feel free to adjust with salt to taste.

Top the salad with the Vegan Parmesan, the croutons, and some freshly ground black pepper.

The Crunchy, Creamy Carrot Salad

Serves 3–4

Carrots

1 pound carrots

2 tablespoons extra-virgin olive oil

1 teaspoon ground cumin

Kosher salt and freshly ground black pepper to taste

Red pepper flakes to taste

Salad

3 tablespoons sesame seeds

8 ounces fresh baby arugula

1 avocado, sliced

1 cup grape tomatoes, halved

¼ cup unsalted toasted sliced almonds (see Note)

NOTE

If you have some untoasted sliced almonds at home, you can dry-toast them yourself using the same method as we do for the sesame seeds.

Za'atar & Lemon Vinaigrette

¼ cup fresh lemon juice

2 tablespoons extra-virgin olive oil

2 teaspoons honey

1 teaspoon za'atar

Kosher salt and freshly ground black pepper to taste

Red pepper flakes

There are some people who love greens so much, they could just eat them straight up with a drizzle of olive oil and lemon juice. I am not one of those people. What excites me most about a bowl of leaves isn't necessarily the actual leaves but rather what's on top of them. This is probably why I (a) lose my cool, (b) lose my dignity, and (c) lose some money when I order a salad or come anywhere near a salad bar. I always seem to black out and forget that toppings are extra.

Anyway, the great thing about varying toppings for salads is that they add different flavors and textures, making the greens a lot more interesting to eat. In this case, it's the tender cumin-roasted carrots working the magic alongside crunchy almonds and sesame seeds, creamy avocado, and a bright lemon vinaigrette. In short, this salad is definitely extra.

Roast the carrots: Preheat the oven to 450°F and line a baking sheet with parchment paper.

Halve or quarter the carrots lengthwise (depending on how thick they are) and put them in a large bowl. Add the olive oil, cumin, salt and black pepper, and red pepper flakes, and toss to coat. Transfer the carrots to the lined baking sheet and roast them, tossing halfway through, for 15 to 20 minutes, or until they are tender and slightly charred but still have a crisp bite to them.

While the carrots are roasting, toast the sesame seeds: Heat a small skillet over medium heat. Once the pan is hot, add the sesame seeds. Toast, tossing, until the sesame seeds turn golden and have a nutty aroma, 3 to 5 minutes. Transfer to a small plate to cool.

Make the Za'atar & Lemon Vinaigrette: In a small bowl, combine the lemon juice, olive oil, honey, and za'atar, and whisk to combine. Season to taste with salt, black pepper, and red pepper flakes.

Make the salad: In a large bowl, combine the arugula, avocado slices, grape tomatoes, most of the toasted sesame seeds, and most of the almonds with the salad dressing and toss to combine. Arrange the roasted carrots on top of the salad, or slice them into 3-inch lengths and mix them into the salad. (Add as much or as little as you'd like; if there's extra, serve it as a side dish.) Sprinkle the remaining sesame seeds and almonds on top before serving.

I am not claiming that these salads are the only cool salads out there. I would *never* come for greens like that. But I do think there's a difference between a regular salad and a cool salad. A regular salad has some greens and maybe a couple stray tomatoes or cucumbers, all tossed in a basic vinaigrette. Those salads might have their time and place…but a cool salad has a little more going on. It's got texture and a dressing that makes you forget you're eating leaves. It's punchy, tangy, a little complex, and might have a secret. You've been getting the cool salads in this chapter. See if you disagree.

Spice Up Your Pomegranate Salad

Serves 1—2

I grew up eating pomegranate in a way that was, well, the only way for me, but could be seen as unusual for others. My mom would deseed the fruit and mix the arils with salt, sugar, and cayenne pepper. It's such a simple combination that you don't really expect it to be as highly addicting and satisfying as it is. The spiciness of the cayenne is quelled by the sugar, which is heightened and brought to life by the salt. I thought I'd give my childhood pomegranate salad a twist by adding some cucumbers, onions, herbs, and lime, similar to what you'd find in a *kachumber*. You can adjust this to taste with the amounts of lime, salt, and sugar. And by the way, feel free to swap out the cilantro for mint because you are absolutely allowed.

**Arils (seeds) from
1 pomegranate**

½ small red onion, thinly sliced

½ cup (packed) cilantro, roughly chopped, plus more for garnish

Juice of 2 limes, plus more to taste

2 or 3 Persian cucumbers, sliced

¼ teaspoon cayenne pepper

1 tablespoon coconut sugar

Kosher salt to taste

In a small serving bowl, toss together the pomegranate arils, onion, cilantro, lime juice, cucumbers, cayenne, coconut sugar, and salt. Taste, and adjust with lime juice, salt, and/or sugar if needed. Garnish with cilantro.

Spice Up Your Pomegranate Salad

Fattoush Salad

Fattoush Salad
with Sourdough Za'atar Croutons

Serves 3–4

Sourdough Za'atar Croutons

2 slices sourdough bread, cut into cubes

½ tablespoon extra-virgin olive oil

1 teaspoon za'atar

Fattoush Salad

1 heart of romaine lettuce, torn

3 Persian cucumbers, sliced

⅔ cup fresh parsley, finely chopped

⅓ cup fresh mint, finely chopped

5 radishes, thinly sliced

½ red onion, diced

Arils (seeds) from 1 pomegranate

Dressing

½ tablespoon ground sumac

Juice of 1 lemon, plus more to taste

2 tablespoons extra-virgin olive oil

2 teaspoons pomegranate molasses, plus more to taste

Kosher salt and freshly ground black pepper to taste

½ teaspoon za'atar

If I could choose a salad to eat for the rest of my life, it would probably be a *fattoush* salad. *Fattoush* has Levantine origins and was historically made as a way to use leftover pita bread. The bread was seasoned, fried, and tossed with greens and vegetables yet remained, and still remains, a main component of the salad itself. That's something I can get behind. To me, the feeling of eating a fattoush salad is like going to the spa (all right, mild stretch, but hear me out). It's zesty, it's fresh, and the tartness of the dressing paired with cucumbers, radishes, herbs, and crunchy fresh lettuce makes me feel pretty zen. If this means anything, I'd choose eating this salad over going to a spa any day.

I highlight the pomegranate molasses in the dressing by adding pomegranate seeds, a crunch factor rivaled only by the za'atar croutons that frequently appear in my dreams.

I also encourage a doubling of the dressing if you like a heavily dressed salad, as this dressing will be on the lighter side.

Make the Sourdough Za'atar Croutons: Preheat the oven to 425°F. Line a baking sheet with parchment paper.

In a medium bowl, toss the bread cubes with the olive oil and za'atar until coated. Spread the cubes evenly on the lined baking sheet, making sure they are in a single layer—they need room to breathe so they can become crispy! Bake, tossing the croutons a couple times, for 10 to 15 minutes, until they are golden brown. Remove from the oven and let cool on the baking sheet. They'll crisp up as they cool.

Make the Fattoush Salad: In a serving bowl, combine the lettuce, cucumbers, parsley, mint, radishes, red onion, and pomegranate arils.

Make the dressing: In a small bowl, mix the sumac, lemon juice, olive oil, pomegranate molasses, salt, pepper, and za'atar together. Adjust to taste with more lemon, salt, pepper, and/or pomegranate molasses as needed.

Add the dressing to the salad and toss to combine. Scatter the sourdough croutons on top. Enjoy immediately.

HEY YOU!

Yes, you! If you're harboring any leftover or stale bread in your pantry, then you have perfect candidates for these croutons and (wink wink) this salad, too.

Chilled Chaat Masala Chickpea Salad

Serves 3–4

It's only now that I realize this undeniable fact: I grew up enmeshed heavily in chickpea culture. My mom used to make this salad all the time as a snack, and it's no wonder I now have such a devout appreciation for the cutest pulse to ever exist (controversial hot take; I stand by my opinion). This salad is zesty, bright, acidic, sweet, and spicy. It's pretty incredible how it takes just a few ingredients and a few minutes to throw together, yet it really has the flavor profile of a dish that says I-spent-longer-than-five-minutes-making-this.

You'll likely find all of the ingredients for this in your pantry except for perhaps the *chaat masala*, which is a spice blend commonly used in Indian street food, with an incomparable flavor thanks to the dried mango powder, coriander, cumin, black salt, and chili powder that commonly make it up. To find it, I recommend the international section of your grocery store or—what would we do without it—the internet.

1 (15.5-ounce) can chickpeas, drained and rinsed

½ red onion, sliced

2 Persian cucumbers, sliced

1 medium tomato, diced

2 tablespoons extra-virgin olive oil

Juice of 2 limes

½ teaspoon *chaat masala*

¼ teaspoon cayenne pepper, plus more to taste

Kosher salt and freshly ground black pepper to taste

¼ cup (packed) cilantro, finely chopped, plus extra for garnish

Put the chickpeas in a medium bowl. Add the onions, cucumbers, tomatoes, olive oil, and lime juice. Mix to combine. Now add the *chaat masala,* cayenne, and salt and black pepper. Season to taste; you can make it spicier with more cayenne pepper, as I often do. Stir in the cilantro. Garnish with cilantro and serve!

Inverted Roasted Vegetable Salad

Serves 3–4

Salad

3 large carrots, scrubbed

5 ounces Brussels sprouts

1 small sweet potato, sliced

2 tablespoons extra-virgin olive oil

Kosher salt and freshly ground black pepper to taste

Red pepper flakes to taste

2 cups fresh baby spinach, chopped

1 cup fresh baby arugula

½ cup cherry tomatoes, quartered

2 to 3 Persian cucumbers, diced

Fresh cilantro, chopped, for garnish

Flaky sea salt to taste

Dressing

1 cup fresh cilantro

¼ cup tahini

Juice of 1 lime

1 tablespoon extra-virgin olive oil

Kosher salt and freshly ground black pepper to taste

Whenever I order a salad with roasted vegetables, typically the greens are on the bottom and the roasted vegetables make themselves perfectly comfortable on top. As a result, the greens become pretty wilty and I am ultimately left with a very sad half-salad. To combat this problem, I decided to invert the salad and lay all the gorgeous vegetables on the bottom with the greens relaxing on top.

While I recognize that this is not a crazy revelation, I do think that peering through the arugula and spinach to see what lies in store for you beneath makes for an exciting salad experience as a whole. I use carrots, sweet potato, and Brussels sprouts here, but you are more than welcome to add (or sub) your favorite roasted vegetables. It should be noted that the dressing also works as a great dip for the vegetables in addition to being an MVP for the greens.

Roast the vegetables: Preheat the oven to 400°F and line a baking sheet with parchment paper.

Slice the carrots in half lengthwise. If you're using extra-large carrots (we love it!), you may need to quarter them. Slice the Brussels sprouts into thirds and the sweet potato into small wedges.

Add the vegetables to a large bowl. Drizzle with the olive oil and sprinkle with kosher salt, black pepper, and red pepper flakes to taste. Toss to coat.

Spread the vegetables out on the prepared baking sheet so that everyone has room to live their best roasted lives. Roast in the oven for about 25 minutes, tossing halfway through, until the veggies are tender and slightly charred around the edges.

While the vegetables are roasting, make the dressing: In a high-speed blender, combine the cilantro, tahini, lime juice, and olive oil, and blend until completely smooth. Add 4 to 5 tablespoons of water and blend to help the dressing come together. You can adjust with water to reach your desired consistency. Season to taste with salt and pepper.

Put the salad together: In a large bowl, toss the spinach, arugula, cherry tomatoes, and Persian cucumbers with about half of the dressing (you can use all of the dressing, but I like to reserve some to dip the roasted veggies in as well).

Arrange the roasted vegetables on a serving plate, and top them with the dressed salad. Garnish with the cilantro, and sprinkle some sea salt and freshly ground black pepper on top.

you will
want to
eat your
vegetables

Masala Cauliflower & Sweet Potatoes
with Cilantro-Mint Chutney

Serves 3–4

2 tablespoons extra-virgin olive oil

½ teaspoon mustard seeds

½ teaspoon cumin seeds

1 yellow onion, sliced

1 (1-inch) knob fresh ginger, minced

4 garlic cloves, minced

1 (15-ounce) can crushed tomatoes, or 4 medium tomatoes, diced

½ teaspoon ground cumin

½ teaspoon cayenne pepper

½ teaspoon ground turmeric

Kosher salt to taste

1 head cauliflower, cut into florets

1 sweet potato, sliced

2 green chiles, stem removed and slit open lengthwise

Juice of ½ lemon

Handful of fresh cilantro, chopped

Cilantro-Mint Chutney
(see Note)

1 cup fresh cilantro leaves (tough stems removed, tender stems okay), packed

½ cup fresh mint leaves

1 green chile

½ teaspoon ground cumin

Juice of 1 lemon

Kosher salt to taste

I have a major thing for cruciferous vegetables, and as embarrassing as that is to say, I can't really hide from the truth. I internally argue with myself all the time (also embarrassing) about whether I like cauliflower or broccoli more, but somehow cauliflower always makes its way to the forefront of my brain and the counter of my kitchen. Its neutral taste and versatile texture allow it to be a lot of different things, and whether it's riced, roasted, steamed, puréed, or sautéed, the common theme is that it absorbs flavors really well.

Cauliflower is no stranger to Indian cuisine, and it frequently appears on the table as *aloo gobi*, a dish of cauliflower and potatoes cooked with spices. My take on aloo gobi here uses sweet potatoes, because I prefer the way their sweeter flesh complements the cauliflower, tomatoes, and onions. And when in doubt, add fresh herbs; I pair this dish with a cilantro-mint chutney that brightens everything up and functions as a zesty condiment for the table.

Heat the oil in a medium skillet over medium heat.

Once the oil is shimmering, add the mustard and cumin seeds. When the seeds start to sizzle after a few seconds, add the sliced onions. Cook the onions for 5 to 7 minutes or until they become lightly browned, then add the ginger and garlic. Cook the ginger and garlic with the onions for another 2 minutes, until they start to get some color.

Add the tomatoes to the skillet and cook for 3 to 4 minutes to infuse with the onions, ginger, and garlic. Then add the cumin, cayenne, turmeric, and salt. Stir, cover the pan, and let the masala cook with the tomatoes and onions for 3 to 4 minutes, until the tomatoes begin to darken in color and reduce slightly.

Now add in the cauliflower florets and sweet potato slices. Stir to coat the cauliflower and potatoes with the tomatoes and onions. Cover the pan again and cook, stirring frequently, until the cauliflower and sweet potatoes are tender, 15 to 20 minutes. Season to taste with salt.

Add the green chiles, lemon juice, and some cilantro, and stir to combine.

Garnish the vegetables with the remaining cilantro and serve with the chutney.

NOTE

To make the Cilantro-Mint Chutney, combine the cilantro, mint, chile, cumin, and lemon juice in a high-speed blender or food processor. You can add a little bit of water to help the blender get going if needed. Season to taste with salt. Serve with the cauliflower.

Cumin-Roasted Carrots
with a Cool Almond Butter

Serves 2–3

I have a carrot problem, and the proof is not in the pudding but rather in my hands. My hands are tinted a gorgeous beta-carotene orange, and if I had to sacrifice my sweet potatoes and carrots in order to restore them to their original color, then . . . I don't want it! Give me orange hands and all the carrots or give me death!

I am being only *mildly* dramatic, but I have to say, this particular preparation of carrots might be the cause for my orange hands. They are so unbelievably delicious, and you will not even believe how much this honey-lime almond butter just makes sense. The sweetness from the honey, richness from the almond butter, and bright acidity of the lime complement and completely take the tender yet still crisp cumin-roasted carrots to the next level.

1 pound carrots

2 tablespoons extra-virgin olive oil

½ teaspoon ground cumin

½ teaspoon ground turmeric

Kosher salt and freshly ground black pepper to taste

Red pepper flakes to taste

Flaky sea salt for sprinkling

Cool Almond Butter

Juice of 1 lime

2 tablespoons creamy almond butter

2 teaspoons honey

Kosher salt

Preheat the oven to 450°F and line a baking sheet with parchment paper.

Scrub the carrots (do not peel them) and trim the ends. Slice the carrots in half lengthwise, or into quarters if they are on the large side. Spread them out on the parchment-lined baking sheet.

In a small bowl, mix together the olive oil, cumin, turmeric, salt and black pepper, and red pepper flakes.

Drizzle the olive oil mixture over the carrots and toss them on the baking sheet until they're completely coated. Roast for 15 to 20 minutes, tossing them halfway through, until they're tender but still have a bit of a bite in them. You may need to roast them for longer if your carrots are bigger, so just keep an eye on them and test their doneness by piercing with a fork.

While the carrots are roasting, prepare the Cool Almond Butter: In a small bowl, mix the lime juice with the almond butter, honey, and a pinch of salt, stirring until smooth and well incorporated. Add a splash of water (about 1 tablespoon or more) to thin the sauce. It should be creamy, but drizzle-able!

When the carrots are done roasting, drizzle the Cool Almond Butter on top. Finish with a sprinkling of sea salt.

Charred Broccoli
with Turmeric Tahini Sauce

Serves 2–3

We've already discussed the fact that cruciferous vegetables give me life, broccoli of course being one of them. My favorite way to eat broccoli is tossed with spices and roasted until the stalks are tender but still crisp, with charred, crunchy florets. I include toasted sesame seeds here because they add a nutty, savory textural element, which we absolutely adore. All of it is complemented by a turmeric tahini sauce that you'll probably want to eat straight up with a spoon. I often pair this recipe with my spiced chickpeas (page 140) for a satisfying snack or meal that is deceptively easy to put together.

1 pound broccoli

3 tablespoons extra-virgin olive oil

½ teaspoon ground cumin

½ teaspoon ground turmeric

Red pepper flakes to taste

Kosher salt and freshly ground black pepper to taste

1 tablespoon sesame seeds

Turmeric Tahini Sauce

2 tablespoons tahini

Juice of 1 lemon, plus more to taste

½ teaspoon ground turmeric

Kosher salt and freshly ground black pepper to taste

Red pepper flakes to taste

Preheat the oven to 425°F and line a baking sheet with parchment paper.

Cut the broccoli into florets with just a couple inches of stalk, and place them on the parchment-lined baking sheet. In a small bowl, mix 2 tablespoons of the olive oil with the cumin, turmeric, red pepper flakes, and salt and pepper. Drizzle this mixture over the broccoli on the baking sheet and toss so that it's evenly distributed. Arrange the broccoli in a single layer on the baking sheet and drizzle the remaining 1 tablespoon olive oil on top. Roast for 20 to 25 minutes, tossing the broccoli a couple times, until it is lightly charred.

While the broccoli is roasting, toast the sesame seeds: Heat a small skillet over medium heat. Once the pan is hot, add the sesame seeds. Toast, tossing them frequently, until they turn golden and have a nutty aroma, 3 to 5 minutes. Set the toasted seeds aside.

Make the Turmeric Tahini Sauce: In a small bowl, combine the tahini, lemon juice, turmeric, salt and black pepper, and red pepper flakes. Stir in 3 to 4 tablespoons of water and mix until smooth. You can add a couple more splashes of water to achieve the saucy consistency of your preference. Adjust as desired by adding additional lemon juice if you'd like more tartness, red pepper flakes for a spicier moment, and salt and pepper to your taste.

Once the broccoli is charred and crisp to your liking, place it on a serving dish. Add a generous amount of the Turmeric Tahini Sauce and sprinkle the toasted sesame seeds on top. Serve immediately.

Turmeric-Roasted Cauliflower
with Cilantro Tahini

Serves 2–3

I could eat an entire cauliflower in one sitting. And by *could*, I mean, I *have*. This recipe makes it easy. Nothing can beat the flavor combination in this cauliflower dish, which is on "repeat" at my home. Also, if you're in the market for slightly yellow tinted fingernails, then you're in luck because turmeric has got you covered!

I toss the cauliflower with some cumin, turmeric, olive oil, red pepper for a kick, and salt and pepper. These are my foolproof roasting ingredients, guaranteed to make everything taste well spiced and delicious. And I would also like to let you know that this green tahini is something that I would like to take with me, in a little mason jar, everywhere I go in life.

3 tablespoons extra-virgin olive oil

3 garlic cloves, smashed

1 teaspoon ground turmeric

½ teaspoon ground cumin

Kosher salt and freshly ground black pepper to taste

Red pepper flakes to taste

1 head cauliflower, cut into 2-inch florets

Handful of fresh cilantro, chopped, for garnish

Cilantro Tahini

¼ cup tahini

⅓ cup fresh cilantro

Juice from 1 lemon

3 tablespoons extra-virgin olive oil

2 garlic cloves

Kosher salt and freshly ground black pepper to taste

Red pepper flakes to taste

Preheat the oven to 450°F and line a baking sheet with parchment paper.

In a medium bowl, mix the olive oil with the garlic, turmeric, cumin, salt and black pepper, and red pepper flakes. Taste a little bit of this marinade and adjust the salt and pepper to your liking. Remove and discard the garlic, and then toss the cauliflower in the marinade until it is evenly coated.

Transfer the cauliflower to the parchment-lined baking sheet, arranging it in a single layer. Roast for 20 to 25 minutes, tossing halfway through, until the cauliflower is tender, golden, and slightly charred.

While the cauliflower is roasting, prepare the Cilantro Tahini:
Combine the tahini, cilantro, lemon juice, olive oil, garlic, salt and black pepper, and red pepper flakes in a high-speed blender or food processor and add 4 to 5 tablespoons of water. Blend until smooth. Adjust the seasoning to taste. If it's too thick, you can add a tablespoon or two more water.

To assemble, spread about three-quarters of the Cilantro Tahini on a serving dish and place the roasted cauliflower on top. Garnish with the cilantro, and serve the remaining sauce on the side for dipping or drizzled on top.

Baingan Bharta
(Spicy Eggplant Masala)

Serves 3–4

I'm huge on Indian vegetarian dishes in general because I absolutely adore the way masala completely transforms the flavor profile of any average vegetable. Maybe my heritage makes me a little biased but still, who can't get behind a perfectly spiced and seasoned, glamorous, ready for their close-up, veggie? When it comes to a traditional eggplant masala (or *baingan bharta*), the process is, well, a process. You first salt the eggplant and let it sit for forty-five minutes, then after drying the eggplant, you roast it until it's tender, so that the skin is blackened and it can be peeled off. Once it is cooled and peeled, you have to mash it until it's a chunky purée . . . have I lost you yet?

I know, it seems like a lot, especially when you want a dinner recipe that's easy enough to whip up after a long day. Here, I do away with the roasting and peeling, so that you can get all the flavors of a traditional baingan bharta but in a lot less time. I want to make all of my recipes approachable and delicious, and completely get rid of the feeling that putting dinner on the table (or the couch—I don't know where you eat!!) is hours away.

2 tablespoons extra-virgin olive oil

1 yellow onion, sliced

5 garlic cloves, minced

1 teaspoon ground cumin

½ teaspoon cayenne pepper

½ teaspoon ground turmeric

½ teaspoon garam masala

1 teaspoon kosher salt, plus more to taste

1 teaspoon tomato paste

1 medium eggplant, diced into 2-inch pieces

1 (15-ounce) can crushed or diced tomatoes

Juice of ½ lemon

1 cup fresh baby spinach

Handful of fresh cilantro, roughly chopped, for garnish

Rice, roti, naan, or quinoa (see Note page 168) for serving

Heat the olive oil in a large saucepan over medium heat.

Once the oil is hot, add the onions. Sauté the onions for 4 to 5 minutes until the onions become translucent and start to brown slightly, then add the garlic. Cook the onions and garlic together for another 2 to 3 minutes until they start to brown.

Now add the cumin, cayenne, turmeric, garam masala, and salt. Roast the spices with the onions and garlic for 1 to 2 minutes, until the spices smell toasty and aromatic and have darkened in color. Then add the tomato paste and cook with the masala and onions for about 1 minute until it deepens in color.

Add the diced eggplant and cook for 15 to 20 minutes or until the eggplant is very soft—you will have to stir, cover, cook, and repeat to get it there. Add about a ½ cup to ¾ cup of water throughout the cooking process to prevent burning, or extra as needed. You want the eggplant to be very tender.

Once the eggplant is soft, add the tomatoes. Continue to stir, cover, cook, and repeat for about 10 more minutes. Adjust to taste with salt.

Now add the lemon juice into the masala.

Add the spinach and cook until it wilts.

Garnish with the cilantro, and serve with rice, roti, naan, or quinoa.

The Broccolini Crunch

Serves 2—3

I'm not throwing any shade at broccoli, but we all know that broccolini is just a little more adorable than its stalkier counterpart. Because it is reminiscent of asparagus, I always find that pairing broccolini with something acidic and crunchy heightens its already sweet and mild taste. Roasting broccolini at a high temperature for a relatively short amount of time allows it to maintain a tender but still crisp stalk, which is complemented here by the nutty crunch of toasted sesame seeds and almonds. The Chile Sesame Vinaigrette is light, tangy, and mildly sweet, designed to be poured over the broccolini as soon as it comes out of the oven, as if to say, "Welcome—you made it to the charred side."

2 bunches (about 1 pound) broccolini or baby broccoli

2 tablespoons extra-virgin olive oil

Kosher salt and freshly ground black pepper to taste

Red pepper flakes to taste

2 tablespoons sesame seeds

3 tablespoons unsalted toasted sliced or slivered almonds

Chile Sesame Vinaigrette

1 tablespoon rice vinegar

1 tablespoon toasted sesame oil

2 garlic cloves, minced

Juice of 1 lime

1 teaspoon honey

Kosher salt and freshly ground black pepper

Red pepper flakes

Preheat the oven to 425°F and line a baking sheet with parchment paper.

In a large bowl, toss the broccolini with the olive oil, salt and black pepper, and red pepper flakes, making sure that everything is coated evenly and thoroughly. Transfer the broccolini to the parchment-lined baking sheet and roast until it begins to char, tossing halfway through, 15 to 20 minutes.

While the broccolini is roasting, toast the sesame seeds: Heat a small skillet over medium heat. When the pan is hot, add the sesame seeds and cook, tossing them frequently, until they turn golden and smell nutty and delicious, 3 to 5 minutes.

Make the Chile Sesame Vinaigrette: In a small bowl, combine the rice vinegar, sesame oil, garlic, lime juice, and honey. Season to taste with salt, black pepper, and red pepper flakes; it should be very light and bright. Stir until thoroughly mixed.

When the broccolini is done roasting, drizzle some of the vinaigrette on top, reserving the extra as a dressing for serving. Top the broccolini with the toasted sesame seeds and almonds (our esteemed crunch factors in this Broccolini Crunch!), and serve.

Honey-Lime & Tahini Brussels Sprouts

Serves 2

I wasn't exposed to Brussels sprouts until I was in college. My parents didn't grow up eating them and never cooked them at home, so consequently, neither did my sister or I. I had always heard through the grapevine that Brussels sprouts were kind of the most evil vegetable on the planet (eat your Brussels sprouts, kids!), but I later found out that I'd been majorly lied to and betrayed. Because what?! Brussels sprouts are delicious! Especially when roasted to a crisp, as they are here, so they yield these irresistible crunchy burnt bits, which always keep me coming back for more. To add some fun, I coat these Brussels in a surprising but divine honey-lime-tahini dressing. Eat this and wonder why Brussels sprouts ever became our enemy in the first place.

8 ounces Brussels sprouts

1 tablespoon extra-virgin olive oil

1 teaspoon ground cumin

Kosher salt and freshly ground black pepper to taste

1 lime, cut into wedges, for serving (optional)

Dressing

2 tablespoons tahini

½ tablespoon honey

½ tablespoon extra-virgin olive oil

Juice of 1 lime

Kosher salt and freshly ground black pepper to taste

Preheat the oven to 400°F and line a baking sheet with parchment paper.

Slice the Brussels sprouts into thirds, or if they are small, slicing them in half will be just fine! You should have about 2 cups after slicing.

In a medium bowl, mix the olive oil, cumin, salt, and pepper together. Toss the sprouts in this mixture. Lay them out on the prepared baking sheet, ensuring that there is space for all of the lil sprouts to breathe and thus cook evenly and fairly.

Roast the Brussels sprouts, tossing them once or twice, until the edges are getting charred and crisp, 20 to 25 minutes.

While the sprouts are in the oven, make the dressing: In a small bowl, whisk together the tahini, honey, olive oil, lime juice, and salt and pepper. The dressing should be thick and creamy.

When the Brussels sprouts come out of the oven, let them cool for a few minutes before transferring them to a serving bowl and tossing them with the dressing.

Season with salt and pepper. Serve immediately with lime wedges for extra juice, if desired.

Roasted Butternut Squash & Co.

Serves 2–3

The creamy sweetness and nuttiness of butternut squash make it a pretty amazing and forgiving canvas. In this case, the paint is a spicy mustard tahini dressing, which you might want to double and keep around for dipping everything you possibly can in. Honestly, I reckon even cardboard would have a fighting chance.

While gremolata is more traditionally made with parsley, lemon zest, and garlic, I spun mine into a cilantro-lime version, swapping cilantro for the parsley and lime for the lemon. This adds a certain brightness and zest, because what is life without a little zest? Not one I'd like to live.

You're welcome to omit the pumpkin seeds if you don't have them or don't like them, but they do add some nice texture and crunch to seal the deal. In conclusion, this roasted butternut squash comes with a lot of company that you won't want to miss.

1 butternut squash, seeds removed, cut into 1- to 2-inch cubes or slices

1 tablespoon extra-virgin olive oil

½ teaspoon ground cumin

Kosher salt and freshly ground black pepper to taste

¼ cup unsalted pumpkin seeds (optional)

Cilantro-Lime Gremolata

1 cup fresh cilantro

2 tablespoons extra-virgin olive oil

3 garlic cloves

Juice of 1 lime

1 teaspoon grated lime zest

1 (1-inch) knob fresh ginger

Spicy Mustard Dressing

1 teaspoon Dijon mustard

⅓ cup tahini

Juice of 1 lemon

Kosher salt and freshly ground black pepper to taste

Preheat the oven to 400°F. Line a baking sheet with parchment paper.

In a large bowl, toss the butternut squash slices with the olive oil, cumin, salt, and pepper.

Arrange the squash in a single layer on the lined baking sheet. Roast for 30 to 35 minutes, tossing the pieces halfway through, until the squash is tender and browning around the edges.

While the squash is in the oven, make the Cilantro-Lime Gremolata: Combine the cilantro, olive oil, garlic, lime juice, lime zest, and ginger in a high-speed blender or food processor. Add 2 tablespoons of water and blend until the ingredients are finely minced and incorporated.

To make the Spicy Mustard Dressing: Combine the mustard, tahini, lemon juice, and salt and pepper in a small bowl. Add 3 to 4 tablespoons of water to thin the dressing. Feel free to add a couple more tablespoons of water to get the dressing to your desired consistency.

To assemble, remove the butternut squash from the oven and arrange it on a plate. Drizzle the Spicy Mustard Dressing over the squash, and then top it with the Cilantro-Lime Gremolata. Sprinkle with the pumpkin seeds, if desired.

Don't Miss a Beet Masala

Serves 2—3

I think we can all agree that beets are definitely the beauty queen among the root vegetables. I mean, what is *up* with that color? I love using beets in the kitchen, not just because I think they're tasty, but because I also appreciate the way they add some color to the table.

If you can get over the fact that peeling beets is sort of annoying, you're well through the most difficult part of this journey. (The good thing about peeling beets before you cook them is that they won't stain your hands as dramatically as they would if you peel after they're cooked.) The onions and masala contrast with the beets' natural sweetness to give you a dish with layered flavor. This is pretty light and bright, so it is best served with heavier entrées or vegetables; I particularly appreciate serving it alongside my *dal saag* (page 131).

2 tablespoons extra-virgin olive oil

1 teaspoon mustard seeds

½ red onion, sliced

3 green chiles, slit open lengthwise

1 large or 2 small beets, peeled and grated

1 teaspoon ground cumin

1 teaspoon ground turmeric

¼ teaspoon cayenne pepper (or up to ½ teaspoon if you like it spicy)

Kosher salt to taste

1 lemon, halved

Fresh cilantro, roughly chopped, for garnish

Heat the olive oil in a large skillet over medium heat. When the oil shimmers, add the mustard seeds.

When the mustard seeds begin to crackle in the oil (after a few seconds), add the onions and green chiles.

Stir-fry the onions and green chiles until the onions begin to turn translucent, 3 to 4 minutes.

Now add the shredded beets to the onions and green chiles. Stir in the cumin, turmeric, cayenne, and salt. Cover the skillet and cook, stirring intermittently, until the beets are tender and soft, 5 to 10 minutes.

Squeeze some fresh lemon juice on top and garnish with the cilantro before serving!

FOR THE PASTA VERSION

Swap out the cauliflower for 8 ounces spaghetti (I like using a brown rice or chickpea spaghetti). Cook the pasta according to the instructions on the box, and follow the directions at right for making the sauce and the Parmesan. Mix the sauce in with the cooked pasta, and top with 5 to 6 tablespoons Vegan Parmesan (or more if you'd like). Season with salt and pepper and enjoy.

Cauliflower Cacio e Pepe

Serves 2–3

As much as we can all raise our eyebrows when we find cauliflower in pizza crust and gnocchi and bread, it's just a versatile little vegetable that wants to be adored. And I adore it.

I find cauliflower to be a great receptacle for all types of flavors, spices, moods, and situations. In this case, I was taking an evening walk to the Upper West Side like the true ancient soul that I am, and into my head popped the idea for a *cauliflower cacio e pepe*. I had just eaten my *cacio e pepe* pasta for dinner (see opposite page for the pasta variation), and my mind was wrapped up in the thought of how crazy delicious it would be if the sauce was embracing the florets of a cauliflower. Enter: salt and pepper roasted cauliflower, a luscious Cacio e Pepe Cream Sauce, and a Vegan Parmesan that can be blitzed up in your blender in less than a minute. There's nothing not to adore.

1 cauliflower, cut into florets

1 tablespoon extra-virgin olive oil

Kosher salt and freshly ground black pepper to taste

Vegan Parmesan

½ cup raw cashews

3 tablespoons nutritional yeast

½ teaspoon garlic powder

½ teaspoon kosher salt, plus more to taste

Cacio e Pepe Cream Sauce

½ cup raw cashews, soaked overnight or "flash-soaked" (see page 21)

2 tablespoons nutritional yeast

Juice of 1 lemon

1 tablespoon extra-virgin olive oil

3 garlic cloves

3 tablespoons unsweetened almond milk

Kosher salt and freshly ground black pepper to taste

Preheat the oven to 425°F and line a baking sheet with parchment paper.

In a medium bowl, toss the cauliflower florets in the olive oil, and season with salt and pepper.

Place the cauliflower on the prepared baking sheet, spreading the florets out in a single layer, and roast, flipping halfway, until they are tender and starting to brown around the edges, 20 to 25 minutes.

Make the Vegan Parmesan: In a high-speed blender or food processor, blitz together the cashews, nutritional yeast, garlic powder, and salt. Be careful not to overblend—you want it just pulverized enough to where a fine meal is achieved. I recommend you do this before making the cream sauce so you don't have to wash your blender twice (the parm is dry, the sauce is creamy). Set the Vegan Parmesan aside.

Make the Cacio e Pepe Cream Sauce: Combine the drained soaked cashews, nutritional yeast, lemon juice, olive oil, garlic, almond milk, and salt and pepper in the blender. Add a bit of warm water to help the sauce thin slightly and move around in the blender if needed. Blend until velvety smooth.

Remove the cauliflower from the oven. Toss in the Cacio e Pepe Cream Sauce. Top with the Vegan Parmesan. (I use 5 to 6 tablespoons here, but you can use as much as you fancy!) Season with salt and pepper to taste.

BY THE WAY

This recipe makes more vegan parm than you'll need here! Reserve the rest for another day—it's great on salads, pasta, or avocado toast for a cheesy kick.

Chic Cabbage & Carrot Stir-Fry

Serves 4–5

Here I am again, talking about cabbage like it's my job. And I guess it *is* my job. Cabbage is sort of a chic, magical thing because even when you sauté it, it still manages to keep a bit of a crisp bite that is texturally very pleasing to eat. Whenever I'd go to India to visit my aunt (hi, Amiya!), she would always make this dish to serve with heartier accompaniments like dal or *chana masala*. You'll typically find this type of dish in South Indian cuisine. I'm going to stop professing my love for cabbage in a second, but I do have one last thing to say: This dish is crunchy, spicy, sweet, and savory—and requires virtually no time to make. Have I sold you yet?

2 tablespoons extra-virgin olive oil

½ teaspoon mustard seeds

2 green chiles, sliced

10 fresh curry leaves (optional)

½ yellow onion, sliced

1 carrot, shredded

1 medium head of green cabbage, thinly sliced or shredded

½ teaspoon ground turmeric

Kosher salt to taste

3 tablespoons unsweetened shredded coconut, plus extra for garnish

Handful of fresh cilantro, roughly chopped, for garnish

Heat the olive oil in a large skillet over medium-high heat. When the oil starts to shimmer, add the mustard seeds, green chiles, and curry leaves, if you have them. Let this sizzle and cook for about 1 minute.

Add the onions and sauté until they turn translucent, 3 to 4 minutes.

Add the carrots, cabbage, turmeric, and salt. Cover the pan and cook on medium-high heat, stirring frequently, about 5 minutes, or until the cabbage and carrots are crisp-tender.

Add the shredded coconut and stir to combine. Remove from heat.

Transfer this Chic Cabbage and Carrot Stir-Fry to a serving dish, garnish with some extra shredded coconut and the cilantro, and serve.

BERKELEY

I was the type of kid who was worried about whether or not I'd get into college by the seventh grade. I wish I could just shake the shoulders of my twelve-year-old self and say "It will be okay. *Please chill out.*" My hindsight vision shows me now that I know I was clinging to perfectionism as a way to prove myself and show that I belonged. I strove for perfect grades and perfect friendships and perfect interactions where I could be as accommodating as possible.

There are just a few times in my life when I've cried from joy and naturally the first was when I got into University of California at Berkeley. I fell in love with the indescribable energy of the Berkeley campus the second I stepped foot on it. And the proximity to San Francisco (a city! finally!) made it feel ideal for me.

At Berkeley I felt surrounded by people who cared fiercely about everything they did, whether it was being on the Quidditch team (yes, there was such a thing) or taking brutal pre-med courses. While I partook in neither, I had always wanted to write and act, so I started taking courses for my Media Studies major and Public Policy minor, signed up for acting classes, and joined the school's TV station, CalTV.

Before school even started, I took it upon myself to compile an obscenely long list on my phone of restaurants to try in Berkeley and in San Francisco. I wanted to explore what would be my home for the next four years, and the only way I could fathom doing so was through food.

I'd go to Vik's Chaat House on Fourth Street in Berkeley with my friends for the best *chana bhatura* and *dosas* around. I would walk down Shattuck Avenue to La Note for their orange flower water–soaked French toast with lavender honey. I took BART into San Francisco for ice cream at Bi-Rite Creamery, Humphry Slocombe, and Mitchell's. I created a food series for CalTV, where I interviewed chefs at iconic restaurants in the Mission District of San Francisco.

Though I'm pretty sure my parents visited me at school exclusively to get *dosas* at Vik's, on one occasion I convinced them to take me to Chez Panisse for my birthday (and was beside myself when I was able to have a conversation with Alice Waters). As a consequence of my newfound obsession with eating to explore and exploring to eat, it was during this time when I became an unofficial text service for friends who needed restaurant recommendations.

I also discovered my rather intense predilection for the ritual of drinking coffee, waking up at 6 a.m. every day to go sit at Caffè Strada, a coffee shop next to campus, right as they opened. I've always looked forward to my mornings, waking up at ungodly hours so that I could maximize every minute of the day. I recognize this behavior is a touch insane (who *voluntarily* wakes up at 6 a.m.?), but having that time with my thoughts when the air was still cold and the café was empty gave me a sense of comfort. The baristas also made my au lait as soon as they saw me walk through the door, so I kind of felt like I had made it.

I didn't realize it at the time, but I was merging my love for media, food, writing, and connecting with people together. I have always felt a certain pressure to water down my ethnicity and my culture to be wholly accepted, something that may have felt necessary to me then, but

feels beyond exhausting to me now. And because of this, one of my primary goals in life is to make people feel seen, because I've always felt that I was not. I want to hear their stories, eat their food, ask them about their lives and kids and dogs. I know we've all been raised not to talk to strangers, but I can't help it. I am curious about everyone.

After interning in New York for a summer, I came back to Berkeley for my senior year. I felt different. Berkeley had become my home, I knew this for certain, but my brief taste of New York had ultimately ruined me for the better. Halfway through my first semester I started to get restless. I wanted to travel, to work, and I realized I wanted to be anywhere but where I was—my normal routines didn't feel like they were serving me like they used to. Who wants college life to end and the real world to begin? I knew this put me in the minority, but I had a feeling that my purpose was about to start outside of school. In October I found out I had finished all my credits, and on a whim I decided to graduate early. I am not an impulsive person at all, but this was entirely a gut feeling. And had I not made that one decision, things might have turned out very differently.

Lemon Rice
with Curry
Leaves

Dal Makhani

Coconut
Rice

Dal Saag

legume
situations

Dal Makhani
(Creamy Black Lentils)

Serves 4–5

While dal makhani is typically made with urad dal (which are whole black gram lentils), feel free to use black beluga lentils, as I do here, as these are more accessible, and the former takes a lot longer to cook!

½ cup black lentils

3 tablespoons extra-virgin olive oil

½ teaspoon cumin seeds

½ teaspoon fennel seeds

1 yellow onion, diced

3 garlic cloves, sliced

1 (1-inch) knob fresh ginger, grated

½ teaspoon ground coriander

1 teaspoon ground cumin

½ teaspoon ground turmeric

½ teaspoon garam masala

½ teaspoon cayenne pepper

½ cup canned crushed tomatoes

1 (13.5 ounce) can full-fat coconut milk

1 cup canned kidney beans, drained and rinsed

Handful of fresh cilantro, roughly chopped, for garnish

1 lemon (optional)

Rice or bread, for serving

Dal makhani literally means "lentils cooked with butter," and the dish is traditionally prepared by cooking lentils with spices and butter over a coal fire for hours and hours. I know this may shock you, but I don't have a coal fire. And even if you do, first of all, congratulations, that is very cool and I'm honestly a little jealous. But I'll contend that maybe you don't have hours and hours to cook lentils over it.

My solution is this: a quicker-to-prepare dal makhani that loses the cream and butter in favor of coconut milk for a spicy, rich, decadent dish that you'll want to eat with a spoon, but that I prefer to scoop up with some rice or naan. *Pictured in chapter opener photo, page 128.*

Place the lentils in a medium bowl and cover them with water. Wash the lentils with your hand, tip out the water, and repeat this process until the water runs clear. Now, cover the lentils with fresh water and soak for 30 minutes to 1 hour (this will allow them to cook faster).

Put the drained lentils in a saucepan, add 1½ to 2 cups of water, and bring to a boil. Boil for 15 to 20 minutes or until the lentils are just tender. Drain any excess water and set aside.

Heat the olive oil in a large skillet over medium heat. Once the oil shimmers, add the cumin seeds and fennel seeds, swirling them in the oil until they sizzle and brown slightly, 1 to 2 minutes.

Add the onions to the pan and cook until they start to become translucent and tender, 3 to 4 minutes. Now, add the garlic and ginger to the skillet and cook with the onions for another 2 to 3 minutes until they start to brown slightly.

Stir the coriander, cumin, turmeric, garam masala, and cayenne into the onions and cook for 2 to 3 minutes until the spices start to roast and the "raw" masala smell disappears.

Now add the crushed tomatoes. Simmer for a few minutes.

Stir in the coconut milk and simmer with the tomatoes and spices for about 5 minutes.

Add the cooked lentils, the kidney beans, and 1 cup of water. Bring the dal to a boil and then reduce it to a low simmer for 20 to 25 minutes, or until the dal has thickened and the lentils are tender.

Garnish with the cilantro and a squeeze of lemon, if desired. Serve with rice, bread, or even just a spoon.